The Juvenile

in Delinquent

Society

The **Juvenile**

in **Delinquent**

Society

by **Milton L. Barron**

The College of the City of New York

1955 **Alfred A. Knopf   New York**

L. C. catalog card number: 52–5081

THIS IS A BORZOI BOOK,
PUBLISHED BY ALFRED A. KNOPF, INC.

PUBLISHED APRIL 1954
SECOND PRINTING, FEBRUARY 1955

To My Parents

Preface

Few of our social problems bring out the lack of a scientific approach to human relations so vividly as does juvenile delinquency. American society is marked by the great value it places upon the scientific method. Yet it manifests very little of it in dealing with the major problem affecting its children. Following World War II this could be observed in the reaction of many Americans to the general decline in cases of juvenile delinquency reported by the police, courts, and other statistics-gathering agencies. The feeling prevailed that in such statistics one had a clear measure of the declining importance of the problem itself; but systematic study at that time would have revealed no sound basis for such optimism. As a matter of fact, soon afterwards in several jurisdictions there was a rise in reported cases. The problem has an underlying tenacity that defies the cyclical influence of war and peace. Careful analysis will demonstrate that it is unrealistic to expect any significant reduction of the problem within the existing framework of programs, agencies, and personnel devoted to treatment and prevention.

The central theme of this book is implicit in its title. It is that the problem of juvenile delinquency can best be understood on the one hand and reduced on the other hand in a comprehensive, societal frame of reference. When juveniles live in a "delinquent" society, juvenile delinquency becomes a major problem of that society. By the same token, the solution of the problem, like that of other social problems, depends on an orderly modification of the American social structure, and some of the values and functions of American society.

The book is designed primarily for use as a text in courses on juvenile delinquency and criminology. It may also be used to supplement other texts and readings concerned comprehensively with social problems and social disorganization or social pathology. Part One represents an effort to define delinquency not only as a social problem but as a unique concept. A statistical profile of delinquent acts is presented, along with a summary of the known characteristics of delinquents. The dynamics of delinquency are also considered, with special reference to the business cycle and the cycle of war and peace.

Part Two is a survey of the major kinds of etiological thought and analysis regarding juvenile delinquency. The key chapter is Chapter XII, which goes into detail on the central theme of the book. Part Three is a discussion of societal reactions to delinquency, ranging from detection and detention, and the juvenile court, to the various types of disposition and treatment of cases and, lastly, delinquency control and prevention.

The task of complete and adequate acknowledgments to the many people who have contributed in one way or another to this book is virtually insurmountable. The writer's debt to the stimulation and ideas provided by his former teachers at Yale and his colleagues and students at St. Lawrence, Syracuse, and Cornell universities is gratefully acknowledged. To Professor William C. Lehmann, who suggested that I organize the course on juvenile delinquency which in turn furnished the motivation for writing this book, a special word of gratitude is expressed. For the careful typing of the manuscript and its revisions, acknowledgments and thanks are due to Mrs. Margaret Anagnost and her staff. Most of all I am indebted to my wife for her bibliographical research and for her patience and persistent encouragement throughout the many evenings and weekends of work required to complete the manuscript.

Ithaca, New York **M. L. B.**

Contents

Delinquent Children—The Multiple Meanings of Juvenile Delinquency—The Impact of the Delinquency Concept on Other Age Groups—Conclusion.

Statistics on Juvenile Delinquency—Limitations of Delinquency Statistics—Efforts to Improve Delinquency Statistics—The Volume of Juvenile Delinquency—The Distribution of Delinquency Offenses—The Age and Sex Composition of Juvenile Delinquents—The Ethnic Distribution of Juvenile Delinquents—The Socio-economic Status of Juvenile Delinquents—The Rural-Urban Distribution of Juvenile Delinquents—Recidivism in Juvenile Delinquency.

Delinquency and the Business Cycle—Delinquency and the Cycle of War and Peace—Delinquency in Wartime: New York City—The Postwar Decline in Juvenile Delinquency—The Resurgence of Delinquency in 1950.

Part **II.** *The Etiology of Delinquency*

The Evolution of Causative Thinking—Variables in Causation—Plurality of Causative Factors—The Interactive Complex in Causation—Correlations in Delinquency —Subjective Assessment of External Factors.

The Individual Approach—The Group Approach—The Institutional Approach—The Communication Approach —The Cultural Approach—The Ecological Approach— The Age-Status Approach.

The Heredity, Physique, and Glands of Juvenile Delin-

Part III. Societal Reactions to Delinquency

Illustrations

FROM WILLIAM HOGARTH (1697–1764)

Charts and Tables

A Note on the Illustrations

THE ILLUSTRATIONS FOR THIS BOOK were selected from the works of WILLIAM HOGARTH (1697–1764), an outstanding English painter and engraver. The London of the eighteenth century which he so realistically depicted was even more "delinquent" or negligent of its commitments than is modern urban society. Crimes were frequent and brutal, and so were the punishments that were meted out. Flogging was universal for children as well as adults. The conditions within prisons, orphanages, lunatic asylums, and hospitals were appalling by the standards society today sets for these institutions.

But all this merely reflected the culture of Hogarth's time. The amusements of most males included such sports as prizefighting, cock-fighting, and bull-baiting. Disputes were generally settled by hand-to-hand fighting; drunkenness was characteristic of all classes. London was unsafe after dark, for on the filthy, cobbled streets of the city thieves, inebriates, and prostitutes roamed virtually unchecked by the ill-paid watchmen.

This was the world that William Hogarth, himself a member of the middle class, observed and reproduced in his art. Although he was primarily a moralist and satirist, Hogarth was able to grasp the sociological relationship between the culture of his native eighteenth-century London and the behavior patterns of its children—not only the pitiful children of the street but also the now pampered, now neglected children of the rich.

The illustrations have been reproduced through the courtesy of THE BETTMANN ARCHIVE.

Introduction

The periodic, dramatic rise and decline in the incidence of juvenile delinquency is one reason for the contemporary widespread interest in the problem. Sudden rises in incidence are often more apparent than real, however, because some of our media of communication find it profitable to manipulate and enlarge delinquency as well as crime coverage. We are indebted to Lincoln Steffens, one of the leading muckrakers of all time, for shedding the first light on the nature and extent of such efforts. Referring to his own experience as a newspaper reporter, he pointed out that many so-called "crime waves" are fabricated to increase newspaper circulation and to enliven an otherwise dull month with newsworthy events.[1]

The current interest in juvenile delinquency also stems from the fact that many politicians, clergymen, and educators have come to appreciate and to exploit its value in the promotion of their respective interests. Many proclamations of political drives

[1] *Autobiography*, New York, Harcourt, Brace, 1931, Part II, Chapter xiv, pp. 285–91.

against "hoodlums," gambling, prostitution, and other evils frequently have the same basis. And so it is with delinquency. The problem lends itself easily to any repertoire for self-righteous speechmaking, lecturing, and sermonizing.

Another reason for the heightened interest in juvenile delinquency today is suggested by Fuller and Myers's theory of the natural history of social problems.[2] According to this theory, each social problem proceeds through phases of (a) attention-getting, in which people become aware or conscious of the problem, and (b) efforts to define the difficulty, which lead to (c) proposals for reform. These phases are followed by attempts at (d) organizing for reform. Once programs for reform are set in motion, they are accompanied by problems of (e) administration of reform. Although this chronological sequence of problem phases is obviously oversimplified and mechanistic, it is conceivable that the pattern is roughly accurate. The "attention-getting" phase of the juvenile delinquency problem may be receiving the greatest emphasis today.

Not to be overlooked as a source of interest in delinquency are the dynamics of American demography. The "vital revolution"—the long-range trend of declining birth and death rates—has focused the attention of American society on the most affected age groups, the very young and the very old.[3] The problems of the juvenile and the problems of the aged have the same demographic foundation.

Not least important in stimulating interest in the problem of delinquency is the multiplication of theories and methodologies seeking to understand and to control the problem. Intense rivalry among these various theories and methods has inevitably attracted considerable attention and stratified the population into diverse schools of thought.

The Approach Used in This Book

It is no longer possible to confine the analysis of any social problem exclusively to the frame of reference of one discipline.

[2] Richard C. Fuller and R. R. Myers, "Some Aspects of a Theory of Social Problems," *American Sociological Review*, 6:24–32, 1941.

[3] See Guy I. Burch and Elmer Pendell, *Human Breeding and Survival*, New York, Penguin Books, 1947, p. 126.

Anthropology, sociology, psychology, and psychiatry constitute highly specialized viewpoints. Much is lost if any one of them is utilized without taking into consideration the contributions of the others. The interdisciplinary approach is an outgrowth of the frustrations inherent in the earlier particularism and parochialism of the nineteenth century—and simultaneously of the modern awareness that a problem like juvenile delinquency demands the broadest possible approach.

Several important precedents exist for such an approach. On the level of academic instruction and research, in recent years many interdepartmental area studies and sequences have been established. In some cases departmental lines between disciplines have been eliminated entirely. For example, in 1946 the Provost of Harvard University announced the establishment of a new department of social relations which was to incorporate all the department of sociology, that part of the department of psychology which had heretofore dealt primarily with social and clinical psychology, and that part of the department of anthropology which had been concerned primarily with cultural anthropology. Defending the step it was taking, Harvard pointed out that World War II had accelerated the synthesis of research in the sociocultural and psychological sciences. Wartime projects had virtually obliterated many of the arbitrary distinctions that were already disintegrating between social scientists engaged in the common study of human relations. Besides having common problems for investigation, Harvard emphasized, today's students of social relations require many of the same skills and tools, such as statistical sampling, interviewing, participant observation, group experiments, coding and machine sorting, community mapping, and life-history analysis.[4]

An outstanding precedent for the interdisciplinary approach, in this case for the specific social problem of alcoholism, has been established by the Yale School of Alcoholic Studies.[5]

Juvenile delinquency itself does not lack such precedence.

---

[4] "Current Items, News and Announcements," *American Sociological Review*, 11:229–30, 1946.

[5] See, for example, *Alcohol, Science and Society*, New Haven, *Quarterly Journal of Studies on Alcohol*, 1945.

Since its earliest days, the child guidance clinic has been distinctive for its interdisciplinary characteristics.[6]

The Juvenile in Delinquent Society

Consistent with an interdisciplinary, wholistic approach is the adoption of "The Juvenile in Delinquent Society" as the title of this book.[7] The concept of a "delinquent society" is not unique; forms occur elsewhere. One is implicit in the chancery proceedings of the juvenile or children's court.[8] Another is to be derived from the cross-cultural evidence provided by the studies of Margaret Mead and other anthropologists.[9] They show that in some societies there is no juvenile problem comparable to delinquency. The significant differential, according to the anthropologists, seems to lie in the social organization and culture of such societies.

One of the most telling arguments of all in support of the conceptualization of American society as a "delinquent society" is to be found in the Children's Charter that was formulated at the White House Conference on Child Health and Protection in 1930. This charter, defining nineteen rights for American children, has been reaffirmed many times since its original statement. The perennial failure to implement these rights involves the same degree of societal shortcoming in the second half of the twentieth century as was true in 1930.

Other, more explicit approximations of the concept of a "delinquent society" are also worthy of mention. Quetelet once observed [10] that "society bears in its womb the embryo of every crime that will be committed, because it creates the conditions

[6] See Chapter XVIII for a description of the organization and functions of the child guidance clinic.

[7] The author is fully aware that the use of such a title, and the implicit theme, may invite two criticisms. Some may say that this is scapegoating, albeit on a plane more inclusive and perhaps more sophisticated than the usual "bad" parents, "unwholesome" neighborhood theme. Another possible criticism is that the title and theme carry the deterministic premises of social science to the point where human beings are conceived as being passive, irresponsible pawns of environmental forces. See Chapter XII for an anticipatory defense against these criticisms.

[8] See Chapters II and XV for analyses of the chancery philosophy.

[9] See Margaret Mead, *Coming of Age in Samoa*, New York, Morrow, 1928; also *Growing Up in New Guinea*, New York, Morrow, 1930.

[10] "Man and Development of His Faculties," in *Essai de physique sociale*, Brussels, 1869, pp. 176–77.

which stimulate crime; it prepares for crime, so to speak, while the criminal is merely the tool." Carr has gone beyond this, stressing that it is parents, teachers, city officials, employers, and other adults who set the behavior models for children, as well as deciding when and where children have failed to conform to that pattern. Delinquency comes, he maintains, when adults permit children to get into situations that frustrate and defeat them. Although technically and legally the child is delinquent, morally, socially, and causally the adults are the ones who have failed.[11]

Leighton, referring to his own earlier consideration of populations as if they were composed solely of adults—omitting, as is commonly done, reference to children—observes that when one does consider the children they cannot in any way be held responsible for the conditions into which they were born. Yet children in many societies are suffering from "stresses" and are reacting to them by building behavior patterns and systems of belief in which hostility, aggression, and hate are ingrained.[12]

In short, the approach of this book and the theme it poses enjoy the support of precedence and unsolicited testimonial. We can turn now from these introductory remarks to an analysis of the problems of "the juvenile in delinquent society."

[11] Lowell J. Carr, *Delinquency Control*, New York, Harper, 1940, pp. 69, 70, 76.

[12] Alexander H. Leighton, *Human Relations in a Changing World: Observations on the Use of the Social Sciences*, New York, Dutton, 1949, p. 108.

Part **I**.

Dimensions of Delinquency

Chapter 1. ∎ *The Case of Howard L.*

"**The** world had produced him, and now he presented himself to the world, not as a child but as a problem, and one beyond the pale." These words appear in the original version of the following nontechnical case history of Howard L.,[1] a juvenile whose offense was recently given considerable publicity throughout the United States. For reasons that appear in the next chapter, *legally Howard's offense was not a delinquency.* Nevertheless there is considerable merit in orienting the study of the problem of juvenile delinquency by examining Howard's case. While no two cases are ever precisely similar, many of the psychological and sociological aspects of Howard's problem are dis-

[1] John Bartlow Martin, "End of a Boy's Life," *McCall's,* July 1948, pp. 25 ff.

cernible among thousands of juvenile delinquents brought to the attention of the police and courts annually.

The Offense

Lonnie F., a seven-year-old boy, had been missing all day. At first the Chicago police were of the opinion that he had fallen asleep in a movie theater and that the ushers would find him. At 1:10 a.m., however, he still had not turned up. The police accordingly set in motion the machinery of search. A teletyped Missing Persons message to other district stations uncovered nothing. Three police squads were assigned to look for Lonnie, but after looking all night they failed to find him.

The next morning detectives were sent to Lonnie's home. His mother said she was afraid Lonnie had run away from home because the family was about to be evicted and she was planning to put him in a foster home. She had last seen him Saturday morning, spinning tops and going off to play with Gerald M., a nine-year-old boy in the neighborhood. She since had learned that they had met a boy a few years older, Howard L.

The police knew Howard L. slightly—he had committed truancy, broken windows, stolen pennies from a newsstand. The police went to his home but he was not there; he was at a motion-picture theater. Howard's mother recalled that Howard, Lonnie, and Gerald had left about 10:30 a.m. the day before for Von Humboldt Park. She promised to ask Howard about Lonnie when he came home.

The police abandoned, after investigation, their first theory that Lonnie's mother, Mrs. F., might have engineered the disappearance to win sympathy in her fight against being evicted from her apartment. But they still thought it possible that the explanation lay in family troubles. When Mrs. F. reported that her husband was in Los Angeles the local police wired the Los Angeles police, who ascertained that Mr. F. knew nothing of Lonnie's disappearance. The pastor who was arranging to have Lonnie placed in a foster home could suggest no explanation either. Nor were there any results when detectives searched the many places where a runaway boy might hide—dark hallways, ruined basements and garages, empty stores, and vacant lots.

By Monday the police concluded that something serious had

happened to Lonnie. Squads were sent out to pick up men with records as sex offenders and purse-snatchers; detectives searched Von Humboldt Park and the lagoon there was dragged. Finally, in an effort to trace Lonnie's movements, the police sent for Howard L. and Gerald M. They talked to Howard first because he was the older of the two.

Howard L. was a twelve-year-old boy, slender, pale, and nervous. He said that Saturday morning Lonnie, Gerald, and he had gone to Von Humboldt Park. There, three unidentified older boys had called Lonnie aside and whispered to him. Howard claimed to have turned around and walked away, never seeing Lonnie again. Gerald told the police the same story, and when the skeptical police questioned the two boys again, they repeated it flawlessly.

During the next two days the police interviewed other adults and children, and also distributed pictures of Lonnie. They picked up several older boys and men with arrest records, but neither Howard nor Gerald could identify any. Howard was confident that he could recognize the boys whom he had last seen with Lonnie, so the police took him to eight schools and had the older pupils march in and out of the classrooms while Howard watched, unable to pick out anyone.

Eleven days after Lonnie disappeared, his dead body was inadvertently found by a postman in a suburban forest preserve eight miles west of Lonnie's home. Identification was difficult because the body was badly battered and decomposed. He had been stabbed with a Boy Scout knife and battered with a large chunk of concrete.

At the inquest Howard said he had been in that forest several times, building a fire and roasting potatoes, but always alone. For some time the police had felt there was something peculiar about Howard and his story, and they questioned him again. When Howard asked for his mother, the police sent for her and also the State's attorney and juvenile authorities. For four days Howard resisted the most intense efforts of the police, juvenile authorities, the Assistant State's attorney and experts with lie detectors and electroencephalographs. But in the meantime the detectives were questioning his friends. One of them, Anna May E., stated that the day following Lonnie's disappearance

Howard had told her he had killed Lonnie. At the suggestion of the police she talked to Howard, and on Sunday, two weeks after Lonnie's disappearance, Howard confessed. He was transferred to the county jail and subsequently brought to trial on an indictment charging first-degree murder.

Life History and Background

Howard L. was born in December 1934 at Chicago Lying-In Hospital. His mother went there in the seventh month of pregnancy after periodic hemorrhages, and the doctors removed the baby by Caesarean section, barely avoiding a miscarriage. His mother was then thirty-nine years old, having been childless since her first marriage at the age of twenty-five. Howard's father was her fourth husband, a cook in a restaurant. They lived in a rooming-house overlooking Von Humboldt Park.

Howard's whole life was spent in the Von Humboldt Park area on the Northwest side of Chicago, described as "a vista of steel trolley poles and neon signs and dingy red brick buildings, old buildings with peaked roofs topped by spires, the ground floors occupied by saloons and auto accessory stores and beauty shops, the narrow unmarked doors between the store fronts opening into black steep stairs that the inhabitants climb to their flats. In the jumbled traffic an old man wrapped in a comforter is driving a horse and wagon, and boys are skipping over the framework behind a billboard in a vacant lot, heading for the White Tower hamburger joint at Northern and Western, the main corner. Against the eastern sky rise the bell-shaped towers and spires of the churches of the foreign born, and not far beyond, near the dirty dock-lined Chicago River, lie the slums."

The delinquency rate in this area has not been so high as elsewhere in Chicago. Its residents are for the most part workingmen and their families. The largest single ethnic group are the Poles, followed by many Jews and Germans, and a few Negroes, Italians, Filipinos, Chinese, and American Indians.

One day when Howard was seventeen months old his father went to work and never returned. Mrs. L. went out to do housework for a few dollars a day in order to support herself and her child. She paid a woman thirty-five cents a day to care for Howard, and lived with him in a three-room flat. In 1940, when

Howard was five, his mother married for the fifth time, her new husband a railroader in relatively good economic circumstances. The family moved into a three-and-a-half-room apartment in a brick apartment-building.

Mrs. L. was now able to take full supervision over Howard. When neighbors or other children complained about his behavior she defended him without qualification. But she punished him severely even for untidiness, losing control of her temper at the slightest provocation. Howard entered the public kindergarten in September 1940. His teacher marked him "Not Efficient" in the only two subjects on which he was graded, and he was found to have an intelligence quotient of 86, indicating "a somewhat slower rate of mental growth than normal rate." He was ill a good deal of the time and had his tonsils and adenoids removed.

In 1942, when he was in the first grade, his mother wrote to his teacher to inquire whether Howard really had bought war-bond stamps with two dimes she had given him, as he said he had. This was the first of several investigations she made, applying pressure on him. Yet when the teachers disciplined him she defended him. At least one of her numerous conferences at school ended in physical violence. The principal found her inconsistent and unpredictable, a difficult person to deal with. When Howard failed in grade 2A during the spring of 1943 he was examined by the Bureau of Child Study of the Board of Education. According to the examiner, Howard was disturbed by conditions in his home —such as his stepfather's treatment of his mother. Because he was under great strain he was unable to apply himself to his schoolwork.

By now Mrs. L. and her fifth husband were quarreling almost constantly, usually over money, and not infrequently over Howard. Late one night an hour-long fight ended when she cut her husband with a knife-sharpener and the police arrived. Howard had been watching in silence from near by. Mrs. L. sued for divorce shortly thereafter, and with Howard left her husband. Soon she was having relations with a man who drank heavily and who became violent when he did so. Howard's tension as a result of all this led to his hospitalization for "psychogenic diarrhea."

Mrs. L. returned to work as a cleaning-woman during the

day and a baby sitter in the evening. Howard took care of himself, making his own meals and going to bed in an empty house. His friends were mostly his own age. He began to come to the attention of police for such offenses as breaking windows, throwing rocks, climbing on shed roofs. Once he was accused of pilfering money from bathers' clothing at the beach and once of stealing pennies from a newsstand. On one occasion he and another boy took a watch at school, sold it for fifty cents, spent fifteen cents and buried the rest in the schoolyard. When the principal investigated, Howard volunteered that although he did not know the name of the thief he could point him out. When his confederate confessed, Howard maintained his own innocence until he was confronted with the burial place of the money.

Howard became known as a problem at school. He failed grade 4B but in 1947 he was advanced into 5B, perhaps because he was so big. His new teacher found that his temper was easily aroused and he lied frequently. Once he wrote an essay in which he said: "I do not like school and I do not like the office. I am in the office every day. What I do like about school is the vacation." He seemed nervous when he arrived in his classroom each morning. When he was truant from school his mother turned him over to the police. She was reported to have told him frequently before he left for school: "Get out of here. I hope you get run over by a truck before you get across the street."

Upon the request of the school principal, Howard was examined by another Board of Education psychologist, who confirmed the previous findings. Mrs. L. agreed to take up the possibility of putting him in a foster home, but nothing was done. During the summer of 1947 he was on the streets most of the time, and spent the rest of his hours in movies, at the beach, in the forest preserve, and sleeping in parked cars.

In September 1947, Howard entered grade 5A. His teacher noted that it was more difficult than ever to get him to work. There were conferences between her, the principal, and the adjustment teacher, but efforts to interest him met with little success. He kept getting into trouble, he was truant, his mother went to see the principal, and soon he was marked unsatisfactory in every subject except art and penmanship.

The principal, contemplating official action that probably

would have brought Howard to a disciplinary school, asked the police Juvenile Officer to take the case. The officer ordered the boy to report to him at the station every Saturday morning; but the very first Saturday morning on which Howard was to report he went off instead with Lonnie F. and Gerald M. The boys played for a while in the neighborhood and then took a streetcar and rode westward until they reached the end of the line. They transferred to a bus that took them through the suburbs to a forest preserve winding along the Des Plaines River.

Howard, Lonnie, and Gerald left the highway and walked down a trail through the woods beside the river. They came to a railroad bridge and stopped to play on it. Tiring of this presently, they went on, crossing a highway and descending into a glen in a bend of the river. Lonnie asked permission to use Howard's knife, and when Howard refused Lonnie cursed him. Howard started smoking a cigarette, and when Lonnie asked for one Howard once more refused. Lonnie swore at him again. Howard pushed him and Lonnie threatened to tell Mrs. L. about her son's theft of ten dollars. Angered, Howard stabbed Lonnie with his knife several times, and then choked and stepped on him. Then he picked up a chunk of concrete and dropped it on Lonnie's chest and face a number of times. Gerald and he buried Lonnie with leaves and returned home, Howard warning Gerald not to tell what happened.

At home Howard changed his clothing and went to a double-feature movie. When Lonnie's brother telephoned, Howard told the story about having left Lonnie in the park with three older boys, and later called back to inquire if Lonnie had returned. He told Anna May E. and two boys the truth after asking them if they could keep a secret.

When Howard confessed, he was lodged in the county jail. In February 1948 he became the youngest person ever to go on trial for his life in Cook County. Juvenile-court jurisdiction, which was established in that county in 1899 for the first time anywhere in the world, could not be used in his case because it involved a capital offense. A plea of guilty was made in behalf of Howard by the defense lawyer. Several weeks later, in April, the judge read his findings preliminary to the sentence. He blamed the mother primarily, but also censured comic books and the movies, concluding that "the Court, after a review of all the evidence in the case, and all matters of mitigation, fixes the limit and duration of the sentence, under the Statutes of Illinois, of Howard L——, for the murder of Lonnie F——, at twenty-two years in the penitentiary." A bailiff led the boy away.

Now that the case of Howard L. has been presented, we can turn to a definition of the problem of delinquency. We will see why Howard was legally not a delinquent, despite the psychological and sociological similarities between his case and many cases of juvenile delinquency in American society.

The term "delinquency" is many centuries old. The Romans used it to refer to failure, neglect of duty, and abandonment of an agreement. Vestiges of these earlier meanings are found today, as in the description of some adults as "tax delinquents." But this is far removed from the prevalent, contemporary usage of the term. When delinquency is preceded by "juvenile," it refers to a major social problem involving a distinctive age group defined by law.

To be sure, the behavior now labeled "delinquent" has been well represented among America's children for countless years. But "juvenile delinquency" as such has been recognized only since 1899. In that year the legislature of the state of Illinois enacted the first juvenile-court law. Until the Illinois legislators acted, all child offenders had technically been "criminals." From 1899 on, many jurisdictions have decided that all child offenders are to be considered delinquents. Others have decreed that juveniles may be looked upon as either criminals or delinquents, depending upon the nature of their offenses.

Differentiation from Crime

Despite its relatively recent emergence, juvenile delinquency has major roots, accounting for its differentiation from crime, which extend centuries back. Other roots date from the years immediately preceding the emergence of the concept of juvenile delinquency itself. What were these historical and recent roots in the process of differentiating delinquency from crime?

EXEMPTION FROM FREE WILL AND RESPONSIBILITY.   One of the earliest roots of the concept of juvenile delinquency is to be found in the idea that immaturity exempts the individual from being a free agent, morally responsible for his choice of behavior. Hebraic law exempted the male child from sinning until his *rite de passage* at the age of thirteen. Roman law divided minors into three categories with regard to responsibility: (a) children under seven were not responsible under any circumstances; (b) those from seven up to the age of puberty were not responsible if the praetor was of the opinion that they lacked understanding of the nature of their acts; and (c) those from puberty up to twenty-five years of age were to have their youthfulness taken into consideration in the prescribing of punishment. The influence of Roman law on the Napoleonic Code appeared in the latter's provision that limited responsibility was to be ascribed to children under sixteen, this age ceiling later being raised to eighteen. English law also qualified responsibility for reasons of age long before the beginnings of American society. Ever since the time of Edward III it has been understood in the law of England that a child under seven years is in all circumstances incapable of guilt for crime, owing to lack of understanding and judgment. From eight to fourteen years of age the English child has been presumed to be incapable of guilt, and therefore irresponsible, unless there is evidence of understanding and judgment or the ability to "discern between good and evil." [1]

EQUITY OR CHANCERY.   A second early root of the concept

[1] Sir William Blackstone, *Commentaries on the Law of England,* 12th edition, London, 1795, Book IV, Chapter ii, pp. 21–4.

of juvenile delinquency is the English principle of equity or chancery. The principle had its first clear-cut expression in the thirteenth century, when a Council of Chancery was established by the king as a reaction against the rigidity of the law and court system of the time as it applied to minors and others in need of special aid. The Council was to receive the petitions of such special cases. In the fifteenth century, a distinct court and chancery jurisdiction evolved, more flexible and informal than the common law-court. But even before the appearance of chancery jurisdiction in England, the idea had developed that the crown was the ultimate parent of all minors and that it should exercise guardianship and protection over them rather than be rigid in its application of punishment. In short, the principle of chancery or equity provided for minors recourse to the king in the face of the strictness of law, so that "more equitable" decisions could be reached for them. The king gave this chancery jurisdiction to his chancellor, and the terms *chancery* and *equity* came to be used synonymously. Here was an application of the ideas that the king was the *parens patriae,* or "father of the country," and in individual cases acted *in loco parentis,* in place of the natural parent. When American independence was attained, the state rather than the crown became the *parens patriae* for minors.

The original English principle of chancery was concerned with such matters of civil law as neglect and dependency, contracts involving minors, property, and inheritance rather than matters found in criminal jurisdiction. With the passage of juvenile-court laws in Illinois and elsewhere after 1899, the principle was extended to cover "antisocial" behavior of persons below a stated age limit. The immunities, privileges, and disabilities that the state had already granted to children under civil law were now set up as a barrier distinguishing the juvenile delinquent from the adult criminal. It was thereafter to be assumed that the child offender was handicapped by a lack of effective parental control, and that the exercise of discretion could not be expected of him, nor the burden of legal responsibility for his behavior placed upon him. His status came to be the equivalent of ward of the state, with the appropriate legal disabilities and immunities.

RECENT ROOTS OF THE CONCEPT OF JUVENILE DELINQUENCY. In the nineteenth century, and early in the twentieth, there took shape certain intellectual and reform movements that undoubtedly contributed to the conceptualization of juvenile delinquency. One was the middle-class humanitarianism that Dickens's novels inspired by virtue of their vivid descriptions of the degrading conditions to which children in English asylums were exposed. This led to the segregation of children from adults in detention and confinement during the nineteenth century. Another influence distinguishing the child from older age-groups was the rise of modern psychology, which stressed the influence of the early years of life on subsequent personality development. Closely related to this has been the gradual realization in modern criminology that the young offender often progresses toward adult criminality unless he is deterred or rehabilitated while he is still relatively malleable.

It is of interest to note that the changed situation regarding children and older minors in our culture has affected legal aspects other than questions of crime and delinquency. At first marriage and gainful employment, as well as responsibility for crime, were expected of the young. Then our laws came to reflect cultural changes in the direction of recognition of the dependency and irresponsibility of such people. Along with the revision in law which raised the minimum age-level for full accountability for crime, other laws (1) raised the minimum age-level for marriage and employment, and (2) raised the maximum age-level for compulsory education.

Emergence of Delinquency

This, in essence, was the background out of which the concept of juvenile delinquency evolved in Illinois at the turn of the century.[2] Like other social inventions, the new concept as expressed in the Illinois law was a combination of such already existing elements as institutional segregation, probation, and separate hearings. But apart from this integrative aspect the law was unique in that it centralized several earlier elements at the ju-

---

[2] For a summary of the process leading up to and immediately preceding its emergence in Illinois law, see Thorsten Sellin, "Juvenile Delinquency," *The Annals of the American Academy of Political and Social Science*, 261:vii–viii, 1949. This is based on a small work compiled by the first chief probation officer of the Cook County Juvenile Court: T. D. Huxley, *Origin of the Illinois Juvenile Court Law*, 3rd ed., 1907, 189 pp.

dicial level and created the status of juvenile delinquency as something quite different from crime, to be treated as doctors treat disease. The law not only conceived of juvenile delinquency but it was also designed to provide care for neglected and dependent children. The joint coverage of the law-breaking child and the needy child by the same law reflected a meaningful association between the two types of children in the minds of the lawmakers.[3]

Extralegal Conceptions of Delinquency

It is clear that the concept of delinquency emerged and developed along legalistic lines and within a judicial frame of reference. Nevertheless, some students of juvenile delinquency, especially social scientists, have maintained that it should be defined otherwise.

There is, for example, the *social psychological* definition. Here the crucial element is that the juvenile is delinquent because he conceives of himself as delinquent, whether it be through official action or by being pointed to as such in the neighborhood. Once a juvenile, whatever his make-up, has been classified as delinquent and has been subjected to various measures, secondary psychological reactions occur, unrelated to the origins of his so-called delinquent behavior but common to all who share his fate. At the same time, "right-minded" people, because he has been labeled delinquent, take up special attitudes toward him, regardless of the individuality of his case. Either action results in ostracism or exclusion from considerable social participation. Some advocates of this definition point out that interference with participation is also interference with the normal socialization process, and it may drive the rejected and ostracized child into groups that have their own sanction and approval for retaliation against the neighborhood. The prevention of delinquency would require action in the neighborhood to keep children from being defined as problems or delinquents. A social psychological process is unquestionably at work in the making of a delinquent.

[3] Although the law applied to the whole state of Illinois, it required that only counties with populations of more than 500,000 need provide a special judge and courtroom for the hearing of such children's cases. See Sellin, *op. cit.*, p. vii.

But an inescapable conclusion is that the legalistic and judicial connotation of delinquency persists as a referent without which the social psychology would be meaningless.

The delinquent as *psychologically* unique is another extra-legal conception. Here the delinquent is a child whose pattern of adjustment deviates from the code of conduct society is attempting to enforce. The delinquent child is one who seeks emotional satisfaction that he cannot find in his environment. He is differentiated at a given time from other children by having a greater degree of egocentrism and a lack of emotional balance. According to this conception of delinquency virtually everyone has probably been "delinquent" at some time or other. There is really nothing here to distinguish the delinquent from other children. Although one may argue that the majority of juvenile delinquents are found among the maladjusted, certainly not all of the maladjusted are delinquent. Furthermore, some delinquents are not maladjusted.

A third extralegal conception of delinquency may be found in *cultural anthropological* efforts, notably that of Sellin. He has suggested that one should study the violations of "conduct norms" rather than artificial legal norms. Every person finds himself in a number of groups, any one of which has a normal or right way of behaving and an abnormal or wrong way of behaving, the norm depending on the social values of the group that formulated it. Conduct norms are universal in the sense that they are found wherever there are social groups, and they are not necessarily embodied in law. These facts, Sellin claims, lead to the conclusion that the study of conduct norms would provide a better basis for the development of scientific categories than a study of either crime or delinquency as defined in law.[4] This conception of delinquency, however, overlooks the fact that conduct norms are just as socially determined and culturally variable as legal norms, yet they lack the latter's traits of precision and specificity.

An interesting compromise between legal and extralegal definitions of the delinquent was attempted by Powers and Witmer.[5]

[4] Thorsten Sellin, *Culture Conflict and Crime*, New York, Social Science Research Council Bulletin #41, 1938, p. 30.

[5] Edwin Powers and Helen Witmer, *An Experiment in the Prevention of Delinquency: The Cambridge-Somerville Youth Study*, New York, Columbia University Press, 1951, pp. 179–81.

Seeking to define the "real" delinquent, the juvenile who makes a career of delinquency, they note that such a child is not necessarily one who is delinquent by legal definition, nor is he the officially adjudged or institutionalized delinquent. Yet it is impossible to escape entirely from the legal concept, for some legally defined overt act is basic to the concept of delinquency. Three additional criteria mark off the "real" delinquent from others: (a) the seriousness of the behavior; (b) its frequency; and (c) the attitude of the offender toward a lawfully constituted society.

Delinquency as Normal, Purposive, and Adjustive

There is little to be gained in denying the basic legal and judicial meaning of delinquency in favor of such extralegal definitions as those discussed above. None of them is successful in usurping the role of the primary definition of the term. This does not imply, however, that the legalists have said all that needs to be said about the nature of delinquency. Accepting the legalistic and judicial foundation of the delinquency concept, some social scientists also suggest that delinquency is normal behavior in the sense that theoretically it is a product consistent with the factors that have gone into the so-called delinquent's development and experience. And just as nondelinquents differ from each other, so delinquents themselves are marked by individual differences in personality and behavior.

Delinquency, like nondelinquency, is adjustive behavior. Frequently it is a means of adjusting to frustrations and deprivations. Certain forms of delinquent behavior are simply useful ways of self-expression which have been adopted where socially acceptable behavior has been thwarted. In short, delinquency, like nondelinquency, is purposive. It meets needs and it is oriented toward goals.

Excellent support for the theory that delinquency is normal, adjustive, and purposive is found in the following interesting parallel drawn between recreation and delinquency: [6]

[6] Henry D. McKay, "The Neighborhood and Child Conduct," *The Annals of the American Academy of Political and Social Science*, 261:36-7, 1949.

As forms of activity, recreation and delinquency have many qualities in common. In its early states, delinquency is clearly a form of play. It is easy to see that running away from home, stealing pies from a pie wagon, or driving a stolen car may satisfy some of the basic needs or desires that are satisfied conventionally by baseball, pleasure riding, or going on a camping trip. In fact, it is easy to see that for those involved in them, many forms of delinquency, although costly to the community, may satisfy more of the immediate needs and wishes of children than are satisfied by more conventional forms of recreation. And this competition between the two types of activity is further complicated if the delinquency becomes financially profitable.

Both delinquency and recreation are essentially group activities. Each can be participated in alone, but in the more prevalent and meaningful forms, two or more persons usually are involved. Each type of activity has a tradition. Children's groups are the recipients and bearers of tradition governing rules, regulations, and mode of play of a great variety of games and means of entertainment ranging from the rhymes which are sung while skipping rope to the techniques for playing third base. Similarly, in those neighborhoods where there are delinquent groups, the members are the recipients and bearers of a tradition on such subjects as how to break into a car, shoplift from a store, or avoid a policeman. The latter groups may be the recipients, also, of the conventional traditions. . . .

Not only are recreation and delinquency both group activities, but in areas of high rates of delinquents the groups resemble each other in terms of physical characteristics, mental abilities, economic status, and family situations. Both delinquent and play groups have in their membership large boys and small boys, smart boys and dull boys, boys from broken homes and boys from integrated homes, and boys from families economically deprived and boys from families economically self-sufficient. In fact, with reference to these and similar characteristics, both kinds of groups are cross sections of the membership of the neighborhoods from which they are drawn.

The importance of this point is that there is no inherent reason why one group engages in delinquent activity and the other in recreation. The delinquent boys might just as well be limiting their activities to conventional games, and vice versa. . . .

The Status of Delinquency

Delinquency involves a unique legal status for the child, quite different from the status of criminality. This status is applied by the juvenile court only after a hearing. It does not affect "protodelinquents," that is, boys and girls who have never appeared in court on an official charge but who have engaged in "antisocial" behavior. Should a child, in the judgment of the court, require protection as a ward of the state on the basis of the criteria of *age, behavior,* and *need,* he is "adjudicated," so to speak, to the status of delinquency. Technically this status differs from that of the adjudicated criminal in a number of ways. The child is not found "guilty." He is not "convicted," nor does his treatment constitute "punishment." There is no "criminal record" against the delinquent. He loses no rights of citizenship. He may subsequently hold public office and secure employment without curb.

But the status of delinquency in practice does not always stand in such contrast to criminality. It too involves contact with the police, and detention and court handling. It entails treatment that is often punitive even though it is disguised by such euphemisms as "correction," "reform," and "rehabilitative therapy." It carries a stigma that is almost as serious as that of being a "criminal" or a "convict." Although the formal legal handicaps are not so great for those with the status of delinquents as they are for those who are adjudicated criminals, the delinquent is nevertheless ostracized and subject to discrimination in home, school, employment, and generally in interpersonal relations.[7]

[7] The fact that the delinquency status shares these traits with the status of criminality may account in part for the widespread misuse of the terms "delinquent" and "criminal" as synonyms. Many writers, for example, often refer to "delinquent adults" and "juvenile crime." Such juxtapositions are legal contradictions, yet they do appear in the following representative titles: Sheldon Glueck and Eleanor T. Glueck, *Five Hundred Delinquent Women,* New York, Knopf, 1934; Liebmann Hersh, "Delinquency Among

Labeling a child a juvenile delinquent is more likely to harm the
child than to aid him. The stigma alienates him still further from
that part of the society toward which he may already feel hostile.

It has been suggested that this dilemma—wherein the "delinquency tag," originally designed to be ameliorative and ad-
vantageous, actually has assumed many of the characteristics of
the status of criminality which it was meant to escape—could be
solved by dropping the labels of "delinquent" and "delinquency"
too. For example, the Standard Juvenile Court Act, formulated
by the National Probation and Parole Association and endorsed
as a model for all states at the National Conference on Juvenile
Delinquency held in 1946, does not define delinquency at all. It
simply describes situations and classifications of children over
which the juvenile court should have jurisdiction. Some juvenile-
court acts, such as those of California and the District of Columbia, already avoid the "delinquency tag." It is felt that this gives
real support to the basic philosophy of delinquency—that a child
should be protected.

Critics of this suggested solution claim that the very same
result was intended and should be evident where the "delinquency
tag" itself is used. Is not the effect of an adjudication to the status
of delinquency meant to be protective and ameliorative? The
critics note further that if the "delinquency tag" is dropped,
thereby no longer distinguishing the delinquent from dependent
and neglected children who are also within the jurisdiction of the
juvenile court, there will be a dangerous though legal possibility
that any child in the latter two categories may be committed to
a training-school or some other institution for delinquents. One
such critic [8] grants the possibility that there are rare cases where
a child not adjudicated delinquent would benefit from commitment to a training-school. But this is more than compensated for
by reducing the danger of unnecessary commitments. Another
danger in the absence of categories is that a court may decide

Jews: A Comparative Study of Criminality Among the Jewish and Non-
Jewish Population of the Polish Republic," *Journal of Criminal Law and
Criminology*, 27:515–38, 1936; Nathaniel D. M. Hirsch, *Dynamic Causes
of Juvenile Crime*, Cambridge, Sci-Art, 1937.

[8] Sol Rubin, "The Legal Character of Juvenile Delinquency," *The
Annals of the American Academy of Political and Social Science*, 261:5–6,
1949.

that a child might benefit from its facilities without bothering with a clear legal test of jurisdiction and proof. When the court does have categories it has to decide whether or not the child is either dependent, neglected, or delinquent, and not merely that it finds the child to be within its general jurisdiction.

Delinquency Legislation

Illinois's leadership in 1899 as the first state to enact juvenile-court legislation establishing the status of delinquency appears at first glance to have been followed reluctantly in other jurisdictions. It was not until 1938 that the federal legislators passed a juvenile-court law to apply to federal offenses by children. Wyoming, the last of the states to enact such a law, waited until 1945. But actually most of the country—all but two states and the federal government—had followed the example of Illinois by the year 1925.[9] Today, in addition to all 48 states and the federal government, juvenile-court legislation exists in the District of Columbia, Alaska, Hawaii, and Puerto Rico. Such legislation either has established separate juvenile courts or has provided for special jurisdiction and procedure in courts already established.[10]

The relationship between federal and state legislative provisions for juvenile delinquency is especially interesting. In 1932, six years before the passage of the Federal Juvenile Delinquency Act, Congress provided for the referral of those under twenty-one years of age who had violated federal laws to state authorities to be treated according to the latter's juvenile-court laws. Beginning in 1938, cases of individuals under eighteen years of age who were charged with violation of federal laws, exclusive of offenses punishable by death or life imprisonment, could be heard before a United States District Court using a procedure based on principles established in the state juvenile-court laws. But this new

[9] Juvenile-court legislation was enacted relatively early in many other countries, especially in western Europe.

[10] Besides delinquency, such legislation has usually assigned cases of dependency and neglect, and often cases of feeblemindedness, health, adoption, guardianship, custody, illegitimacy, consent of marriage, and annulment of marriage by children to the jurisdiction of juvenile courts. Adults who have either parental or quasi-parental relationships to children, and other adults who may influence children so as to "contribute" to their delinquency, may also be found in this court's jurisdiction.

act did not supersede the earlier provision permitting the referral of such cases to the state authorities. As a matter of fact, the policy of the Department of Justice has been to refer cases of juveniles to state authorities whenever possible.

For example, in the fiscal year that ended June 30, 1952, there was a total of 2,433 federal juvenile offenders. In the majority of these cases, 1,549, the federal juvenile delinquency procedure was employed; in 150 cases, there was the "regular" court procedure; and in 734 cases the children were either diverted to state authorities or dismissed.

An interesting question that appears from time to time about the Federal Juvenile Delinquency Act has to do with its legality. Is the Act constitutional? The only answer that can be given for the time being is that *provisionally* it is constitutional. Whether or not it is *absolutely* constitutional cannot be ascertained until the Supreme Court has had the opportunity to consider the question in a test case. Some legal scholars maintain that the statute is unconstitutional for three reasons. First, it legislates for a class (juveniles); second, it deprives a person of the right of trial by jury, and the "consent" that is supposed to overcome this defect cannot be executed by a minor; and last, it abrogates all existing criminal statutes, and by means of a proceeding converts these crimes into a status called "juvenile delinquency." [11]

With regard to the substance of delinquency and the characteristics of delinquents, what common denominator can one extract from the juvenile-court laws of the various jurisdictions? The laws generally agree in defining a delinquent child as one who is over seven years of age and under sixteen to under twenty-one years of age, and who (a) violates any law of the state or commits any act that if committed by a person above this age group would be *an offense punishable other than by death or life imprisonment;* [12] or who (b) is habitually truant from school, in-

---

[11] See also the discussion of the constitutionality of the juvenile court in Chapter XV.

[12] That is, any offense, from misdemeanor up to homicide, committed by a legally defined juvenile or child is considered to be an act of juvenile delinquency. But if the same person commits an offense that, when committed by an "adult," is punishable by death or life imprisonment, then the juvenile or child is held as accountable as if he were an adult. The significance of this qualification of delinquency is discussed in a later section of this chapter.

corrigible, ungovernable, habitually disobedient and beyond the
control of his parents or other persons in custodial charge of him.
In short, the laws generally cover not only most violations for
which adults are held responsible, but they also burden children
with the responsibility for the avoidance of a number of ambiguous and indefinite acts, conditions, and behavior problems presumably peculiar to children and representing no violation of law
if committed by adults. The list of "other acts or conditions" that
may bring a child within the jurisdiction of the juvenile court—
aside from the common denominator of incorrigibility, ungovernability, and habitual disobedience—includes immoral and indecent
conduct, immoral conduct at school, knowing association with
vicious or immoral persons, growing up in idleness or crime,
knowing entrance and visit of a house of ill repute, patronizing a
policy-slip or gaming place, patronizing public poolrooms,
wandering about railroad yards or tracks, jumping a train or
entering a car or engine without authority, habitually using ob-
scene or vulgar language in public places, loitering and sleeping
in alleys, using intoxicating liquors, deporting oneself so as to
injure oneself or others, smoking cigarettes, being in an occupation or situation dangerous to oneself or others, begging or receiving alms or being in the street for the purpose thereof, etc.
No state includes all these items in its definition of delinquent
behavior. The various state laws have an average of eight or nine
of these items in addition to violations of already enacted laws.

Some critics maintain that delinquency laws are inconsistent
in their embodiment not only of those activities proscribed for
adults but additional proscriptions as well. A child is more
egocentric than an adult and cannot be expected to subordinate
his needs and drives to the demands of the social group as well as
an adult can. Yet the law actually sets higher standards for the
child. A child who associates with immoral persons or a child
who leaves home without consent is doing nothing that in the
case of an adult would be considered criminal behavior. Indeed
a child who smokes or drinks is engaging in behavior that among
adults in some strata is considered a social grace. Society also
legally defines as delinquent in the case of the child or adolescent
other behavior that in the adult is socially acceptable, such as
attaining sexual goals by direct means and exploratory sex be-

havior. Another criticism is that delinquency laws falsely assume that the parents of children are always worthy of respect and that the home is an adequate refuge.

The Standard Juvenile Court Act, the model to which reference has been made above, includes in its provisions corresponding to the usual legal definition of delinquency only two items supplementary to violation of law or ordinance. These items are (1) a child who deserts his home or who is habitually disobedient or is beyond the control of his parent or other custodian; and (2) a child who, being required by law to attend school, willfully violates rules thereof or absents himself therefrom.

Comparable Legislation in Other Societies

A concise picture of comparable legislation in two other societies is useful in broadening one's perspective on the American situation. In England in 1933, a Children and Young Persons Act was passed that created a "petty sessional court of summary jurisdiction" to deal with offending individuals under seventeen. A "child" was defined as a person over eight but under fourteen years of age, and a "young person" was defined as one over fourteen and under seventeen years of age. With the measure of responsibility differing somewhat from one age group to the next, the new court was given jurisdiction to try all summary offenses committed by both age groups and all indictable offenses other than homicide. The age limit has since been raised to include as "young persons" those under twenty-three years of age.

In the Soviet Union new legislation was enacted in 1935 whereby young people were classified into three groups: (1) those up to twelve years, regardless of their offenses; (2) those between twelve and sixteen charged with what the Soviets consider to be minor infractions; and (3) those between twelve and sixteen charged with serious offenses. All people over sixteen years of age are considered adults and are handled by the regular criminal courts. Children in the first two groups are not criminally prosecuted or even brought before the court as defendants. Whether or not they committed the offense with which they are charged, they are held to be innocent of criminal act. Their misbehavior is the responsibility of others—their parents, a teacher or some other adult, the school, the neighborhood, or society in general.[13]

The Age Criteria of Juvenile Delinquency

Chronological age evidently is considered to be a crucial factor both in the United States where the modern beginnings of the concept of delinquency took shape and in other societies that have adopted the concept either literally or in some modified form. Yet even in American law there is so much variation—more so in the upper than in the lower age limits of delinquency—that what constitutes a delinquent act in one locality often does not elsewhere.[14]

Most juvenile-court laws have no floor or minimum age limit regarding delinquency. According to such laws, a person is defined as delinquent exclusively in terms of the one age-dimension of the upper age limit—"children under eighteen"—or whatever the age limit may be. In practice, however, a four-year-old, let us say, or anyone else up to seven years of age who is found to have committed a violation, is not classified as delinquent but as a dependency or neglect case, inasmuch as the jurisdiction of most juvenile courts includes cases of dependency and neglect.

Where the law does set a specific minimum-age limit to delinquency, it is usually seven years of age. This has its origin in the English common law, whereby a person under seven years of age was conclusively presumed to be incapable of "felonious intent." In several states the law provides that a child under such a specified age is presumed to be incapable of delinquency, but given certain conditions or circumstances he may be found delinquent. This has raised the following rhetorical question: Is not the reason for the rule exempting older children from criminal responsibility also applicable to these younger children as far as delinquency is concerned? The result is that in some juvenile-court acts the provision appears that a child under a stated age cannot under any circumstances be adjudicated a delinquent.

---

[13] Dyson Carter, *Sin and Science*, New York, Heck-Cattell, 1946, pp. 181–2.

[14] For the impact this variation has on the validity of comparative statistics of delinquency, see the next chapter.

It has already been observed that the maximum or upper age limit is much more variable and, for that reason, controversial. The range is from a maximum of the sixteenth birthday in some states to the twenty-first birthday in others. A number of states place the limit at seventeen, but by far the majority name eighteen years as the limit of juvenile-court jurisdiction. An interesting, although obviously rare, question is whether or not marriage by a "child" challenges and supersedes the maximum age qualification for juvenile-court jurisdiction. A judge in New York City's Children's Court faced such a question and resolved it by denying discharge from probation to a fifteen-year-old boy who had slipped away to another state and married, misrepresenting his age. The boy was originally placed on probation as a juvenile delinquent after having been found in possession of a dangerous weapon. In rejecting the challenge to the court's continued jurisdiction, based on a newly attained marital status, the judge said:

> The problem with which the court is confronted is whether the fact, as it has been urged, that he is now "a married man" ousts the court of jurisdiction in law. He is still a child. The duties and obligations delegated to the court to protect this boy have not been dissolved by his misconduct. That is the law. Marriage does not as a matter of course emancipate. Under some conditions it does the opposite—it enslaves. It adds nothing to the age. It may add to responsibility but to bear responsibility one must be mature not only chronologically—that is physically—but intellectually and, moreover, socially. The law as enacted is good. Most persons continue to be children not only up to sixteen years of age, but way beyond that.[15]

A significant point is that a person beyond the maximum age limit may still be placed under the jurisdiction of the juvenile court if the act he allegedly committed occurred when he was within the age limits. Furthermore, the laws usually provide that once jurisdiction is obtained it may continue until the child reaches the age of majority or adulthood. Jurisdiction in dependency and neglect cases involves the same age limits as in de-

[15] New York *Herald Tribune*, December 14, 1949, pp. 1, 51.

linquency cases, except for a few states where it is lower than the latter and one state where it is higher.[16]

One complication is that some states set higher age limits of juvenile-court jurisdiction for girls than for boys, and a few states even have different limits as to sex and age in different parts of the state. But the trend is toward uniformity. Until 1940 most of the courts reporting to the Children's Bureau in Washington, D.C., had jurisdiction over boys under the age of seventeen, and the second most frequent age of jurisdiction over boys was under sixteen. The modal age of jurisdiction over girls was also under seventeen, but the second most common was under eighteen. Since 1940 the trend has been to raise the age limit of juvenile-court jurisdiction over both boys and girls, particularly boys. The result is that most reporting courts now have the same age jurisdiction over both sexes; namely, up to eighteen years of age.

A more serious complication is that many juvenile courts do not have exclusive jurisdiction over *all* children within the prescribed age limits. They have exclusive jurisdiction over most— but not all—cases of children, or they may have concurrent jurisdiction with some other courts over the children. This is an outcome of the incomplete evolution of the concept of delinquency as distinguished from criminality in law. That is, for most cases of children within the defined age limits, the transition is complete from full responsibility for crime to exemption from responsibility under the principles of chancery and equity. But often the law either withholds the logical extension of these principles to other children who have allegedly committed acts punishable by death or life imprisonment, declaring in effect that legally they are adults who know the difference between right and wrong and who know the nature and quality of their acts by virtue of the "serious" acts they have committed, or it grants joint or concurrent power both to the juvenile and criminal courts to try such "serious" cases as those involving homicide, robbery, burglary, and rape. Often these exemptions of children from the jurisdiction of juvenile courts apply only to the older years within the age

16 See Alice Scott Nutt, "Juvenile and Domestic Relations Courts," *Social Work Year Book*, 1947, p. 272. Also useful is Sol Rubin's chart on "Jurisdiction of Juvenile Courts in the United States," *Probation*, June 1946, pp. 144–5.

limits, or only to cases within certain counties of the state. In concurrent jurisdiction the decision as to which court should hear the case may be in the hands of the judge, or the district attorney, or the grand jury, or even be left to the child himself to decide. There is little doubt that this conflict between juvenile and criminal court jurisdictions for children betrays the diehard reluctance of the legal system to bypass completely the older ideas of retribution, deterrence, and protection of the public in favor of the new idea of promoting the child's welfare. That legalists do not stand alone in this respect can be seen in Durea's study of the attitudes of various academic adults toward delinquent behavior in children. Psychologists, sociologists, and graduate students as well as juvenile-court judges were asked to rate fourteen types of delinquent behavior with the use of a scale developed on the basis of paired comparisons. Murder was considered the most serious offense and truancy the least serious.[17]

The following critical questions directed at the arbitrariness and inconsistencies in law as they appear in the age factor are inevitable:

Why should one offender fifteen years of age go to juvenile court on a delinquency charge, whereas a co-offender who may be only a few days or months older goes to criminal court on a charge of felony? Why should a male of fifteen be subject to a different court system than a female the same age? Why should a boy of sixteen in one jurisdiction go to criminal court for an offense that sends another boy of eighteen or twenty elsewhere to a juvenile court? Why should a boy of sixteen who steals in one jurisdiction be subject to the chancery procedure of the juvenile court, whereas a boy of ten who kills in the same jurisdiction is sent to criminal court?

One rebuttal in answer to the first of these four critical questions is that, despite its apparent arbitrariness, the law must use clearly defined systems of age classification in order to function effectively. This promotes justice, it is maintained, more than would be possible if judges were not restrained by considerations of age. The second and third critical questions regarding sex and

[17] Mervin Arnold Durea, "An Experimental Study of Attitudes Toward Juvenile Delinquency," *Journal of Applied Psychology*, 17:522–34, 1933.

jurisdictional differentials obviously cannot be rebutted except in terms of the cultural biases that make for such differentials. Yet the weakest of all rebuttals is given in answer to the fourth criticism, which concerns dual or concurrent jurisdiction. The rebuttal is that society cannot afford to "coddle a killer" and other serious offenders. This is so weak that the most vociferous of all demands for legislative reform is to be found here. The demand is that all children within the given age limits be subject to juvenile court jurisdiction regardless of the nature or "seriousness" of the offense. It is voiced most frequently in connection with specific cases of alleged murder by schoolboys who, under the present system, are prosecuted in regular criminal court procedure and are liable to death or life imprisonment if found guilty, just as in cases involving adults. It is estimated that two homicides a day are committed by American boys and girls under twenty years of age—and one of the two is committed by someone under eighteen.

The Paradox of Jurisdictional Exemption

The boy stood in Albany Police Court yesterday, leaning forward a bit, his body tense with fright, his hands clutching his cap. He looked younger than his 14 years. He wore patched and faded blue dungarees and a lumber jacket. It was a special Sunday session and it lasted just five minutes. His mother and father, Mr. and Mrs. Carl M. D. stood nearby, weeping. The charge was brief enough. Carl D., a freshman at Philip Livingston High School in Albany, standing in this adult court, heard the District Attorney say that he had hanged his eight-year-old playmate Robert W. Saturday, by winding a rope with a slipknot around his neck three times, swinging it over a tree and securing the end of the rope to the branch of another tree. . . . Three boys found the body hanging from the tree in an isolated district. . . . They called the police. . . .

The white-faced boy blinked at Judge ——. The judge read the charge, quoted a lot of legal language. Carl didn't have to plead. A plea of innocent is automatic under the State Law. He was charged with first degree murder. That means he faces the possible penalty of the electric chair. . . .[18]

[18] *PM*, March 17, 1947, p. 12.

Many professional observers point out that there is a striking paradox in the maintenance of a statewide system of children's courts employing a concept of clinical treatment for delinquents while at the same time other children like Carl D. are held as accountable as adults. They claim that those who defend the paradox because it works against the "coddling of killers" do not realize that many juries, when facing the alternatives of convicting a child for a capital crime or setting him free, choose the latter course. The child is released with his potentially dangerous maladjustments untreated.

Aside from this general paradox, there are specific paradoxes in this arrangement of dual or concurrent jurisdiction. Suppose a child who had been hanged by another child subsequently survived? Suppose the noose slipped, or he was cut down in time to save him? In that case the defendant would automatically be assigned to juvenile court jurisdiction instead of being tried in an adult criminal court for murder, even though his intent would conceivably be the same whether his victim lived or died.

Or suppose a child has a gun and aims it straight at another person's heart? If his aim is accurate and he kills, he is deemed responsible and subject to adult trial and penalties. If his aim is bad and he misses, he goes to children's court. His treatment as an offender thus actually depends not on his intent, but on his aim. Lastly, suppose one object of a child's homicidal assault has a strong physique and survives, whereas the victim of another child has a weaker physique and dies. Both homicidal children may have the same intent, but they receive widely different handling because of a circumstance that has nothing to do with the nature of their behavior.

The Strain toward Consistency

Indicative of the broad demand for reform is the fact that prosecutors themselves in criminal court cases involving children are among the most vociferous advocates of the amendment of the paradoxical laws. Many urge the adoption in their own states of the "progressive" legislation enacted by California, Connecticut, Indiana, Michigan, and Wisconsin, where all juvenile offenders under the age of eighteen, including those charged with murder, have been placed under the jurisdiction of the juvenile courts.

In the state of New York the situation is unique. In 1947, largely as a result of the case of Carl D. and similar cases, the Young Bills were introduced in the state legislature to permit the children's courts of the state to deal with all children under sixteen, regardless of their offense. When some opposition developed in the legislature on the basis of "coddling" the older child, the Bills were revised to apply to those under fifteen only. This was a compromise to assure enactment. In March 1948 the Bills became laws, providing that in New York State all children under fifteen years of age were thereafter not to be placed on trial for capital crimes or for any other degree of crime. As a concession to the opposition referred to above, an intermediate zone of concurrent jurisdiction was established whereby discretion was thereafter to be left to the courts as to whether the fifteen-year-old charged with a crime punishable by death or life imprisonment should be treated as a criminal or as a juvenile delinquent in the children's court. In short, it is still possible in New York State to try a child for murder in criminal court providing he or she has passed the fifteenth birthday.

The Trend of the Definition of Delinquency

Some view such amendments of law as only one part of a trend whereby the legal definition of delinquency is yielding ground to a more eclectic definition with clinical implications. For alongside the strain toward consistency of children's court jurisdiction, there are in some states deliberate efforts to attain an unrestricted statutory definition of delinquency. Indeed two jurisdictions, California and the District of Columbia, now have no statutory definition at all.

Supporters of the trend say that an unrestricted definition is administratively useful as well as a logical outgrowth of the philosophy of delinquency—that children should be given individualized treatment based on their needs as individuals rather than on the nature of their offenses. The child's welfare is advanced if the court's interest is not fixed on particular isolated offenses. If the definition of delinquency is unrestricted the court is in a position to protect and treat as many children as possible who may benefit by its help. From the standpoint of society, children who steal, beg, or run away may not be as difficult problem cases as children who develop pathological lying and mental conflicts. An unrestricted definition permits delinquency coverage of the latter as well as the former.

Others, however, claim that the trend in definition carries several dangerous possibilities. One is that without the check of precise terms in law there is nothing to prevent inadequate parents from having their children assigned to the status of delinquency if they so desire. A second danger is that the ethnic and class biases of the police and other officials against some children may be rationalized in the respectable vagueness of the law.

Bias in the Identification of Delinquent Children

Considerable evidence is available that such biases are very frequently exercised in the process of identifying some children as delinquent while others, whose behavior and personality traits are similar, are exempt from such identification. Porterfield's comparison of the offenses of 2,049 cases of alleged delinquents in the Fort Worth, Texas, area with the admitted conduct of several hundred students at three colleges of northern Texas showed that many college students have committed one or more of the "delinquency offenses," but seldom have they been so charged as in the case of "their less fortunate counterparts." [19] Sometimes the influencing factor comes from within the family rather than an outside source in the identification of delinquent children. A comparison of delinquent and nondelinquent Negro boys in Philadelphia revealed that although the so-called delinquents actually participated in more overt delinquency, the nondelinquents also participated to a significant degree. The family situation seems to have prevented the latter's offenses from becoming known to the authorities.

The Multiple Meanings of Juvenile Delinquency

Out of this perplexing situation has come a vigorous demand for clarification, for uniqueness and consistency of reference as far

---

[19] Austin Porterfield, *Youth in Trouble,* Austin, Texas, Leo Potishman Foundation, 1946, p. 41.

as juvenile delinquency is concerned. The champion of such clarification, and at the same time perhaps the most successful in achieving it, has been Carr. The chart below [20] is his own answer to the following questions and comments about the term "delinquent":

What Is a Delinquent?

TERM APPLIED		MEANING
Total juvenile population	1 —	All children in given area, below given age (in Michigan, age 17).
Juvenile deviates	2 —	All children showing deviant behavior, whether or not antisocial.
Legal delinquents	3 —	All deviants committing antisocial acts as defined by law.
Detected delinquents	4 —	All antisocial deviants detected.
Agency delinquents	5 —	All detected antisocial deviants reaching any agency.
Alleged delinquents	6 —	All apprehended antisocial deviants brought to court.
Adjudged delinquents	7 —	All court antisocial deviants "found" delinquent.

Adapted from the Original. *It is of course obvious that the respective categories, from "1" to "7," become ever narrower in scope.*

As used in literature, does it describe just one particular group of individuals, or does it refer now to one class of children and then to another? Is it uniformly designative or does it occasionally express an evaluative judgment about the class designated? "Morally it may mean one thing, legally something else; practi-

[20] Lowell J. Carr, *Delinquency Control*, New York, Harper, 1940, p. 59.

cally a third thing, and statistically still a fourth. . . . The best that can be done is to define the reference that it shall carry within the framework of a given discussion. . . ." [21]

The Impact of the Delinquency Concept on Other Age Groups

It would be inappropriate to conclude this chapter without some comment on the influence of the concept of delinquency on age groups other than children.

There have been many developments in the field of adult crime adjudication which owe their existence to prior demonstrations of their utility in the juvenile court. These are, among other things, the indeterminate sentence, behavior clinics, and presentence investigation. But the impact of the delinquency concept has been much more pronounced in age groups contiguous to juveniles or children. In New York City, for example, a law enacted in 1943 established a "Youth Section" of the Court of General Sessions for offenders sixteen to nineteen years of age. This law provides that if the offense with which a youth is charged is not punishable by death or life imprisonment, he may be eligible for treatment as a "youthful offender," a legal status resembling that of the juvenile delinquent as far as the principles of equity or chancery are concerned.

Conclusion

The primary purpose of this chapter has been to trace the emergence of juvenile delinquency as a concept from its earliest beginnings and to define and analyze its legal characteristics. Few, if any, other social problems are as dependent on a legal orientation as is juvenile delinquency. In the next two chapters, attention is turned to the profile of juvenile delinquency, an analysis of the incidence, participants, and spatial and temporal distribution of the problem. The profile in turn should be of some value in facilitating subsequent efforts to answer basic questions about the etiology of juvenile delinquency and the tasks of treatment and prevention.

[21] *Ibid.*, p. 58.

QUESTIONS AND RESEARCH SUGGESTIONS

1. *Why is juvenile delinquency considered to be a concept as well as a social problem?*
2. *What are the strengths and weaknesses of extralegal conceptions of delinquency?*
3. *In what sense is delinquency "normal" behavior?*
4. *Why was the final offense of Howard L. discussed in Chapter I legally not a delinquency in the state of Illinois?*
5. *What is the trend of the definition of delinquency?*
6. *Make use of the survey method to determine the extent of "proto-delinquency" among the students living in your residence unit.*
7. *Look up the juvenile-court law in your home jurisdiction and compare it with the common denominator of such laws throughout the United States.*
8. *Examine the Standard Juvenile Court Act and list the points of resemblance and difference between that model and the law in your home state.*
9. *Compare the juvenile-court legislation of one European country, one Asiatic country, and one South American country with the law of the United States.*
10. *In a small-scale survey of public opinion, determine the extent to which your sample is for or against concurrent jurisdiction.*

SELECTED READINGS AND REFERENCES

Banay, Ralph S., *Youth in Despair*, New York, Coward-McCann, 1948.

Brown, Fred, "Social Maturity and Stability of Non-delinquents, Proto-delinquents and Delinquents," *American Journal of Orthopsychiatry*, 8:214–19, 1938.

Courthial, Andree, "What Is a Juvenile Delinquent?" *Family*, 14: 169–71, 1933.

Lou, Herbert H., *Juvenile Courts in the United States*, Chapel Hill, University of North Carolina Press, 1927.

Partridge, E. DeAlton, "Social Antecedents of Delinquency," *Journal of Juvenile Research*, 21:1–10, 1937.

Rubin, Sol, "The Legal Character of Juvenile Delinquency," *The Annals of the American Academy of Political and Social Science*, 261:1–8, 1949.

Schramm, Gustav L., "Philosophy of the Juvenile Court," *The Annals of the American Academy of Political and Social Science,* 261: 101–8, 1949.

Standard Juvenile Court Law, New York, National Probation Association, 1946.

Chapter **III.** *Profile of Juvenile Delinquency*

In an analysis of juvenile delinquency it is customary, and justifiably so, to consider the profile of the problem before examining its etiology and control. How much delinquency is there? What is the relative incidence of the various types of delinquency? Who are the delinquents and how many of them are there? Where are they? When are they delinquent? These are major profile questions whose answers, regardless of their present degree of accuracy, logically precede attempts to answer the crucial questions of why there is delinquency and what can be done to prevent and control it. A recent national conference on the prevention and control of juvenile delinquency [1] concluded

[1] National Conference on Prevention and Control of Juvenile Delinquency, *Report on Statistics*, Washington, D.C., U.S. Government Printing Office, 1947, pp. 3–4.

that the kinds of "profile" facts needed may be classified as follows: (1) the numbers and characteristics of children dealt with as delinquents by agencies, both public and private, having a major responsibility in this field; (2) the character of and circumstances surrounding delinquent acts, such as the time and place of the delinquency, whether the delinquent act was that of an individual or a group and whether it is the first delinquency or one of a series; (3) the socio-economic and psychological factors involved in delinquency—that is, the age, sex, race, school status, psychological and psychiatric diagnosis, and recreational interest, the economic status of the family from which the delinquent comes, its organization, neighborhood location, and mobility, and the neighborhood in which the family resides classified according to housing, economic, and social type.

This chapter concentrates on a static profile of juvenile delinquency and the following chapter is concerned with its dynamics. Because it is obviously unrealistic to maintain rigidly this artificial division of labor, the lines are occasionally crossed in each chapter. Preliminary to a consideration of both the static and dynamic profiles, it seems necessary to evaluate the technique that is utilized in each case.

Statistics on Juvenile Delinquency

The most important technique in the measurement of delinquency's profile is that of statistics. As in the case of other applications of statistics, statistical procedures in juvenile delinquency have two distinct phases. One phase has to do with the collection and tabulation of accurate, representative information. But what is the value of masses of figures in and of themselves? Hence, the second phase, the analysis of data, is necessary; that is, "a fundamental obligation of those who are responsible for delinquency statistics is to present an interpretation of the statistics which will give explicit recognition to limitations of the data and to the basic assumptions upon which the analysis is made." [2]

There are many private organizations and governmental agencies active in the collection and distribution of statistics relating to juvenile delinquency. Most prominent are the federal agencies whose statistics have nationwide coverage as their objective,

[2] *Ibid.*, p. 1.

namely (1) police arrests based on fingerprint records reported to the Federal Bureau of Investigation, (2) the juvenile-court cases reported to the Children's Bureau, and (3) the reports on institutionalized delinquents to the Children's Bureau, Bureau of the Census, and Bureau of Prisons. Most of these reports are obtained from state and local agencies on a voluntary basis and thus fall short of complete nationwide coverage. Police arrests and juvenile-court statistics are more frequently used than the others because they obviously cover a larger proportion of the total group of children with "behavior problems."

POLICE ARRESTS. It is not merely their extensive coverage that makes police arrest statistics so important. They are significant, too, because they infer that many children in society have a traumatic experience—interaction with the official agents of social control. This differentiates them from children who otherwise often resemble them in personality and behavior. Statistics on police arrests of children are part of the larger uniform crime-reporting program of the Federal Bureau of Investigation, originally formulated by a committee and technical staff sponsored by the International Association of Chiefs of Police for the purpose of improving general police statistics. Since 1930 the F.B.I. has received reports from local and state police on a voluntary basis in two forms. One is in summary form and the other is in the form of individual fingerprint records.[3] The summary reports contain such information as state and municipal offenses known to the police, offenses cleared by the police, persons released without being charged, and persons formally charged by the police. The fingerprint records contain information on the age, sex, race, offense charged, and history of offenses of the arrested person. These records received during a given year are tabulated for the items mentioned above and the totals are published by the F.B.I. in *Uniform Crime Reports for the United States and Its Possessions.* They constitute the only source of national statistics of adults as well as children arrested by the police. Yet such a compilation is limited to instances of arrests for violations of state law and municipal ordinances. Fingerprint cards represent-

---

[3] In 1949 a new form was introduced that recorded the characteristics of the child arrested whether he or she was fingerprinted or not. See the subsequent section on "Efforts to Improve Delinquency Statistics."

ing arrests for violations of federal laws or representing commitments to any type of penal institution are excluded. Furthermore, the *Uniform Crime Reports* themselves point out that the data compiled from fingerprint cards do not represent all persons arrested, inasmuch as there are many persons taken into custody for whom no fingerprints are forwarded to Washington. This would apply especially to children, because in many places it is a matter of law or public policy not to fingerprint children who are arrested. Despite these omissions, it is the belief of the F.B.I. that for many years the majority of the law-enforcement agencies making arrests throughout the country have transmitted fingerprint records to them regularly. Therefore, while the figures may be an understatement since they are limited to those arrests where the offenders are fingerprinted, the F.B.I. believes that the trends reflected periodically do represent a reasonably reliable index of all arrests throughout the country. The assumption here, of course, is that the same policies as to who are fingerprinted prevail, in general, year after year.

JUVENILE-COURT STATISTICS. The desirability of collecting the second of the more frequently used national statistics on delinquency, juvenile-court statistics, was recognized in 1923, but it was not until 1927 and periodically thereafter that they were collected and published by the Children's Bureau. Initially, the plan for uniform reporting of juvenile-court data called for voluntary and direct reporting from the individual court to the Children's Bureau in Washington. The method used was to send statistical cards to each court willing to co-operate with the Bureau. These cards were so arranged that most of the information could be entered by checking, thereby reducing clerical work considerably. Blanks were also provided the courts so that they could compile their own tables and send them to the Children's Bureau, or, if the courts preferred, they could send the cards to the Bureau for compilation. Franking privileges were given to co-operating courts. But this system of individual court reporting was never successful in terms of coverage—a mere 15 per cent of the population in 1927, the first year of its operation, and only 37 per cent in 1945, the last year of its existence. The following year, 1946, the system of reporting was revised. In a number of states, state welfare departments had been given responsibilities for providing services to local juvenile courts and, in a few states, state-administered juvenile courts had been organized. These provided the statewide machinery for the conversion in 1946 to a local-state-federal reporting system by which the Children's Bureau now receives summary reports only from a single agency in each state instead of directly collecting reports from individual courts. It is hoped that over a period of time the new system will improve the national collection of court data. The revised reports, still voluntary, include all children's cases of dependency, neglect, and special proceedings other than delinquency, and delinquency cases disposed of unofficially as well as officially.[4]

Limitations of Delinquency Statistics

The limitations of statistics on juvenile delinquency have long been recognized. One of the most penetrating inquiries into both crime and delinquency statistics was undertaken by the National Commission on Law Observance and Enforcement—better known as the Wickersham Commission—in its Report on Criminal Statistics, published in 1931. Some of its observations about such statistics are no less pertinent today than when they were first published. It noted that there is general agreement as to the importance of official and trustworthy statistics of crime and delinquency. "The eagerness with which the unsystematic, often inaccurate, and more often incomplete statistics available for this country are taken up by text writers, writers in the periodicals, newspaper writers, and public speakers, speaks for itself. Most . . . assume certain things to be well known or incontrovertible. But as one looks for the facts underlying such assumptions he soon finds they are not at hand. Even when tables and masses of figures are given one soon finds that for the most part the material is . . . uncritical. . . . Accurate data are the beginning of wisdom in such a subject, and no such data can be had for the country as a whole." [5]

[4] One child may appear before the court a number of times during the year, yet each appearance is counted as a unique case if a new complaint is filed and dealt with separately.

[5] See National Conference on Prevention and Control of Juvenile Delinquency, *op. cit.*, p. 2.

Some reputable scholars go so far as to question seriously whether delinquency can ever be satisfactorily measured.[6] Others even doubt the wisdom of attempting national compilations. What major shortcomings do the critics of delinquency statistics see? They may be classified and summarized as follows:

1. LACK OF UNIFORMITY AND AMBIGUITY IN LEGAL DEFINITIONS. Between jurisdictions and even within one jurisdiction from one year to the next, some legal definitions of delinquency vary in such important respects as age and conduct. The impact this has on the validity of comparative police and court statistics in the dimensions of both space and time is self-evident. The ambiguity of many conduct items in legal definitions—for example, "injuring or endangering the morals or health of himself or others"—encourages considerable variation among police and court personnel in the identification of delinquents. This variation, in turn, it may readily be deduced, also undermines confidence in comparative statistics.

2. VARIABLES IN THE EXPOSURE, DETECTION, AND APPREHENSION OF CHILDREN. Many families of high socio-economic status have a strong aversion to police referral, discreetly diverting their misbehaving children to the attention of private agencies, psychiatrists, and boarding-schools. Other families, especially those who are members of cohesive ethnic groups, avoid police referral and other "outside" sources, dealing with their wayward children themselves whenever possible. This happens partly out of disagreement with the value attached to such waywardness by outsiders, partly because of belief in self-help, and partly as a defense measure in order not to increase antagonism toward themselves.

The accuracy of delinquency statistics is also allegedly affected by variation in place and time of the members, efficiency, and policy of the police in the detection and apprehension of delinquents. There are variations too in the exposure, detection, and apprehension of children on the basis of their age, sex, and ethnic affiliation. For example, the family and the police are not likely to consider stealing on the part of a child of seven as serious as stealing on the part of a boy of fifteen. Boys are seldom referred to authorities for sex offenses other than homosexuality and rape,

---

[6] See, for example, Sophia M. Robison, *Can Delinquency Be Measured?* New York, Columbia University Press, 1936.

whereas girls are seldom referred for anything but sexual misconduct. For most offenses, Negro children are more likely to be exposed to, or detected and apprehended by, police officials than are white children, many of whom are often known only by private agencies.

3. VARIABLES IN POLICE ADMINISTRATION. Lack of time, training, and interest among some police results in the recording of inaccurate and fragmentary data about the children they detect and apprehend. Different police departments have different policies regarding the fingerprinting of children, and not all of those who do fingerprint children send their records to the Federal Bureau of Investigation.

4. VARIABLES IN COURT PRACTICES. Court statistics are affected by the fact that many children never reach the courts. They are given terminal treatment by the police, school authorities, and private social agencies. The latter organizations often do not label their child clients as delinquent, even when the conduct involved is similar to that adjudicated in courts.

The proportion of children referred to juvenile courts fluctuates from place to place and from year to year in the same place, depending upon differences and changes in policy. Some courts call burglary by children "trespassing"; sex offenses are often called "incorrigibility." All this results in lumping together in court statistics activities of different character. There is variation from one court to the next in the extent of official versus unofficial or informal handling of cases, and there is no agreement between courts about the inclusion in their reports to the Children's Bureau of those cases disposed of unofficially. Furthermore, the statistical recording of court cases handled officially is more complete than that of cases dealt with unofficially.

In some localities, repeated court referrals are reported as additional cases each time; in other localities this is not the practice. Courts that co-operate in the Children's Bureau coverage do not constitute a representative sample of all juvenile courts in terms of either geographic location or rural-urban distribution. Urban communities and the Northeast and the West Coast are overrepresented.

5. VARIABLES IN INSTITUTIONAL INTAKE. Statistics on the population of institutions for delinquents are qualified by varia-

bles of place and time in commitment policies and housing facilities. Judges differ in their decisions in dealing with essentially the
same types of cases. For example, four New Jersey judges were
compared for three selected years, and differences were noted
of more than ten per cent in the use of institutionalization versus
probation. One judge would institutionalize heavily for one type
of delinquency; another would use probation for the same type
but institutionalize for another type. The judges differed in the
agents they consulted before making decisions about commitment.
They also disagreed in their attitudes toward children of different
nationalities as far as commitment and its alternatives were concerned.[7] Smaller counties have been found to favor commitments
more than the larger counties, and commitment to an institution
instead of probation in some communities is found to be the practice in a much larger percentage of girls' cases than of boys' cases.[8]

It is clear that there is an incomplete coverage of their respective universes in all three nationwide types of delinquency statistics: by the police, the courts, and institutions. The fact that
institutional statistics cover their universe more accurately than
the others because of the relative ease of "nose-counting" behind
lock and key has led some students to conclude that of all types
of statistics they serve best as an index of the dynamic incidence
of delinquency. The index notion is based on the assumption that
a certain consistency exists over long periods of time in the
proportionate relationship of the total incidence of delinquency
to that recorded. But, as Sellin observed long ago,[9] police and
court statistics, despite the fact that their universes are not so
easily and accurately counted, are more likely to furnish a sound
basis for such an index. This is because the value of a crime or
delinquency rate as an index decreases as the distance from the
acts of crime or delinquency themselves, in terms of procedure,
increases. The more the variables between the act and the statis-

---

[7] Emil Frankel, "The Offender and the Court: a Statistical Analysis
of the Sentencing of Delinquents," *Journal of Criminal Law and Criminology*, 31:448–56, 1940.

[8] Benedict S. Alper and George E. Lodgen, "The Delinquent Child
in Pennsylvania Courts," *Mental Hygiene*, 20:598–604, 1936.

[9] Thorsten Sellin, "The Basis of a Crime Index," *Journal of Criminal
Law and Criminology*, 22:335–56, 1931.

tical compilation, the less reliable the statistic is as a reflection of the act.

Efforts to Improve Delinquency Statistics

Some of the limitations of delinquency statistics which have been described above are being corrected. For example, the Federal Bureau of Investigation data, until recently, were limited to children arrested and fingerprinted, thereby covering only part of the children arrested. The Bureau in 1949 inaugurated a new report that would show the age, race, and sex of all persons arrested, whether fingerprinted or not.

In the case of the Children's Bureau's statistics on court cases, it has already been mentioned above that, effective in 1946, data on unofficial as well as official cases are sought for inclusion in reports. The reports under the revised system also attempt to group together jurisdictions with similarities in age and other statutory definitions. If this is successful, obviously it will result in a more valid comparability of data.

In 1943–4, an experiment in the central registration of delinquency in an entire community, the District of Columbia, was undertaken co-operatively by the Children's Bureau and the District of Columbia Council of Social Agencies.[10] It demonstrated what is possible in the direction of comprehensive and accurate statistical coverage when all types of cases that *might* be dealt with under the law are reported to a central register by all agencies dealing with such cases. The six public agencies in the District of Columbia which are concerned with juvenile behavior registered in a central file each case of "delinquency" coming to their attention. In this way it was found that less than half of the children alleged to be delinquent during the period covered were known to the juvenile court during the same period. It was also found that many children were dealt with by the police without court referral and that a large number of children registered were unknown to the police. The study showed that because of duplication of statistics gathered by any two agencies, a central registration file is probably the only feasible method for

[10] Edward E. Schwartz, "A Community Experiment in the Measurement of Juvenile Delinquency," *Yearbook of the National Probation Association,* 1945, pp. 157–82.

gathering locally in complete, unduplicated fashion the count of children alleged to be delinquent. Edward Schwartz, who played a leading role in the original experiment, later cautioned that the central registration approach was hardly feasible on a nationwide or statewide basis, but that complete and unduplicated communitywide statistics on juvenile delinquency can be obtained by collecting records of children known to all agencies, or by the current reporting to a central register by all agencies of children referred to them.[11]

That authorities are impressed by the technique of central registration is to be seen in its adoption. New York City registered its so-called problem children from March 1, 1950 to March 1, 1951. The register cost $20,000 and was financed by the city and the state. Between the ages of six and twenty-one there were found to be 37,515 boys and girls who were either delinquent or had behavior problems bordering on delinquency. These constituted all people in the aforementioned age span whose behavior in any way brought them to the attention of any of twenty-three public and voluntary social agencies as well as the police, courts, and schools. Excluded from the register were more than 3,000 youths over sixteen but under twenty-one who were arrested for felonies, and not treated as juvenile delinquents. Of the 37,515 children registered, 29,042 were boys and 8,473 girls. The median age of the entire group was fourteen years.[12]

The present status of delinquency statistics, despite the aforementioned improvements, still leaves much to be desired. They are nevertheless useful, say some analysts, because "they measure the volume of certain kinds of business transacted. . . ."[13] They have significance not as measures of the children's behavior or of the totality of police, court, and institutional contact with children, but as minimum indexes of such contact. Such children represent at least a portion of all children whose

[11] Edward E. Schwartz, "Statistics of Juvenile Delinquency in the United States," *The Annals of the American Academy of Political and Social Science*, 261:20, 1949.

[12] See Alfred J. Kahn, *Police and Children*, New York, Citizens' Committee on Children of New York City, 1951; see also the *New York Times*, April 25, 1952.

[13] Lowell J. Carr, *Delinquency Control*, New York, Harper, 1940, pp. 61–2.

behavior might be dealt with by the police, courts, and institutions. *Is it possible to assume, then, that changes in the number of children coming to the attention of law-enforcement, judicial, and institutional agencies give some indication of changes occurring in the total incidence of delinquency?* [14] Perlman [15] believes that such an assumption is possible, but only for comparisons of year-to-year changes in *national* data rather than for local data or for inter-area comparisons. This is so, he claims, because local changes in law or administrative practice which affect time series are less significant in national totals. Support of the assumption is found in the fact that despite the limitations of police arrest statistics and juvenile-court statistics individually, both present a somewhat similar picture in year-to-year changes. We find, he says, despite the fact that neither of these series represents a completely accurate measurement of juvenile delinquency, and despite the differences in unit of count, extent of coverage, and geographic representation, that nevertheless there is a remarkable similarity between the direction of changes indicated by the two lines. Both increased sharply from 1942 to 1943, both decreased between 1943 and 1944, both increased again in 1945 to the ten-year peak and both showed sharp decreases in 1946 and 1947. This striking similarity, he claims, cannot be accounted for on the grounds that the police arrest data composed a large proportion of the cases referred to court, for the police data were based on fingerprint records and were therefore only a small proportion of those referred to court. Schwartz [16] agrees with Perlman, for he asserts that the marked similarity in the movement of the two series, despite their differences in source and coverage, strongly suggests that they are subject to common determining factors. Nationally pervasive social forces, which could well have affected both the number of arrests of children and the number of juvenile-court delinquency cases, were operative for the period under consideration. It seems likely, therefore, according to Schwartz,

[14] This is evidently of basic importance to the question of the dynamics of delinquency, which is discussed in the next chapter.

[15] I. Richard Perlman, "The Meaning of Juvenile Delinquency Statistics," *Federal Probation*, 13:64–6, 1949.

[16] Edward E. Schwartz, "Statistics of Juvenile Delinquency in the United States," *The Annals of the American Academy of Political and Social Science*, 261:12, 1949.

Chart I

Comparison of Delinquency Cases Disposed of by Juvenile Courts, with Police Arrests of Children under Eighteen Years of Age, 1938–47.[17]

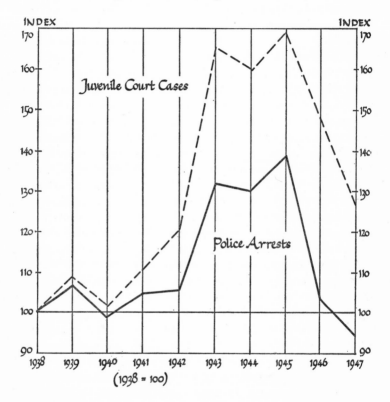

[17] Adapted from Edward E. Schwartz, "Statistics of Juvenile Delinquency in the United States," *The Annals of the American Academy of Political and Social Science,* 261:11, 1949.

that statistics available on a national basis do indicate for ten years [18] the direction of the large change in the number of children who were in conflict with the law.

The Volume of Juvenile Delinquency

Now that the characteristics of delinquency statistics have been examined and their limitations realized, it is appropriate to turn to the static profile of the problem which they present. What, for instance, do statistics reveal of the volume of juvenile delinquency?

The available data, of course, do not claim to measure the absolute volume of *delinquent behavior* in the United States. There are estimates, however, of the size of the juvenile population marked by "deviant" behavior, based on teachers' surveys of the children in their classrooms. At any given time, it is claimed, teachers can spot from two to twenty per cent of their pupils being "deviant," with five per cent the most frequent number.[19]

Before World War II, nationwide statistics pointed to approximately two million of the country's forty-three million children under eighteen years of age as "coming to the attention" of the police annually. After the war, the Federal Bureau of Investigation revealed that one person in every six reported arrested was under twenty-one years of age. These "minors" constituted half of all arrests for auto theft, a third of all arrests for robbery, burglary, and larceny, one in four of those arrested for rape, and one in eight of all arrests for murder.

On another level, that of court cases, it is estimated from the available federal-state juvenile-court statistics that *alleged delinquents* constitute roughly one per cent of the child population aged ten to sixteen, inclusive. Another estimate is that about six of every thousand children under eighteen years of age are involved in court cases. In 1952 some observers estimated that 3,000,000 juveniles annually reach the courts, more than 500,000 are detained in jails, and about 35,000 are committed each year to 300 training schools. At the same time the Bureau of the Census predicted that within ten years the child population between ten

---

[18] See the accompanying Chart I. This period covers the prewar and postwar years of World War II.

[19] See Carr, *op. cit.*, pp. 58, 136.

and seventeen years of age—the age span when delinquency most frequently occurs—will increase at least 50 per cent. In other words, if nothing new is done in prevention, there may be 450,000 juvenile delinquents in the courts of the United States by 1960. These estimates, of course, do not take into consideration many of the unofficial cases and all of the children known to agencies other than the courts. If they could be estimated, the percentage would undoubtedly be much larger.

The Distribution of Delinquency Offenses

Analysis of court cases [20] in most jurisdictions shows that theft is the most common type of offense for male delinquents, with "mischievous behavior" a close second. Endangering the morals of oneself and others and running away from home are third and fourth, with other offenses trailing behind. Among girls, sex offenses rank first, and running away, second. Theft and sex offenses, which are statistically the leading offenses of boys and girls respectively, have something in common according to one school of thought. They both provide libidinous gratification. The claim is that stealing brings with it the thrill of excitement in entering restricted places; physical violence and the use of dangerous weapons involved in many cases of robbery are aggressive acts that are substitutes for the male sexual act. The male before sixteen years of age usually cannot meet his sexual needs directly as easily as can the female, so he must resort to sexually symbolic acts such as stealing.[21]

The relative order of distribution of offenses, as measured in specific jurisdictions and areas, does not vary much from the over-all picture. For example, more than half of the cases of children charged with violations of federal laws have been in connection with the National Motor Vehicle Theft Act, and other forms of larceny and theft are the next most frequent federal offenses. In Merrill's study of delinquency on the West Coast,[22] the distribution of offenses was as follows: theft, 59.7 per cent; beyond control, 18.3 per cent; sex, 7.9 per cent; malicious mischief, 4.8

[20] For arrest cases, see accompanying Table I.
[21] Ralph S. Banay, *Youth in Despair*, New York, Coward-McCann, 1948, pp. 84–5.
[22] Maud A. Merrill, *Problems of Child Delinquency*, Boston, Houghton Mifflin, 1947, p. 346.

Table I   *Arrests by Age Groups, 1951* *

Offense charged	Total all ages	AGE						
		Under 15	15	16	17	18	19	20
Total	119,676	3,492	4,276	10,931	18,560	28,775	27,369	26,273
Criminal homicide	687	16	20	50	110	147	153	191
Robbery	5,063	70	128	414	786	1,246	1,178	1,241
Assault	5,941	44	86	372	773	1,404	1,517	1,745
Burglary—breaking or entering	17,099	1,134	1,069	2,467	3,197	3,705	3,017	2,510
Larceny—theft	18,196	622	620	1,930	3,282	4,523	3,874	3,345
Auto theft	9,852	528	873	1,610	1,882	2,054	1,631	1,274
Embezzlement and fraud	1,239	8	6	77	140	271	342	395
Stolen property, buying, receiving, etc.	542	13	12	51	87	123	146	110
Arson	181	14	9	24	33	40	35	26
Forgery and counterfeiting	1,390	19	32	107	190	327	360	355
Rape	2,576	13	40	163	388	657	706	609
Prostitution and commercialized vice	706	1	4	11	67	168	220	235
Other sex offenses	2,052	35	48	138	255	495	496	585
Narcotic drug laws	2,440	14	28	134	305	529	692	738
Weapons, carrying, possessing, etc.	1,621	5	19	118	229	429	411	410
Offenses against family and children	664	2	1	16	32	112	188	313
Liquor laws	1,771	10	18	74	155	541	530	443
Driving while intoxicated	2,152	3	5	39	159	446	634	866
Road and driving laws	3,577	6	12	123	344	1,037	1,077	978
Parking violations	42	—	—	—	—	10	10	22
Other traffic and motor vehicle laws	2,803	13	30	110	299	738	827	786
Disorderly conduct	6,507	41	81	314	810	1,779	1,764	1,718
Drunkenness	6,851	34	57	187	621	1,631	2,038	2,283
Vagrancy	6,610	40	82	450	1,034	1,862	1,648	1,494
Gambling	567	4	8	20	65	148	153	169
Suspicion	8,993	233	292	723	1,790	2,292	1,903	1,760
Not stated	833	11	20	63	87	247	201	204
All other offenses	8,721	559	676	1,146	1,440	1,814	1,618	1,468

* Adapted from *Uniform Crime Reports* issued by the Federal Bureau of Investigation, U.S. Department of Justice, Washington, D.C., Volume XXII, Number 2, 1951, p. 109.

per cent; vagrancy, 4.6 per cent; truancy, 1.7 per cent; assault, 1.6 per cent; and forgery, 1.4 per cent. In an analysis of the records over a period of three decades in the Children's Courts of New York City, the two most frequent offenses were "stealing" and "disorderly conduct." [23]

But it is very clear that petitions issued for court referrals and court adjudications do not present an accurate picture of the order of frequency among delinquency offenses. Truancy is but one of several offenses that occur more frequently than the court

[23] Julius Bernard Maller, "Juvenile Delinquency in New York: a Summary of a Comprehensive Report," *Journal of Psychology*, 3:1–25, 1937.

statistics indicate. This can be seen in the Washington, D.C., community experiment in central registration described above, which shows the following distribution of offenses: [24]

Table II *Washington, D.C., Central Registration*

(1) Reason for reference	(2) Children registered by all agencies for reason specified in (1)	(3) Children registered by juvenile court for reason specified in (1)	(4) Per cent of all children registered for specified reason who were registered by juvenile court for that reason
Truancy	3,488	177	5
Stealing	1,870	1,487	80
Acts of carelessness or mischief	951	733	77
Running away	819	16	2
Traffic violations	591	585	99
Being ungovernable	456	244	54
Sex offense	258	61	24
Assault, injury to person	187	148	79

A breakdown of 1,148 offenses by 368 boys confined in an institution is suggestive of the pattern to be found on that level. The five most common types of offense, in the order of their frequency of occurrence, were: stealing, incorrigibility, burglary, truancy, and larceny. Delinquencies involving acquisitive behavior predominated over those involving nonacquisitive behavior, while those against property exceeded those against persons.[25]

Truancy, which neither court nor institutional statistics portray accurately in the profile of delinquency, is important for reasons other than its high rank in the distribution of offenses. It so often accompanies other delinquencies and it so frequently

[24] Edward E. Schwartz, "A Community Experiment in the Measurement of Juvenile Delinquency," *Yearbook of the National Probation Association*, 1945, p. 173.

[25] Mervin Arnold Durea, "A Survey of the Extent and Nature of Offenses Committed by Delinquent Boys," *Journal of Juvenile Research*, 19:62–74, 1935.

makes an early appearance that it has been called the kindergarten of both delinquency and crime. It is important too because it is one kind of delinquent behavior that can easily be defined and accurately measured. This can be illustrated with reference to New York City where, like elsewhere, truancy is a violation of school regulations, handled by an official bureau in the Board of Education. The following points from the regulations of the Board of Education show the basis of definition and measurement:

1. Regular uninterrupted attendance at a full-time day school or upon equivalent instruction is required of every child from seven to seventeen years of age, who is not regularly and lawfully employed, unless suspended from attendance. Every such child is required to attend the entire time that the public schools are in session in the city or district where he resides.

2. When a pupil is absent except for such known causes as severe storm, personal illness, quarantine, death in the family, or religious observance, the principal shall notify the parent or guardian of said pupil by mail or otherwise on the day on which such absence occurs; if the pupil is not promptly returned to school by his parent or guardian, or if a satisfactory explanation of his absence is not made, said principal, if possible, shall interview the parent or guardian, either in person or through a teacher. *On the fifth day* of absence, if a satisfactory explanation has not been made, said principal shall forthwith report the case to the Bureau of Attendance. In case of unexplained absence of a pupil known to have been a truant, or when truancy or illegal detention of such pupil is suspected, immediate notification shall be given to the Bureau of Attendance on the day on which such absence occurs.

Children who fail to obey these regulations are called with their parents or guardians before a district officer for a hearing. The officer, after listening to the complaint and questioning the child and the parent, disposes of the case with the truant officer by either a dismissal with a warning, a period of reporting to the officer, or referral to the children's court.

Based on the records in the Bureau of Attendance covering truancy hearings, the rate of truancy per 1,000 school population in New York City at one time was calculated as being approximately 3.8. Since truancy is defined in terms of five days of unexcused absences from school, and there is no reason to assume that its recording would be influenced by the age, sex, race, religion, or nationality affiliation of the truant, it is probable, according to one authority, that the ratios of six boys to one girl, one child under ten to thirteen children over ten years of age, five children of Roman Catholic affiliation to one child of Jewish affiliation, more nearly indicate the relative frequency of occurrence of truant behavior among the two sexes, the two age groups, and two of the more prominent religious affiliations than is true for statistics describing other types of delinquency.[26]

The Age and Sex Composition of Juvenile Delinquents

What age pattern emerges from the statistics of juvenile delinquency?[27] The predominant or modal age of delinquents in both police arrests and court cases is from fourteen to eighteen years of age. In peacetime the fourteen- and fifteen-year-olds are more prominent. In wartime the sixteen- and seventeen-year-olds take the lead, more so in court cases than in police arrests, and largely as a result of fluctuations in boys' cases. Children under ten years of age do not appear in delinquency statistics of any kind in accord with their proportion in the population.

Although both girls' and boys' cases are generally concentrated in the same years, namely the period of adolescence, the mean age of girl delinquents is higher than that for boys. One possible reason for this is that up to the age of sixteen girls are more closely supervised by their parents than are boys. This supervision may be partially responsible for the delayed appearance of girl delinquents in the courts. Furthermore, the majority of girl delinquents are apprehended for sexual delinquency, and the girl usually does not become desirable or accessible before the age of fifteen or sixteen.

[26] Robison, *op. cit.;* see also New York City Joint Committee on Maladjustment and Delinquency, *The Psychological and Sociological Implications of Maladjustment and Delinquency,* New York, Board of Education, 1938, pp. 30–4.

[27] Any such pattern is obviously qualified by the bias against the referral of younger children to the courts when other agency care is available and considered preferable. Another qualification stems from the maximum legal age limits of delinquency, ranging from sixteen to twenty-one, which have an understandable influence on the decline of statistical recording of delinquency offenses for ages above sixteen years.

Delinquency, according to the available statistics, involves more adolescent boys than girls. The sex ratio in arrest cases has recently been approximately one girl to every ten boys, whereas court cases are generally reported to be about 1:5. In federal offenses as many as 93 per cent of the court cases have involved boys. One reason why the proportion of girls' to total cases has been consistently higher in courts than in arrests is the difference between boys and girls in the source of their referral to the juvenile court. A larger proportion of girls are referred to the courts from non-police sources. Delinquency statistics report more boys than girls partly because boys are apprehended more often, whereas even when girls are detected and apprehended, they are often just reported to their parents, an expression of differential cultural expectations for the two sexes. Another reason is derived from the previous discussion of the distribution of delinquency offenses. Whereas most boys come before the juvenile courts because of stealing or other aggressive behavior injurious to others, the bulk of the girls' cases are brought into court because of problems of personal behavior or sex difficulties which primarily endanger the welfare of the girl rather than constitute offenses against others.

Although we are concerned here mainly with a static profile of juvenile delinquency, it is appropriate to observe that the trend in sex ratio over a number of years has been marked by a striking decline in the proportion of boys alleged by the courts to be delinquent, and a correspondingly striking increase in the relative number of girls. For example, a survey of the records of the Children's Court of New York City for thirty years from 1902 to 1932 revealed that in the first decade the ratio of delinquent boys to girls was about 60 to 1; in the last decade it dropped to 8:1. The director of this survey [28] interpreted this to be a real change in ratio rather than a function of altered court procedures. The greater similarity in recent years in the environmental conditions to which boys and girls have been exposed, and revisions in the definition of delinquency were held responsible for the change.

[28] Julius Bernard Maller, "The Trend of Juvenile Delinquency in New York City," *Journal of Juvenile Research*, 17:10–18, 1933.

The Ethnic Distribution of Juvenile Delinquents

Statistics about the ethnic distribution of delinquents are subject to the same qualifications as are other aspects of the profile. That is, they probably do not provide a true index of distribution because of such variables as bias, which lead to differences in police, court, and institutional policies in the disposition of cases. With this in mind, what do the statistics say at any given time about the ethnic identity of delinquents? The children represented in disproportionate numbers are Negroes and many second-generation whites of Southern and Eastern European and Latin-American backgrounds. For example, about five times as many Negro children are arraigned as delinquents in the children's courts of New York City as are white children in proportion to their relative frequencies in the total population. One important reason is the fact that Negro children seldom come to the attention of anything other than official agencies. Among institutionalized delinquents, the racial differential is also explained in large part by such factors. The case records of 300 institutionalized delinquents, 179 of whom were Negroes and 121 whites, were analyzed to determine whether the courts were committing these children on the same basis. This study discloses that Negro children are committed younger, for less serious offenses, with fewer previous court appearances, and with less prior institutionalization.[29] Other studies show that the foreign-born children, the second generation of Oriental parentage, and Jewish and white Protestant children are represented in the statistics in much lower proportions than they appear in the general population.

Social scientists are not disposed to explain the disproportionate representation of Negroes and of native white children of foreign-born, Catholic parentage (such as Italians) in terms of their race, religion, or recency of immigration *per se*. Their explanation, instead, is in terms of the inequitable psychological, social, and economic status of the children in these groups as contrasted with other groups. For example, in the case of Italian and Jewish children in New York City, where the two groups are approximately equal in nativity status as native-born Americans of

[29] Sidney Axelrad, "Negro and White Male Institutionalized Delinquents," *The American Journal of Sociology*, 57:569–74, 1952.

foreign-born parents, how does one account for their different proportions in delinquency courts? It has been suggested that in addition to such factors as different attitudes on the part of each group toward the question of reporting their children to officials, there is the possibility that problems of adjustment to the American scene differ for each. Italian-Americans have the handicap of a highly urbanized environment after a predominantly rural European background. Then, too, they are a selected population representing chiefly unskilled labor. The Jews, however, represent an unselected sample of Eastern European Jewry with a close-knit family system, who also have had the advantage of a background of highly competitive and urban European life.

The explanation for the low representation in delinquency statistics of the foreign-born and those native-born who are of Oriental parentage is that their family systems too are closely knit, characterized by strong parental control that is rarely broken in the age span of juvenile-court jurisdiction. As for white Protestant children, their low delinquency rates stem largely from their overwhelming middle-class status and from the fact that their families usually have been in this country for generations with a continuity and cohesion of tradition and culture.

The Socio-economic Status of Juvenile Delinquents

According to the available police, court, and institutional statistics, juvenile delinquents include a disproportionate number from families of lower socio-economic status. For example, the occupational distribution of the parents of 761 delinquents in Passaic, New Jersey, was compared with the distribution of all male and female members of the "labor force" in the community in 1940. In the delinquent sample, significantly fewer parents were in the professions, or working as proprietors, clerks, sales personnel, and draftsmen. Significantly greater numbers of parents were factory operatives, laborers, and domestic servants.[30] There is good reason to believe, however, that the statistics do not accurately reflect the actual situation; some special surveys such as central registrations reveal that there is practically as much behavior resembling delinquency in relatively privileged homes,

[30] William C. Kvaraceus, "Juvenile Delinquency and Social Class," *Journal of Educational Sociology*, 18:51–4, 1944.

private schools, and "good" neighborhoods as there is in the lower economic classes, public and parochial schools, and blighted ecological areas. As a matter of fact, even in arrest and court cases, the trend is for more and more of the children to come from homes in the middle-income and high-income brackets.

The Rural-Urban Distribution of Juvenile Delinquents

Delinquency cases, proportionately as well as in absolute numbers, are drawn more characteristically from urban industrial communities.[31] This may be so partly because in rural areas the family, the church, and the neighborhood are more likely to assume the responsibility for, and treatment of, such cases instead of depending on the police, judges, and probation officers. Another likely explanation for the difference in rates is that juvenile courts are generally located in urban communities and draw their cases from their immediate urban surroundings more readily than from their rural jurisdictions. But even if juvenile courts were more extensive in rural counties, and a greater effort were made to deal with cases of offenders there officially, it is still doubtful that this would materially alter the reported delinquency ratio.

Recidivism in Juvenile Delinquency

Last in this static profile of the problem of juvenile delinquency is recidivism. Recidivists or "repeaters" are found in every police department, court, and institution that keeps accurate records. Sellin [32] gathered extensive statistical data supporting the conclusions that (1) the probability of a child's committing a subsequent offense increases with each new adjudication; (2) offenses against property appear to be more recidivistic than other forms of offense; and (3) the younger persons are when they commit delinquency, the more apt they are to become recidivists than are those who begin their delinquency later in life. In Merrill's sample of juvenile delinquents,[33] there were among the

---

[31] It was observed some time ago, however, that there is a tendency for rural areas to surpass urban population in proportion of offenses against persons and to lag behind the urban population in offenses against property. See Pitirim Sorokin and Carle Zimmerman, *Principles of Rural-Urban Sociology*, New York, Holt, 1929, p. 384.

[32] Thorsten Sellin, *The Criminality of Youth*, Philadelphia, American Law Institute, 1940.

[33] Merrill, *op. cit.*, p. 296.

recidivists a disproportionate number who had foreign-born and unskilled parents, and a low proportion who had professional parents. "But," she concluded, "none of these differences is statistically significant. There is significance only in the fact that the recidivists are the ones who deviate in all of these respects in the direction of inferior status."

It is obviously impossible to present a static profile of juvenile delinquency unless the dynamics of the problem are also delineated. The next chapter represents an effort to examine such questions as the alleged increase of incidence in war and prosperity and the alleged decrease of incidence in peace and economic depression.

QUESTIONS AND RESEARCH SUGGESTIONS

1. *What are the major criticisms of delinquency statistics?*
2. *Why are police statistics a better index of the incidence of delinquency than are institutional statistics?*
3. *What is the technique of central registration and why is it an improvement over the traditional methods of statistics-gathering?*
4. *Why is truancy such an important delinquency offense?*
5. *How do you account for the fact that delinquency statistics generally report a much higher proportion of boys' cases than girls'?*
6. *Compare the statistics on police, court, and institutional cases of delinquency in your jurisdiction for the most recent year.*
7. *Ascertain whether or not the proportion of children in your jurisdiction arrested by the police for alleged delinquency was higher than the nationwide proportion during some recent year.*
8. *Assuming that you are asked to construct a central registration file for your community, list the agencies there which you would call upon to co-operate with you in gathering your statistical data.*
9. *Analyze Table I and show to what extent the various age groups differ from each other in the distribution of their alleged offenses.*
10. *Write a short essay on the problems involved in the interpretation of the profile of delinquency.*

SELECTED READINGS AND REFERENCES

Axelrad, Sidney, "Negro and White Male Institutionalized Delinquents," *The American Journal of Sociology*, 57:569–74, 1952.

Blanchard, Paul, "Negro Delinquency in New York," *Journal of Educational Sociology*, 16:115–23, 1942.

Durea, Mervin Arnold, "A Survey of the Extent and Nature of Offenses Committed by Delinquent Boys," *Journal of Juvenile Research*, 19:62–74, 1935.

Frankel, Emil, "The Offender and the Court: a Statistical Analysis of the Sentencing of Delinquents," *Journal of Criminal Law and Criminology*, 31:448–56, 1940.

Judicial Criminal Statistics, Bureau of the Census, Washington, D.C.

Kvaraceus, William C., "Juvenile Delinquency and Social Class," *Journal of Educational Sociology*, 18:51–4, 1944.

Lunden, Walter A., *Statistics on Crime and Criminals*, Pittsburgh, Stevenson and Foster, 1942.

Maller, Julius B., "Juvenile Delinquency in New York: a Summary of a Comprehensive Report," *Journal of Psychology*, 3:1–25, 1937.

National Conference on Prevention and Control of Juvenile Delinquency, *Report on Statistics*, Washington, D.C., U.S. Government Printing Office, 1947.

Perlman, I. Richard, "The Meaning of Juvenile Delinquency Statistics," *Federal Probation*, 13:63–7, 1949.

Prisoners in State and Federal Prisons and Reformatories, Bureau of the Census, Washington, D.C.

Robison, Sophia M., *Can Delinquency Be Measured?* New York, Columbia University Press, 1936.

Schwartz, Edward E., "A Community Experiment in the Measurement of Juvenile Delinquency," *Yearbook of the National Probation Association*, 1945, pp. 157–82.

Schwartz, Edward E., "Statistics of Juvenile Delinquency in the United States," *The Annals of the American Academy of Political and Social Science*, 261:9–20, 1949.

Sellin, Thorsten, "The Basis of a Crime Index," *Journal of Criminal Law and Criminology*, 22:335–56, 1931.

Social Statistics (Juvenile Court Statistics), United States Children's Bureau, Social Security Administration, Federal Security Agency.

Uniform Crime Reports for the United States and Its Possessions, issued by the Federal Bureau of Investigation, United States Department of Justice, Washington, D.C., quarterly.

United States Congress, *Juvenile Delinquency*, Washington, U.S. Government Printing Office, 1950.

Chapter IV. *The Dynamics of Delinquency*

As in many other social problems, there are marked cycles or swings in the measured incidence of juvenile delinquency. These "ups" and "downs" from one period to the next provoke a broad gamut of emotional response among laymen, ranging from alarm and indignation when the problem appears to be growing, to complacency when the trend is downward. Repetitive patterns of increase and decrease also lead to a considerable amount of dubious cause-and-effect thinking. For example, when the problem seems to subside, organizations that deal with the problem frequently become self-congratulatory. Yet when the problem is marked by a rise in incidence a short time thereafter, the same organizations point to the increase as evidence that the budgets for their programs should be expanded.

A fundamental question here is whether or not the measurements of delinquency actually reflect the trends of the problem. Another basic problem is to account for whatever cycles do exist.

There is no need here to discuss in detail the limitations of most delinquency statistics as they affect the validity of trends or dynamics of the problem. In the previous chapter it was seen that despite (1) the ambiguity and lack of uniformity in legal definitions, (2) variables in the exposure, detection, and apprehension of children, (3) variables in police administration, (4) variables in court practices, and (5) variables in institutional intake, there is reason to believe that *national* changes in the number of children coming to the attention of arrest, court, and confining agencies give some indication of the dynamics occurring in the total incidence of delinquency. "The available statistics on juvenile delinquency, which show increases or decreases but not the actual frequency of the phenomena constitute, in effect, an instrument somewhat like a weather vane, which shows the direction of the wind but not its velocity." [1]

Locally, of course, one cannot be certain that measured dynamics of delinquency are genuine reflections of increase or decrease in the problem itself. An increase may result from an intensive drive on the part of the local police force; a decrease may come from the opposite—namely, a reduction in the police force or the distraction of the police by some other aspect of police work. Changes in court policy or in the intake philosophy of social agencies also may bring forth apparent rather than real rises and falls in the incidence of the problem. But to the extent that facilities and administrative methods remain constant, changes in the number of cases counted are a fair index of fluctuation in the volume of actual delinquency.

Statisticians recognize four kinds of dynamics in delinquency. These are: (1) the long-time trend; (2) cycles or swings covering a number of years; (3) seasonal variations or variation in days, weeks, or months; and (4) fluctuations "due to accidental or nonforeseeable factors."

With the exception of cyclical fluctuations, it is virtually im-

---

[1] Edward E. Schwartz, "Statistics of Juvenile Delinquency in the U.S.," *The Annals of the American Academy of Political and Social Science,* 261:12, 1949.

possible to deduce any broad patterns or generalizations. Consider, for example, seasonal fluctuations. While it is true that communities generally show "ups" and "downs" in measured incidence of delinquency in accordance with the progression of seasons, each community has its own peculiar seasonal pattern and it varies somewhat from year to year. In cyclical fluctuations, however, two patterns are alleged to emerge: (1) the incidence of juvenile delinquency has a positive correlation with the business cycle, and (2) delinquency is positively correlated with war and negatively correlated with peace. On the other hand, the incidence of adult crime in each case is inversely correlated. It has a negative correlation with the business cycle, a negative correlation with war, and a positive correlation with peace.

Delinquency and the Business Cycle

The claim that delinquency increases in periods of economic prosperity, and decreases in periods of economic depression marked by extensive unemployment, is supported by the count of juvenile-court cases in given jurisdictions covering the years from 1928 to 1944. In the depression years from 1929 to 1939, American communities showed a clear decline in the incidence of juvenile court cases. From 1939 to 1944, as the business index reversed itself, the court cases of delinquency moved upward likewise. In a study made of Los Angeles County Juvenile Court cases over this very same sixteen-year period from 1928 to 1944, these fluctuations were true of both boys' and girls' cases.[2] But there was some deviation from the upward trend of the business index in 1939 and 1940 in the incidence of girls' cases. One reasonable explanation for this deviation is that the decline in the case load of relief agencies during those years led to a reduction in the number of court petitions for delinquent girls. This becomes clear when one understands the difference in the referring sources of boys' and girls' cases. Police are the referring source for virtually all boys' cases, whereas a large proportion of girls' cases are referred to the Los Angeles juvenile court by social agencies, especially the public relief agencies. As economic conditions improved in 1939 and 1940, fewer and fewer families came

[2] David Bogen, "Juvenile Delinquency and Economic Trends," *American Sociological Review*, 9:178–84, 1944.

into contact with these agencies. Therefore fewer delinquent girls were detected by them and brought to the attention of the court.

One student of the dynamics of delinquency has tried to demonstrate that the economic prosperity accompanying World War II had an impact on the incidence of delinquency over and above any effect that the war itself may have had. This point first requires recognition of the fact that the economic "boom" of the war period was greater in the industrial communities of the Great Lakes, the Gulf, and the East and West coasts than those of the interior states. The migration of workers from communities in the latter area to communities in the former areas became a rough index of the differential impacts of the economic boom. The larger the population growth of a community, the larger its boom. The effect of this economic boom in the more prosperous areas on juvenile behavior, aside from any effect the war itself may have had, became evident in the fact that 36 big-city courts in areas that increased in population in the period 1940 to 1944 showed a seventeen per cent greater increase in delinquency cases than 42 big-city courts in areas that lost population.[3]

The reverse pattern is the case in adult crimes. Studies of court and prison statistics have long indicated that such offenses, especially those against property, increase in periods of depression and decrease in periods of prosperity.[4]

Why should the trends of delinquency and crime be diametrically opposed in relation to the business cycle? In an economic depression adults commit more offenses, especially those against property, because of enforced idleness, financial needs, and excessive worry, whereas in prosperity these factors are removed or considerably reduced. For children, on the other hand, depres-

[3] Lowell J. Carr, *Delinquency Control*, New York, Harper, rev. ed., 1950, pp. 107–10.

[4] See, for example, Wm. A. Bonger, *Criminality and Economic Conditions*, Boston, Little, Brown, 1916; Dorothy Swaine Thomas, *Social Aspects of the Business Cycle*, New York, Dutton, 1925; Emma Winslow, *Relationships between Employment and Crime as Shown by Massachusetts Statistics*, Report of U.S. National Commission on Law Observance and Enforcement, Vol. I, Part IV, U.S. Government Printing Office, Washington, D.C., 1931; Mary Van Kleeck, *Notes on Fluctuations in Employment and in Crime in New York State*, Report of U.S. National Commission on Law Observance and Enforcement, Vol. I, Part V, U.S. Government Printing Office, Washington, D.C., 1931; Sam Bass Warner, *Crime and Criminal Statistics in Boston*, Cambridge, Harvard University Press, 1934.

sion and prosperity presumably have different effects than those on adults. A depression, because there is less money, tends to bring the family more closely together and to reinforce the controls of that primary group over the children. In prosperity, there is more money and recreation outside the family for both parents and children, and controls are weakened. The family tends to become disorganized. The divorce rate and other forms of marital separation increase. Furthermore, as Bogen observes, the difficulty of finding employment and of supporting two households tends to hold the family together as an economic unit in depression years. But this loses much of its force at times when money flows more freely and jobs are easy to find. Besides, the employment of women increases in prosperous times, the consumption of alcohol increases, and the patronage of commercialized recreation reaches higher levels. Unquestionably there are other factors which contribute to the increase in juvenile delinquency in prosperous years, such as the carelessness with which people handle property at such times, but it seems likely that the relaxation of parental supervision and the tendency for family disorganization are of primary importance. Whereas the temptations and opportunities for stealing or other mischief are sharply limited by parental supervision in the case of children, adults normally are restricted in their activities by the routines of regular employment. In periods of economic depression, the combination of enforced idleness and financial need probably leads to the increase in adult offenses against property, while in periods of prosperity the weakening of parental supervision leads to increased juvenile delinquency.[5]

Delinquency and the Cycle of War and Peace

The accompanying chart of delinquency-court cases from 1938 to 1947 graphically presents the problem's second cyclical pattern, increase in war and decline in peace, with reference to World War II.[6] But even in World War I this cyclical pattern was

[5] Bogen, *op. cit.*, p. 183.

[6] Notice that boys' cases, comprising about four fifths of all delinquency cases, increased from the peacetime year of 1938 to a peak in the war year 1945. There were minor reversals from the trend in 1940 and 1944. From the peak in 1945, the boys' cases decreased substantially in 1946 and continued downward in 1947. For girls' cases, the peak was reached in

Chart II

*Juvenile Delinquency Cases Disposed of from 1938
to 1947 by 76 Courts in Areas of Population
100,000 or More.*

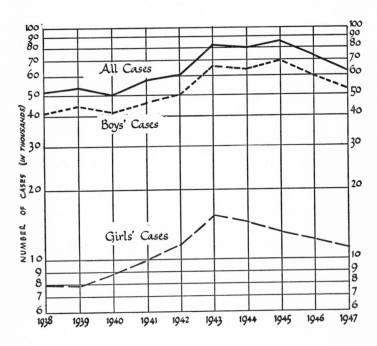

recognized. Then, as now, the wartime increase in delinquency and the decrease in crime as measured by arrest, court, and institutional cases were followed by postwar decrease in juvenile cases and increase in adult cases.[7] One student of delinquency [8] has suggested that the increased volume of literature on delinquency at that time was a reflection of the wartime increase in delinquency. For example, there was little significant systematic research before 1914, but coincident with World War I there appeared such notable pioneer publications as the *Yearbook of the National Probation Association* (1915), the *Journal of Delinquency* (1916), *Mental Hygiene* (1917), Healy's *The Individual Delinquent* (1913), and Leeson's *The Child and the War* (1917). In World War II, juvenile offenses again were reported to have increased while adult offenses decreased.

That war as war—apart from its economic effects of increasing jobs and stimulating migration—actually does something to increase the incidence of delinquency is shown by statistics taken during World War II from 42 big-city courts that served areas of *decreasing* population. These 42 big cities were clearly not booming economically as were 36 others whose populations increased. Yet their courts reported a 42 per cent increase in all delinquency cases and a 58 per cent increase in girls' cases alone. In other words, over and above the effects of the economic boom and population influx into war production centers, the war as war sent court cases climbing in American cities.[9]

Why is this so in children's cases in wartime but not adult

1943 and was followed by constant decreases each year. In spite of the decrease in delinquency cases, the year 1947 showed all delinquency cases were still 25 per cent above the cases reported in 1938. The 76 courts were used in this chart primarily because they had voluntarily supplied the data. Although they do not represent all juvenile courts in the country, it is believed that the general direction of change shown by the trend line from 1938 to 1947 for these 76 courts would hold true even if data were available for a better representation of courts throughout the United States. See *Juvenile Court Statistics*, 1947, Division of Statistical Research, Social Statistics Section (Children's Bureau), Federal Security Agency, Social Security Administration, December 1948, Washington, D.C., p. 3.

[7] See Benjamin Malzberg, "Demobilization and the Crime Rate," *Journal of Delinquency*, 4:152–7, 1919.

[8] P. S. DeQ. Cabot, *Juvenile Delinquency: A Critical Annotated Bibliography*, New York, H. W. Wilson, 1946.

[9] Carr, *op. cit.*, pp. 107–10.

cases? The answer is usually that war has some compensations for adults but few for juveniles. Income rises for adults in wartime, and accordingly there is less provocation for crimes of acquisition. Furthermore, because there is an acute need for manpower, there is a tendency to be lenient toward those who commit minor crimes. They are sent back to their jobs rather than to prison. But at the same time there is a weakening of home ties for juveniles, and a slackening of parental control, particularly when both parents are drawn into war work. There is an inevitable restlessness among adolescents not old enough to join the armed forces, a demand for some equivalent action and excitement. Significant, too, is that welfare agencies and community services lack funds or personnel, or they are focused on the needs of adults in war work or in the armed services.

The war-peace cycle of delinquency and the reverse pattern for crime have generally been confirmed in other societies. A considerable increase in the number of juvenile offenders in England and in Germany was noted after the outbreak of World War I, and the phenomenon was repeated in World War II. In Japan before World War II juvenile delinquency had not been a serious problem because the powerful controls of parental discipline in the family, public opinion in the community, and respect for the authority of the police tended to keep it low. Sex delinquents were absorbed into the brothel system. Yet during World War II the problem increased greatly, much as it did elsewhere.

Most studies agree that the wartime rate of increase in girls' cases is larger than that in boys' cases.[10] This may be explained by the fact that girls are more often convicted for sex violations than are boys and that wartime creates more opportunities for such violations. A second refinement about the wartime rise in delinquency is that large urban areas usually report larger increases than do less densely populated areas, primarily because war has a harder impact on urban than rural areas as far as the behavior of children is concerned.

[10] See the chart above on differential increases in girls' and boys' cases from 1938 to 1947.

Delinquency in Wartime: New York City

Locally—*e.g.*, in a given community—there is often consider-able disagreement about allegations of increase and decrease in the incidence of juvenile delinquency. Do the statistics genuinely reflect the dynamics of delinquency? Do all delinquency offenses show the same trend? For example, late in 1942 and early in 1943, some citizens of New York City expressed much concern about the rise of the problem since the beginning of the war. Mayor La Guardia had a different impression; namely, that delinquency had not materially increased. Nevertheless he agreed to organize an investigation. He appointed a Committee on Juvenile Delin-quency in February 1943, headed by William B. Herlands, City Commissioner of Investigation. In August 1943 the Herlands Report was released, an exhaustive analysis of 16,059 Children's Court cases for the period of 30 months from January 1941 to June 1943, covering the transition from peace to war. It was by far the most detailed and careful statistical analysis of the local problem New Yorkers had ever had. It brought out the following points:

1. Offenses centering around the home and school—running away from home, disobeying parents, and truancy—together with burglary, accounted for most of the increase in delinquency since Pearl Harbor. Misconduct in the home made up 96 per cent of the net increase of juvenile delinquency in 1942 over 1941. To-gether with truancy and burglary, it accounted for four fifths of the increase, during the first four months of 1943, over the same period in 1942.

2. It is an unwarranted conclusion that since most delinquent acts during the period covered occurred at home or in the school, parents and teachers must have been mainly responsible. Another unwarranted conclusion is that social and economic factors—inadequate recreation, inferior housing, discrimination against minorities, poverty—were relatively negligible. The Herlands Re-port stressed that the statistics merely showed where the delin-quency *occurred*, not where it was *caused*.

3. A total of 3,560 children were found delinquent by the Children's Courts of New York City in 1942, compared with 3,197 in 1941. During the first four months of 1943, those found delin-quent totaled 1,618, compared with 1,248 in the same period in

1942. The 29 per cent increase in adjudged delinquents in the first third of 1943, coming on top of an 11 per cent increase in 1942 over 1941, could be considered *prima facie* evidence that there was a real increase in war over peace. There was no "joker" in this increase as there had been in the 1939 rise in court cases over 1938, which was brought about mainly by a concentrated police drive on children using slugs in subway turnstiles and slot machines. The 1942–3 rise was the "real thing," occurring at a time when police supervision was weakened by a loss of over a thousand patrolmen from the Police Department.

4. The wartime rise in juvenile delinquency was not uniform throughout the city, for while some neighborhoods showed rises others showed clear declines.

5. Despite the general rise in juvenile delinquency in New York City in wartime since 1941, the following specific types of offenses actually decreased: stealing, destruction of property, ungovernable behavior, auto stealing, using vile language, and stealing from vending machines.

In short, as shown by the Herlands Report, the dynamics of juvenile delinquency in a specific locality may vary somewhat from the two cyclical patterns of war and peace and prosperity and depression appearing in the nation as a whole.

The Postwar Decline in Juvenile Delinquency

With the end of World War II and the return to peace, most local statistics concurred with such nationwide coverages as the arrest statistics of the Federal Bureau of Investigation in describing a decline in juvenile delinquency. Arrests of boys over the country under eighteen years of age fell 19.4 per cent during the first six months of 1946 as compared with the same period in 1945. Arrests of girls under twenty-one declined 34.7 per cent during the first half of 1946. As the decade came to an end the decline continued. For example, the New York City Youth Board reported a citywide drop of three per cent from 1947 through 1949.

Once again there was substantiation of the maxim that when delinquency decreases, agencies and organizations become self-congratulatory, thereby inferring that there is a causal relationship between their programs and the decline in incidence. Illustrative of this type of questionable etiology to account for postwar declines in the incidence of the problem is the following editorial [11] entitled "Good Work":

> The report of Judge —— of Children's Court to the Board of Supervisors shows an encouraging trend downward in juvenile delinquency. A decrease from 1,225 to 1,130 in the number of children's cases before the court indicates that efforts against juvenile delinquency here are bearing fruit. Yet the number of adult cases has increased in a year from 1,190 to 1,238. More and more effort through the agencies that have taken up the work of saving children from the wrong path will have increasingly beneficent effect as the months and years pass. The report, itemized, shows what an excellent instrument the Children's Court is from year to year. Its administration has brought good results and it is one of the community's best assets, now and for the future.

The Resurgence of Delinquency in 1950

That such words might have been spoken in haste came to be realized in 1950. The Korean War and the defense preparation associated with it seemed to provoke an upward trend once again. Dispositions of juvenile cases by the federal courts, for example, rose that year for the first time since 1946.[12] The Children's Bureau reported that court cases of delinquency were four per cent higher than in 1949. Reports to the Federal Bureau of Investigation on police arrests of children under eighteen years of age showed that the 1950 figure was five per cent over 1949. Such arrests during the first six months of 1951 were nine per cent above those in the 1950 period. In New York State the Youth Commission noted a substantial increase of cases during 1951 for the first time since 1943. Increases were particularly noted in the defense-industry and metropolitan areas. The Children's Courts of New York State reported to the New York State Department of Correction an increase of 1,415 cases received by such courts in 1951 over 1950. The accompanying chart makes it possible to

---

[11] *Syracuse Herald-Journal*, February 25, 1948, p. 24.

[12] United States Congress, *Juvenile Delinquency*, printed for the use of the Special Committee to Investigate Organized Crime in Interstate Commerce, Washington, U.S. Government Printing Office, 1950, p. 10.

observe all the cycles of increase and decrease in delinquency in that state accompanying war and peace from 1938 to 1951.[13]

Chart III

Official Delinquency Cases Disposed of by the Children's Courts of New York State, 1938–51

Yr.

Year	Cases		Period
1938	|||||||||||||||||		
1939	||||||||||||||||||||||	⎫	
1940	||||||||||||||||||	⎬	*Defense Preparation*
1941	||||||||||||||||||	⎭	
1942	|||||||||||||||||||	⎫	
1943	||||||||||||||||||||||||	⎬	*War*
1944	||||||||||||||||||||||	⎬	
1945	|||||||||||||||||||||	⎭	
1946	|||||||||||||||||||||	⎫	
1947	|||||||||||||||||	⎬	*Postwar*
1948	||||||||||||||||	⎬	
1949	|||||||||||||||	⎭	
1950	|||||||||||||||	⎫	*Defense Preparation*
1951	||||||||||||||||	⎭	*and Korean War*

EACH \| REPRESENTS 500 CHILDREN'S-COURT CASES

Statistics on court and arrest cases in the country as a whole covering the same period of time show a similar pattern of cycles.[14]

In 1953 the Associated Press reported the results of a survey, conducted by its bureaus, of the juvenile-court records in cities having more than 100,000 population. Sixty-one of the 106 cities throughout the country falling within this category co-operated, four of them showing a decrease in court cases since 1948, and nine revealing no trend either upward or downward. But in the remaining forty-eight cities the number of delinquency cases increased. Some of this increase, of course, was accounted for in some cities by the increase in population, or by changes in sys-

[13] *Youth Service News,* New York State Youth Commission, Vol. 4, No. 5, May 1952, pp. 1, 5.

[14] *The Child,* Vol. 17, No. 4, December 1952, p. 64.

tems of keeping records and changes in age limits for juveniles. In a few cases the increase could be explained by the extension of city boundaries. On the whole, however, one could conclude that there was a general increase in the incidence of the problem.

It is now appropriate to turn to the next major concern, the etiology of juvenile delinquency. Why does juvenile delinquency occur? What makes a juvenile delinquent? What are the principal approaches, hypotheses, and theories in answer to these questions?

QUESTIONS AND RESEARCH SUGGESTIONS

1. *What evidence is there to support the argument that economic prosperity has an impact on the incidence of delinquency apart from that of war?*
2. *How do you account for the fact that the trends of delinquency and crime are diametrically opposed to each other in relation to the business cycle?*
3. *In World War II, juvenile offenses were generally reported to have increased, whereas adult offenses decreased. Why?*
4. *What significant finding about the dynamics of delinquency came out of the Herlands Report?*
5. *Determine what seasonal variations, if any, exist in the measured incidence of delinquency in your community, and construct some hypotheses to account for them.*
6. *Compare the statistics on delinquency and crime over the past ten years in your home state, and account for the fluctuations that have occurred during that period.*
7. *Compare the statistics on delinquency and crime in a given locality during the nineteen twenties, and explain the patterns you find.*

SELECTED READINGS AND REFERENCES

Abbot, Edith, "Juvenile Delinquency During the First World War; Notes on the British Experience, 1914–18," *Social Service Review*, 17:192–212, 1943.

Aitken, G. A., "Juvenile Offenses in Wartime," *The Child*, 7:110–18, 1916.

Bell, Marjorie, "Delinquency in War-Time England," *Probation*, 20: 97–102, 111–15, 1942.

Bogen, David, "Juvenile Delinquency and Economic Trends," *American Sociological Review*, 9:178–84, 1944.

Chute, Charles L., "Juvenile Delinquency in Wartime," *Probation*, 21:129–34, 149–53, 1943.

Evjen, Victor Harold, "Delinquency and Crime in Wartime," *Journal of Criminal Law and Criminology*, 33:136–46, 1942.

Overholser, Winfred, "Who Are the Juvenile Delinquents?" *Journal of Social Hygiene*, 30:304–8, 1944.

Schwartz, Edward E., "Statistics of Juvenile Delinquency in the United States," *The Annals of the American Academy of Political and Social Science*, 261:9–20, 1949.

Thomas, Dorothy Swaine, *Social Aspects of the Business Cycle*, New York, Dutton, 1925.

United States Congress, *Juvenile Delinquency*, Washington, D.C., U.S. Government Printing Office, 1950.

Part **II.**

The Etiology of Delinquency

Chapter **V**. *The Philosophy of Causation*

The New York State Youth Commission recently announced that it would analyze and make an inventory of the most significant delinquency causation studies.

Lee C. Dowling, Executive Director of the Youth Commission, in explaining the objectives of this project, stated, "What causes juvenile delinquency is the $64 question for which everyone has an answer. Some of the answers are merely opinions, while others are based upon research. Some are similar, while others are widely diversified. Some experts feel that we should put our present knowledge of delinquency causation to greater use rather than add to the number of research studies, many of which are merely gathering dust on the shelves of libraries. Other experts point out that effective

preventive programs must be based upon scientific research
and decry the lack of such valid data. Still other experts take
a middle of road course and suggest that we use our present
knowledge of causation while further refining our research
in this area."[1]

There is no serious challenge to the generalization
that the goal of all systematic inquiry is the discovery of significant
relations within the subject matter studied. For example, one may
say that the common objective of statistical studies on the static
and dynamic profiles of juvenile delinquency is to facilitate the
discovery and expression of significant relationships between delinquency and other phenomena. Just as data have been collected
on the number of industrial accidents and the hours of employment in several factories in order to discover whether the two
sets of phenomena have a causal relationship or whether they are
partly or completely independent, so the central purpose of inquiry about the socio-economic status of juvenile delinquents and
the trend of delinquency in war and peace is to discover whether
some particular socio-economic status on the one hand, and the
conditions of war on the other hand, are causally connected with
juvenile delinquency or whether the problem is partly or completely independent of each.

Most causal inquiries regarding problems of human relations,
not merely those in connection with delinquency, fail to confront
the basic question of what is meant by a causal relationship. One
sociologist[2] maintains that if the question were confronted, the
concept of causation would soon fall into disuse. This is because
the first characteristic of a cause is the element of pressure or
compulsion about it. *A cause is that which makes something happen.* The cause of some *effect* refers to an invariant relationship
between two phenomena. But the search so far for causes of delinquency reveals no such relationship. One cannot yet say, for
example, that if *A commits a delinquency at time t,* we can understand as its cause a certain factor *C,* so that the following holds:

[1] *Youth Service News,* New York State Youth Commission, Vol. 4,
No. 5, May 1952, p. 1.
[2] Albert Morris, "Crime Causation," *Federal Probation,* 7:18, 1943.

If C takes place, then A will commit delinquency at time t; and this is true where A is an individual of a certain type, C an event of a certain type, and t the time.

The Evolution of Causative Thinking

The evolution of man's cause-and-effect thinking is, in a sense, a record of his struggle to understand himself and his environment. One of the earliest forms taken by this kind of thinking assumed that one thing, A, was the cause of another thing, B, without any sufficient evidence either that there was such a relationship or that A even existed. An "evil spirit" brought on a plague, or a plague following the appearance of a comet or an eclipse was considered to be the result of it. The Latin phrase *post hoc ergo propter hoc* ("after this, therefore because of it") describes the fallacy of this kind of causative thinking. Although most people no longer think of an evil spirit as the cause of delinquency, there is still considerable expression of the fallacy of *post hoc ergo propter hoc*, even among delinquency specialists.

A later form of cause-and-effect thinking has involved, on the one hand, the recognition of actual cause-and-effect relationships, but on the other hand it has maintained that these relationships are true in all situations and contexts and that one need not verify the specific relationship before taking preventive action. The reasoning is: Physical punishment has a deterrent effect on some kinds of behavior. Therefore it would be useful in any manner to deter children from delinquent behavior. There is no need to hesitate about immediate action.

The most recent form of causative thought poses hypotheses or "educated guesses" and seeks verification in experimentation and other scientific methods of research for facts and data to test the hypotheses. Quantitative thinking is usually involved here; *i.e.*, thinking in terms of units susceptible to counting. Facts are classified into categories based on the assumed identity of units. Whatever uniformities emerge are called scientific laws. One kind of scientific law, the positive law, poses an invariant relationship. It is conspicuous by its absence in the study of human relations. We have already noted, for example, that the search for "causes" of juvenile delinquency reveals no such relationship. The second kind of scientific law, the statistical law, states a degree of probability in the relationship between phenomena. It goes almost without saying that statistical laws are characteristic of human relations, for although family traits, economic pressures, neighborhood associates, personality handicaps, and other variables in a behavior situation interact in such complex ways that no invariability between any one of them and the ultimate behavior can be established, these so-called variables may still condition and control that behavior.

Variables in Causation

Statistical laws, but not positive laws, are discernible in delinquency causation. One reason is that variables—uncontrolled factors in social situations—preclude invariability in a relationship but allow probable relationships. Let us assume, for example, that a greater frequency of certain delinquent acts is detected among the children of businessmen than among the children of teachers. An invariant relationship has not been established in this case, probably because many other conditions besides the mode of occupation distinguish the social groups to which the children of businessmen belong from the social groups to which the children of teachers belong. One can say the same thing when one finds a greater frequency of crime among bachelors than among married men. To proceed to the question of why the marital condition acts as a deterrent from crime is foolish, because there may very well be other factors than marital status distinguishing the unmarried, as a broad social category, from the married.

A good, practical example of the part variables play in delinquency causation is found in connection with the question of whether a causal relationship exists between broken homes and delinquency. Research findings show not only that the rate of broken homes varies widely for different nationality groups but that the rate of increase of broken homes in the successive age groups is almost as great as the variation in the ratio between nationalities. This means that the effects of age and nationality differences have to be held constant before valid comparisons of broken homes can be made between a delinquent group and a nondelinquent control group.

Plurality of Causative Factors

Another reason why positive laws based on invariant relationships are not true of delinquency causation is that causative factors in social situations are usually plural. Many years ago, John Stuart Mill, the famous logician and philosopher, made this point clearly and emphatically.[3] "It is not true," he said, "that one effect must be connected with only one cause, or assemblage of conditions; that each phenomenon can be produced only in one way. There are often several independent modes in which the same phenomenon could have originated. One fact . . . may follow, with equal uniformity, any one of several antecedents, or collections of antecedents. Many causes may produce mechanical motion; many causes may produce some kinds of sensations; many causes may produce death. A given effect may really be produced by a certain cause, and yet be perfectly capable of being produced without it."

In the case of delinquency specifically, the consensus among experts is that causation is plural rather than singular, even in individual cases. One of the most comprehensive surveys of juvenile delinquency ever made was that by the Pepper Subcommittee on Wartime Health and Education, reporting to the United States Senate in 1944. The committee called witnesses who were authorities on child development, protection and education, recreation, religion, law enforcement, and various agencies concerned with delinquency. A general point of agreement was that it is impossible to "blame" any single factor for the problem. Today only the naïve and credulous accept theories of unit causation of delinquency. An examination of the most elementary case shows that behavior, socially approved or not, is a product of the individual's many experiences, reaching far back into his early development.

But apparently the naïve and credulous are numerous. Students of human relations and its problems have always tried to explain a given situation in terms of their own specialties. This has been especially true with regard to crime and delinquency. Anthropologists, sociologists, psychologists, and psychiatrists have made a long series of erroneous efforts to attribute crime and delinquency to some particular human trait or environmental

[3] *A System of Logic*, Vol. I, 1875, p. 505.

condition. Their monistic theories of delinquency or crime causation have one thing in common: errors of inadequate sampling and lack of control. One of the earliest and most famous of these erroneous monistic theories was that of Lombroso and his followers, representing what has come to be known as the Italian school of criminology.[4] The Lombrosians, a generation before the concept of delinquency emerged, claimed there was a born criminal type with certain stigmata of degeneracy which distinguished the criminal from "normal" people. These stigmata included a cleft palate, a low forehead, an unusually shaped head, nose, and jaw, protruding ears, low sensitivity to pain, and in the case of males, lack of beard. All such traits were alleged to constitute a reversion to a hypothetical savage (atavism) and in some mysterious manner they were associated with a predisposition to crime.

Shortly thereafter, the Lombrosian theory was discredited by more rigorous scientists, especially the Englishman Charles Goring. They showed that Lombroso's sample was inadequate and that he and his followers had ignored the possibility that the alleged criminal traits might be as prevalent among law-abiding people. When Goring used such a control group—a representative sampling of the unincarcerated population—along with his study of prison inmates, he found the so-called "stigmata" to appear no more frequently among prison inmates than among the population at large.[5]

Yet some investigators continue to explain the delinquent solely in terms of personality maladjustment; others look at the family and see the source of all trouble there. Still others concentrate their analyses on the child's associates, or the neighborhood. The inevitable result is that panaceas are recommended to solve the problem. Those who explain delinquency in terms of personality believe that clinical guidance programs in the schools, or more and better psychiatrists, psychoanalysts, and psychologists are the answer. Those who regard the family as the cause emphasize family training and counseling, and, in some cases, punish-

[4] See Cesare Lombroso, *Crime: Its Causes and Remedies*; translated by H. P. Horton, Boston, Little, Brown, 1911.
[5] Charles Goring, *The English Convict*, H.M. Stationery Office, London, 1913.

ment of parents. Those who see the source of the problem in juvenile gangs claim that organized and supervised recreation offers the solution. If the neighborhood is thought to provoke delinquency, co-ordinating and neighborhood councils are offered as the most satisfactory means of dealing with the problem.[6]

Overlooked by proponents of singular or unit causation is that delinquency is a legal category, and probably the only thing that is alike in all delinquencies is that they are violations of law. Otherwise delinquency has no inherent quality or property applying to all types under all conditions. Since it has no inherent universal property, one cannot expect to find, in the variety of persons who are adjudicated delinquent, any one psychological type, any one character trait, that differentiates delinquents from all other persons. The endless vicissitudes of circumstance, opportunity, and personal history preclude the expectation of any single inclusive formula.

The Interactive Complex in Causation

It is possible for some people to comprehend the pluralistic nature of causation in juvenile delinquency, but to be unaware of a related characteristic; namely, that the various causative factors constitute an interactive complex. This can be an oversight of serious consequences, in that the abstraction of one factor —separating and itemizing it out of its functional context—may divorce it from reality. MacIver in this connection warns [7] that when a number of diverse factors are interactive, and when a particular result stems from their interaction, it is erroneous to treat them as though they were independent, homogeneous units each of which produces a measurable portion of their joint product. This assumption is found among writers who list in an order of priority or importance the diverse "causes" they postulate for delinquency. The assumption is not only false but mechanistic because it treats the various components of a social situation, or of any organized system, as though they were detachable, isolable, homogeneous, independently operative, and therefore sus-

[6] Marshall Clinard, "Secondary Community Influences and Juvenile Delinquency," *The Annals of the American Academy of Political and Social Science*, 261:42, 1949.
[7] Robert M. MacIver, *Social Causation*, Boston, Ginn, 1942, pp. 93–5.

ceptible of being added to or subtracted from the causal complex, increasing or decreasing the result by that amount.

Even in the case of relatively unbiased observers, attempts to separate factors on the basis of frequency into major and minor "causes" of delinquency often represent subjective evaluations rather than objective classifications. The fact that highly regarded authorities on juvenile delinquency differ from other equally eminent authorities in reporting the influence of, let us say, peer groups as a factor in delinquency bears witness to the evaluative rather than the statistical character of such abstractions.

Correlations in Delinquency

Qualifications of the validity of the concept of causation in delinquency, such as are found in variability, plurality of factors, and the interactive complex, have been given so much weight that many scholars and students now avoid the term "causation" in favor of "correlation" or "functional configuration." These presumably permit cause-and-effect thinking while at the same time they absolve the analyst from some of the intolerable commitments involved in the concept of causation. Among the alternatives to causation, the concept of correlation is the most widely used.

The meaning of correlation becomes clear if the reader assumes that he has before him several thousand shells of different length and width.[8] The problem he is called upon to solve is whether or not there is any correspondence or relationship between the length and width of the shells. His general impression is that the longer the shell, the greater its width. But this impression is unreliable because the large number of shells makes it impossible to recall the dimensions of each one. What he may do, then, is to order the shells systematically, from left to right, in a pattern of increasing length. If, as a result of this arrangement, the shells are also found to fit into a coinciding order of increasing width, the reader may conclude there is a "co-relation" between the length and width of the shells. Even if the numerical measurement of the two dimensions of length and width shows a correspondence only in part, there may still be some correlation. In

---

[8] See Morris R. Cohen and Ernest Nagel, *An Introduction to Logic and Scientific Method,* New York, Harcourt, Brace, 1934, pp. 313–14.

short, two variables are correlated if in a number of instances a change in one of them accompanies a change in the other, whether the change be in the same or opposite directions. Changes in the two variables in the same direction mean a positive correlation, whereas changes in opposite directions (such as when one increases and the other decreases) signify a negative correlation.

In the study and analysis of juvenile delinquency, the following four types of correlations are sought most frequently:

1. The incidence of a trait in a group of delinquents is compared with the incidence in nondelinquents or in one or more different categories of delinquents.

2. The incidence of delinquency or delinquents in a group or area possessing a trait is compared with the incidence in a group or area possessing the same trait in different degree, or possessing a different trait.

3. The incidence of delinquency or delinquents in a group or area possessing a trait is compared with that incidence in the same group or area subsequent to the modification or disappearance of the trait.

4. The trend of delinquency or delinquents in a group or area possessing a trait is compared with the trend in a group or area possessing the same trait in different degree, or a different trait.

It is very important to note here that some correlations between delinquency or delinquents and a trait are accompanied by comparisons with a control group of nondelinquents or a control situation of nondelinquency. The argument supporting such comparisons is that if any given percentage of delinquents is found to have a particular trait, it means nothing unless we know that, with respect to the trait, delinquents differ significantly from a nondelinquent but otherwise similar group. Similarly, if 90 out of 100 redheaded people have quick tempers, there can be no valid inference that red hair and quick tempers are causally connected unless we also have information about the relative number of people who are not redheads and who are quick-tempered. The point is that if one wishes to discover the connections of an attribute A with an attribute B, he must not only discover the proportion of A's that are B's, but also the proportion of a's (the absence of A) that are B. When one correlates delinquency with a factor like broken homes, then, there are four possible combinations to consider: broken homes and delinquent children, broken homes and nondelinquent children, unbroken homes and delinquent children, and unbroken homes and nondelinquent children.

It becomes clear, on the basis of these observations, that a high correlation does not necessarily mean causation. One or more factors may be associated with delinquency without being causally related to it. To insist here that there is a causal relationship is to submit to the fallacy of *post hoc ergo propter hoc,* the error in reasoning that in a temporal sequence the prior factor has caused the subsequent one. A simple correlation merely directs our inquiry in a particular direction. Where causation exists, there one also finds correlation, but where there is correlation there may be no corresponding causation. Among the many things that happen together or in sequence, some are causally independent, some are interdependent, and some are dependent alike on the same larger causal scheme but not on each other.

One may say that a correlation is a clue or a question mark, the significance of which is what we can infer from it or what we may learn by following its lead. Sometimes no inference can be drawn because the lead peters out. Correlations are useful in many areas of investigation but their value is small where the correlated variables do not fall within or cannot be brought within one coherent order. Illustrations of this point may be found in the observations that the expenditure for the British navy has a high correlation with the trend of consumption of bananas, and the spread of cancer in England likewise has a high correlation with the increased importation of apples.[9] To conclude from this that a smaller consumption of bananas and an embargo on apples would reduce the navy's expenditure and the incidence of cancer is an absurdity because it is inconsistent with the causal knowledge we already possess. Both illustrations bring out the principle that the discovery of a correlation serves merely as the starting-point for further investigations and analyses.

Many correlation studies in delinquency may conquer all these hurdles and still fail to satisfy the vigorous demands of scientific causation. Frequently a group of delinquents is found to

---

[9] Cohen and Nagel, *op. cit.,* p. 317.

differ in a statistically significant way from a nondelinquent control group with which it is compared. Nevertheless, the diffentiating trait may not be at all characteristic of the delinquent group. Suppose, for example, that a researcher compares 100 delinquent girls with 100 nondelinquent girls with respect to broken homes. He finds, let us say, that 10 per cent of the nondelinquents come from broken homes, whereas this is true of 30 per cent of the delinquent girls. Although the difference between the two groups is significant, the researcher has not demonstrated that the broken home is characteristic of delinquents. The fact is that 70 per cent of them come from unbroken homes. Again, ecological studies showing a high correlation between residence in interstitial areas and delinquency, as compared with lower rates of delinquency in other areas, overlook the fact that even in the most marked interstitial area nine tenths of the children do not become delinquent.

One answer to these questions about correlations is offered by psychiatrists; namely, that each individual has his own "breaking point," which is not the same for individual A as it is for individual B. A second answer is provided by what may be called a person's subjective assessment of the meaning of his experiences.

Subjective Assessment of External Factors

Some scholars maintain that it is here, in a person's subjective assessment of the meaning of his experiences, that broken homes, interstitial areas, and other external factors correlated with delinquency either succeed or fail to influence "causally" his behavior. An illustration may be useful here.[10] Let the reader assume that a boy is returning home from school and sees an unexpected group of people at his doorstep, including a policeman, several neighbors, and some strangers. He may suppose that they have gathered to welcome him and congratulate him as the winner of a nationwide contest he entered several months ago. On the other hand, his supposition may be that they have discovered that he was one of several boys who broke some windows in the neighborhood on Halloween. If his interpretation is that they are a welcoming group he will respond one way; but if he feels that they have come to "get" him, his response is likely to be quite

---

[10] See Morris, *op. cit.*, pp. 18–19.

different. In either case he may be entirely wrong in his interpretation. The important point, however, is that the external situation is relatively unimportant. Rather, what the boy himself thinks of them and how he interprets them is the crucial factor in his response.

The child's own story or life history, the delinquent's own account of his experiences, has long proved its value in this respect, not only for research into the factors "causing" delinquent behavior, but also for the practical purpose of treatment.[11] One can presumably distinguish thus between the factors really operative on the child and the factors merely present; between the environment merely around the child and that to which he responds. To be specific, a broken home, because it has a different meaning to one child than it has to another, will not lead consistently to delinquent behavior. The nondelinquent also comes from such a home, responding to a psychological environment that is different from that of his delinquent brother.

Our next concern is an examination of the approaches and methods found in the etiological [12] analysis of delinquency. This will provide the background for the various theories to be considered in subsequent chapters.

QUESTIONS AND RESEARCH SUGGESTIONS

1. *Why is there considerable scepticism about employing the concept of causation in the study of human relations?*
2. *How has causative thought evolved since its earliest form?*
3. *What is the difference between a positive law and a statistical law?*
4. *Why are monistic theories of causation in delinquency subject to criticism?*
5. *Why are delinquency correlations usually accompanied by a control group or a control situation?*

[11] See Clifford R. Shaw, *The Jack Roller*, Chicago, University of Chicago Press, 1930.
[12] In social science the term "etiology" is often used instead of "causation" because it connotes cause-and-effect thinking while at the same time it avoids the commitment to invariant relationships implied in causation.

6. *Does a high correlation mean causation? Explain.*
7. *Give some of your own examples of the fallacy of* post hoc ergo propter hoc.
8. *Outline the research method you would use to test the Lombrosian theory of delinquency and crime.*
9. *Give some plausible illustrations of your own, showing the subjective assessment of the meaning of experiences that could lead to delinquency.*
10. *Write your own life history, showing the factors really operative on your coming to college, contrasted with the external social and cultural factors of your situation.*

SELECTED READINGS AND REFERENCES

Cohen, Morris R., and Ernest Nagel, *An Introduction to Logic and Scientific Method*, New York, Harcourt, Brace, 1934.

Glueck, Sheldon, "Crime Causation," *National Probation Association Yearbook*, 86–108, 1941.

Lejins, Peter, "Pragmatic Etiology of Delinquent Behavior," *Social Forces*, 29:317–21, 1951.

MacIver, Robert M., *Social Causation*, Boston, Ginn, 1942.

Morris, Albert, "Crime Causation," *Federal Probation*, 7:17–20, 1943.

Selling, Lowell S., *Diagnostic Criminology*, Ann Arbor, Mich., Edwards, 1935.

Chapter **VI** . *Approaches and Methods*

In his *Study of Sociology* Herbert Spencer tells the story of a Frenchman who after spending three weeks in England proposed to write a book about it. At the end of three months he felt that he was not quite ready and by the end of three years he had decided that he knew nothing about it. Anyone who spends three years mulling over the question of crime [and delinquency] causation may find himself in much the same position. . . .[1]

There are two general types of approach utilized in the etiological analysis of delinquency. One, given various labels such as the *individual, internal,* or *constitutional approach,* con-

[1] Albert Morris, "Crime Causation," *Federal Probation,* 7:17, July–September, 1943.

stitutes those efforts which seek causation in the organism and personality of the child; the second, called the *environmental, external,* or *situational approach,* covers the theories that seek causation in the geographical, human, and manmade world confronting the child.

Such a classification may be criticized for being mechanistic and misleading in its "either-or" implication. For example, social psychological theories cannot accurately be classified as either constitutional or situational. More correctly, they fit in both schemes. In defense of the classification, however, one may say that sophisticated students will not think of the various theories in "either-or" fashion. A classification is a convenience, and no more. A theory is classified in one category and not in another on the basis of its emphasis; it may still share characteristics with theories placed in another category for their different emphasis.

A second criticism of the classification, perhaps more legitimate than the first, is that it is needlessly oversimplified. To generalize that there are only two approaches to the etiology of delinquent behavior conceals several important refinements. For this reason there is justification in considering the following seven approaches and their corresponding methods rather than merely the two traditionally discussed.

The Individual Approach

The individual or "case method" approach is the oldest and still probably the most widely used of all in modern etiological studies of delinquency. Healy's work with individual delinquents in the Juvenile Psychopathic Institute in Chicago is generally considered to be the pioneer effort of its kind.[2] Examining several hundred cases, he factorized and enumerated the various causative elements he found present in each child. Tabulation of the proportional occurrence of the causative factors gave him a picture of what might be more or less frequent, and hence important, in the etiology of delinquency.

The underlying assumption of this approach is that if knowledge can be acquired of all the facts about the individual delinquent, especially his mental life, the etiology of the child's

[2] William Healy, *The Individual Delinquent,* Boston, Little, Brown, 1915.

behavior can be determined. What needs of the child are met by the delinquent behavior? What personal characteristics and goal-activities differentiate the delinquent from the nondelinquent child?

Those who have employed this approach have analyzed individual delinquents by two types of methods: (A) longitudinal or genetic methods, and (B) cross-sectional methods. With longitudinal or genetic methods the attempt is to penetrate the developmental process of the child for causes; in the case of cross-sectional methods the effort is to learn all that can be learned about the child as he or she is at the time of the examination.

(A) LONGITUDINAL METHODS. Of all longitudinal methods, *psychoanalysis* is probably the most penetrating. It seeks to uncover the early, deeply embedded, hidden forces of personality which are alleged to find expression in delinquency and other deviant symptoms of behavior. The psychoanalytic method, however, has very limited utility in dealing with children. This is not only because it is too costly and requires a long period of probing, but also because some intellectual maturity in the subject is needed for successful analysis.

The *child's own story* or *life history* is a longitudinal method that Healy himself developed but never used extensively. It remained for Clifford Shaw to apply this method fully. In the prefatory remarks to one of his better known life histories, Shaw described the method as follows: [3]

> The life record itself is the delinquent's own account of his experiences, written as an autobiography, as a diary or presented in the course of a series of interviews. It has already demonstrated its value, not only for research into factors contributing to delinquent conduct, but also for the more practical purposes of social treatment.
>
> As a safeguard against erroneous interpretations, it is extremely desirable to develop the "own story" as an integral part of the total case history. Thus each case study should include, along with the life-history document, the usual family history, the medical, psychiatric and psychological findings,

[3] *The Jack Roller,* Chicago, University of Chicago Press, 1930, pp. 1–3.

the official record of arrest, offenses, and commitment, the description of the play-group relationships, and any other verifiable material which may throw light upon the personality and actual experiences of the delinquent in question.

The validity and value of the personal document are not dependent upon its objectivity or veracity. It is not expected that the delinquent will necessarily describe his life situations objectively. On the contrary, it is desired that his story will reflect his own personal attitudes and interpretations, for it is just these personal factors which are so important in the study and treatment of the case.

The *case-history method,* as Shaw indicated, is a more comprehensive longitudinal method than the life history. Case material on an individual child may be secured from laymen possessing knowledge about the child; by direct examination of the child at the hands of physicians, psychologists, psychiatrists, and social workers; and from documents, records, etc. The data form a case record that may be very voluminous or a mere statement of relatively few facts. Whether full or scanty, the case record may be literary; *i.e.,* prepared as a story with topical divisions, or abbreviated by the use of symbols, checks, or numbers similar to those found on the face sheets or record cards used by police departments and probation offices. It is in the latter type of record that the quantitative character of the underlying etiological thought emerges.

One outline of the data sought in a case history of a delinquent child is suggested by the following: [4]

1. *Identifying Information*
   Names (including nicknames, aliases, etc.)
   Addresses (past and present)
   Age and place of birth
   Color, nationality, or descent
   School grade
   Names and addresses of father and mother
   Occupations of father and mother
   Names and ages of siblings

[4] Adapted from Donald R. Taft, *Criminology,* New York, Macmillan, 1943, pp. 46–51.

2. *Behavior*

Details of the present difficulty

With whom was the first delinquency committed?

What is the child's explanation and motive for delinquency?

Did the delinquency bring a sense of shame, achievement, fear, or other emotions?

Is delinquency unusual in the family and neighborhood?

Is the delinquent behavior the first offense or is it occasional, frequent, or habitual?

Under what particular circumstances is the behavior repetitive?

Under what circumstances does the child refrain from the behavior?

Who has tried to help the child and how has this been done?

What effect has there been from attempts to help the child?

What is the child's attitude toward attempts to help him?

What punishment has the child received and what effect has it had?

What is the child's attitude toward his punishment?

Has the child been institutionalized, and if so, what effect has it had?

What relationships has the child had with local or other social agencies?

3. *Developmental History*

Pregnancy and conception

The infancy of the child: its pattern of health, walking, talking, and feeding

Was the child wanted or unwanted, and if unwanted, did it come to know this?

Was the child legitimate or illegitimate, and if illegitimate, did the child or anyone else come to know this?

Nervous or other deviant habits

Sex knowledge and habits, homosexual tendencies, and heterosexual experience

Experiences associated with adolescence and puberty

4. *Medical History*
   General health
   Diseases
   Hospital, clinic, and dispensary experiences

5. *Present Personality Traits*
   Physical appearance and its effect on the child
   Intelligence
   Child's attitudes toward himself and others
   Temperament and emotional stability
   Character traits and interests

6. *Family History and the Home*
   Age and place of birth of parents
   Health, income, education, and intelligence of parents
   Parents' personality traits
   Parents' understanding of the child's difficulties
   Police record of the parents
   Evaluation of the home by the child in comparison with
      other homes
   Physical aspects of the home, and degree of overcrowding
      and privacy
   Occupants of the home
   Social relations in the home and their effect on the chil-
      dren
   Tension and conflict in the home
   Discipline in the home and reactions to it
   Differential treatment of the child and siblings
   Prevalent attitudes in the family
   Status of the family in the neighborhood and community
   Characteristic behavior of family members
   Intellectual, work, and recreational activities in the home

7. *The Neighborhood*
   Physical appearance, reputation, and economic status
   Ethnic composition
   Stability and mobility of population
   Patterns of behavior which are approved, tolerated, and
      condemned
   Attitudes toward law, police, courts, schools

Agencies of social control
Typical leisure-time activities
Delinquency incidence

8. *Other Group Affiliations*
To what other groups has the child ever belonged?
What has been his status in them?
What effect have they had on him?
Friendships of the child
What membership has the child had at the time of delinquency?
From what groups has the child been excluded?
What attitudes toward law, delinquency, and crime are prevalent in the child's groups?
What is the status of the child's peer groups in the neighborhood and the larger community?

9. *Recreational Opportunities and Activities*
The child's use of leisure time
Forms of recreation available
Forms of supervision
The child's definition of "a good time"

10. *Occupational Opportunities and Activities*
Positions held and length of time
Attitude toward and interest in work
Income and its expenditure
Effect of work on status and associations

11. *School Life*
Child's scholastic progress and record
Behavior and activities in school
Personalities of teachers and the child's attitudes toward them
Interests of the child which the school meets and fails to meet
School discipline and the child's reaction to it
Truancy and how it is handled
Child's status among schoolmates

(B) CROSS-SECTIONAL METHODS. Cross-sectional methods were defined above as those methods in the individual approach to the etiology of delinquent behavior which are utilized to learn all that can be learned about the child as he or she is at the time of the examination. These are, in effect, personality tests.[5] They seek to identify the personality traits of the delinquent child in four ways:

1. By rating the degree to which a child possesses certain defined traits, such as self-sufficiency, submissiveness, emotional stability, and honesty.

2. By sampling the interests, attitudes, and adjustment of the child through the use of questionnaires and inventories.

3. By securing a direct record of conduct on performance tests to ascertain honesty, trustworthiness, inhibition, etc.

4. By projective techniques.

Representative of *rating tests* is the Haggerty, Olson, and Wickman scale, which the tester applies to the child and then compares with a number of other children of the same age with respect to thirty-five different intellectual, physical, social, and emotional traits. These ratings are made by placing a cross (x) above the appropriate descriptive phrase for each trait rated. For example, one of the items of social behavior is:

How does he react to frustrations or to unpleasant situations?   Score

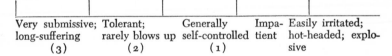

| Very submissive; long-suffering (3) | Tolerant; rarely blows up (2) | Generally self-controlled (1) | Impatient | Easily irritated; hot-headed; explosive |

Others of these ratings are self-ratings; *i.e.*, the child writes on the subject "How I feel" or on "How most boys feel" or "How I think I ought to feel" about the various situations such a test presents.

Among *questionnaires and inventories* that get at interests, attitudes, and adjustment, one finds that the schedule most widely used by clinics engaging in personality research in delinquency is the Woodworth Psychoneurotic Inventory. This consists of questions based on symptoms associated with psychopathic trends. It assumes that delinquency is frequently the result of failure to make satisfactory life-adjustments; therefore a questionnaire that

[5] The discussion here is based on the excellent description of such tests by Maud A. Merrill, *Problems of Child Delinquency*, Boston, Houghton Mifflin, 1947, pp. 25–50.

can differentiate between children with respect to emotional stability may contribute to an understanding of emotional factors in delinquent behavior. Another attempt to measure delinquent personality is the Pressey Interest-Attitude Test, which actually comprises four tests. They measure attitudes toward things considered wrong, anxieties, fears, worries, likes, and interests, and the types of people liked or admired. Those who use the tests find that with increasing age the attitudes of children change in the direction of emotional maturity but that delinquent children are found to be emotionally retarded in comparison with nondelinquents. A more revealing response is alleged to be obtained by disguising the purpose of the test, as in the case of Zucker's Story-Completion Method. Here the child subjects finish three short stories, the beginnings of which are presented to them, and in this manner delinquents are alleged to be differentiated from nondelinquent subjects. "The interpretation of the conduct of others with whom the child identifies has important bearing on the understanding of his own needs. Especially when the subject is free to interpret a situation in any way he wishes is he apt to reveal his own ways of thinking and feeling." [6]

Performance tests endeavor to measure personality directly; they may be illustrated by the test for honesty, which offers the child subject an opportunity to cheat and scores him on the basis of whether or not he takes advantage of that opportunity to increase his score. These tests are no longer considered to be very useful, for little relationship exists between the scores on dishonesty when dishonesty is measured in terms of stealing pennies and dishonesty measured in terms of lying about cheating. In other words, there is little tendency for children to be consistently honest or dishonest in the various situations in which different expressions of dishonesty are involved.

Projective techniques are relatively new devices for personality analysis of delinquents in comparison with nondelinquents. They are "unstructured," in the sense that the subject's response to them is largely free from predetermined limitations inherent in the material or technique itself. The goal of these techniques is the disclosure of how the subject selects and organizes his experience, his meaning, his areas of sensitivity, and how he protects

[6] *Ibid.*, p. 35.

his vulnerability. "He . . . projects his private world upon an unstructured external medium." [7] Of the three projective techniques enjoying broad adoption—the Rorschach, the Thematic Apperception, and the Play techniques—the Rorschach is the least structured. The individual taking such a test is expected to reveal his private world by expressing what he sees in ten ink-blot pictures. Murray's Thematic Apperception Test, on the other hand, is a story-telling test consisting of a set of pictures, each of which shows one or more persons in some kind of situation or action. Some of the pictures are either drawn especially for the test or are taken from photographs and magazine illustrations. As each is exhibited the subject is asked: "What story does this picture tell?" The diagnostic, etiological purpose behind the question is to lead the subject, by association perhaps, to the possible dominant drives, emotions, and conflicts of his personality. The kind of story he tells, it is believed, will reveal these facets of his personality. [8]

The third of the principal projective techniques, play techniques, use the play artifacts of children in our culture—dolls, toy animals, blocks, etc.—as material for projecting the child's world. One advantage of the play field as a projective technique

---

[7] *Ibid.*, p. 45.

[8] At the test's inception, it was not realized that these pictures, portraying white persons exclusively, might distort the responses of non-white subjects. In 1948 the Thompson Revision of the test was announced, a year after Thompson, a former Army psychologist, noticed that a Negro patient in a Veterans Administration hospital was giving particularly flat, unimaginative responses to the original pictures. Inspired by a hunch, Thompson asked the man to imagine that the persons in the pictures were Negroes. Immediately the responses were more colorful and imaginative, apparently because the subject identified himself with the figures in the pictures and expressed a new insight into the situations portrayed. This case illustrates ethnocentrism, the "in-group, out-group" feeling sociologists have long stressed as crucially important in a multi-group society. The in-group person has difficulty understanding that the outsider has his own feelings and emotions and personality characteristics. Thompson's subject had run into this psychological and cultural wall, but as soon as he imagined the people in the pictures to be Negroes—members of his own in-group—he developed more complex and refined stories. After several impromptu experiments, Thompson decided to modify the original plates by changing the white figures to Negroes, but to retain the expression on the faces and the situations as originally pictured. Thereafter he found that Negroes almost invariably gave longer, more detailed responses to the modified pictures, and hence responses of greater diagnostic and etiological importance.

among children is that it has none of the restrictions of the "world of reality." The child at play is largely free from the limitations he would face in other situations because of small size, lack of strength, or inarticulation.

The Group Approach

It is easily understandable why the individual approach to the etiology of delinquency has been supplemented by the group approach. One could expect that students of human relations, especially sociologists, would come to interpret delinquent behavior as a product of social interaction in the family, the play, or peer group, and the neighborhood, as well as a phenomenon of the individual person. In the words of two sociologists who pioneered in the study of delinquency: [9]

It is quite generally assumed among students of human behavior that the attitudes and habits underlying the behavior of the child are built up in the course of his experiences, developing in the process of interaction between the child and the successive situations in which he lives. The character of this process is determined, therefore, both by the condition in the organism and by the nature of the social . . . situations to which the child is responsive. The child is born into the world a physical organism endowed with certain physical characteristics, reflexes, capacities and undefined impulses. Furthermore, he is always born into a social world in which certain personalities . . . and social relationships already exist. The social world thus precedes the child and has certain expectations with reference to him. It functions in relation to his original impulses as a defining agency, giving meaning to these impulses and largely determining the course of their development.

If the attitudes underlying behavior traits are formed in the process of social interaction, it follows that an understanding of the behavior of the child necessitates a knowledge of

[9] Clifford R. Shaw and Henry D. McKay, "Social Factors in Juvenile Delinquency; a Study of the Community, the Family, and the Gang in Relation to Delinquent Behavior," *Report on the Causes of Crime*, Washington, D.C., National Commission on Law Observance and Enforcement, No. 13, Vol. II, 1931, p. 3.

the social world in which he lives. Children always live and act in association with other persons. They live as members of groups, as participants in the activities of a dynamic social world; it is artificial to view them and their behavior apart from the various groups of which they are members.

A refinement of these associational processes in the approach to crime as well as to juvenile delinquency is seen in Sutherland's theory of differential association, whereby a person is said to become delinquent by virtue of an excess of situations, arising out of his social interaction, favorable to violations of law over situations unfavorable to such violations.[10]

Obviously, some of the very same methods in use in the individual approach—for example, the case history—are also useful in the group approach. Nevertheless, there are other methods originating in the group approach itself. One that has long been used is the *family interview.* Here the interviewer arranges for a meeting of the members of the immediate family of the delinquent subject and proceeds to elicit the different dimensions of parent-child and sibling relationships. Usually one question has been sufficient to orient the family interview, the members of the family thereafter verbally unfolding their characteristic roles, attitudes, and reactions in the group. Occasionally the interviewer inserts questions to steer the verbal interaction. The interview may be taken down stenographically so that the very words of the family are recorded. The family interview presents the family in action, exposes the inner life of the family, the manner in which the child responds to the family, and the place the family has in his social world.

More recently devised methods that may be used in the group approach to the etiology of delinquency are represented by *situational analysis* and *sociodrama.* Situational analysis involves the selection—or the creation if necessary—of specific conflict situations in a group including one or more delinquent children. Planted in the locale are two observers who study what is happening and later record it. After the session is over, the participants are interviewed in detail concerning their perception of the event. Their evaluations of what went on, their images of

[10] Edwin H. Sutherland, *Principles of Criminology,* Philadelphia, Lippincott, 1947, Chapter i.

their own behavior and that of the other participants, their justifications for that behavior, and the motivations they impute to the other participants are later compared with the original record of the observers.

Sociodrama involves a brief outline, given by the observer-analyst to a group of participants including one or more delinquents, of a conflict situation that requires decision and choice. The roles of the participants are defined to them and the situation briefly specified. Their instructions are to present the essence of the conflict to the audience, and to act out resolution to it. Here the useful data to the analyst consist of the justifications selected and developed by individuals interacting in conflict; the justifications underlying the compromises made in resolving the conflict; the type of resolution; and the reactions of approval or disapproval on the part of the audience in the ensuing discussion.

The Institutional Approach

A third approach to the etiology of delinquency is the institutional approach. This has involved systematic inquiries into the extent to which educational, religious, and recreational experiences of delinquent and nondelinquent children are comparable, and the impact of the values and processes of such experiences. With the exception of inquiry into recreation for children, this approach has largely been speculative, lacking in empirical, fact-gathering methods of investigation.

The Communication Approach

A fourth approach to the etiology of delinquency involves the analysis of delinquency in terms of the media of communication to which children are exposed. The underlying assumption here is that newspapers, comic books, motion pictures, radio, and television may motivate—or at least stimulate—children to engage in delinquent behavior. The methods used in this approach include content analysis of the media for such themes as crime, sex, and violence, and for the presence or absence of artifacts and techniques that children may adopt for delinquencies. Some sampling of delinquent and nondelinquent children has been done with regard to their exposures to such media, and the incidence has been quantified and correlated in each case.

The Cultural Approach

The cultural approach to the etiology of delinquency is so close to the group approach that some students are willing to consider them as one. This approach has employed two somewhat different assumptions: (1) much of delinquent behavior is cultural behavior, in that it is quite consistent with several values and cultural traits in American society; (2) in a multi-group society, culture conflict exists as a result of the chronological succession of groups populating the society, each marked by a different culture. The child is caught in this cultural conflict, one expression of which is delinquent behavior. The cultural approach employs many of the methods described in connection with the previously discussed approaches. It also makes use of questionnaires and value inventories which are applied to delinquent and nondelinquent children, seeking out cultural differentials.

The Ecological Approach

The ecological approach to delinquency examines the spatial distribution of delinquency offenses and the residences of delinquent children in relation to other variables that may be distributed in spatially similar patterns. It is based on the assumption that delinquency shows patterns of spatial concentration in so-called delinquency areas, not because of the spatial factor as such, but as a result of the cluster of variables in some areas that promote a higher incidence of delinquency and other social problems. The method employed in this approach has been to plot on a community map the distribution of delinquency and delinquents over a specific period of time and to correlate the findings with other maps of the community plotted for other variables.

The Age-Status Approach

The last approach to the etiology of delinquency is the age-status approach. Here one explores the significance of the age span of the juvenile in American society with relation to the rights, duties, roles, and expectations of childhood as a status. The underlying assumption of this approach is that the lack of clearly defined status and roles in childhood may be conducive to delinquent behavior. Many of the aforementioned methods of other approaches are used, along with the comparative method, which introduces ethnographic material on the status and roles of children in other societies where juvenile delinquency and other problems of childhood and adolescence are conspicuous by their absence.

Now that the approaches and methods utilized in the etiology of delinquency have been outlined, it is appropriate to turn to the theories and empirical findings that have emerged from the respective approaches. They are discussed in the following chapters in the same sequence in which the approaches were taken up in this chapter.

QUESTIONS AND RESEARCH SUGGESTIONS

1. *What is the underlying assumption of the individual or "case-method" approach in the etiological analysis of delinquency?*
2. *What are the resemblances and differences in the life-history and the case-history methods?*
3. *Why are projective techniques called "unstructured"?*
4. *What is the difference between situational analysis and sociodrama?*
5. *How do the two assumptions underlying the cultural approach to the etiology of delinquency differ from each other?*
6. *Utilizing the outline in this chapter of data sought in a case history of a delinquent, point out the gaps in the* Case of Howard L., *which appears in Chapter I.*
7. *Construct a sociodrama that you, as an observer-analyst, would be willing to outline and offer to a group of participants including one or more delinquents.*

SELECTED READINGS AND REFERENCES

Healy, William and Augusta Bronner, *New Light on Delinquency and Its Treatment,* New Haven, Yale University Press, 1936.
Lindesmith, A. R. and H. Warren Dunham, "Some Principles of Criminal Typology," *Social Forces,* 19:307–14, 1941.
Merrill, Maud A., *Problems of Child Delinquency,* Boston, Houghton Mifflin, 1947, pp. 25–50.

National Commission on Law Observance and Enforcement, *Report on the Causes of Crime*, Washington, D.C., 1931.

Plant, James S., "The Search for Causes," *Social Work Year Book*, New York, Russell Sage Foundation, 1933, pp. 35–40.

Reckless, Walter C., *The Etiology of Delinquent and Criminal Behavior*, New York, Social Science Research Council, Bulletin #50, 1943.

When he was a little boy everyone thought that Tom would grow up to be a doctor or a lawyer. He was such a serious child, so quiet and polite and so thoughtful of his mother. Tom came from "decent" folk. His father was a streetcar conductor who worked nights, never drank or ran around. When he came home after work he would go to sleep. In the afternoon when he woke up, he would read the paper and perhaps listen to the news or the ball game over the radio. Then he would go to work again. His mother took pride in their home which was almost paid for and kept it "neat as a pin." She had only two children, Tom and his brother, Bud, who was two years younger. Everyone fussed over Bud when he was a baby because he was always gurgling and had deep dimples and laughing eyes. Even Tom's mother seemed to prefer Bud, though she would deny it vigorously if you asked her. But she was always showing Bud off and quoting the smart things he said when people came to visit. Tom would look on with that serious expression of his.

At five years of age Tom began to wet the bed. His mother didn't know what was wrong with him. She would spank him for the bed wetting, but it didn't do any good. Finally, she took him to a doctor. But he found nothing wrong with the boy. Once when Tom was about eight years old his mother discovered that he had been stealing pennies from her purse to buy himself candy. She tried to shame him by pointing out that Buddy would never do anything like that. When Tom was twelve, the bed wetting stopped, but he still was a "nervous boy." He bit his nails and had a habit of jerking his head back sometimes. And he would toss in his sleep and grind his teeth.

Tom never had trouble at school, but neither did he receive honors as Bud did. Bud was president of his class and captain of the baseball team. He took the lead in the school play, and when he was awarded a prize for his art work his mother was elated.

Tom had no close friends and played mostly by himself. He would have wonderful daydreams of triumphing over Bud, over his schoolmates, over everybody. First he would dream that he was the fastest cross-country pilot, breaking all records. Then he was a G-man, tracking down counterfeiters, becoming a hero. Wouldn't his mother be surprised when she saw his picture in the paper!

Summer came and Tom's mother sent him to camp because she thought it would build him up and make a "real boy" of him. He was unhappy there and hoped his mother wouldn't make him return next year. Perhaps it was because he couldn't do any of the things as well as the other boys such as swimming, boxing, or pitching horseshoes. Once when two of the boys were teasing him and called him a sissy, Jimmy came by and chased them away. He said he'd knock their tops off if they didn't leave Tom alone. Jimmy

THE IDLE APPRENTICE AT PLAY IN THE CHURCHYARD DURING DIVINE
SERVICE: *Plate III in the* INDUSTRY AND IDLENESS *series*

In the engravings of his Industry and Idleness *series,*
Hogarth portrayed the development of two fellow apprentices.
He attempted to contrast the happy rewards of industry on the
part of one of them, Francis Goodchild, with the woeful con-
sequences of idleness on the part of the other, Thomas Idle. In
Hogarth's day, no more than now, a prevailing middle-class no-
tion was that idleness led inevitably to immoral and criminal be-
havior; industry was the key to a life of righteousness. Thus the
apprentice Francis Goodchild is at divine service with his master's
daughter, while outside in the churchyard Tom Idle is seated on
a grave in the company of three ruffians, playing "hustle cap." He
is attempting to cheat by furtively pushing some coins under the
brim of his hat. But the others have discovered his trick and a
quarrel is under way. The Industry and Idleness *series strikes a*
note of irony not intended by Hogarth: Idle's failure is not, in
truth, very different morally from Goodchild's ultimate success.
Goodchild marries his master's daughter in order to promote his
ambitious ends. Idle emerges as the victim of a social system in
which the norms define his behavior as punishable. In eighteenth-
century England, "white collar" and lower-class behavior patterns
were given different evaluation and sanction, just as they are in
contemporary American society.

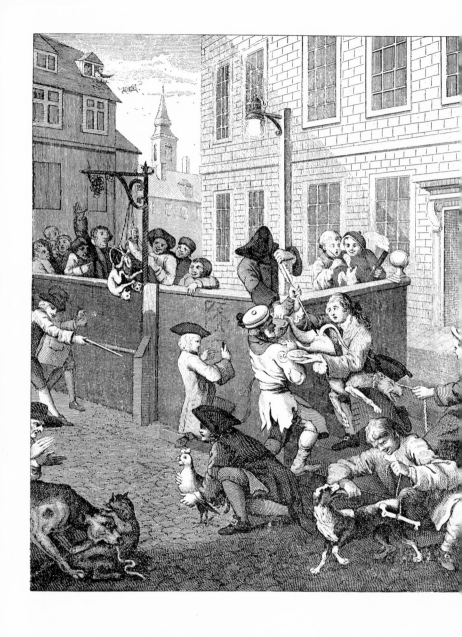

THE FIRST STAGE OF CRUELTY: *Plate I in* THE FOUR STAGES OF
CRUELTY

In The First Stage of Cruelty, *issued in 1751, Hogarth
shows some boys at what he considers the beginning of careers of
cruelty. The children in this startling scene are busy demonstrating several ingenious methods of tormenting animals. The artist
was struck by the prevalence of cruelty in English culture—a
trait that was exhibited for him, offending his strong middle-class
morality, daily in the streets of London. In Hogarth's eighteenth-
century world, this kind of behavior was most often accounted
for as an expression of innate disposition. Since Hogarth's day, society's prevailing ideas have changed; today such behavior is no
longer explained in terms of inherent characteristics. Cruelty in
our contemporary culture, no matter the age group, is usually
looked upon as learned or acquired behavior.*

was only a year older than Tom, but Tom heard one boy say Jimmy had a "record" and that the probation officer had sent him to camp to reform him. But Tom didn't care. He thought Jimmy was great and he hoped they could be friends. Jimmy didn't like the place either because there were too many rules.

When the police caught Jimmy, Tom, and another boy stripping tires off a sports roadster later that year, Tom stood still and gave himself up without a struggle. To an observer it might have seemed, for a moment, that he was glad to be caught.[1]

Constitutional theories explaining delinquency and crime have gone through a common chronological pattern. Largely because of Lombroso's efforts in the nineteenth century, attention was first directed toward the possibility of unique hereditary and physical traits among criminals distinguishing them from the rest of the population. At the turn of the century the careful anthropometric studies of the Lombrosian school gave way to equally meticulous psychometric studies by those who saw the etiology of delinquency and crime in differential types of intelligence. More recently, constitutional theories have sought the answer in the differential development of personality. Earlier theories, of course, have not succumbed to those which appeared at a later date. Today one can still find many modified versions of the Lombrosian and psychometric schools of thought.

The Heredity, Physique, and Glands of Juvenile Delinquents

The theory of the born or congenital delinquent had its origin in the nineteenth century, the era preceding the differentiation of delinquency from crime. It has long had more enthusiastic supporters in Europe than in America. Lombroso, an Italian criminologist, was the most vociferous proponent of this theory of innate criminality that allegedly manifests itself in physical stigmata. Shortly after the legal distinction was made in the United States between delinquency and crime, Healy reported that his clinical findings were negative with regard to this

---

[1] *Understanding Juvenile Delinquency,* Federal Security Agency, Children's Bureau, Publication #300, 1949, pp. 3–4.

theory.[2] Nevertheless the theory persisted, albeit in somewhat modified form. If the child could not be said to inherit a trait of stealing as he does a physical trait like blue eyes, one might still say that the child inherited the predisposition or tendency to steal.[3] The genealogies of such notorious families as the Jukes, Kallikaks, Nams, and Zeros were offered as evidence. When Spaulding and Healy in Chicago [4] and Burt in London,[5] after their investigations of the family backgrounds of several hundred delinquents, were unable to support the claim that there is an inherited tendency toward delinquency and crime, a new technique emerged in efforts to substantiate the diehard theory. This was the comparison of monozygotic or identical twins with dizygotic or fraternal twins, the former presumably being biologically the same individuals, whereas the latter are two biologically different individuals. For example, Johannes Lange, a German criminologist, searched in the prisons of Bavaria for criminals who had twins, and found 13 identical and 17 fraternal sets. Of the 13 sets of identical twins, 10 were found to have a criminal record for each twin while the remaining three sets had one twin criminal and one noncriminal. On the other hand, of the 17 sets of fraternal twins, two were found to have a criminal record for each twin and 15 had one criminal and one noncriminal. These data, as one might suspect, were interpreted to mean that criminality was inherited; otherwise the monozygotics would not be predominantly "concordant" and the dizygotics "discordant." [6] Several points, however, undermine such an interpretation. It is doubtful, for instance, that twins, especially when they are mature, can accurately be classified as monozygotic or dizygotic. It is also doubtful that the environmental influence

[2] William Healy, *The Individual Delinquent*, Boston, Little, Brown, 1915, p. 783.

[3] It is not difficult to understand the persistence of this theory. Darwin's work was so influential from its inception in the nineteenth century and thereon that many notions of hereditary-biological types have been able to retain the respectable aura of "science."

[4] Edith R. Spaulding and William Healy, "Inheritance as a Factor in Criminality," *Physical Bases of Crime: a Symposium*, Easton, Pa., American Academy of Medicine Press, 1914, p. 19.

[5] Cyril Burt, *The Young Delinquent*, New York, Appleton, 1925, p. 56.

[6] Johannes Lange, *Crime as Destiny*; translated by Charlotte Haldane, London, Allen and Unwin, 1931, p. 41.

was entirely eliminated from Lange's findings. To support his theory Lange should have shown, but actually failed to show, that criminality existed in the family background of all monozygotics in his sample. He should have proved, but he did not even attempt to prove, that all noncriminal monozygotics lack criminality in their family lines.

Following Lange's work, investigations by Stumpfl, Kranz, A. Rosanoff, Handy, and I. Rosanoff have all claimed to demonstrate, although to a lesser extent than Lange, a higher incidence of delinquency in identical than in fraternal twins. But other investigators, such as Guttmacher, Healy, and Bronner, have denied the validity of these research efforts, pointing out that they contain many sources of error.[7]

A work by another European, Kretschmer, in 1925 [8] fostered a revival of the Lombrosian theory of physical stigmata. Many European criminologists accepted his claim that he had isolated three major and several minor and mixed types of body builds, as well as his claim that characteristic temperaments were associated with these types of physique. They applied his typology to offenders, alleging that the more serious and chronic ones were preponderantly "athletic-schizothymic" and "asthenic schizothymic" or "leptosomeschizothymic," whereas the less serious and malleable offenders were "pyknic-cyclothymic." In the United States the typology and theory were discredited, for there was no success in isolating the types of body builds described by Kretschmer, nor in proving that mental traits followed Kretschmer's specifications, nor in demonstrating a significant relation between body build and either delinquency or crime. More recently, however, a few American scholars have themselves proposed the theory. One of the more conspicuous efforts to show a causal re-

---

[7] See F. Stumpfl, *Die Ursprunge des Verbrechens*, Leipzig, 1936; H. Kranz, *Lebensschicksale krimineller Zwillinge*, Berlin, 1936; A. Rosanoff, L. M. Handy, and I. Rosanoff, *The Etiology of Child Behavior Difficulties, Juvenile Delinquency and Adult Criminology with Special Reference to their Occurrence in Twins*, Sacramento, California, Department of Institutions, Psychiatric Monographs, No. 1, 1941; Lucien Bovet, *Psychiatric Aspects of Juvenile Delinquency*, Geneva, World Health Organization, Monograph Series No. 1, 1951.

[8] F. Kretschmer, *Physique and Character*, New York, Harcourt, Brace, 1925.

lationship between physical features and delinquency and crime was made by Hooton.[9] His claim was to have found a reliable difference not only between types of offenders in physical and morphological traits and body builds, but also between offenders and the civil population of two states. His conclusion was that offenders represent a biologically inferior aggregate although, he admitted, there is no more unity of type among offenders than there is in the civil population. The sharpest criticism made of Hooton's work has been with reference to his comparison of offenders and nonoffenders. The latter were represented by Nashville firemen, members of the Massachusetts state militia, and patrons of bathing beaches. Says Reckless: [10]

As far as interpretation goes, one should bear in mind that in Hooton's conclusions slight deviations under the average become the basis for inferiority. While there may be some justification for this, he assumes without further ado that the discerned biological inferiority is hereditary. After making the inferior hereditary, he finds that the biologically inferior gravitate to sociologically inferior environments; again an unproven assumption. Lastly, the weakest of the inferior succumb to the pressures of the bad environment, thereby becoming criminal; once more an unproven assumption. Hence, inherited biological inferiority receiving the impact of environment is the cause of crime.

Another recent attempt in America to show that behavior is a function of an organic structure is Sheldon's study of delinquents.[11] In his earlier studies he had concluded that there are three body types, and that correlated with these are three temperamental types as well as three psychiatric types. In his various writings Sheldon's hypothesis has been that all variations in personality and behavior are related to variations in these basic indices. From 1939 to 1946 he observed 200 subjects who

[9] Earnest Hooton, *The American Criminal: An Anthropological Study,* Cambridge, Harvard University Press, 1939.

[10] Reckless, *op. cit.,* pp. 14–16.

[11] William H. Sheldon *et al., Varieties of Delinquent Youth: An Introduction to Constitutional Psychiatry,* New York, Harper, 1949.

had been referred to a South Boston social center by several Boston agencies. But in the words of one critic: [12]

> The futility of this study in constitutional psychology should have been obvious in advance from previous failures of analogous studies. Sheldon is added to the list of Lombroso, Kretschmer, Hooton and other failures who attempted to demonstrate a physical difference between criminals and non-criminals.

A few critics have not been willing to go quite so far in minimizing the work of Sheldon and his predecessors. They maintain that it is possible that, rather than the physical constitution of a person directly determining his behavior toward others, the attitudes of the group predispose certain types of behavior toward, and consequently from, individuals of that constitution. Irritation, discomfort, a lowering of social status, and feelings of inferiority—such psychological conceptions of self and others based on physical traits may motivate delinquent behavior where the physical traits do not do so directly. The same point is often made by some critics of the related theory that physical handicaps, poor health, and malnutrition cause delinquency.[13] The critics here maintain that delinquents are not clearly differentiated from nondelinquents in these respects, for although many delinquents are found in poor physical condition, others are not. The same is true of nondelinquents. The same critics maintain that there is no more reason to believe that these physical defects directly cause delinquency than in the case of body types. But, they caution, the possibility remains that individual children with defects, should they suffer ridicule and other forms of differential

[12] Edwin H. Sutherland, "Critique of Sheldon's Varieties of Delinquent Youth," _American Sociological Review_, 16:10–13, 1951.

[13] Such a theory is implicit in Maller's study of the rate of delinquency in fourteen neighborhoods in New York City. He found that delinquents who had been brought into the juvenile courts were suffering from many more physical defects than was the child population in general. These defects included defective vision, carious teeth, and malnutrition. In areas of high rates of delinquency, 42 per cent of the children were found by the Department of Health to be suffering from malnutrition, compared with an average of 19 per cent for the city as a whole. J. B. Maller, "Juvenile Delinquency in New York City," _Journal of Psychology_, 3:1–25, 1937. See also his reports for the New York State Legislative Committee on Juvenile Delinquency, _Legislative Documents_ Nos. 62 and 75, 1939, 1940.

social treatment, may build self-images that become sources of inferiority feeling, resentment and, subsequently, delinquent behavior. There are many alternative responses, however, for other individual children with similar defects may become timid and withdrawn, or play the fool to conceal their distress and retain contact and rapport with their social world. (For example, it is interesting to note the varying interpretations of the effects of physical disability to be found in such works as Somerset Maugham's *Of Human Bondage,* Edith Wharton's *Ethan Frome,* Robert Louis Stevenson's *Dr. Jekyll and Mr. Hyde,* and Thomas Mann's *Mario and the Magician.* A good example of contrast is found in Charles Dickens's treatment of Tiny Tim in *The Christmas Carol* on the one hand, and Victor Hugo's Quasimodo in *The Hunchback of Notre Dame* on the other.) What of the many children with physical defects in our society who do not become delinquent or engage in alternative reactions? Only by including all other social elements along with the physical elements can one understand such variations in behavior.

There are a few advocates of the theory that nearly all delinquency and crime is an expression of one or more of the several types of glandular disturbance, hereditary and otherwise. But when it is a matter of demonstrating the exact relationship between these disturbances and either delinquency or crime, there is an obvious impasse. There is nothing in the make-up of a glandularly disturbed child which makes delinquency inevitable. The most that can be said with assurance in behalf of the theory is that in some cases of delinquency there may indirectly be a basis of glandular disturbance. For example, thyroid deficiency may result in physical and mental retardation; hypersecretion, on the other hand, may produce acceleration in body growth, as well as tension and impulsiveness. Both kinds of effects may lead to delinquent behavior, depending on the social situation and the cultural interpretations surrounding children who are so affected. The important point is the manner in which people interact with the individual who has glandular malfunctioning.

The Intelligence of Juvenile Delinquents

H. H. Goddard, the man who introduced the Binet scale into this country, was the person most responsible for the theory that delinquency and crime are products of mental deficiency.[14] On the basis of the large proportion of mental defectives he seemed to have found in institutions for delinquents, he concluded that the greatest single cause of delinquency and crime was "low grade mentality" and that every mental defective was a potential delinquent. During the first ten years of both the Binet and Simon scales' use in the measurement of intelligence, almost 200 reports of the result of tests given to delinquents appeared in the journals. On these scales, the intelligence-test scores of institutionalized delinquents were, in a large proportion of the cases, found to be below what was assumed to be the lower limit of normal intelligence. From this it was easy to infer that delinquency was caused by feeblemindedness.

There have been several refinements of this theory of a differential in intelligence between delinquent and nondelinquent. A common one is that it is in verbal and abstract intelligence that the delinquent is inferior, not in mechanical or manual aptitude. The protest of the inarticulate boy with good practical ability, seeking some means of expression, is reflected in overt delinquency.

Another theoretical refinement is that the intelligence level of institutionalized delinquents is inferior to that of juvenile court cases. Still another is that certain types of offenders brought to juvenile court are alleged to have lower IQ scores than other types. Merrill found that in such categories as forgery, parental control, and malicious mischief there were more children whose IQ was above the average of the delinquent group than there were below. On the other hand, in the sex, truancy, vagrancy, and assault categories the reverse was true: more of the children whose offenses fell into such groups were below the average IQ of the entire group she investigated than were above it. In the stealing category she found little difference in the percentage of cases above and below the average.[15]

The results of the Stanford-Binet test given to about 600 delinquents brought before the judge of the juvenile court of

[14] See his *Feeblemindedness, Its Causes and Consequences*, New York, Macmillan, 1914.

[15] Maud A. Merrill, *Problems of Child Delinquency*, Boston, Houghton Mifflin, 1947, pp. 173–4.

Lucas County in Toledo showed that the average IQ of the boys was slightly less than three points higher than the mean IQ of the girls. The Negro delinquents rated slightly lower in IQ than did the whites. Those charged with running away had the highest IQ's, whereas those charged with stabbing, holdup, and assault had the lowest.[16]

In recent years the theory has lost strength because of a decline in the proportion of the mentally deficient found among delinquents and criminals. This decline, according to some analysts, has been largely the result of changing conceptions of normal intelligence and feeblemindedness which grew out of the army tests of World War I, when drafted men were found to have an average intelligence of about thirteen years. Thereafter it was realized that the early scales of Binet and Simon were crude measures of intelligence, for they gave mental-age scores that were too high at the lower end and too low at the upper end. Apparently the early intelligence-scores of institutionalized delinquents had been considered inferior in such a large percentage of cases because the lower limit of the range of normal intelligence was assumed and not actually known.

In those early days of testing the influence of Goddard was very great. In those days, too, there were many poorly trained and inexpert testers, and Goddard, on the assumption . . . that the finer the sieve the better job of screening, also commented that the more expert the mental tester the larger proportion of delinquents he would find to be feebleminded. And, as one writer has sardonically pointed out, many testers attempted to demonstrate their superiority in that manner.[17]

Lane and Witty have gone so far as to conclude from several studies that the average IQ among 699 delinquent boys did not fall below that of nondelinquents drawn from largely the same racial and socio-economic groups. Groups of recidivists and non-recidivists who were compared did not differ from each other in intelligence. There was no relation discovered between IQ and such variables as age at first arrest, age at first commitment,

[16] William Evans McClure, "Intelligence of 600 Juvenile Delinquents," *Journal of Juvenile Research*, 17:25–43, 1933.
[17] Merrill, *op. cit.*, pp. 158–60.

number of convictions in court, and seriousness of delinquent activities.[18]

Others have pointed out that because mental defectives are more easily caught and more readily brought to court, owing to a poor school record, and because overcrowded conditions in institutions for defectives have led many to be charged with delinquency and sent to corrective institutions, there is often an apparent rather than a real differential in intelligence between court and institutionalized delinquents and nondelinquents. Furthermore, it is now understood that intelligence does not play an isolated role and accordingly needs to be evaluated in the context of the total personality and the social and cultural situation.

What can one conclude about the relationship of intelligence to delinquency?

1. The average intelligence level among delinquents who are apprehended and among institutionalized delinquents is lower than that of unselected school children but approximately the same as the intelligence level of nondelinquents who have the same ethnic and socio-economic background.

2. There are delinquents with very high as well as very low intelligence.

3. The exact relationship between intelligence and delinquency is unknown.

4. It is conceivable that in individual cases low intelligence leads to isolation, a sense of inferiority, and aggressive behavior defined as delinquency.

5. The greater suggestibility in some children of low intelligence because they are less critical may lead them to delinquency through the example and persuasion of others.

The Personality of Juvenile Delinquents

The twenty-fifth anniversary of the founding of the juvenile court highlighted the emergence of a new type of constitutional theory about the etiology of delinquency: the problem is effected through differentials in personality structure. In 1925 the delinquent personality in court was described as "a compound of

[18] Howard A. Lane and Paul Andrew Witty, "The Mental Ability of Delinquent Boys," *Journal of Juvenile Research*, 19:1–12, 1935.

insolence, bravado, scorn, poise, wit, youthful cunning, and resourcefulness in lying, impossible to describe unless witnessed." [19] Not too different is a more recent characterization of the delinquent personality in court:

> As we see him in court, the young delinquent is loath to admit that he is afraid of anything. . . . There is nothing, he says with obstinate bravado, of which he is afraid. While this tough exterior is not by any means the only *persona* seen in the juvenile court, it certainly occurs with such frequency that no one who works with delinquent children can fail to recognize it. . . .[20]

One of the most ambitious characterizations of the delinquent personality came out of the work of the Gluecks.[21] The delinquent is distinguishable from the nondelinquent, they claimed, in the following respects: (1) physically, in being mesomorphic in constitution (solid, closely knit, muscular); (2) temperamentally, in being restlessly energetic, impulsive, extroverted, aggressive, destructive (often sadistic); (3) in attitude, by being hostile, defiant, resentful, suspicious, stubborn, socially assertive, adventurous, unconventional, nonsubmissive to authority; (4) psychologically, in tending to direct and concrete, rather than symbolic, intellectual expression, and in being less methodical in his approach to problems.

There have been several theories attempting to account for the delinquent personality. One is usually identified with the work of W. I. Thomas.[22] It begins with the recognition of such basic psychological needs or wishes as security, response, recognition, and new experience as motivating forces common to every child. Failure to satisfy these needs in socially approved institutions such as the family provokes emotional disturbance in the personality which drives the child to seek methods of reducing the tension in socially disapproved channels outside the family.

[19] Miriam Van Waters, *Youth in Conflict*, New York, Republic, 1925, p. 149.

[20] Merrill, *op. cit.*, p. 109.

[21] Sheldon and Eleanor Glueck, *Unraveling Juvenile Delinquency*, New York, The Commonwealth Fund, 1950, pp. 281–2.

[22] *The Polish Peasant in Europe and America*, Boston, Richard C. Badger, 1918–20, and *The Unadjusted Girl*, Boston, Little, Brown, 1923.

Psychologically, then, the delinquent is a child seeking emotional satisfaction that he cannot find in his environment.

One of the most frequently utilized supports for this theory of the wish-thwarted delinquent personality came out of the Healy and Bronner study, which compared delinquents with their nondelinquent siblings.[23] The authors claimed that 91 per cent of the delinquents, as compared with only 13 per cent of the control group, were marked by feelings of being rejected, deprived, insecure, unloved, and misunderstood, a feeling of being thwarted, feelings of inadequacy or inferiority, and so forth.

The theory has been used extensively with special reference to the sex offender. Puberty, especially for the girl, makes possible an outlet for the satisfaction of the wishes of response, recognition, and new experience, the satisfaction of which may have been frustrated in socially sanctioned channels. Such frustrations are quite common in the status of adolescence which puberty introduces. No longer a child biologically, the adolescent is nevertheless still a child legally and, in many cases, socially. His activities are circumscribed, self-assertion suppressed, possessions limited, and economic independence not tolerated. It is to be expected, then, that the "child" of thirteen years of age and over, dominated by parents, and thwarted by them from wish-satisfaction, often manifests many aggressive personality traits and seeks substitute response and satisfaction.

So much for the wishes for response, recognition, and new experience. What about the wish for security? A definite lack of security is said to be a common denominator in the attitudes of many children. This is related to the present insecurity of the adult world and is reflected, according to some students, in increasing juvenile delinquency.

Insecurity gives rise to anxiety, which in turn tends to set free aggressiveness, expressing itself by delinquent acts of all kinds. In most people this aggressiveness will give rise to feelings of guilt, which in turn produce further anxiety. In this manner the vicious circle is completed. The experiences during World

[23] William Healy and Augusta F. Bronner, *New Light on Delinquency and Its Treatment*, New Haven, Yale University Press, 1936. For a later statement, see the article by the same authors in the *Social Work Year Book*, New York, Russell Sage Foundation, 1939, pp. 37–43.

War II have been used to substantiate the point. American children who were affected by the wartime disruptions tended to react in terms of their own sense of security. That is, children who felt secure in relation to their parents showed fewer signs of deviant behavior, such as delinquency, than did children whose home situations were less secure.

Enuresis (bed-wetting) is a common symptom of the child's insecurity. Some studies show a higher incidence of persistent enuresis among delinquents than among nondelinquent controls, which suggests that enuresis and delinquency are both expressions of some common fundamental disorder in personality. At one time it was assumed that enuresis was brought on by some kind of physical weakness or defect. Today, the prevailing interpretation is that enuresis is the result occasionally of a physical factor such as kidney trouble, a slight local infection or a small bladder, but that the great majority of cases are psychological rather than physical or biological in origin. Psychiatrists say about such cases that enuresis is an expression of the child's unconscious wish to regain the passive security he enjoyed in infancy, to be taken care of as he was when completely dependent. In many cases of bed-wetting, whether by delinquents or others, there is a large element of resentment by one child who feels he is being neglected in favor of another child. Often the bed-wetter is afraid to show his resentment openly, or even to acknowledge it to himself. Such a child is very likely to develop exaggerated fears in addition to enuresis. He is afraid of what his parents might do if he showed his feelings. He is afraid to recognize them himself. It is easy to translate these fears into fear of the dark, or into frightening dreams that may in turn intensify the bed-wetting. Enuretics are said to have in common the need for reassurance, the need to have their confidence in themselves restored.

Yet we have already seen that delinquents, to a greater extent than nondelinquents, say they are not afraid of anything. Are such personality traits as insolence, bravado, and scorn compensatory mechanisms that cover up the underlying fear and insecurity of the child? It is interesting to note that Willard Motley's famous novel [24] about an Italian boy in Chicago's West

[24] *Knock on Any Door*, New York, Appleton, 1947.

Side is based on such a theme. Nick Romano's development is traced from the time he was an altar boy in the Catholic Church through his adolescence, when he gradually became involved in delinquency, crime, and homosexuality. His career is ended when he becomes a "cop-killer" and is electrocuted at the age of twenty-one. In the words of one reviewer: [25]

> Motley has exposed, in the subtlest way, the essential passivity of the killer. He has shown that the real motivation is fear. He has demonstrated that it is not by accident that there is such a high rate of homosexuality among these frightened personalities. The protagonist of Motley's book, the Chicago gangsters of the twenties, and the Hitler legions of the thirties, have characteristics in common—the compulsion to rush into danger in an attempt to conquer anxiety arising out of their fear of their own passivity. If the book says anything, it says: "Frighten people and you either make abject creatures or killers of them."

Another theory of the delinquent personality as distinct from the nondelinquent is offered by the psychoanalytic school of thought.[26] Freud's concepts of unconscious repression, the need for punishment, and the feeling of guilt have all been employed in the study and understanding of delinquency. A basic point made by the psychoanalytic school is that it is folly to ask ourselves why a particular child becomes a delinquent instead of asking why all children do not become delinquent. It teaches that all infants come into the world with impulses and instincts that are not adjusted to life in society; that they are born potentially delinquent—meaning by this that if a little child could realize the demands of its instincts, it would behave as a delinquent. Every child, the psychoanalytic school maintains, is born with a feeling of insecurity, giving rise to tension and fear. Unless this is relieved, the tension accumulates and psychological pressure is enhanced. This pressure can be discharged temporarily by aggression or avoided by escape into fantasy. It can be alleviated

[25] Horace R. Cayton, *New Republic*, May 12, 1947.

[26] One of the most recent books dealing with delinquency from a psychoanalytic point of view is K. R. Eissler and Paul Federn, eds., *Searchlights on Delinquency: New Psychoanalytic Studies*, New York, International Universities Press, 1949.

by socializing bonds such as with one's parents, the result being the formation of conscience. Conscience repels and dissuades the psychic tension from breaking out in aggression. When psychic tension does break out into aggression, conscience determines the limit and direction of the individual's behavior in terms of what the conscience deems the least wrong. Delinquency and crime are forms of aggressive activity, but they are channeled in a given direction according to the conscience of the individual. Sometimes what appears to be a delinquency or crime may represent a symbolic gratification of a forbidden sexual act blocked by the inhibitions of conscience. The similarity of the gun to the male phallus has often been noted in psychoanalytic literature. The "stick-up" may contain strong elements of a suppressed homosexuality or sexual impotency. Even when this is not the case the persistence of "gun-toting" in the face of serious penalties and meager returns can be explained by a deep-rooted psychological, probably infantile, craving. The little boy with the gun becomes like the father, powerful, fear-inspiring, and dominant, and the hostile outsiders of the adult world acknowledge his strength. Another example of symbolic sex gratification appears in many cases of repeated shoplifting by girls. The articles they take are of a masculine nature and are associated with sporty and flashy attire, representing an unfulfilled love tryst.

The delinquent personality differs from the nondelinquent in the intensity of his psychic tension, the extent and direction of his resistance, and in the frequency with which his psychic tension breaks through the bonds of conscience.[27]

In connection with this theory it is of some interest to note the three psychological types of delinquents and their social correlates identified by Reiss.[28] On the basis of official court records and psychiatric reports of more than a thousand white male juvenile-delinquent probationers in Cook County, Illinois, the following types were isolated: (1) the relatively integrated delinquent; (2) the delinquent with relatively defective superego controls; and (3) the delinquent with markedly weak ego con-

[27] See James S. Wallerstein, "Roots of Delinquency," *Nervous Child*, 6:399–412, 1947.

[28] Albert J. Reiss, Jr., "Social Correlates of Psychological Types of Delinquency," *American Sociological Review*, 17:710–18, 1952.

trols. *The relatively integrated type of delinquent,* according to Reiss, is an adolescent whose personal controls are such that there is high probability he will become an adjusted adult. Although he comes from one of the less desirable residential areas in the community, his family has a relatively stable pattern of mobility, in that it does not move at frequent intervals. The family is structurally intact, the parents maintain stable marital relations and they have conventional moral ideals and utilize effective techniques of control over their children. The relatively integrated delinquent usually participates in the culture of his age group, frequently leaves school and seeks employment. When he is attending school he is less often truant, demonstrates good deportment and generally is no different from other delinquent types in scholarship patterns. Although he does not commit any particular kind of offense with significantly greater frequency than do the other delinquent types, he resembles the defective superego type in participating more often in such delinquent acts as burglary and larceny, particularly auto larceny. These offenses tend to be characteristic of the one-time delinquent or the members of organized gangs. The relatively integrated delinquent, in short, tends to be less often a recidivist than are the other delinquent types.

The delinquent with defective superego controls is labeled as such because he does not internalize the conventional social norms and he feels little sense of guilt about his delinquent acts. His social correlates suggest a personality developed in nonconventional situations. Seldom does he come from a settled residential area. He often leaves school seeking regular employment, but unlike the relatively integrated type he does not generally complete his grade school education. While he is in school he rejects its social control, demonstrating poor deportment and scholarship and frequent truancy. Most often his family is characterized by separation, desertion, or divorce, as well as the death of a parent. In those cases where both parents are present their interaction is hostile and they seldom represent conventional moral ideals and adequate techniques of control. This type of delinquent is usually a member of a gang and participates with several associates in his offense. Lastly, he has the highest rate of recidivism of the three types.

The delinquent with relatively weak ego controls is insecure, has low self-esteem, and is hostile toward other people and their environment. He generally shows anxiety and experiences much conflict internally over his behavior. In most cases he comes from a settled residential area, but his family moves about frequently within the community as well as from community to community. This suggests that he is not integrated into his age group in the community, partial substantiation of which is the fact that he is seldom a participant in "peer groups." Seldom does this type leave school, but when he does he is usually unemployed. His scholarship tends to be average for his grade level, although he generally shows poor deportment and frequent truancy. While the parents are usually together, their marital relations are often marked by conflict. The delinquent with relatively weak ego-controls is frequently the eldest child in a small family. This suggests that his emotional instability in part stems from the fact that he is often the victim of parental anxiety. Lastly, he is more often a lone offender, because he participates in group life with his peers far less often than do the other types.

The psychoanalytic theory of delinquency, of course, has not escaped criticism. As Merton says: [29]

It no longer appears so obvious that man is set against society in an unceasing war between biological impulse and social restraint. The image of man as an untamed bundle of impulses begins to look more like a caricature than a portrait.

The theory is useful but not essential to the conception of the delinquent as a neurotic or emotionally unstable personality. Some neurotics are inhibited and engage in social withdrawal, but others find their outlet in exaggerated aggressiveness. Neurotics who are delinquent are said to be more aggressive and extroverted than the nondelinquent neurotic.[30] The severity of the neurotic tendency increases from the less to the more "seriously"

[29] Robert K. Merton, Chapter v, "Social Structure and Anomie," in *Social Theory and Social Structure*, Glencoe, Illinois, The Free Press, 1949, p. 125.

[30] See Margery Stern, "Some Differences between Neurotic Delinquents and Other Neurotic Children," *Smith College Studies in Social Work*, 16:62–81, 1945; Banay, *op. cit.*, p. 141.

delinquent children. The Rorschach ink-blot test, when applied to delinquents and a control group of nondelinquents, has supported the position that delinquents are more neurotic and emotionally immature. They are less critical and more aggressive and they have more intense feelings of anxiety.

The psychotic or mentally disordered personality is less often found among delinquents than among adult offenders because for the most part mental disorders are characteristic of maturity. The hallucinations and delusions of mental disorder require an experience and development that children are not likely to have had. A small number of delinquents are psychotic, and some forms of disorder are almost direct in effecting delinquency. For example, a schizophrenic or paranoiac may have a vigorous delusion of persecution which may lead to homicidal attack upon the alleged persecutor. But a more likely process is that the disorder lowers the social status of the child, not only aggravating his deviant personality traits but also leading to delinquent behavior in order to satisfy his wishes.

There is as yet no universal agreement on the question of differentials in the personality structures of delinquent and nondelinquent. One extreme is represented by Merrill,[31] who maintains that personality tests show delinquents to differ from nondelinquents in the following ways:

1. In emotional stability, measured by symptoms associated with psychopathic trends.

2. In emotional maturity, measured by kinds of persons liked and admired; anxieties, fears, and worries; things considered wrong; likes and interests.

3. In social adjustment, measured by responses to questions interpreted as indicating interest in people, sympathy, poise, and self-control.

4. In attitudes, measured by self-criticism, feeling of being different from the average, feeling of superiority, social insight.

5. In honesty, measured by amount of cheating on performance tests of deceptiveness.

On the other hand, Schuessler and Cressey summarized 113 studies—the entire number of such studies available—that had used objective tests of personality traits of delinquents and

[31] *Op. cit.,* pp. 40–1.

criminals in comparison with control groups. Their conclusion was that this series of 113 studies did not provide a consistent demonstration that delinquents and criminals differ from nondelinquents and noncriminals in any personality trait.[32]

Hathaway and Monachesi,[33] bemoaning the fact that there has been virtually no *predictive* value stemming from these studies, believe they can account in part for the situation. They note that in general the majority of research studies attempting to reveal how delinquents and nondelinquents differ in personality have been inclined to relate the background of the delinquent to the behavioral difficulty *after* his "maladjustment" has occurred. That is, much of what is known about the personality factors allegedly indicative of probable maladjustment is derived only from an historical reconstruction of the child's personality development. The reliability of such reconstructions is so questionable that it may be largely responsible for the indifferent results obtained when the reconstructions are utilized to predict the behavior of other children whose personalities seem to resemble those of the already known and studied delinquents.

There is general agreement, however, that an understanding of delinquency is incomplete unless the social situation is taken into consideration. *Delinquency depends partly on the kind of person one is and partly on the social and cultural factors.*

The chapter that follows is an examination of the first of such situations, the primary group of the child.

QUESTIONS AND RESEARCH SUGGESTIONS

1. *Is it correct to conclude that the physical constitution of a child can have no influence on his behavior leading to delinquency? Why?*
2. *Why has there been in recent years a decline of the theory that delinquency is caused by low intelligence?*
3. *How does the theory of W. I. Thomas account for the delinquent personality?*

[32] Karl F. Schuessler and Donald R. Cressey, "Personality Characteristics of Criminals," *American Journal of Sociology*, 55:476–84, March 1950.
[33] Starke R. Hathaway and Elio D. Monachesi, "The Minnesota Multiphasic Personality Inventory in the Study of Juvenile Delinquents," *American Sociological Review*, 17:704, 1952.

4. What criticism can one make of the psychoanalytic theory of delinquency?
5. What is meant by the "relatively integrated" type of delinquent?
6. Compare the theories of Lombroso and Sheldon and show to what extent they resemble and differ from each other.
7. Analyze and compare the varying interpretations of physical disability in the works of Somerset Maugham, Edith Wharton, Robert Louis Stevenson, and Thomas Mann.
8. List the main points you would make in an essay on the relationship between intelligence and delinquency.

SELECTED READINGS AND REFERENCES

Babcock, Marjorie E., A Comparison of Delinquent and Non-delinquent Boys by Objective Measures of Personality, Ph.D. Thesis, Columbia University, 1932.

Blumgarten, A. S., The Scientist Looks at the Unstable Child, Child Research Clinic Series, Vol. 1, No. 3, Woods School, Langhorne, Pa., 1935.

Dollard, John, et al., Frustration and Aggression, New Haven, Yale University Press, 1939 (revised edition, 1945).

Durea, M. A., "Personality Characteristics and Degree of Delinquency: An Empirical Analysis of Blameworthy Circumstances and Anxiety States," The Journal of Social Psychology, 13:329–39, 1941.

Eissler, K. R., and Paul Federn, eds., Searchlights on Delinquency: New Psychoanalytic Studies, New York, International Universities Press, 1949.

Foxe, Arthur N., "Freud's Contribution to an Understanding of Delinquency," American Journal of Orthopsychiatry, 10:863–6, 1940.

Friedlander, Kate, The Psychoanalytical Approach to Juvenile Delinquency, New York, International Universities Press, 1947.

Glueck, Bernard, "Psychological Motive in Criminal Action," Journal of Criminal Psychopathology, 2:21–53, 1940.

Glueck, Sheldon, and Eleanor Glueck, Unraveling Juvenile Delinquency, New York, The Commonwealth Fund, 1950.

Hartman, A. A., "Recidivism and Intelligence," Journal of Criminal Law and Criminology, 31:417–26, 1940.

Hathaway, Starke R., and Elio D. Monachesi, "The Minnesota Multiphasic Personality Inventory in the Study of Juvenile Delinquents,"American Sociological Review, 17:704–10, 1952.

Healy, William, and Augusta F. Bronner, New Light on Delinquency and Its Treatment, New Haven, Yale University Press, 1936.

Jastak, Joseph, "The Manual-Minded Child," *Delaware State Medical Journal*, 14:126–9, 1942.

Jastak, Joseph, and H. Allen, "Psychological Traits of Juvenile Delinquents," *Delaware State Medical Journal*, 16:100–4, 1944.

Johnstone, E. L., "The Relation of Mental Deficiency to Delinquency," *Federal Probation*, 6:27–8, 1942.

Lane, Howard A., and Paul A. Witty, "The Mental Ability of Delinquent Boys," *Journal of Juvenile Research*, 19:1–12, 1935.

McClure, William Evans, "Intelligence of 600 Juvenile Delinquents," *Journal of Juvenile Research*, 17:25–43, 1933.

Merrill, Maud A., *Problems of Child Delinquency*, Boston, Houghton Mifflin, 1947.

Michaels, Joseph J., "The Incidence of Enuresis and Age of Cessation in One Hundred Delinquents and One Hundred Sibling Controls," *American Journal of Orthopsychiatry*, 8:460–5, 1938.

Michaels, Joseph J., "Parallels between Persistent Enuresis and Delinquency in the Psychopathic Personality," *American Journal of Orthopsychiatry*, 11:260–74, 1941.

Michaels, Joseph J., "Note on the Incidence of Enuresis in Twenty-five Delinquents," *American Journal of Orthopsychiatry*, 13:644–8, 1943.

O'Leary, W. D., "Mental Hygiene Problems of Childhood," *Catholic Schools Journal*, 42:267–9, 1942.

Reichenberg, W., and L. Chidester, "Lack of Imagination as a Factor in Delinquent Behavior," *Menninger Clinic Bulletin*, 1:226–31, 1937.

Reiss, Albert J., Jr., "Social Correlates of Psychological Types of Delinquency," *American Sociological Review*, 17:710–18, 1952.

Rowe, A. W., "A Possible Factor in Behavior Problems of the Young," *American Journal of Orthopsychiatry*, 1:451–75, 1931.

Schuessler, Karl F., and Donald R. Cressey, "Personality Characteristics of Criminals," *American Journal of Sociology*, 55:476–84, 1950.

Selling, Lowell S., and Seymour P. Stein, "Vocabulary and Argot of Delinquent Boys," *American Journal of Sociology*, 39:644–7, 1934.

Sheldon, William H., *et al.*, *Varieties of Delinquent Youth: An Introduction to Constitutional Psychiatry*, New York, Harper, 1949.

Slawson, John, *The Delinquent Boy: a Socio-Psychological Study*, Boston, Badger, 1926.

Chapter **VIII.** *The Family and Juvenile Delinquency*

The "inquiring reporter" of a newspaper in a large upstate New York community [1] once asked this question of five people: "What do you believe is the most important factor contributing to juvenile delinquency?" They responded as follows:

A veteran's counselor:

"I would say that broken homes constitute a prime factor in the rise of juvenile delinquency. Another factor is the lack of proper guidance and supervision of the children's activities by the parents. I believe that all agencies including the home, school, religious organizations, etc., should bring their influences to bear upon this matter."

---

[1] *Syracuse Herald-Journal*, May 20, 1947, p. 30.

A teacher:

"I believe that the home conditions surrounding a child are the chief factor influencing his conduct. A lack of supervision seems to be at the root of a great deal of juvenile delinquency and I think a lack of recreational activities also aggravates the situation."

A receptionist:

"I believe that children are almost entirely a product of their early training and home life and that juvenile delinquency is a result of failure by the parents. 'As the twig is bent the tree's inclined' and insecurities known by the child foster personality maladjustments which lead to delinquency."

A Children's Court Assistant District Attorney:

"I believe a poor family background and lack of beneficial training in the home are responsible for a large number of juvenile delinquency cases. There is no easy cure for delinquency because each case is a problem in itself requiring individual study and a special plan for correction."

Another teacher:

"In my opinion parental indifference is the cause of considerable juvenile delinquency. Many parents are more interested in their jobs and the money they are earning than in their children. I think mothers should remain in the home unless it is absolutely necessary that they work, because the children's welfare is all-important."

Obviously the one common denominator in all five of these opinions is that family life is the most important factor contributing to juvenile delinquency. Laymen do not stand alone in this respect. Among social workers, administrators, and academic specialists, "family" theories in etiology have long been prominent. Their feeling has been that, of all social background data, the more important influences are those in operation for a long period of time, and the most important is that covering the earlier years of childhood, namely the home and family. A judge of a well-known Domestic Relations Court in New York City which has jurisdiction over delinquency cases has stated as his fundamental premise that no child is born into the world to be "bad" or "good." "Under this premise," he continues, "the question: 'What causes juvenile delinquency?' instead becomes: 'Who, in the first instance, makes it possible for a child to be bad or good?' And there is only one answer—the parent." [2]

Empirical support of family theories in etiology in general has been so voluminous that it is almost unnecessary to provide documentation. Representative of such support is the Gluecks' study of 500 institutionalized boys, and a control group of identical numbers, which concluded that the kind of relationships that existed in a home between the boy and his parents had far more to do with delinquency than whether he lived in a slum area, or grew up among conflicting cultures, or had a high or low intelligence quotient. They maintained that if the child's family life was "adequate," the chances were only 3 in 100 that he would turn out to be delinquent, whereas if his family situation was "poor," the chances were 98 out of 100 that he would become a delinquent. [3]

The Gluecks found that their sample of delinquents came from homes where the families were more mobile and homes that had a greater scarcity of sanitary facilities, less tidiness, and more overcrowding. The families of the delinquents had more often been dependent on relief agencies for support, and their standard of living and income were lower. Delinquents were generally found to be more often making their homes with people other than their own parents, and more often to come from homes of separated or divorced persons, or parents who had never been married to each other, or who were no longer alive. The delinquents' families also differed from the control group's families in the ability or willingness of the parents to assume family responsibilities. Parents of delinquents were not only more frequently on relief, but were more often dependent because of the reluctance of the head of the family to assume responsibility than because of unforeseeable crises. They were more often afflicted by emotional disturbance, drunkenness, criminality, physical ailments, or mental deficiency. Delinquents were also found to be more often the victims of indifferent or hostile parents, and, as a

[2] *New York Times Magazine*, December 22, 1946, p. 20.
[3] Sheldon and Eleanor Glueck, *Unraveling Juvenile Delinquency*, New York, The Commonwealth Fund, 1950.

consequence, they were less attached to their parents than were the members of the control group. This emotional deprivation led the delinquents to feel that their parents did not care about their welfare. Accordingly, they made little attempt to emulate or respect their parents. Finally, in the homes of delinquents the pattern of discipline was more erratic than in the homes of the control group, ranging from extreme physical punishment to extreme laxity.[4]

Family theories in the etiology of delinquency have taken such a firm hold, especially among legislators, that it is no longer unusual to find the logical consequences in treatment and prevention. This can be seen in legislation to make parents liable at least for the partial support of their institutionalized delinquent children,[5] and the arrest and punishment of parents for "contributing to the delinquency of a minor."[6] In short, it is no exaggeration to observe that parents have increasingly become scapegoats, assigned the entire burden of causation in delinquency. Theories about the family and delinquency, when they do not lead to scapegoating of this sort, select one aspect of family life as influential, at the same time conceding that there are other important explanations of the problem.

The family is thought to provoke delinquency in the following ways:

Affection and Discipline in Parent-Child Relationships.

Unsatisfactory parent-child relationships have long been suspected of causing delinquency. The theory is that the child engages in delinquent and other antisocial behavior as a result of parental failure in socialization of the child. The theory is substantiated, its adherents maintain, when intrafamily tension and emotional disturbance are found to be more prevalent in the family relationships of delinquents than of nondelinquents.

Industrialization and urbanization have brought on individ-

---

[4] In an even larger scale study of 5,000 cases of juvenile delinquency in Canada, the conclusion was that for the most part the children had lived in homes that had presented heavily weighted factors contributing to the insecurity of the child during its developmental years.

[5] See Harriet F. Pilpel and Theodore Zavin, *Your Marriage and the Law*, New York, Rinehart, 1952.

[6] See Chapter XVIII for a more detailed account of such practices.

ualization in the home and have promoted the decline of the family's common objectives without offering substitute forms for the socialization of the child. At the same time industrialization and urbanization have led to an impermanence of the family's relationships to the community. Family mobility means, among other things, that the child lacks identification with the community. Excessive family mobility is generally accompanied by an increase in delinquency. Merrill claimed that her delinquent sample was significantly differentiated from her control group in this respect. Nearly half of the delinquents she studied were either indifferent or antagonistic to their community. The non-delinquents, on the other hand, were found to be much more likely to identify themselves positively with the community.[7]

Thus juvenile delinquency is believed to involve a breakdown in the emotional attachment between parent and child and a minimizing of the child's sense of responsibility to the community. Usually this covers several aspects, such as the parent's feeling of helplessness in the situation, his desire to protect the child and at the same time to injure the child for rejecting parental protection, and a feeling of shame as a result of the exposure of family incompetence. The child often feels neglected and therefore rejected by his parents. Inasmuch as his parents typify the community to the child, he is likely to become aggressive, rebellious, hostile, and hyperactive, engaging in such delinquency as truancy and thievery.

Parents are expected to be the primary agents of both discipline and affection. These contradictory roles are often pointed to as important factors in creating family tension. "We still control children by fear and force," observes one sociologist, "but many parents, fearful of Freudian complexes and repressions, abjure all discipline and control. . . . We 'love' children too much and too little; frequently the same child is a victim of this emotional polarity, indulged and frightened in almost the same breath."[8] In her study of delinquents, Merrill found it useful to

[7] Maud A. Merrill, *Problems of Child Delinquency*, Boston, Houghton Mifflin, 1947, pp. 87–8.

[8] See Bain, "Our Schizoid Culture," *Sociology and Social Research*, 19:266–76, 1935.

define "good" discipline as control that was firm but not so strict as to cause fear; "fair" discipline was sometimes inconsistent, but generally moderately firm; "poor" discipline was very lax, or extremely rigid, or very erratic. Affection was defined as "good" if it involved a parental relationship that was sympathetic and kind; "fair" affection was somewhat indifferent, and "poor" affection involved a clearly hostile attitude by the parents. The main differences between Merrill's delinquent and control groups were the poor discipline in the delinquent group and the fact that although relationships of affection were generally good in both groups, in the delinquent group a significantly greater number of parents were actually hostile toward their children. The nondelinquent boys' attitudes toward their relationship with parents, with respect to parental discipline and affection, were less resentful.[9] In other studies, too, such as that done by Healy and Bronner,[10] nondelinquents were found to have more satisfying social relationships with the family than had delinquents.

A study by Zucker[11] began with the hypothesis that affectional identification with the parent is deficient or lacking in the delinquent child. A delinquent group and a nondelinquent group of twenty-five boys each, from two different public schools in Manhattan, were studied. The two groups were approximately equivalent in age, race, socio-economic background, and tested intelligence. The delinquents, in comparison with nondelinquents, tended to show less affectional attachment to their parents, to exhibit less regard for the welfare of their parents, to retaliate against their parents more often by engaging in disapproved behavior, and to obey parents less often.

Delinquents have reported that their fathers punish more than their mothers, fathers favor daughters, and mothers favor sons.[12] A closely related finding by Merrill was that antagonism

[9] Merrill, *op. cit.*, pp. 72-3.
[10] *New Light on Delinquency and Its Treatment*, New Haven, Yale University Press, 1936.
[11] Herbert John Zucker, "Affectional Identification and Delinquency," *Archives of Psychology*, No. 286, New York, 1943.
[12] H. W. Newell, "Family Attitudes as Revealed by the Psychiatric Examinations of 107 Juvenile Delinquents," American *Journal of Orthopsychiatry*, 2:377-83, 1932.

toward the father was greater among both her delinquents and nondelinquents than was antagonism toward the mother, but the intensity was greater among the delinquents than among the nondelinquents.[13] But before Newell and Merrill's studies are accepted as "proof" of the validity of the Freudian Oedipus and Electra complexes, mention should be made of one more study: that of the background of 116 delinquent boys resident in a specific period of three months at the Cedar Knolls School of the Jewish Board of Guardians. Maternal rejection was reported in 47 per cent of the cases, compared with paternal rejection in 34 per cent.[14]

Affection and discipline are clearly important factors in the etiology of delinquency. Further research will undoubtedly throw light on the subtleties of their influence which are still not fully understood.

Social Class Patterns in Child-Rearing

The social class studies in American sociology, beginning in the 1930's, now provide new etiological thought about delinquency. As Shulman [15] observes, the different patterns of child-rearing in different social classes suggest that these differences may have an effect on such behavior as delinquency. Middle-class parents are more strict with their children and frustrate their impulses, whereas lower-class parents are more permissive; *i.e.*, the child is less restricted in his range and choice of action. Furthermore, obedience of parents by the middle-class child gives him an acceptable status to achieve, that of his parents. But the lower-class child would not find such obedience attractive in our culture because to inherit his parents' status is not rewarding. In short, frustrations imposed by parents are readily tolerated in one case because they lead to upward mobility, an acceptable goal in our culture, whereas in the other case any frustrations are intolerable because they do not lead to that goal.

[13] *Op. cit.*, pp. 127–8.

[14] Joseph Lander, "Traumatic Factors in the Background of 116 Delinquent Boys," *American Journal of Orthopsychiatry*, 11:150–6, 1941.

[15] Harry M. Shulman, "The Family and Juvenile Delinquency," *The Annals of the American Academy of Political and Social Science*, 261:30–1, 1949.

Less is known about the upper-class patterns of child-rearing and their relation to juvenile delinquency. This is an area which invites intensive investigation. It is conceivable that a concept of "white collar delinquency" would emerge which would revolutionize the field of delinquency in the manner that Sutherland's "white collar crime" has affected criminology.[16]

The Broken Home

Closely related to the above is the theory that the complete family (also known as the normal or natural family), in which both parents are present in the same household as their children, is a preventive of delinquency. Conversely, the broken home, in which one or both parents are absent because of divorce, desertion, separation, death, or commitment to an institution, is thought to be conducive to a high incidence of juvenile delinquency because of deficiencies in parental affection and discipline.

Empirical studies have failed to agree with regard to this theory.[17] Some show a high proportion of broken homes among delinquents, whereas others show a much lower incidence of broken homes. Recent studies have frequently concluded that broken homes are less important as a causal factor than was concluded by earlier studies.[18] The latter overlooked the fact that the incidence of broken homes increases with the age of the children studied. Also, they did not recognize any selective bias in the fact that there is an increase in the frequency of broken homes as one progresses from court arraignments to institutional commitments. They did not take into consideration the fact that the delinquent child from a broken home is more likely to be

[16] See Edwin H. Sutherland, *White Collar Crime*, New York, Dryden, 1949; see also discussion of the concept of white collar delinquency in Chapter XIII.

[17] See Edwin H. Sutherland, *Principles of Criminology*, rev. ed., Philadelphia, Lippincott, 1947, pp. 158–60.

[18] One of the first was Clifford R. Shaw and Henry D. McKay, "Are Broken Homes a Causative Factor in Juvenile Delinquency?" *Social Forces*, 10:514–24, 1932. Data on the incidence of broken homes among 7,278 unselected schoolboys in 29 public schools of Chicago suggested that the then accepted assumption of the broken home as an important factor in delinquency rested on an inadequate basis, and that the underlying factors were aspects of family relations which were more subtle than a formal break.

institutionalized than the delinquent from a complete home whose problem is otherwise adjusted. Those who report the offense and make the arrest, the teacher and the juvenile-court judge, are more likely to think that the broken home is unsatisfactory and commitment would be preferable, than they would in the case of a complete home. Investigators in earlier studies were naïvely impressed by the much higher percentage of broken homes among institutionalized delinquents than that in the general population. One such investigator [19] compared the proportion of broken homes among reform school cases with that of children in three New York City public schools. He found not only the expected differential but also a closer connection between delinquency and the loss of the mother than the loss of the father. In so doing he failed to consider that the comparison was distorted on the one hand by the possibility that children from broken homes are more likely to be institutionalized than are those from complete families, and on the other hand the fact that public school children were drawn largely from Jewish families, which have an unusually low rate of broken homes. We now realize that in the measurement of the extent of broken homes among juvenile delinquents and control groups consideration must be given to the ethnic background of the samples. The incidence of broken homes shows wide variation by race, nativity, and nationality. Inasmuch as the proportion of delinquents known to the courts varies by ethnic groups, the general child population is not represented unselectively in court intake for ethnic background. For example, Jewish delinquents with a low broken-home rate tend to be underrepresented because of the provision of private facilities for their care; Negro delinquents, however, with a high rate of broken homes, are overrepresented because of a lack of private facilities for their care. This shows how the disproportionate number of broken families among court and institutionalized cases may be a result of the ethnic distribution of such cases.

An example of studies of broken homes using a more scientific methodology was one made of a group of 362 delinquent girls in Chicago. They were matched for age and nationality with the

[19] John Slawson, *The Delinquent Boy: a Socio-Psychological Study,* Boston, Badger, 1926, p. 354.

same number of schoolgirls who lived in the same ecological areas. Defining broken homes as those from which *one or both parents* were absent, it was found that 67 per cent of the delinquents, compared with 45 per cent of the nondelinquents, came from broken homes. When the broken home was defined as a home containing *only one parent,* the difference between delinquents and nondelinquents was not so great.[20]

On the basis of the findings in a Spokane study of 515 delinquents one may say that the incidence of broken homes among delinquents varies by offense, sex, and source of referral to court. Broken homes were found to be associated more frequently with cases charged with ungovernability, running away, and truancy, and less frequently with cases charged with property offenses, traffic violations, and misdemeanors. The former offenses, which had a high proportion of broken homes, were those in which girls were more often involved, whereas the latter offenses, which had a lower proportion of broken homes, involved boys more frequently. But a comparison of broken-home rates for boys and girls apprehended for *comparable* delinquencies showed an insignificant difference.[21]

Most research studies today, while they agree with earlier studies that the incidence of broken homes is higher for delinquents than for nondelinquents even when such factors as age and ethnic background are considered (although they disagree about the *degree* of differences), claim that this does not necessarily prove a causal relation, but merely strongly suggests one. An important obstacle to causal conclusiveness here is the lack of data about the proportion of broken homes for the whole population. Perhaps if such information were available a much greater proportion of the nondelinquent children would be seen to have broken homes than is now assumed. One student of this question says her data suggest that a minority of children today arrive at the age of eighteen without some such major break in the family. Consideration of the divorce rate and the rate of mental illness (one adult in twenty is said to spend some time of his life in a

[20] Margaret Hodgkiss, "The Delinquent Girl in Chicago, II. The Influence of Broken Homes and Working Mothers," *Smith College Studies in Social Work*, 3:259–74, 1935.

[21] H. Ashley Weeks, "Male and Female Broken Home Rates by Type of Delinquency," *American Sociological Review*, 5:601–9, 1940.

In his series on The Election, Hogarth dealt with a political contest in which the candidates were compelled, by custom as much as necessity, to spend money freely. The setting of Canvassing for Votes is the village street between two rival inns. A freeholder who possesses a vote is being bribed by both innkeepers, who are acting as agents for opposing parties in the current political campaign. Leering in self-satisfaction, the freeholder is accepting both bribes. Behind the group stands one of the candidates in the election, engaged in buying from a wandering peddler some trinkets for the two ladies on the balcony. The scene being eighteenth-century England, these ladies of course have no votes—but they may well be able to influence men who have. Hogarth is ridiculing the corruption he observes riddling the political life of England, a country that boasts all the while of its democracy and political freedom. From satires like this it is easy to see why an election in eighteenth-century England was widely referred to as a "popular farce." And it must unfortunately be admitted that our own society is almost as ripe for such satire. Two centuries after Hogarth, corruption is still an integral part of the political affairs of the day. And it is no easier in our time than it was in Hogarth's to build integrity and moral virtue in children when they are exposed daily to the evidence of immorality and "delinquency" in the public life of their elders.

GIN LANE

A dead man, a hawker of gin and ballads, sits in the foreground of this famous picture. Above him is one of Hogarth's most gruesome figures, a ragged woman so intoxicated that she lets her shrieking child fall from her arms. Behind her a famished man shares a bone with a dog, while two people haggle with a pawnbroker, presumably for gin money. At a coffin-maker's shop in the background, a woman who has drunk herself to death is being lowered into a coffin as her naked child sits wailing near by. Another child has been impaled on a spit by a man, mad with drink, who rushes to join a free-for-all at a distiller's shop. A woman, apparently too weak to stand, is about to be taken home in a wheelbarrow by a kind friend, but not before her daughter pours a parting drink down her gullet. At the right two children, inmates of a charity home, are having a congenial drink together. Another drunken mother at the extreme right is introducing her infant to the pleasures of gin. High above the grisly scene, in the rafters of a ramshackle house, hangs the body of a man who has committed suicide. Although Hogarth intended this engraving to be a satiric indictment of the gin craze that seized the British people in the mid-eighteenth century, his picture is, incidentally, a vivid demonstration of the impact of adult drunkenness on children.

mental hospital) should lead one to see how unreal the usual concept of normal family experience actually is.[22] Another point that has emerged in contemporary evaluation of broken homes is that it is not so much the physical break in the home as the child's reaction to it that is important. The break itself may solve as much of the problem as it creates. A complete home that is marked by dissension may be psychologically and socially more broken than a physically broken one in which the remaining members of the family carry on as a close family unit.

Intergenerational Conflict

In a dynamic culture, according to some etiologists, there is an inevitable conflict between parents and children. The conflict is especially intensive when cultural differences between generations are magnified by nativity differences. In other words, conflict between immigrant parents and their native-born children is apt to be greater than that found between native-born parents and their children. For the children of those recent immigrants whose culture differs extensively from that of earlier American stock a psychological conflict often develops. Delinquency may result as an expression of rebellion and a desire to flee from the less rewarding ways of foreign-born parents. This is more likely among those second-generation children whose parents' Old World culture includes highly developed forms of parental authoritarianism in contrast to the relatively equalitarian family ways of older-stock Americans. Support for this theory is alleged to be found in the fact that the children of foreign-born parents become delinquent more frequently than those of American-born parents. Some students of the problem, however, urge caution at this point. They say the fact that the delinquency rate among second-generation children is so much higher may be largely due to the tendency of most foreign-born families to be economically underprivileged and ecologically segregated in areas of greater delinquency risk.

[22] Lois Barclay Murphy, "Cultural Factors in the Development of Children," *Childhood Education*, 23:53–8, 1946.

Size of Family, Sibling Relations, and Order of Birth

Some etiological theories have been based on the suspicion that the presence or absence of siblings, and the number and ordinal relation of siblings, are significant factors at work leading to critical interpersonal relationships and juvenile delinquency.

One theory is that the only child and the child in the large family are both inclined to be delinquent more frequently than others. A supporting study was made of 700 cases in Chicago, and the indication was that while the only child is more frequently delinquent than children with one brother or sister, most delinquents appear in very large families.[23] The findings of most studies, however, generally show that delinquencies occur disproportionately in families where there is more than one child. But this may be interpreted in more than one way. It may mean that the child in a large family of siblings is neglected by his parents, unwanted by them, and driven to the streets by crowding, whereas parents take greater interest in their only child and exercise more careful control over him. On the other hand it may mean that the large family is merely part of the configuration of traits (such as poverty and foreign-born parents), characteristic of so many apprehended delinquents. These traits inherently are not necessarily causal factors. The only child is more likely to come from a home of higher social status, which in turn implies private treatment and concealment of delinquent behavior.[24]

Sletto found that, in general, delinquent boys in the "only child" position did not differ significantly from other delinquent boys in types of offense. But a greater proportion of "only girl" offenders were charged with theft; a much lower proportion were charged with sex offenses than in the case of offenders from families of other sizes.[25] In another comparative study of 37 "only" children and 133 children who had siblings, in the New York State Training School for Boys, the "only" children were found to a significant degree to be more frequently emotionally

[23] John Levy, "A Quantitative Study of Behavior Problems in Relation to Family Constellation," *American Journal of Psychiatry*, 10:637–54, 1931.

[24] See Paul W. Tappan, *Juvenile Delinquency*, New York, McGraw-Hill, 1949, pp. 140–1.

[25] Raymond F. Sletto, "Delinquency and the Only Child," *Sociology and Social Research*, 18:519–29, 1934.

unstable, overaggressive, and seclusive, and given to lying and running away. Children with siblings showed more revenge feelings, suspiciousness, and temper outbursts, and had more undesirable companions.[26]

Where there are other siblings, does the child's relation to his brothers and sisters, and their order of birth, have an effect on delinquency? The theory here is that sibling rivalry may express itself in one extreme of regression to infantilism, accompanied by passivity and anxiety, or in the other extreme of well-planned aggression and destructive behavior. One of the New York State Crime Commission studies [27] called attention to the fact that when some of the children in large families were delinquent the second child in the family committed the most serious delinquencies, the next to the youngest child was least likely to become delinquent, while the youngest child was less likely to be truant than were the oldest and intermediate children. Sletto's study of the significance of sibling position in delinquency was a further refinement.[28] He made a comparison of 1,046 Minneapolis schoolchildren who had been legally adjudicated delinquent with nondelinquent children matched for age, sex, and number of siblings. Delinquency ratios were higher for girls whose siblings were all brothers than for girls whose siblings were all sisters. For boys this was true only in the intermediate positions. Delinquency ratios were generally high for children who were in sibling positions involving the presence of younger siblings of each sex, and low for children in positions involving the presence of older siblings of each sex. The ratios were somewhat higher for both boys and girls when older siblings were of the same sex and younger siblings were of the opposite sex than when the reverse was true. To explain the intricacies of this complex pattern of differences in delinquency ratios among children of varying sibling positions is obviously a formidable task. The answer may lie in the different roles that children play in family life on the basis

[26] Henry H. Hart and Sidney Axelrad, "The Only-Child Delinquent Contrasted with Delinquents in Large Families," *Journal of Criminal Law and Criminology*, 33:42–66, 1941.

[27] Harry M. Shulman, *Crime and the Community*, Albany, The Crime Commission of New York State, 1928, p. 12.

[28] Raymond F. Sletto, "Sibling Position and Juvenile Delinquency," *American Journal of Sociology*, 39:657–69, 1934.

of order of birth. Or younger children may not have so high delinquency ratios as their older siblings simply because they are not old enough to have had as many opportunities for delinquency.

Economic Status of the Family and Projection of Parental Ambition

It has long been thought that poverty in the family is a causative factor in juvenile delinquency, even though on the surface this appears to be a contradiction of the statistics of apprehension and court intake, which show a rise in rate in periods of economic prosperity and a decline in depression. The theory is that a family of low income, even when it enjoys prosperity, demonstrates relative neglect of the children by the hard-pressed parents, together with such concomitants as crowding and ecological segregation in areas of high delinquency risk. Most studies of arrest, court, and institutionalized cases reveal a large proportion of economic marginality in the families. The occupational backgrounds of fathers of delinquents show a disproportionate number of unskilled and semiskilled workers, and there is a similar disproportion of employed mothers, more so in the case of delinquent girls than boys. But a pattern of low economic status may be largely an outcome of skewness in arrest, court, and institution intake. That is, the assumption of police and administrators is that children of such families are more likely to be delinquent and that their parents are unable to care for them. At the same time the wealthy and otherwise privileged families are more able to shield their delinquent children from the police and courts. In other words, there may be an apparent rather than a real substantiation of the theory.

It is conceivable that deviant behavior such as delinquency is induced by the compensatory projection of parental ambition. Many parents of low occupational level and limited financial resources may try to reach their goals vicariously through their children. Merton has reported that in a research project on the social organization of public housing developments he found that the lower the occupational level of the parent, the larger the proportion who aspired for a professional career for their children. Should this finding be confirmed in other research one may be enabled to say that those parents least equipped to provide opportunity for their children exert the most intense pressure upon their children for high achievement, a pattern that invites deviant behavior.[29]

Maternal Overprotection: Momism

A popular although controversial theory is that excessive mother love ("momism") and overprotection of the child produce personality traits that lead to delinquent behavior. Rebellion against the father is caused by these mother-child relationships. The father is actually an accomplice because he fosters the development of such behavior by giving the mother free rein in the care of the child, thereby allowing the overprotection of the child to develop unchecked. When the father permits the situation to continue for a time and then tries to check it, rebellion by the child almost inevitably follows.

Although the name of Philip Wylie is usually associated with the origin of the theory of "momism,"[30] its most prominent advocate has been Edward Strecker, a psychiatrist.[31] A basic premise he employs is the differentiation between "mom" and "mother." A mom is a maternal parent who fails to prepare her offspring emotionally for living on an adult social plane, for she does not untie the emotional "apron string" that binds her children to her. A mother, on the other hand, encourages the development of a mature child. The answers of a maternal parent to the following forty questions, according to Strecker, reveal whether she is a mom or a mother. The typical mom, Strecker claims, would answer "yes" to all questions except 1, 3, 8, 14, 18, 27, 28, 29, 31.

1. Do you think it wise to give intelligent, honest answers to all the questions your youngsters ask regarding sex?

2. Do you consider children of eight or nine years of age too young to spend their vacations away from home in summer camp?

[29] Robert K. Merton, "Social Structure and Anomie," in *Social Theory and Social Structure*, Glencoe, The Free Press, 1949, p. 148.
[30] See his *Generation of Vipers*, New York, Rinehart, 1942, pp. 184–204.
[31] *Their Mothers' Sons*, Philadelphia, Lippincott, 1946.

3. Do you think even very young children should be allowed the adult privilege of making some decisions for themselves, even though in instances their decisions are unwise in your opinion?

4. When you and your husband have a serious disagreement, do you look to your children for sympathy?

5. Do you think a home should be run in such a manner that the primary consideration is almost *always* that the children's wants and comforts come first?

6. Do you find your sympathies tend in the direction generally of the child who you think is most like yourself?

7. Would you *forbid* your son or daughter to marry someone of whom you do not approve and make him uncomfortable if he were not willing to obey?

8. Do your children take an active part in school and community life?

9. Do you find yourself "running down" or belittling your husband to the children?

10. Do you ever resort to weeping to gain a point with your children?

11. Do you frequently have outbursts of temper when your children misbehave?

12. Do you habitually and secretly discuss your daughter-in-law (or son-in-law) with your married son (or daughter)?

13. Do you ever complain to your married children of the treatment or attitude you receive from their husbands or wives?

14. Do you consider it your duty to help your children form a healthy, normal, and beautiful concept of sex?

15. When you don't feel well, do you complain to your children and look to them for sympathy?

16. If your husband punishes a child, do you interfere or argue about it before the child?

17. Do you comfort, pet, and reward a child after it has been justly punished?

18. If you felt you had unjustly punished or scolded a child because you yourself were in a jittery state, would you afterward acknowledge this to the child and talk it out frankly?

19. Do you try to force your children to accept or acknowledge your personal prejudices and ideas of right and wrong as best, even though they may not agree with them?

20. Are you hurt or angry when your children do not accept your judgments and decisions?

21. Are you hurt, openly or secretly, when your children are happy away from home—even though you know they are happy at home also?

22. Do you get your children to obey by giving or promising them presents and rewards?

23. If your children get into difficulties in school, do you usually think it is the fault of the teacher and school?

24. Do you worry when your children are quiet and do not tell you what they are thinking?

25. If your children quarrel with other children, do you generally defend your children and take their side?

26. If your children quarrel between themselves, do you take the part of one consistently?

27. Are you happy and satisfied to see your children going forward as a part of their own times when it means breaking away from the traditional past of your own?

28. Do you consider your children's requests in the matter of clothing and personal appearance and encourage them to make their own selections?

29. When their selections are unwise do you talk over the problem with them adequately?

30. Do you oppose your children's, particularly your son's, participation in rough games like football for fear they might be hurt?

31. Do you accept your share of the responsibility in meting out and carrying through just and necessary punishments of your children?

32. Do you worry about your children's health and spend a great deal of energy and time warding off the *possibility* of colds, sicknesses, or injuries?

33. Do you impress on your children the various family physical weaknesses?

34. When your children make friends of whom you do not approve, do you try to force them to give them up, rather than depend on your child's own ability to come to a proper decision about the friend in question?

35. If you are unhappily married and not well mated sexually, would you (or do you) try to influence your children's selection of marital partners so that their husbands or wives will be as unlike your own as possible?

36. Have you advised or influenced your son or daughter either not to marry or to wait a long time before so doing?

37. Do you believe that an adult son or daughter should devote his life to the care of an aged or chronically ill parent rather than put that parent in a good institution or home where he or she will receive adequate care and comfort?

38. Do you think you should bring your aging father or mother into your home to live if your husband objects?

39. If there were an alcoholic in your family, would you consider it reasonable and proper to try to exact promises from your children never to touch alcohol?

40. If the men of your family had all been professors, ministers, professional men or white-collar workers, and your son, who had a real flare for mechanics and a very low scholastic aptitude, wanted to go into a garage business, would you refuse to accept his decision gracefully and belittle his choice?

Despite the variety of situations these questions cover, and their intrinsic merit in distinguishing between "mom" and "mother," they are probably not very useful in their present form. Most of the forty questions are "leading" questions. For example, question 19 asks the maternal parent whether or not she *forces* her children to accept or acknowledge her personal *prejudices*. The discerning "mom," easily realizing what answer is preferred, will be reluctant to express her actual attitude.

Van Ophuijsen, a co-worker of Freud and a pioneer psychoanalytic practitioner in the Netherlands, has taken issue with Strecker and his followers for presenting only half of the theory in "momism." "Popism," he maintains, is a necessary supplement in accounting for much delinquency. Paternal influence determines the child's social behavior even more decisively than does maternal tutelage. There is a distinction between "fathers" and "pops." Fathers pilot their sons and daughters to social responsibility with reasoned correction and praise, imparting self-discipline by example. Pops are both "the lord and master" whose word is law and the "dear Dad" who "worships the little woman and children" and wants nothing but that the youngsters have more opportunity than he had. They are unwilling to take responsibility for helping to put psychologically "wise" limitations upon the child. There are several types of pops. There is the autocrat who barricades himself behind the newspaper and seldom condescends to answer a question at the table. Another is the ne'er-do-well who comes home after a few drinks to pick a quarrel. More numerous are the retreating pops whose only reason for being seems that of making money. Some pops are "assistant moms." They act as if mom, who works in an office, were neglecting her home and children, and so they have to sacrifice themselves by taking over the mother role, thereby confusing the child. American culture, especially the urban subculture, fosters "popism," according to Ophuijsen. Away from home long hours, the male parent finds that the overbearing mom type of wife or some other female is all too ubiquitous. The father's role is ignored, as though the family were entirely the mother's responsibility.[32]

Differential Association

Edwin H. Sutherland's theory of differential association describes another way in which the family is now held accountable for juvenile delinquency. The theory holds that delinquency, like other behavior systems, is learned in interaction with others. A

[32] An interview reported in the *New York Herald Tribune*, April 20, 1947, Section II, p. 5.

person becomes delinquent because of an excess of social situations, arising from his associations, favorable to delinquency over situations unfavorable to delinquency.[33] As far as the family is concerned, these associations are both horizontal or lateral (that is, involving the interaction of sib with sib) or vertical (that is, a transmission from parent to child). The most frequently used evidence to support this theory is the large proportion of other members of the families of delinquents who are also known to be delinquent and criminal.[34] The Gluecks, for example, reported that over 80 per cent of their subjects were from families in which other members were violators of the law.[35] Shulman's studies point to the greater importance of the lateral transmission of delinquency within the family over vertical transmission.[36]

Sutherland's theory is often criticized for its minimizing of individual differences, for it claims that such differences are causal factors only as they affect differential association. The theory does not adequately explain why two or more children in the same home often respond differently to the situation of delinquent and criminal members of the family.

Appraisal of the Family in the Etiology of Delinquency

The various theories discussed in this chapter leave no doubt about the importance of the family in the etiology of juvenile delinquency. But there is one important question which these theories do not adequately answer. Why is it that in the same family there are both delinquent and nondelinquent children? An answer often suggested is that the family of the delinquent child is really different from that of the nondelinquent child, even when the two children are nominally members of the same family. Another suggested answer, as we have already seen, is that there are personality differences between delinquents and nondelinquents. A third is that the family is not self-contained, for there are other social and cultural influences in the lives of children, which must be considered. We turn now to one such in-

[33] Sutherland, *op. cit.*, pp. 6–9.

[34] This, of course, does not prove that the child directly learned the delinquent behavior from his parents or siblings. See Shulman, *op. cit.*, p. 27.

[35] *One Thousand Juvenile Delinquents*, Cambridge, Harvard University Press, 1934.

[36] *Op. cit.*, p. 27.

fluence, the horizontal associations of children outside the family context.

QUESTIONS AND RESEARCH SUGGESTIONS

1. *Why do academic specialists as well as laymen feel that family life is the most important etiological factor in delinquency?*
2. *What have been the logical consequences in treatment and prevention of family theories concerning the etiology of delinquency?*
3. *In what eight ways is the family thought to provoke delinquency?*
4. *In what way would you say that the family situation of Howard L., described in Chapter I, contributed to his problem behavior?*
5. *How do you account for the fact that delinquents and nondelinquents are frequently members of the same family?*
6. *Examine the Gluecks'* Unraveling Juvenile Delinquency *and critically evaluate their methodology and findings.*
7. *The author has alleged that Strecker's forty questions distinguishing between "mom" and "mother" are not very useful in their present form. Show what revisions you would make to enhance their usefulness.*

SELECTED READINGS AND REFERENCES

Bonney, M. E., "Parents as Makers of Social Deviates," *Social Forces*, 20:77–88, 1941.

Davis, Allison, and Robert J. Havighurst, "Social Class and Color Differences in Child-Rearing," *American Sociological Review*, 11: 698–710, 1946.

Glueck, Sheldon, and Eleanor Glueck, *Unraveling Juvenile Delinquency*, New York, The Commonwealth Fund, 1950.

Hart, Henry H., and Sidney Axelrad, "The Only-Child Delinquent Contrasted with Delinquents in Large Families," *Journal of Criminal Law and Criminology*, 33:42–66, 1941.

Hodgkiss, Margaret, "The Delinquent Girl in Chicago, II. The Influence of Broken Homes and Working Mothers," *Smith College Studies in Social Work*, 3:259–74, 1935.

Knickerbocker, L., "Treatment of Conflicts Arising in Sibling Rivalry," *Menninger Clinic Bulletin*, 4:12–22, 1940.

Lander, Joseph, "Traumatic Factors in the Background of 116 Delinquent Boys," *American Journal of Orthopsychiatry*, 11:150–6, 1941.

Levy, John, "A Quantitative Study of Behavior Problems in Relation to Family Constellation," *American Journal of Psychiatry*, 10:637–54, 1931.

Miller, Justin, "Foreign Born Parentage and Social Maladjustment," *Psychological Clinic*, 19:19–25, 1930.

Newell, H. W., "Family Attitudes as Revealed by the Psychiatric Examinations of 107 Juvenile Delinquents," *American Journal of Orthopsychiatry*, 2:377–83, 1932.

Ross, H., "Crime and the Native-Born Sons of European Immigrants," *Journal of Criminal Law and Criminology*, 28:202–9, 1937.

Shaw, Clifford R., and Henry D. McKay, "Are Broken Homes a Causative Factor in Juvenile Delinquency?" *Social Forces*, 10:514–24, 1932.

Sletto, Raymond F., "Delinquency and the Only Child," *Sociology and Social Research*, 18:519–29, 1934.

Sletto, Raymond F., "Sibling Position and Juvenile Delinquency," *American Journal of Sociology*, 39:657–69, 1934.

Shulman, Harry M., "The Family and Juvenile Delinquency," *The Annals of the American Academy of Political and Social Science*, 261:21–31, 1949.

Strecker, Edward, *Their Mothers' Sons*, Philadelphia, Lippincott, 1946.

Weeks, H. Ashley, "Male and Female Broken Home Rates by Type of Delinquency," *American Sociological Review*, 5:601–9, 1940.

Zucker, Herbert John, "Affectional Identification and Delinquency," *Archives of Psychology*, No. 286, New York, 1943.

Chapter IX. Peer Groups and Juvenile Delinquents

My earliest recollections of the neighborhood go back to the time I used to play with a small group of kids. We played Cowboy and Indians and very often we would go to the river and throw stones in the water and play around in the railroad yards. We would spend all day fooling around in this way, only going home to secure our meals. Our mothers would worry about our whereabouts on these days when we did not appear and would scold us and threaten to have our fathers give us a licking, but the next day we would go back again doing the same things.

I started to school when I was a little past six years of age which is the time when most of the boys in the neighborhood started school. After school all of us kids would play all kinds of games in the streets, alleys, or on the school play-ground. After we had our supper all of us kids would get together and go to shows. There was no restraint exercised by our parents. In those days two of us used to get into a show for a nickle. We always managed to get our hands on a few nickles. If we didn't have any nickles and sometimes even if we did, we would manage to sneak through one of the back doors. We liked Cowboy and Indian pictures and when one of these was showing there was nothing that could keep us away from the shows.

One of our favorite places of play was the railroad yards, but the cops from the railroad always tried to make us leave because we would get noisy and very often we would break into the box cars. I shall never forget one time when we were playing in the yards and we broke into two cars that were loaded with pickles. The cars were on different tracks and some of the kids got into one car and some into the other car and one of the greatest free-for-all pickle battles ever staged took place. Pickles were strewn from one end of the yard to the other. Now I ask you what kid would not prefer the company of the gang when such interesting events took place? Very few of them, I believe, would not like it, es-pecially boys of spirit. And that poor railroad cop! He de-served whatever salary he received. I imagine that many times he stood on the carpet before the officials because of the many depredations that we committed. Expense meant noth-ing to us. We always acted and then considered the conse-quences after we were caught.

Another time when we were playing in the railroad yard there was a car filled with horses on a side track. Some kids said that we could have a lot of fun if we opened the door and let the horses out. Every kid dared the other kid to open the car. For a long time everyone was afraid to, but finally one boy got enough nerve and opened the door. The horses didn't even wait until we put the runway up to the door; they just jumped out. What a rodeo we had! We really en-joyed outselves watching those horses run up and down the railroad yard. Everything went well until the railroad police-man came around. He tried to chase all of us kids and at the same time tried to corral the horses. At that time the real fun began. The horses ran out of the railroad yard and into the streets. In a few minutes there were stray horses all over the neighborhood. They were in people's front yards, alleys, streets, and vacant lots. Finally the fire department was called and came out and rounded up the horses. They found all of the horses and the only bad effects noticeable were that they were full of burrs and stickers. There was so much excitement and so many people on the streets that the policemen were not able to find the boys who had done the deed.

We used to have a great time on the railroad tracks fighting with other gangs of kids. There was one gang in particular from across the river who were our mortal enemies and we fought them every time we could. The fights usually took place on the railroad tracks where all the gangs would congregate for the purpose of taking coal. Each gang would fight the other gang to see who could get the best coal or the most coal. Stealing coal from the cars on the tracks was one of the things that we did most. It was more fun than anything else.

This bunch of kids was made up of roamers. They managed to roam around everywhere and do all kinds of things. During the summer-time we would sleep out in the public parks and wait for the milkmen and bakery wagons to start their deliveries in the morning. As they would deliver their milk, bread, and cakes in front of the neighborhood stores, we would lie in wait and be ready as soon as they would leave so we could rush the place and grab what we wanted. If the bread boxes were closed we would use a jimmy to open them. When we got a little more experienced we had keys made to do away with the jimmys. It was a great life to me while it lasted.[1]

The growth of the Gestalt school of psychology with its insistence upon seeing the delinquent and other behavior-problem types in their configurational setting has led to many

[1] Clifford R. Shaw, editor, *Brothers in Crime*, Chicago, University of Chicago Press, 1938, pp. 109–11.

studies of the social contexts of delinquents. It is now common-place that life in modern, Western societies has increasingly been influenced by human associations outside the family. As far as juveniles are concerned, few extrafamilial associations are con-sidered to have as significant an impact on personality and be-havior as those which they form among their peers. Peer (they are occasionally called "horizontal") groups are so intimate and pervasive in their influence that sociologists and anthropologists often place them in the same category with the family and the neighborhood and classify them all as primary groups. Peer groups are believed to be more influential in urban than in rural settings. This is because urban family controls are more tenuous, and urban children can organize themselves without the consent and with only the partial knowledge of their parents. Thus the peer group takes up the child where the family's influence ends.

A clear, useful definition of "peer" is offered by Bossard: [2]

A peer in the common social sense of the word is a person whom one meets on terms of approximate equality, a companion or fellow. For the child, a peer, negatively considered, is a non-adult, a non-parent, a non-teacher; on the positive side, it means another child, relatively of the same age, in certain instances of the same sex, with whom he can associate on terms of equal status, at least as far as his elders are concerned. It is important that this dual nature of the peer concept be recognized, for the peer group is more than an association of equals whose concern is with each other; it is, in a certain very specific sense, also a group-ing in which the adult is assigned the status of alien and the purpose of which is to maintain that status.

The Role of Peer Groups among Juveniles

Peer groups of juveniles tend to fall into two main categories: informal peer groups such as the play group, the clique, and the gang; and the more formally organized groups such as clubs.[3]

Even if the family experience on the whole serves as a deterrent from delinquency, it cannot shelter children from

[2] James H. S. Bossard, *The Sociology of Child Development*, New York, Harper, 1948, pp. 493–4.

[3] *Ibid.*, pp. 494–5.

other forces, such as those found in many peer groups, that may work counter to the family influence. This is not to say, of course, that all peer groups are oriented toward delinquency. But the pattern of family control is more likely to be explicitly in accord with legal norms than is the pattern of the peer group.

The personal relationships of most kinds of peer groups are extremely effective in the transmission of attitudes and values. Communication in such groups has emotional overtones that arise out of identification with members of the group. Because communication is so effective in the peer group the latter is important in the personality development and behavior patterning of the juvenile.

The juvenile peer group is very effective in producing conformity. The individual member is more sensitive to its sanction and disapproval than to those of any other groups. The family, for example, may decide what the child's mode of dress will be, but the peer group's reaction is crucial in determining whether or not the form of dress is satisfactory to the child. The same is usually true about the child's speech, manners, relationships with the other sex, and so on.

Another reason why the peer group is important as far as delinquency is concerned is that it often constitutes the dominant social medium for satisfying the juvenile's wishes for security, response, recognition, and new experience. In the case of new experience, this may take the form of games or athletics, the use of stimulants, or gambling and predatory exploits. Says Thrasher on this point with regard to the juvenile gang member:[4] "He lives in a world of adventure which it is difficult for the unseeing adult to comprehend. His imaginative exploits are often meaningless to the unsympathetic outsider but full of significance for the group itself."

All studies of peer groups [5] bring out two major facts. One is that individual status within such a group is for most members a very real and important matter, providing keen and vivid satisfaction. These statuses are achieved in the child's own world,

[4] Frederic M. Thrasher, "Gangs," *Encyclopaedia of the Social Sciences,* Vol. VI, p. 565. See also Clifford R. Shaw, "Group Factors in Delinquency among Boys," *Proceedings Third Biennial Meeting of the Social Research Child Development,* 14:1–26, 1939.

[5] See Bossard, *op. cit.,* p. 515.

involving recognition by his peers. Many children find greater satisfaction in being the doorkeeper or errand boy for the gang than in receiving the approval of adults. Roles in peer groups become a powerful determinant in the formation of the child's conception of himself. The second fact is that peer group status has special significance for children whose opportunities otherwise are relatively limited. The boy and girl who have not succeeded in gaining satisfactory statuses within their family; whose family is nonexistent, inadequate, or in perennial conflict; whose relations with their parents and other older people at home involve a constant struggle against domination or neglect; whose school performance is unsatisfactory; whose opportunities to engage in other community activities are limited—these frustrated and underprivileged children can find in peer groups, especially conflict gangs, the opportunities for individual achievement otherwise denied. One may say that, as a general rule, the less rewarding and the more drab the child's life outside the peer group, the more does a role within the group mean to him. In short, peer roles are often compensatory.

The peer group background of a major part of delinquent behavior has long been recognized. It goes almost without saying that the gang is the most conspicuous peer group in relation to delinquency. The conclusion of various studies of delinquency by Shaw and McKay, the Gluecks, Healy and Bronner, and Puffer has been that it is largely a gang operation. Although solitary individuals do commit delinquency, the greater part of it is committed in companionship with others. Even in the case of delinquent acts by solitary individuals, such as truancy and running away from home, gang association may be at the basis of the outlook and habits involved. This is because juvenile gangs are by and large conflict and nonconformist groups that avoid supervision and organized agency programs. They thrive on independence from outside discipline and authority. When gangs are enticed into agency buildings, the agencies complain that they disrupt programs and that they have a deleterious influence on the more conforming children within the agencies' fold.

Of 5,480 offenders, Shaw found that only 18.2 per cent had committed their offenses alone. Among the remaining cases, 30.3 per cent had had a single companion; 27.7 per cent two companions; 10.8 per cent three companions; 7.1 per cent four companions; 3.9 per cent five companions; and 1.0 per cent six or more companions. Stealing was found to be especially group-centered, for 89 per cent of those charged with theft were brought into court with accomplices.[6] The Gluecks in one of their early studies found that approximately seven tenths of 1,000 delinquent boys had committed their offenses in the company of others.[7] Comparisons between nondelinquent and delinquent cases by Healy and Bronner and by Atwood and Shideler suggest that the latter are more gregarious and less solitary in interests than the former, which can be taken to mean that delinquents are exposed socially more than are nondelinquents to the risks of getting into trouble.[8] Shaw in a later study [9] claimed to have discovered that there are carriers of delinquency patterns from one companionship situation over to another. Carriers of delinquency "infection" in present situations had received their "infection" from carriers in previous situations—"a sort of 'laying on of hands' process as in apostolic succession." [10]

Despite this kind of evidence, there has been a divergence among students of delinquency regarding the degree to which they accept peer companionship as an etiological factor. Reckless and Smith represent those who have virtually no qualifications regarding the causal relationship.[11] They see the peer companionship factor operate to bring about delinquency in any one of three ways: (1) There may be an association of predelinquents who come together by chance and who remain together as com-

[6] Clifford R. Shaw and Henry D. McKay, "Social Factors in Juvenile Delinquency," *Report on the Causes of Crime*, National Commission on Law Observance and Enforcement, Vol. II, pp. 195–6.

[7] Sheldon and Eleanor Glueck, *One Thousand Juvenile Delinquents*, Cambridge, Harvard University Press, 1934, pp. 94, 100–1.

[8] William Healy and Augusta Bronner, *New Light on Delinquency and Its Treatment*, New Haven, Yale University Press, 1936, pp. 63–64; B. S. Atwood and Ernest H. Shideler, "Social Participation and Juvenile Delinquency," *Sociology and Social Research*, 18:436–41, 1933–4.

[9] *Brothers in Crime*, Chicago, University of Chicago Press, 1938, pp. 109–26.

[10] Walter C. Reckless, *The Etiology of Delinquent and Criminal Behavior*, New York, Social Science Research Council Bulletin #50, 1943, pp. 30–1.

[11] Walter C. Reckless and Mapheus Smith, *Juvenile Delinquency*, New York, McGraw-Hill, 1932, p. 146.

panions because of similar attitudes and other personality traits. In the course of time this group becomes delinquent as a group without any member having been previously delinquent. (2) Another way may be that previous delinquent behavior by individuals attracts them to each other. (3) A third way is that previously nondelinquent juveniles are attracted into association with those who have been delinquent.

Tappan, on the other hand, represents those students of delinquency who have reservations about the influence of peer companionship on delinquent behavior.[12] He claims that one cannot measure the probabilities of an individual's delinquency by his associates alone. He suggests that the importance of the factor is exaggerated somewhat by reason of the fact that the child already disposed to delinquency prefers to associate with others whose values and conduct are similar. Delinquency, he maintains, results not from contact alone but from numerous variables that may be associated with that contact, especially what the individual himself brings to it. While some types of offenses require training in technique which comes only from association, many offenses, especially by young offenders, require no prior group inculcation. The maladjusted child needs no instruction or stimulation to play truant, to disobey his parents, to run away from home, or to take the property of others.

The Social Structure of the Gang

Three types of gangs are found, from the standpoint of development. Each type merges into the other, so that all three constitute stages through which a single gang may pass. The *diffused type* is a loosely knit gang in the early process of integration. The *solidified type* is found at the completion of the process of integration and accordingly has a high degree of solidarity and morale. The *conventionalized type* appears when the gang assumes the external characteristics of a club or some other formal pattern.[13]

The organization of a gang usually calls for a leader, an inner circle, the rank and file, and finally the "fringers" or

[12] Paul W. Tappan, *Juvenile Delinquency*, New York, McGraw-Hill, 1949, pp. 146–7.
[13] Thrasher, *op. cit.*, pp. 564–5.

hangers-on.[14] Gang leaders, sometimes called president or "big shot," are seldom elected. On the other hand their elevation is not a matter of force, for the neighborhood bully is seldom the gang leader. The leader may actually be a relatively puny boy physically who, nevertheless, through a lively imagination can always improvise and suggest something for the gang to do. The well-organized conflict gangs also may have an officer who may be called the war councilor. His task is to set dates and agree on battlegrounds for "rumbles" with enemy groups. He is also the master of war tactics and strategy. With pencil and paper, he works out logistics, and sees that weapons are assembled so as to avoid seizure by the police. Gangs, like other peer groups, also have their custodians of group membership, who are often members who themselves just "shaved in" and who rather quickly become "zealous keepers of the keys." Most of these groups have their "funny boys" whose irresponsible behavior is tolerated because of the humor they contribute. Virtually every group has its "loud-mouthed" member, the show-off or braggart, whose account of anything comes to be discounted by the gang. Then there is the aggressive member, an ambitious personality always reaching out for more territory, always willing to engage in a fight, provided that the others do the fighting. Every gang and most other peer groups have "goats." These are the boys of lower intelligence, slow of wit and frequently combining some special peculiarity of manner, speech, or appearance with their subnormalities. They are the members who invariably are apprehended, or who are often sacrificed or used as a decoy by the group.

The overwhelming number of juvenile gangs are composed of boys. Only in rare cases do girls form gangs. Thrasher's explanation of this is that girls in our society are too well incorporated in the organized life of the community to escape adult control. Another explanation may be the cultural differential between the sexes in expectations of conflict behavior.[15]

One of the central themes of gang life, it has already been made evident, is conflict. This has been recognized by all students of the juvenile gang, beginning with Puffer in 1905 when

[14] *Ibid.*, p. 566.
[15] *Ibid.*, pp. 565–6.

he defined a gang in terms of the "conflict test." [16] He was followed by McCormick in 1912, who concluded that a gang can
never thrive without another gang to fight.[17] Thrasher, who is
generally recognized as the modern expert on the sociology of
gangs, defined the gang as "an interstitial group originally formed
spontaneously, and integrated through conflict. . . . To become
a true gang the group as a whole must move through space
(linear action) and eventually . . . must meet some hostile element which precipitates conflict." [18] In Whyte's analysis of an
Italian-American "street corner society" one of his principal informants described gang conflicts as "rallies." Said he: "It usually
started this way. Some kid would get beaten up by one of our
boys. Then he would go back to his street and get his gang.
They would come over to our street, and we would rally
them. . . ." [19]

Membership based on clearly defined territorial lines is
crucial in the social structure of most urban gangs. Recalling his
own childhood in Brownsville, an area of Brooklyn, one writer
reports:

> Inclusion in the gang was absolute, and human relations
> outside it were cut to a minimum. Even its territory was
> staked out with minute precision. When two Brownsville kids
> who were strangers had some contact, the first question was
> "What's your block?" and the answer established identity.
> A gang might not inhabit a full block but only a specific
> sector of it. Thus "my block" was Osborne Street between
> Pitkin and Glenmore Avenues, and the region my gang re
> garded as its domain took up one-third of this area, starting
> from Pitkin Avenue. Our territory ended where a small
> group of Italian families and their offspring took over. The
> section of the block nearest to Glenmore Avenue belonged

[16] J. Adams Puffer, "Boy's Gangs," *Pedagogical Seminary,* June,
1905, p. 175, cited in Bossard, *op. cit.,* p. 497.
[17] William McCormick, *The Boy and His Clubs,* New York, Fleming
H. Revell, 1912.
[18] *The Gang,* 2nd rev. ed., 1936, pp. 54, 57.
[19] William Foote Whyte, *Street Corner Society,* Chicago, University
of Chicago Press, 1943, p. 5.

to a second Jewish group. Small as the area was, the three juvenile clans were as tightly contained as primitive tribes.[20]

This recollection, of course, refers to another very important aspect of gang organization and conflict—racial, religious, and nationality lines. Chambers, who has made intensive studies of juvenile gangs in New York City [21] notes that it is in the borderline districts of diverse ethnic groupings and racially segregated areas that gangs fight and kill each other. In Manhattan, gang warfare takes place almost exclusively in uptown areas, where the overcrowded, segregated Harlem Negroes and Puerto Ricans have been striving to move into better housing areas. In recent years these groups have been moving into the Bronx, and gang fighting has broken out there too. In 1939, Chambers points out, jobs became abundant and Manhattan Negroes began to acquire the income necessary to leave the worst of the restricted slum districts. As the war brought higher wages and a fresh wave of migration from the South, the Negro influx into white areas was accelerated. It was about then that the large proportion of conflict gangs came into existence. Before that time, street-corner clubs of whites in upper Manhattan had served mainly as outlets for athletic activity. When the traditional colored districts began to expand, however, the white boys' clubs turned to conflict.

This is true of ethnically homogenous or segregated neighborhoods. In heterogeneous neighborhoods, however, there is a crude form of democracy which enables boys of various ethnic identities to belong to a gang on a basis of equality.

Gang conflict is in many ways a struggle for power very much like that of political units engaged in warfare. Each gang has its locality that it defends against outsiders, the center of which is the "hangout" or territorial headquarters. Every gang is on the defensive or offensive for play privileges, property rights, the physical safety of its members, and the maintenance of its status in the neighborhood.

Like other human groups, the gang uses several mechanisms of membership control in order to achieve the rapport necessary

[20] William Poster, " 'Twas A Dark Night in Brownsville," *Commentary*, Vol. 9, No. 5, May 1950, p. 461.
[21] Bradford Chambers, "The Juvenile Gangs of New York," *American Mercury*, April 1946, pp. 480–1.

to accomplish its goals. These include punishment, ridicule, and praise. Underlying such techniques of social control is the gang code, which is often at variance with the prevailing laws. It is quite all right, according to such codes, to steal or commit other offenses against the outgroup, but to "squeal" on each other is a serious breach of the gang code.

Both Thrasher and Bossard make a point about juvenile gangs which supports the major premise of this book. It is that, *in developing their gangs, boys cannot go beyond their experiences and the observations and activities of their families and other elders. Hence their codes and chosen activities must be studied with reference to the moral codes and activities they meet in the communities where they live.*[22]

The Juvenile Gangs of Metropolitan New York

Largely because it was the setting for Thrasher's classic study entitled *The Gang*, Chicago has been the major source of illustrative material about juvenile gangs. The most recent analyses, however, have been made of New York City's gangs.[23]

In earlier days in New York City, juvenile gangs were organized as "cellar clubs," but now headquarters are more likely to be in candy stores, poolrooms, and cafeterias. Gang members are brought to court for the same charges as in the "cellar club" era: rape, theft, beatings, rioting, and extortion. Gangs have been known to overturn ash barrels systematically and then demand weekly payments from apartment house superintendents to prevent recurrences. The most serious change in juvenile offenses has been the increase in drug addiction.

Most of the conflict gangs are found in one or another of the eleven areas marked out by the New York City Youth Board as having high rates of juvenile delinquency.[24] The estimate in 1950 was that there were between 150 and 180 active juvenile

---

[22] Thrasher, *The Gang*, 1927, p. 255; Bossard, *op. cit.*, p. 510.

[23] The material here is derived largely from Charles Grutzner's series of articles in the *New York Times*, May–August, 1950.

[24] These areas are West of Central Park, Manhattanville-Washington Heights, Central Harlem, and East Harlem in Manhattan; Williamsburg, South Brooklyn, Bedford-Stuyvesant, and Brownsville in Brooklyn; Morrisania-Belmont and Mott Haven-Longwood in the Bronx; and South Jamaica, Queens.

gangs in New York City with such names as Slicksters, Puerto Rican Dukes, Gay Nineties, and Robins; and for girls, Wildcats and Shangri-la Debs. Some gang names are found diffused over two or more boroughs of the city. In some cases this is because members have moved into another neighborhood and set up a new gang with the old name. Another way in which names come to be shared by two or more gangs is through contact in correctional institutions such as the State Training School for Boys at Warwick. Gang lines are retained by boys in such institutions, and nonmembers released from there often take the gang concept home and use the name of a gang that was prestigeful and powerful at the institution.

Some gangs perpetuate themselves, even to the third generation. That is, twice their leaders have outgrown their teen-age activities and turned over the names of their gangs to young recruits.

Not all juvenile gangs in New York City are found in lower socio-economic levels. One gang has been composed of upper-income boys, chiefly children of broken homes, on and near Manhattan's West End Avenue. The gang has specialized in intruding on parties in wealthy homes, breaking furniture, and stealing.

Although girls' gangs are rare, it is not unusual to find groups of teen-age girls who act as adjuncts or auxiliaries of the boys' gangs, in some cases carrying their conflict weapons. The boy gangsters know that to search a female suspect the police must call a police matron, a time-consuming process and therefore one seldom used. When a fight is about to take place, the girls hide weapons on their persons and accompany the boys to the scene. After the fight they again hide the weapons until they reach a designated rendezvous removed from the battle area. Frequently the girls furnish the boys with an alibi, saying that they were at a dance or a movie with them at the time of a fight.

A variety of weapons are used in juvenile gang wars, such as switch blades (which are procurable at sporting goods stores) and fish-knives, which have a long blade on one end and a hook on the other. Side handles from ash and refuse barrels are also used, the metal handles fitting over the knuckles, inflicting severe gashes when the rounded surface is filed into sharp ridges. Although the knife is the favorite weapon, most notoriety has been given to "zip-guns," named after the sound they make. The zip-gun is a home-made device in which rubber bands project a firing pin with enough force to shoot a .22 caliber cartridge out of a metal tube. Curtain rods provided the tubes for the first zip-guns. Then juvenile gangs discovered that automobile radio antennae provided a truer bore for a .22, and this led to an epidemic of antennae thefts. Later a super-zipper was developed by adapting the mechanism of the toy gun that is sold to project model airplanes into flight. The cartridges are secured in shooting galleries where the boys pump them out of guns while pretending to fire them. The guns, which cost less than fifteen cents to make, have been tested by the police ballistics division and have been found capable of penetrating a one-inch pine board after traveling 25 to 30 feet, and then continuing on their way some distance.

The Influence of the Gang on Delinquency

It is clear that the juvenile gang does have some influence on delinquency. It may create heightened feelings of in-group and out-group, with an accompanying system of dual morality; it may develop attitudes of conflict; frequently it teaches and transmits techniques of delinquency.

Many of its values and processes are thought to be conditioned by "secondary" community influences, such as religion, recreation, the school, and other institutions. An analysis of such influences is presented in the following chapter.

QUESTIONS AND RESEARCH SUGGESTIONS

1. *Why are peer groups believed to be more influential in urban than in rural settings?*
2. *Why is the peer group considered to be important in the personality development and behavior patterning of the juvenile?*
3. *What two major facts come out of all studies of peer groups?*
4. *What are the reservations some students of delinquency hold about the influence of the peer group on delinquent behavior?*
5. *Is it possible to grant any delinquency influence at all to the juvenile gang?*
6. *Study the social structure of a gang in your community and com-*

pare it with the abstraction of gang organization described in this chapter.

7. *Read Shulman's* The Amboy Dukes *and show whether or not the author supports the thesis that "gang conflict is in many ways a struggle for power."*

SELECTED READINGS AND REFERENCES

Atwood, B. S., and Ernest H. Shideler, "Social Participation and Juvenile Delinquency," *Sociology and Social Research*, 18:436–41, 1933–4.

Bossard, James H. S., *The Sociology of Child Development*, New York Harper, 1948.

McKay, Henry D., "The Neighborhood and Child Conduct," *The Annals of the American Academy of Political and Social Science*, 261:32–41, 1949.

Shaw, Clifford B., "Delinquents and Delinquency Areas," *Mental Health Observer*, 3:1–8, 1935.

Shaw, Clifford B., *Brothers in Crime*, Chicago, University of Chicago Press, 1938.

Shulman, Irving, *The Amboy Dukes*, New York, Doubleday, 1947.

Thrasher, Frederic M., "Gangs," *Encyclopaedia of the Social Sciences*, Vol. VI, pp. 564–7.

Thrasher, Frederic M., *The Gang*, Chicago, University of Chicago Press, 1927.

Whyte, William Foote, *Street Corner Society*, Chicago, University of Chicago Press, 1943.

Chapter **X**. *Institutional Omissions and Commissions*

Jimmy is a handsome lad, going on 16 and big for his age. He might have made a good tackle on the high-school team—that is, if he had ever reached high school. He quit grammar school in the eighth grade. It was against the law, but the school was glad to be rid of him. He only made trouble, anyway.

Jimmy had hated school from the day he began, and he started to play hookey almost at once. Not that he wasn't bright. There wasn't a smarter child in the neighborhood. But for such a restless, active boy sitting in a seat all day reading about lambs and fairies and trips to the country was more than he could stand. And later he had to learn about the inches of rainfall in Tibet and how many gallons of paint it takes to paint a house! Who wanted to know about that, anyway? His father had once been a painter and where had it gotten him? A bad lung, out of work, and drunk most of the time.

Besides, Jimmy never liked his teachers. They were always scolding him. There was one in the fifth grade who was different. She was young and seemed to understand him. She made him monitor and let him help her with the blackboard. When she found him playing with an airplane model he had made instead of studying his grammar, she didn't scream and send him to the principal. Instead she kept him after school and talked to him about airplanes and how he could join a group at the church where the boys learned to make different kinds of models. He said nothing but he knew he wouldn't go. Only sissies went there—and besides the stuff cost money. Jimmy didn't "skip" school once that year.

But that teacher was transferred, and the next one was a "sourpuss." His older brother, Jack, whom Jimmy adored, had been in her room long ago and had made her life miserable. When Jimmy started "acting up" in class, she said he was no good and would end up in the penitentiary like his brother. Jimmy quit after that and refused to go back until the truant officer found him one day loitering around the railroad tracks and took him to "Juvenile." They kept him in the detention home two weeks. Several doctors asked him questions and made him play with blocks. They told the judge he needed supervision and something they called "a good relationship." After that, the probation officer came around once in a while to check up on how he was behaving and to warn him to be "a good boy."

After Jimmy left school, he bummed around a bit. He made an occasional dollar delivering orders for the corner liquor store. Sometimes he would get a good tip on the races in the back of the cigar store. He ran away to another city and tried to enlist in the army, but the recruiting officer found out how young he was and would not accept him. He remained in the strange city, sleeping in the subway. But the police picked him up one day, and the Travelers' Aid arranged a ticket back home. After that, he was anxious more than ever "to do something," but he didn't know what. He got into fights all the time. It was shortly after this that he and two other boys stole a roadster. They "borrowed" it at first just to go for a ride. That was Jimmy's idea when he spotted the key in the ignition. Stripping the tires off came later. But the police pulled up before Jimmy even had the first tire.[1]

It is often taken for granted in American society that religious, educational, and organized leisure-time experiences have only salutary effects upon juveniles and other participants. The assumption is that they provide children with stimuli that either reinforce legally sanctioned behavior or deter delinquent and other deviant behavior. A closely related assumption is that the only etiological relationship of these social institutions to delinquency is passively that of omission, not actively that of commission. The purpose of this chapter is to present evidence that indicates the inadequacies of these assumptions and, more positively, to propose a dynamic etiological relationship between the institutions and delinquency.

Religion and Delinquency

It has been impossible to ascertain with any assurance the relationship between religion and delinquency. This is because much of religious experience is so subjective and subtle that no adequate index is available. At the same time it is inadequate to study the relationship between the formal and external aspects of religion—such as denominational or sectarian identification, Sunday School attendance, knowledge of the Bible—and delinquency. How one can be misled in this respect is clearly illustrated in the interpretations of European criminologists like Bonger and Aschaffenburg. Their studies of the religious affiliation of criminals concluded that Catholics tend to be more criminal than Protestants, and Jews are the least criminal of all

[1] *Understanding Juvenile Delinquency*, Federal Security Agency, Children's Bureau, Publication #300, 1949, pp. 1–3.

ENSNARED BY A PROCURESS: *Plate I in* THE HARLOT'S PROGRESS

Hogarth's portrayal of Mary Hackabout's career in harlotry begins at the Bell Inn in Cheapside, London, where Mary and her father, a country curate, have arrived in search of better fortune than their county of York provides. Mary, a girl of sixteen, is greeted flatteringly by a procuress whose custom it is to welcome such attractive young newcomers. The woman pretends to engage the girl as a companion or maid, but her real intent is obvious. Mary, for her part, wears a look that can be construed as either naïve or knowing. On the steps of the inn stands one of the woman's clients. His hand is thrust in his pocket to indicate his willingness to pay both the procuress for the introduction and the girl for her compliance. Beside him stands a pander, surprised and delighted at Mary's good looks. It is almost unnecessary to add that promiscuity was the most prominent form of deviant behavior among girls in Hogarth's world, just as it is in ours.

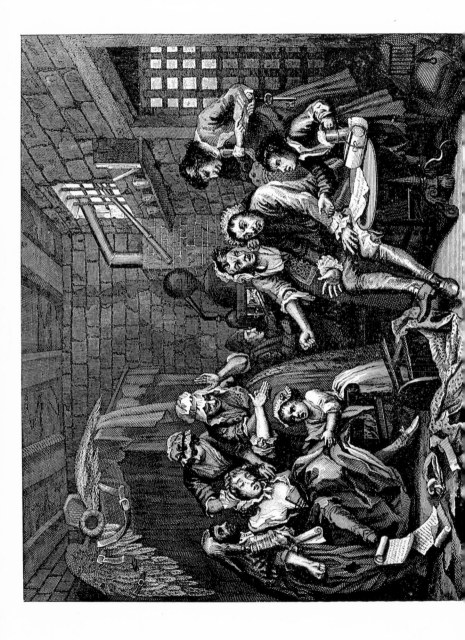

THE FLEET PRISON: *Plate VII in* THE RAKE'S PROGRESS

In this engraving from his series on The Rake's Progress, *Hogarth shows the interior of an eighteenth-century London prison, where his hero, Tom Rakewell, has been confined for debt. This dark, damp stone room, with its ragged bed serving several inmates, is characteristic of London prisons in the artist's day. Rakewell is shown besieged by three tormentors: a turnkey badgers him for a tip, a small boy wants money for bringing beer, and his wife berates him for causing her degradation. At the left are Rakewell's mistress and child, who have followed him into prison. A demented inmate in the rear conducts a search for the philosopher's stone; above the bed is a pair of wings used by another disturbed unfortunate. Hogarth's works touch frequently on institutionalization in the eighteenth century, when such places of confinement as prisons, lunatic asylums, and hospitals were little more than dumping-grounds for custodial care. Virtually no differentiation was made among the inmates on the basis of age, sex, and need. Although contemporary society has made great progress in differentiating on the basis of age and sex, modern institutional confinement is still subject to criticism for its failure to make adequate segregations on the basis of need.*

three denominations. Presumably these criminologists would come to the same conclusion about delinquency in an American community such as Passaic, New Jersey, where most of the delinquent children studied by Kvaraceus claimed to be connected with some church. Two thirds were found to be members of the Roman Catholic and Eastern Orthodox churches; slightly over one fifth had membership in a Protestant church, and two per cent were Jewish. The remainder had no church affiliation.[2]

Etiological interpretations stemming from statistical generalizations of this sort about delinquency as well as crime overlook the fact that in European countries, and to a certain extent in the United States, Roman Catholics have lived in the poorest economic conditions. Since most apprehended offenders come from the lower economic levels, Catholics have tended to show up unfavorably in the statistics. Relevant, too, is that in any survey dealing with the religious affiliation of apprehended offenders, there may be false statements of affiliation and attendance, inasmuch as the subjects will exaggerate their religious connections in the hope of making a favorable impression on the authorities. In fact a superficial interpretation of the statistics gathered by Kvaraceus and others suggests that there is a direct causal relationship between the incidence of delinquency and attendance at religious services. That is, the delinquency rate is usually highest among Catholic young people who belong to the group most likely to attend church regularly, and it is lowest among Jews, the religious group in which attendance at religious services is least frequent.

The evidence, however, indicates that affiliation, churchgoing, or regular Sunday School attendance can have no measurably significant relationships in themselves to delinquency or its avoidance. Hartshorne and May [3] could find no significant difference in honesty between children attending Sunday School and nonattending children, *all other things being equal.* Hightower, after testing some three thousand children for lying, cheating, and deception, concluded that there was no relationship of any consequence between Biblical information and the different phases of

[2] William C. Kvaraceus, *Juvenile Delinquency and the School*, New York, World Book Co., 1945, pp. 101–2.
[3] *Studies in the Nature of Character*, New York, Macmillan, 3 vols., 1928–30.

behavior studied.[4] Marsell examined comparable groups of boys in the Ohio Reform School and of supposedly nondelinquent boys outside, finding that the reform school inmates had received just as much religious training as the outsiders. "It seems safe to conclude," he said, "that there is no significant relation between religious training and delinquent or nondelinquent behavior." [5]

Perhaps even more interesting have been studies such as the one in which three of Thurstone's scales for the measurement of social attitudes were given to 83 delinquent and 100 nondelinquent girls, all from the eighth- to tenth-grade level. Here the delinquents actually showed attitudes more favorable to Sunday observance and the Bible than the control group.[6] In a similar study, 164 delinquent boys and girls in the ninth and tenth grades were compared with 133 nondelinquents in the same grades, using Thurstone's attitude scales on law, God, and the church. Statistically significant differences showed that (1) delinquent girls had more favorable attitudes than nondelinquent girls had toward the law, God, and the church; (2) delinquent girls had more favorable attitudes than delinquent boys had toward God and the church; and (3) nondelinquent boys had more favorable attitudes toward God than had nondelinquent girls.[7] In 1950 a survey of the national council of the Young Men's Christian Association concluded that fewer than 20 per cent of 1,935 young people living in an area embracing 75 per cent of all American Y.M.C.A.'s found in religion a compelling guide for their everyday behavior.

We have already observed that the usual contention is that religion is a deterrent from delinquency because it is generally in agreement with the civil and criminal law. But it is equally arguable that religious experience may provoke certain forms of delinquency and crime. Ethnocentrism and prejudice readily evolve

[4] *Biblical Information in Relation to Character and Conduct,* Iowa City, University of Iowa Press, 1930.
[5] *A Study of Religious Training as a Psychological Factor in Delinquency,* Unpublished Ph.D. Dissertation, Ohio State University, 1930.
[6] Warren C. Middleton and Paul J. Fay, "Attitudes of Delinquent and Nondelinquent Girls toward Sunday Observance, the Bible, and War," *Journal of Educational Psychology,* 32:555–8, 1941.
[7] Warren C. Middleton and R. R. Wright, "A Comparison of a Group of Ninth and Tenth Grade Delinquent and Non-delinquent Boys and Girls on Certain Attitude Scales," *Pedagogical Seminary and Journal of Genetic Psychology,* 58:139–50, 1941.

out of denominationalism and sectarianism, setting up a duality of morals as a concomitant of the marked psychology of in-group versus out-group.[8] In a heterogeneous American society of well over two hundred religious groups, it is possible for people to be deterred from committing illegalities against their fellow in-group members, but at the same time to feel justified about behaving aggressively against the out-group. Thus many intensely religious Protestant whites have been members of the Ku Klux Klan, taking part in its sporadic violence not only against Negroes but against Jews and Catholics as well. Presumably these forces are at work on the juvenile level of the population too.

This has been implicitly acknowledged by some clergymen who have deplored the extent of religious differences, noting that religion as a unifying force is impotent today because of misplaced emphasis on sectarian differences that divide, instead of on the fundamental "truths" that unify; on special modes of baptism; on this or that way of serving communion; on seemingly endless differences in creedal statement and ritual custom. More explicit acknowledgment of the point has been made by other clergymen who have maintained that religion can be a "detriment" when it is the sanctifier and one of the bearers of the prejudices that exist among groups, as in the case of the Ku Klux Klan in the South, anti-Semitism in northern cities, and in related manifestations of minority-group hatred. Religion is also a major force in social conservatism. When child-labor legislation was proposed in the early years of the twentieth century in New York State, clergymen rose in self-righteous indignation to denounce this "invasion" of the home by the state. Religious divisions, each unit of which often seeks to protect its vested institutional interests even at the price of individual human welfare, disrupt American society. One may be justified in speaking of the "invasion" of the home by the church, for where differences of religious affiliation exist within a marriage, the child is often confronted with a serious conflict in loyalties. Increasingly, Protestant, Catholic, and Jewish spokesmen are urging their respective adherents

---

[8] An upper-class Englishman was once asked whether he thought anybody could get to heaven without first becoming a member of the Church of England. In reply, he said: "I don't know, but I am sure of one thing. No gentleman would ever try it."

to avoid mixed marriages. Where they do occur, however, they provide an occasion where an authoritarian religious body can divide the home and create tension, having a seriously impairing effect on the socialization of children in that home.

Somewhat more direct etiological hypotheses and theories about the relationship between religion and delinquency are suggested by Kvaraceus in connection with his study of Passaic children.[9] He observes that maladjustments among children—such as delinquency—are sometimes a reaction against parental strictness associated with religious beliefs. They may also occur among children whose parents are affiliated with sects whose practices seem strange to the majority and which subject the children to ridicule from their peers. On occasion, too, an emotionally unstable child will seek, either alternately or concurrently, release from his tensions both in extreme participation in the external aspects of religion and in delinquent behavior.

The School and Delinquency

It is not commonly known that the concept of free and universal public education took hold in the United States in the nineteenth century in response, first, to the insistence of the Protestant churches that all people be able to read the Bible.[10]

As the American public school system evolved, its shortcomings were soon apparent. Says Ellingston: [11]

> Knowledge seemed to be power and the public school set out to provide all children with the kind of knowledge and intellectual training which had theretofore been reserved for the chosen few who were going into commerce or the professions. In other words, the public school was set up to load and train the child's mind on a mass-production basis. Thereby the public school became the prisoner of an extremely limited purpose; to cram into the heads of all chil-

[9] Kvaraceus, *op. cit.*, p. 105.
[10] Secondly, the response was "to the demands of a democratic society for equal opportunity for all its citizens; and thirdly in response to the demand of an expanding commerce and industry for literate workers." See John R. Ellingston, *Protecting Our Children from Criminal Careers*, New York, Prentice-Hall, 1948, p. 201.
[11] *Ibid.*, pp. 201–2.

dren the same conglomerate mass of information at the same speed. Preoccupation with that narrow goal tended to blind the school (always excepting, of course, its inspired teachers) to the differences in the mental capacities, interests, and speed of development of different children. It functioned as though it were preparing all children for white collar jobs. It paid little or no attention to the fact that the child is a physical being, an emotional being, and a social being, as well as a mental being and that he does not park outside his anger or his hunger or his undeveloped and uncoordinated muscles or his shame for his poverty-stricken home or his need to belong and to be competent while he carries only his memory like a bucket into the classroom. In general the school saw only its chosen mass of facts to be learned and the pupil only as a mind to be stuffed. Moreover, for its mass-production job, the public school developed authoritarian methods of instruction—the regimentation of grades, the imposed silence, the compulsion of the switch and of the dunce's cap, repetition, and a destructive competition that for the duller children was often cruel.

In the etiology of delinquency, is the school's role that of omission or of commission? Several students of the problem say the answer is omission. Boynton is quite explicit about this when he says that "the school's most frequent relationship to delinquency is a passive rather than an active one. That is, the school does not make as many delinquents as it permits children to leave its doors and become delinquent. To this extent, its sin is one of omission rather than commission." [12]

Yet Ellingston's general observations quoted above and data collected in community and segmental studies imply that the school's role is also actively that of commission in its etiological relationship to delinquency. The literature on juvenile delinquency consistently refers to the unsatisfactory school adjustments in the background of the majority of adjudged delinquents. Retardation is unusually high; there is a preponderance of low school achievement and of poor marks, a high incidence of tru-

[12] Paul L. Boynton, *Psychology of Child Development*, Minneapolis, Educational Publishers, 1940, p. 384.

ancy, and an intense dislike for school and teacher. Leaving school early is frequently the end of a most unsatisfactory situation. It has been said that while the delinquent child may be an inescapable headache for the school, at the same time it is also true that the school is frequently an even greater headache for the child. Some of the major factors of omission and commission in the school which are thought to contribute to the etiology of delinquency are as follows:

1. THE ROLE OF THE TEACHER AND THE SCHOOL ADMINISTRATOR. A long-standing suspicion is that unwittingly many teachers help make delinquents. For example, in the second decade of the twentieth century Wickman ascertained the attitudes of teachers in Cleveland and Minneapolis schools toward behavior problems in children. These were set against a norm composed of the judgments of thirty professional mental hygienists. The teachers consistently regarded as serious those forms of behavior which they interpreted as an attack on the established order or as a frustration of the immediate purposes of teaching. On the other hand, they consistently rated as insignificant in importance the withdrawing or submissive forms of behavior. These judgments were virtually reversed by the mental hygienists.[13] A review of the experiments by Haggerty, McClure, and Yourman yields similar findings; namely, that teachers tend to identify the problem child as one who is antagonistic to authority (presumably theirs), who fails to make stringent application to imposed schoolwork, and who violates the teacher's social conceptions and moralities. On the other hand the same studies show that teachers tend to ignore or underestimate the personal problems of children, such as shyness, timidity, and dejection, because these do not interfere with classroom order.[14]

Coinciding with Wickman's work, Miriam Van Waters saw teachers as being somewhat like parents in their relations with children. Unless a teacher has developed insight into problems of personality, including her own, Van Waters pointed out, she is likely to inculcate her pupils with destructive emotional attitudes.

[13] E. Koster Wickman, *Children's Behavior and Teachers' Attitudes,* New York, The Commonwealth Fund, 1928.
[14] Charles Uger, "The Relationship of Teachers' Attitudes to Children's Problem Behavior," *School and Society,* 47:246–8, 1938.

This can come about far more readily through what the teacher is and does than what she teaches.[15]

Teaching is not infrequently in the hands of emotional misfits and frightened, inferiority-ridden men and women seeking a safe, respectable, and quickly attainable higher social status. Some psychologists maintain that there is a positive correlation between the classroom "atmosphere," almost entirely a product of the teacher, and the degree of emotional disturbance among children there. Moralizing and scolding by teachers are widespread. Many teachers force children to admit they are "bad" boys and girls and "needle" them into admitting what they want them to say.

Much of this is not really the shortcomings of teachers, but more accurately a reflection of the low estate of primary and secondary education in contemporary American society. Relatively inadequate salaries, which become even more inadequate in times of inflation, do not attract the best caliber of people into the teaching profession and are not conducive to high morale among those who are already in it.

According to a nationwide study,[16] in-service training programs for teachers are frequently left to chance or do not exist. In a mass system of education, classes are often so large that the teacher is unable to reach the individual pupil. Teachers in many schools seldom have contact with a pupil's parents except on occasion of complaint. Teachers often are unaware of the factors in the home and elsewhere that make a child what he is, and they have little knowledge of the community agencies or resources that deal with children. There are few specialists trained to measure pupil abilities, interests, aptitudes, and personality traits. Special educational programs for atypical children are inadequate, and there are few specialists to aid the classroom teacher in coping with unusual problems that arise in the classroom or on the playground.

Furthermore, some school board members are so politically minded that they fail to act in the best interests of the children. School administrators frequently do not care to assume increased

---

[15] Miriam Van Waters, *Youth in Conflict*, New York, Republic, 1925.
[16] National Conference on Prevention and Control of Juvenile Delinquency, *Report on School and Teacher Responsibilities*, Washington, D.C., 1947, pp. 9–10.

responsibility in the problem of juvenile delinquency, at the same time discouraging originality and initiative by the teacher or principal.

2. STANDARDIZATION OF CURRICULUM. Many schools still operate on the false assumption of uniformity among all pupils who happen to be in the same classroom, regardless of differences in aptitudes and capacities. Says Clinard: [17]

> Schools are generally not operated with the purpose of developing interested, creative minds with some degree of individuality. Most professional educators would agree that in reality schools are places where juveniles, during a process of several hours a day, are routinized, bored, crushed in their individuality, and thrown into needless competition with others rather than aided in the development of co-operation.

It is well known that teachers occasionally rid themselves of pupils of low achievement by promoting them into the next higher grade, thus making room for those below who are moving up. In this manner children are sent on to upper grades when they are still unable to cope with subjects taught in the lower grades. Forcing children from class to class when they cannot keep up with the scholastic requirements is frequently emotionally disturbing to them, leading to feelings of inferiority and compensation by aggressiveness both in and out of school. The scholastic inaptitude of many delinquents is brought out in the following exchange between a juvenile-court judge and an apprehended delinquent.[18]

QUESTION: *In what year of high school are you, John?*
ANSWER: *In the third term.*
QUESTION: *What course do you take?*
ANSWER: *The academic course.*
QUESTION: *Tell me, Johnny, what subjects do you take in that course?*
ANSWER: *Well, I have history, literature and art appreciation.*
QUESTION: *What phase of history have you studied?*
ANSWER: *Ancient history.*

[17] Marshall B. Clinard, "Secondary Community Influences and Juvenile Delinquency," *The Annals of the American Academy of Political and Social Science*, 261:44–5, 1949.

[18] See Jacob Panken, *The Child Speaks; the Prevention of Juvenile Delinquency*, New York, Holt, 1944.

QUESTION: *Just let me understand what you mean by ancient history.*

ANSWER: *Well, sir, the history of people who lived 2000* B.C.

QUESTION: *What people are those?*

ANSWER: *The people who lived 2,000 years ago.*

QUESTION: *But which people, John?*

ANSWER: *Oh, the Spinx.*

QUESTION: *The Spinx? I never heard of that people. Where did they live?*

ANSWER: *Right here.*

QUESTION: *Do you mean that the Spinx people lived on the American Continent?*

ANSWER: *Oh no—they lived in Egypt.*

QUESTION: *And you say they lived in Egypt 2,000 years before the birth of Christ?*

ANSWER: *Yes, sir.*

QUESTION: *John, I really never heard of the Spinx. Will you tell me something about them?*

ANSWER: *You ought to know about the Spinx people.*

QUESTION: *Spell it, please.*

ANSWER: *S–P–H–I–N–X* (very slowly).

QUESTION: *Oh—you mean the Sphinx! That isn't a people. It is a monument in Egypt.*

ANSWER: *Well, I thought they were people who lived there.*

QUESTION: *What do you study in literature?*

ANSWER: *I don't know what you mean.*

QUESTION: *What period in literature do you study?*

ANSWER: *The modern.*

QUESTION: *Whom are you studying?*

ANSWER: *I don't know; we read story books.*

QUESTION: *Tell me what you read.*

ANSWER: *Well, I read* Midsummer Night's Dream.

QUESTION: *You say that is modern?*

ANSWER: *Yes, sir.*

QUESTION: *Who wrote it?*

ANSWER: *I don't know.*

QUESTION: *If I should tell you that William Shakespeare wrote it, would you say it was written by a modern?*

ANSWER: *Sure.*

QUESTION: *Who was Abraham Lincoln?*
ANSWER: *He was the first President of the United States.*
QUESTION: *For what was he noted?*
ANSWER: *Well, he was the first President of the United States.*

The course of study this delinquent experienced is typical of the academic curriculum, traditionally aimed at the acquisition of verbal and literary skills more than manual skills. In large part this is because of the origins of formal education in the preparation of professional aspirants for theology, law, and medicine. In the public school system there is an obvious incompatibility when children with a "manual" type of intelligence and "slow learners" (who may not be inferior in intelligence but too disturbed emotionally to be able to learn) strive for success in a "lingual" type of school environment. Some analysts have strongly suggested that by creating social failures this actually contributes to delinquency. The insistence of schools in teaching children subjects in which they cannot succeed often damages self-confidence, leads to rejection by teachers and classmates, and makes them vulnerable to neurotic and delinquent behavior. As a matter of fact there are several empirical studies, comparing delinquents with nondelinquents, which conclude that the former are on the whole less skilled in the use of verbal symbols and have greater reading difficulties than the latter, but have a higher manual or mechanical aptitude.[19] The Gluecks' ten-year study of 500 delinquent boys in Boston, compared with a control group of 500 boys from the same ecological area, held that the former were distinguishable from the latter in tending to direct and concrete, rather than symbolic and intellectual expression.[20]

Many of the problems encountered by adolescents (as well as by delinquents specifically) are centered around the fact that

[19] See Joseph Jastak and H. Allen, "Psychological Traits of Juvenile Delinquents," *Delaware State Medical Journal*, 16:100–4, 1944; John Slawson, *The Delinquent Boy: a Socio-Psychological Study*, Boston, Badger, 1926; A. D. Glanville, "Psychometric Patterns in Industrial School Boys," *Delaware State Medical Journal*, 9:11–14, 1937; Henry Feinberg and Clyde L. Reed, "Reading Level of a Group of Socially Maladjusted Boys," *Journal of Social Psychology*, 12:31–8, 1940; Joseph Jastak, "The Manual-Minded Child," *Delaware State Medical Journal*, 14:126–9, 1942.

[20] Sheldon and Eleanor Glueck, *Unraveling Juvenile Delinquency*, New York, The Commonwealth Fund, 1950, Chapter vi.

they cannot see why they are in school. They do not perceive school as something that will help them achieve the values important to them. Indeed, to many of them, school is actually detrimental as far as the achievement of many important values is concerned. An interesting variation of this thesis has been applied to the education of girls in American high schools.[21] Some of the problems encountered by adolescent girls are thought to result from the subservience of their education to masculine values, more specifically, the values of those boys who are preparing for college and professional schools. Half of the girls who begin high school leave before being graduated, and the main reason given by forty per cent of these girls for leaving is significantly: "I'm not interested in my course." Eleven per cent fewer boys than girls give this as their reason.

A highly publicized case that brought out the relationship between a standardized curriculum, the pressure to adjust to it, and delinquency, involved a fourteen-year-old schoolboy in a large metropolitan community.[22] Panicked by the thought of parental retaliation should he again fail a scheduled examination in high school algebra, he persuaded a friend to telephone a threat to the mathematics teacher that she would be killed if she did not pass every pupil. Still panicked, he formed a group of his friends into a rifle squad. Riding in a stolen car, armed with rifles and ammunition stolen from a shooting gallery, they fired at the home of the mathematics teacher. Nobody was harmed. Finally, the terror-stricken boy persuaded another to take the examination for him, and thereby was apprehended. It is worth noting, especially in connection with this case, that some educators are disturbed by the mechanical formula of memorizing-by-rote which continues to dominate a large portion of teaching. They look with particular disfavor on archaic methods of teaching arithmetic and algebra to children, emphasizing that such mathematics as taught in many schools has no relation to the normal learning development of children, and that mathematical tests are often grossly unfair indices of a child's actual intelligence or ability to learn.

[21] Charles G. Spiegler, "Are Our Girls Getting Boys' Education?" *New York Times Magazine*, May 14, 1950, p. 29.
[22] See Albert Deutsch, *PM*, May 12, 1948, p. 11.

3. THE COMPETITIVE PROCESS. American school systems generally reveal their dependence on the competitive process most clearly by the use of symbols called "marks" or "grades," which stratify children into what appears to be an academic social class system. Great emphasis is placed on these symbols. The pupil who receives low marks is treated as a failure, often regardless of his nonacademic assets and achievements. Kvaraceus's study shows that the marks received by delinquents are inferior, and he suggests that the dissatisfaction and thwarting accompanying each report of marks might well result in some form of aggressive, delinquent behavior.[23] In his Passaic sample, delinquents almost without exception did not receive a mark of E (Excellent), VG (Very Good) or G (Good).[24] The figures there also showed 43.5 per cent of the 661 delinquents as having had to repeat one term or more in a semiannual promotion system. This compared unfavorably with 17 per cent of the total school population in elementary grades who were found to have repeated one or more terms. Kvaraceus maintains that a child who is continually kept back with younger children will develop feelings of insecurity, inferiority, and distaste for the entire school program. Such a child lacks any real school satisfactions. Being the oldest and usually the largest pupil in the class, the repeater (like the child of low achievement who is automatically promoted into an intolerable situation) will adopt aggressive behavior to demonstrate some superiority or gain some satisfactions, even though in a way that provokes the disapproval of adult society.[25]

Measurements of School Experience as an Etiological Factor

Truancy, as we have already seen in Chapter IV, is not only a major type of delinquent behavior, but also one that is readily measurable. If failure and frustration in school lead to truancy, then it is self-evident that truancy can serve as a criterion or measure of the etiological relationship between school experiences and delinquency. Although such variables as the weather, ethnic and cultural backgrounds (that is, how parents of a given background value education), employment opportunities for

[23] Kvaraceus, *op. cit.*, pp. 140–3.
[24] *Ibid.*, pp. 155–6. See also his "Delinquency—a By-Product of the School?" *School and Society*, 59:350–1, 1944.
[25] Kvaraceus, *op. cit.*, pp. 139–40.

teen-agers, and the mood of the times are also at work in bringing about truancy, school conditions are believed to be at the core of truancy absences.

Kvaraceus claims that there is another index in support of an etiological relationship between frustrating school experiences and juvenile delinquency. In the community Kvaraceus studied, the lowest monthly incidence of delinquency referrals was found to occur when school was not in session, during the summer vacation. The peak of referrals, on the other hand, was at the height of tension and dissatisfaction with school, namely, during the spring and autumn. This was found to be the case despite the widespread belief that summer freedom and leisure are conducive to deviant behavior by children. The closing of school, a frustrating agency, more than offset the situation of "plenty of time to get into trouble." [26]

Confidence in this criterion is qualified by the fact that communities other than Passaic may not show a decline in the measured incidence of delinquency during summer vacations from school. As we have already seen in Chapter IV, each community has its own peculiar seasonal pattern, which varies somewhat from year to year.

Delinquency and the Use of Leisure

Juvenile delinquency is widely assumed to be a product of the misuse of leisure time. As a matter of fact, the alleged leisure-time problem of children ranks with the family and comic books as leading etiological scapegoats of delinquency. In rural societies of the past (and to a large extent of the present) the problem of leisure for children was negligible because they were part of the household's productive economy. But in urban societies children are not ordinarily economically productive, the result being that when they are not in school they are free from systematic activity a large part of the time. Inasmuch as there was no problem concerning idle children among country folk before they migrated to the city, they had no institutional forms to transplant to the city areas to meet the need. At the same time the large city, a comparatively new social phenomenon, has not developed adequate institutions for this purpose. The end result has been

[26] *Op. cit.*, pp. 151–2.

that children, especially boys, have few meaningful, acceptable ways to use their leisure time, and inevitably they fill some of the vacuum with delinquent behavior. Support for this view comes from people who work with "street corner gangs" and who receive such explanations for delinquency as: "We had no place to go," or: "There was nothing else to do."

It is true that the majority of young people in the United States do not participate in any organized or supervised program of recreation in their leisure time. Several studies of the extent to which adolescents use organized group recreation have come to the same conclusions; namely, that only one third of the boys and one fourth of the girls in urban areas have any organized affiliation at all. This refers to and includes affiliations such as with churches, schools, fraternities, private clubs, and youth-serving agencies. There are marked inequalities in the organized services that do exist. That is, there are fewer services for girls than for boys, for children in the less privileged neighborhoods, for Negro children and those of some other minority groups, and for children with mental, physical, and emotional handicaps. One theory is that lack of supervised and organized programs for children in leisure time leads to delinquency in the following manner:

> There are a great many frustrating things that happen to children who are in the process of growing up and learning to adjust to an adult world. . . . Play activities, especially in the younger years, but also in adolescence, games and recreations, serve an important compensatory function for some of these thwarted motives of children. In the world of play where one can do as one pleases, the conditions imposed by reality can be changed readily by the child. . . . In play, children can be as powerful as adults . . . and sometimes play serves to release tensions that arise in conflict situations. It is easy to see that play which serves the child as a substitute for lack of real adventure may easily shade into delinquency. Indeed, many of the escapades which land their youthful participants in the juvenile court can best be understood in the light of what we know about the dynamics of play.[27]

[27] Maud A. Merrill, *Problems of Child Delinquency*, Boston, Houghton Mifflin, 1947, pp. 88-9.

One of the most popular empirical tests of the theory that unorganized and unsupervised play in leisure time leads to delinquency is the ecological or spatial distribution of juvenile-court cases in their relation to the location of playgrounds in a community. Sullenger,[28] for example, using a base map of Omaha, spotted the homes that furnished delinquents to the juvenile court in a given period. His next step was to spot the location of the community playgrounds and to measure their spatial relationship to the delinquents' homes. A circle of one-half-mile radius was drawn from the center of each playground and the number of delinquents' homes was counted in each case. Sullenger found that 90.4 per cent of the delinquents lived more than one-half mile from the nearest playground. The arbitrary distance of one-half mile was utilized because the national child welfare and playground associations had found that this was the maximum distance most urban children would walk to a playground.

OTHER FACTUAL DATA ON LEISURE AND DELINQUENCY. There have been methodologies other than ecology to check empirically on the theory. Harris found that the findings of a questionnaire investigating the play practices of teen-age boys differentiated sharply between delinquents and nondelinquents. The data indicated that what the delinquent individual considered as play frequently involved activities that were technically violations of the law.[29]

The most comprehensive empirical study of the relationship between recreation and delinquency was made in Chicago for the Chicago Recreation Commission. This was a factual analysis of data collected during 1938 and 1939 on the recreational activities of approximately 15,000 boys and 8,000 girls between the ages of ten and seventeen. They were stratified into three groups: delinquents having court records, nondelinquents, and unofficial delinquents. The findings included the following: (1) Boys over fourteen years of age did not participate in recreational programs in so large numbers as did younger boys; (2) proportionately more nondelinquents than delinquents took part in supervised

[28] Thomas E. Sullenger, *Social Determinants in Juvenile Delinquency,* New York, Wiley, 1936, pp. 13–16.

[29] Dale B. Harris, "A Play Activities Blank as a Measure of Delinquency in Boys," *Journal of Abnormal and Social Psychology,* 37:546–59, 1942. See also Dale B. Harris, "Relationships among Play Interests and Delinquency in Boys," *American Journal of Orthopsychiatry,* 13:631–8, 1943.

recreation; (3) delinquents preferred competitive sports and non-supervised activities; (4) delinquents attended movies more often than did the nondelinquents; (5) all boys and girls spent twice as much time at the movies as in supervised recreation; and (6) participation in supervised recreation was correlated with a low rate of recidivism.[30]

These findings suggest some reservations about a clear-cut etiological relationship between leisure and delinquency. Evidently, organized recreation and delinquency are not mutually exclusive activities. To suggest that a boy will not be delinquent because he plays organized ball is no more valid than to say that he will not play ball because he is delinquent. He may do either, neither, or both. Participation in organized recreation represents a very small proportion of the total life experience of the child. In the Shanas study just summarized, it was found that during any one three-month season, between one third and one half of the participants took part in supervised recreational programs for less than ten hours.[31]

It is perfectly understandable that organizations interested in the promotion of group programs, such as recreation commissions, will "discover" that delinquency is a product of unsupervised play, but the fact that most delinquencies occur during the leisure time of children does not in itself reveal anything about the basic causation of delinquency. Obviously, other factors need to be explored to account for the problem behavior.

The task in the next chapter is to examine media of communication to which children in American society are exposed during their leisure time. The question is whether or not juveniles are stimulated to engage in delinquent behavior by the content of movies, radio programs, television, and the comic book.

[30] Ethel Shanas and C. E. Dunning, *Recreation and Delinquency: a Study of Five Selected Chicago Communities*, Chicago, Chicago Recreation Commission, 1942.

[31] See the comments of Henry D. McKay, "The Neighborhood and Child Conduct," *The Annals of the American Academy of Political and Social Science*, 261:38, 1949.

QUESTIONS AND RESEARCH SUGGESTIONS

1. *Why has it been difficult to ascertain the relationship between religion and delinquency?*
2. *What is the basis of the argument that religious experience may provoke certain forms of delinquency and crime?*
3. *In what ways may the school be said to play an active role etiologically with regard to delinquency?*
4. *What methodological technique is most frequently used to test the theory that unorganized and unsupervised play leads to delinquency?*
5. *Are organized recreation and delinquency mutually exclusive? Why?*
6. *Construct an ecological map of your community and show the correlation, if any, between the location of playgrounds and the residences of police-arrest cases of delinquency.*

SELECTED READINGS AND REFERENCES

Clinard, Marshall B., "Secondary Community Influences and Juvenile Delinquency," *The Annals of the American Academy of Political and Social Science,* 261:42–54, 1949.

DiVesta, Francis J., *Process Concepts and Values in the Social and Personal Adjustments of Adolescents,* Ithaca, Cornell University Agricultural Experiment Station, Memoir No. 287, November 1949.

Dougherty, Frances D., "A Study of the Mechanical Ability of Delinquent Children of the Los Angeles Juvenile Court," *Journal of Delinquency,* 102:293–311, 1926.

Fine, Benjamin, *Our Children Are Cheated,* New York, Holt, 1947.

Harris, Dale B., "A Play Activities Blank as a Measure of Delinquency in Boys," *Journal of Abnormal and Social Psychology,* 37:546–59, 1942.

Harris, Dale B., "Relationships among Play Interests and Delinquency in Boys," *American Journal of Orthopsychiatry,* 13:631–8, 1943.

Healy, William, and Augusta F. Bronner, "How Does the School Produce or Prevent Delinquency?" *Journal of Educational Sociology,* 6:450–70, 1933.

Johnson, Arthur C., "Our Schools Make Criminals," *Journal of Criminal Law and Criminology,* 33:310–15, 1942.

Kahn, Alfred J., "Who Are Our Truants?" *Federal Probation,* 15:36–47, 1951.

Kanner, Leo, "Cultural Implications of Children's Behavior Problems," *Mental Hygiene*, 25:353–62, 1941.

Kvaraceus, William C., "Delinquency—a By-Product of the School?" *School and Society*, 59:350–1, 1944.

Kvaraceus, William C., *Juvenile Delinquency and the School*, New York, World Book Co., 1945.

McKay, Henry D., "The Neighborhood and Child Conduct," *The Annals of the American Academy of Political and Social Science*, 261:32–41, 1949.

Middleton, Warren C., and Paul A. Fay, "Attitudes of Delinquent and Non-Delinquent Girls toward Sunday Observance, the Bible, and War," *Journal of Educational Psychology*, 32:555–8, 1941.

National Conference on Prevention and Control of Juvenile Delinquency, *Report on School and Teacher Responsibilities*, Washington, D.C., 1947.

National Conference on Prevention and Control of Juvenile Delinquency, *Report on Recreation for Youth*, Washington, D.C., 1947.

Shanas, Ethel, and C. E. Dunning, *Recreation and Delinquency: a Study of Five Selected Chicago Communities*, Chicago, Chicago Recreation Commission, 1942.

Sullenger, Thomas E., *Social Determinants in Juvenile Delinquency*, New York, Wiley, 1936.

Uger, Charles, "The Relationship of Teachers' Attitudes to Children's Problem Behavior," *School and Society*, 47:246–8, 1938.

Wickman, E. Koster, *Children's Behavior and Teachers' Attitudes*, New York, The Commonwealth Fund, 1928.

Chapter **XI.** *The Mass Media of Communication*

In the basement of St. Philip's Episcopal Church parish house in uptown New York an eleven-year-old boy who had been charged with deliberately breaking windows was talking to a psychiatrist. He was telling about the comic books he had read and how he and his friends liked to act out the stories. "My sister always likes to play the handsome man," he said. "I like to play the crook or the cop. She lots of times plays an actress getting captured. We used to make her walk along the street; then we used to come and take her into the playroom and tie her up. And then we go sit at a table and make plans how to get rid of her. In the meantime she is trying to escape."

Dr. Frederic Wertham, director and founder of the Lafargue Clinic located in that basement, later said: "The comic books, in intent and effect, are demoralizing the morals of youth. They are sexually aggressive in an abnormal way. They make violence alluring and cruelty heroic. They are not educational but stultifying. If those responsible refuse to clean up the comic-book market—and to all appearances most of them do, the time has come to legislate these books off the newsstands and out of the candy stores.[1]

The mass media of communication—especially the newspaper comic strip, the comic magazine, radio, cinema, and television—are now of major importance in the transmission of American society's culture and subcultures to the juvenile population. They are carriers of culture norms and patterns as well as news and propaganda. It is conceivable that their increasing accessibility to larger and larger audiences will eventually lead them to be placed alongside (and in some cases above) such traditional social and cultural forces as the family, the peer group, and the institutions of religion, education, and leisure in any scale measuring the conditioning of juvenile behavior.

A verifiable generalization is that every medium of communication, especially when it is introduced, arouses suspicion, criticism, and opposition among adults regarding its impact on children. All mass media mentioned above have been suspected at one time or another of being an etiological factor—in some cases, *the* cause—of juvenile delinquency. This suspicion has been enhanced by knowledge of the effectiveness of propaganda, which uses the same channels of communication.

The most conspicuous of these media, as far as the juvenile audience is concerned, is the comics that appeared first in newspaper strips and later in magazine or book form. The following analysis and evaluation of the etiological relationship between the mass media and delinquency is largely in terms of the comics. The justification for this is twofold: first, many of the characteristics of and responses to one medium are shared by the others; [2]

[1] Judith Crist, "Horror in the Nursery," *Collier's*, March 27, 1948, p. 22.
[2] "Whether they look at pictures, listen to words and sounds, or read the printed word—and they do all of this together some of the time—they

secondly, perhaps more thought has been given to the possible impact of comics on delinquency than to the impact of any other medium.[3]

The Evolution of the Comics

Today's comics trace their origin back to picture strips of "Max and Moritz" created by German artist Wilhelm Busch over a century ago. Direct descendants of the two boys are "The Katzenjammer Kids" and "The Captain and the Kids." Of course the art of telling stories in picture strips is almost as old as man himself; examples of such art have been traced back to prehistoric cave dwellers. Early hunters of the stone age, ten thousand years or more before the birth of Christ and long before the invention of written language, depicted in vegetable coloring on the walls of their caves the animals they had confronted and slain. Ancient peoples delineated day-to-day scenes in pictures on the walls of their tombs. Early mosaics, in shells, lapis lazuli, and pink limestone, dated 3000 B.C., told of the Sumerian army at war, and showed the royal family at peace. Scenes of daily life in ancient Egypt appear on tombs; for example, that of two girls engaged in a hair-pulling contest. The medieval monks frequently told their Bible stories by pictures in panel form, known as blockbooks. Interestingly enough, these blockbooks attempted to tell their stories without words, but when words were used they were enclosed in a "balloon" very similar to the device used in contemporary comics.

The comics were introduced in American newspapers at the beginning of this century. They were originally intended for adults, but children proved to be a more responsive audience. Shortly thereafter, other strips appeared, designed for children only. It is generally agreed that the comics were misnamed, for although they were meant to make their audience laugh, today many of them are not amusing, nor do they pretend to be.

The historical relationship between comics in newspapers and later in magazines or books has its contemporary vestige in

---

perceive the same world-view. . . ." See Norbert Muhlen, "Comic Books and Other Horrors," *Commentary*, 7:82, 1949.

[3] Many references throughout this chapter are dependent on "The Comics as an Educational Medium," an issue of *The Journal of Educational Sociology* edited by Harvey W. Zorbaugh in December 1944.

the fact that twenty per cent of comic magazines consist of reprints from newspaper strips. The transition from one to the other occurred in 1911 when the first modern comic book appeared as a collection of Bud Fisher's "Mutt and Jeff" newspaper strips. Hayden Weller summarizes its interesting beginnings as follows: [4]

> Calvin Harris, then promotion manager of the [Chicago] *American,* persuaded the Ball Publishing Company of Boston to produce the book as a circulation builder for newspapers. The papers were to offer it to readers for a few cents a copy and six coupons clipped from succeeding issues of the paper. Other newspapers carrying the Fisher strip were slow to accept the idea and Harris was finally forced to place an advance order for 10,000 copies at 17½ cents each before the Ball Company would publish.
>
> Harris, now a successful magazine writer, recalls that the 10,000 copies arrived at the *American* a week before the coupons were due to appear and were stacked in the hallway outside his office. On the same day Andrew Lawrence, cost-conscious managing director of the Hearst papers, also arrived in Chicago. When Lawrence learned the size of the order he went into the livid act of the legendary newspaper efficiency expert and fired Harris.
>
> The first week's sales reached 35,000 and netted the *American* a profit of more than $6,000 in addition to the circulation. Harris was rehired at an increase in salary. The comic book was launched!

The Volume and Audience of the Comics

A recent estimate is that whereas most children go to the movies four to eight times a month and listen to radio dramas practically every afternoon or evening for several hours, they read more than a dozen comic books or magazines per month.[5] This is aside from the fact that the daily comic strips in newspapers are read by two thirds of all children over six. The most reliable information on the variety of comic books in the United States

[4] "The First Comic Book," *The Journal of Educational Sociology,* 18:195, 1944.
[5] Muhlen, *op. cit.,* p. 82.

comes from the files of the Library of Congress. The law requires a publisher to file a copy of his magazine with the Library if he wishes it to be copyrighted. Currently there are approximately 315 different titles, which means that there are at least that many different ones available for juveniles and other readers to purchase.

Between fifty and sixty million comic magazines are sold each month in this country, and there are three to four readers of each copy, considerably above the rate for other magazines or books, owing to circulation by resale and "swapping." Surveys by Gallup and others confirm what these figures imply; namely, that the comics are America's favorite literary form. Regional differences are insignificant in this respect. Furthermore, readers are found in all socio-economic strata and subcultures of American society. Intelligence quotients seem to make very little difference, for the comics are read by bright as well as dull children. One difference is that bright children are likely to abandon the comics earlier.[6]

The Content of Comics and Related Mass Media

A central question is whether or not there are any patterns or themes in the comics and other mass media. If such patterns are discernible, presumably one can deduce the reasons for their appeal to the juvenile audience. One content analysis reaches the following conclusion: [7]

> In contrast to the official pattern of the American Drama, and its world of peace and progress in which people get along with each other, the American daydream . . . of the media of mass entertainment is acted out in a world in which human relations are opened and settled by daggers, whips, tommyguns, or atomic exterminators. In psychoanalytic terms, the entertainment of a large part of the nation's adults, and of the overwhelming majority of its youth, is directed toward *mortido* rather than *libido:* toward destruction rather than procreation, toward hate rather than love, toward aggression rather than understanding, toward death rather than life. Its common denominator is violence. . . .

[6] Josette Frank, *Comics, Radio, Movies—and Children*, New York, Public Affairs Pamphlet #142, 1949, p. 3.
[7] Muhlen, *op. cit.*, p. 82.

Not infrequently the comic book demonstrates pictorially to the juvenile reader how to gouge eyes out with the thumb, choke off the windpipe, kick an opponent in the stomach or shins, flatten his arch with the heel, bite his ears, kick him in the liver area, and punch him in the spine. The essence of such violence, according to one psychiatrist, is sadism.[8] For example, in the case of Donald Duck he is repeatedly victimized, falling through space, landing on a rock which he picks up and lets fall on his toe, after which he looks up only to be hit on the head by a coconut hurled by an unseen foe.

A useful perspective is gained by examining the values mass media uphold. Happiness is measured in terms of material accumulation, and masculinity in terms of nimbleness with knife, gun, and fist. Power, aggression, and even murder are glorified by the subtle insinuation that in some situations it is justifiable to take the law into one's own hands.[9]

One of the most thorough analyses of comic magazines was done by the Children's Book Committee of the Child Study Association of America.[10] It was an examination and evaluation of a sample of 100 current comic magazines which fell into the general categories of adventure, fantasy, animal stories, war, crime and detective, real stories and biography, jungle adventure, fun and humor, love, and retold classics. The favorite category is adventure, which as a matter of fact was found to permeate most comics, regardless of their other characteristics. In the crime and detective comics, offenses are usually on a grandiose scale, involving gangs and plots, sabotage and racketeering. Although the inevitable pattern is that criminals are brought to justice and the righteous are avenged, right triumphs by force and violence.

[8] Ralph S. Banay, *Youth in Despair*, New York, Coward-McCann, 1948, p. 64.
[9] *Ibid.*, pp. 62–3.
[10] For a summary of this analysis, see Josette Frank, "What's in the Comics?" *The Journal of Educational Sociology*, 18:214–22, 1944.

The Appeal to Juveniles

There is no simple answer to the question: Why do children like comics? Nevertheless, there are at least three outstanding theories contributing to an answer.[11]

1. *Action.* Children like action and the comics provide them with it in its most dynamic form. The action is easy to follow, for the relation of cause and effect is clear and immediate. It is of the "biff bang" variety, which is especially pleasing to juveniles to whom physical encounters are fascinating and forbidden.

2. *Security.* In the comics, children can count on everything turning out as they would have it. The "good guys" overcome and defeat the "bad guys," no matter how insurmountable the odds.

3. *Reflection of own fantasies.* The comics enable easy identification by the juvenile reader with the hero or villain. It is conceivable that they find in these fancied roles some escape from the frustrations that accompany the subordinate status of childhood and adolescence in a world of superordinate adults.

The Controversy about Comics

For many years there has been a violent controversy over whether or not the comics lead to delinquency and other forms of deviant behavior. In 1940 the book reviewer of the *Chicago Daily News* articulated the feelings of the "accusers" among laymen when he wrote:

> Virtually every child in America is reading color "comic" magazines—a poisonous mushroom growth. . . . Frankly we were not perturbed when we first heard about the rise of the action "comics." We imagined (as do most parents) that they were no worse than the "funnies" in the newspapers. But a careful examination of the . . . periodicals now on the stands shocked us into activity. At least 70 per cent of the total were of a nature no respectable newspaper would think of accepting.
>
> Save for a scattering of more or less innocuous "gang" comics and some reprints of newspaper strips, we found that the bulk of these lurid publications depend for their appeal

[11] See, especially, Lauretta Bender, "The Psychology of Children's Reading and the Comics," *The Journal of Educational Sociology*, 18:223–31, 1944.

upon mayhem, murder, torture and abduction—often with a child as the victim. Superman heroics, voluptuous females in scanty attire, blazing machine guns, hooded "justice" and cheap political propaganda were to be found at almost every page.

The old dime novels in which an occasional redskin bit the dust were classic literature compared to the sadistic drivel pouring from the press today.

Badly drawn, badly written and badly printed—a strain on young eyes and young nervous systems—the effect of these pulp-paper nightmares is that of a violent stimulant. Their crude blacks and reds spoil the child's natural sense of color; their hypodermic injection of sex and murder makes the child impatient with better, though quieter, stories. Unless we want a coming generation even more ferocious than the present one, parents and teachers throughout America must band together to break the "comic" magazine.[12]

On the professional level of the controversy, the accusers claim that juveniles can be so deeply impressed by crime and horror stories that they accept a world so depicted as the real world to which they have to adjust themselves. Apparently supporting such a theory is the case of the boy who received a Superman cape on his birthday, wrapped it around himself, and sprang out of the window of his apartment house. The defenders of comics, on the other hand, maintain that juveniles, finding it necessary to suppress their aggressive behavior under the restrictions of adults and education, can do this in an acceptable way by finding an outlet through imaginative participation in the violence-play and aggression-fantasies of the comics or other media. According to this reasoning, these mass media are the "aspirin" and "penicillin" of children which help them to overcome the irritations accompanying the task of growing up into a peaceful adult world. This is in contrast to the accuser's theory that the comics are an "opium," leading children spellbound into the road of delinquency.

An inescapable fact about this controversy is that both ac-

[12] Quoted in Harvey Zorbaugh, "Editorial," *The Journal of Educational Sociology*, 18:193–4, 1944.

cusers and defenders have very little systematic, scientific observation to support their positions. Whereas the accusers may be able to point to Blumer and Hauser's study of the effects of another medium, the movies, on delinquency to support their positions,[13] the defenders can point to Healy[14] and Burt[15] for "proof" that the impact of the mass media is negligible. The latter did case studies, and as is generally true when such a methodology is used, the authors were so engrossed in finding other causative factors that they gave little attention to the effects of mass media. The opposite was true in the Blumer and Hauser study. The methodological "moral," as Reckless so aptly puts it, is that when one looks for certain effects he finds many instances of them, and when one does not look for the effects he is likely to find few instances of them.[16]

The Etiological Argument: Accusation

Psychiatrists (some, not all) are the best-known proponents of a theory of causal relationship between the mass media and delinquency. They argue that the suggestive effect of the media upon the minds of juveniles is profound, judging from the time children spend discussing them. By emphasizing wealth, materialism, and immorality in our culture, the mass media furnish juveniles with models conducive to delinquency. As they read, listen to, or watch the exploits of hero and villain, the emotions of juveniles are aroused but the tensions remain unsolved until there is overt physical activity, often of an imitative delinquent type.

The argument continues that there is ample evidence, other than delinquent behavior, of the direct effects of mass media on our culture. (The implication is that there must be direct effects

[13] Herbert Blumer and Philip M. Hauser, *Movies, Delinquency and Crime*, New York, Macmillan, 1933. The authors used the life history, interviews, and the questionnaire to find that ten per cent of the male and twenty-five per cent of the female delinquents in their sample believed they had been motivated to commit their offenses by movie stimulation.

[14] William Healy, *The Individual Delinquent*, Boston, Little, Brown, 1915, p. 136.

[15] Cyril Burt, *The Young Delinquent*, New York, Appleton, 1925, p. 521.

[16] Walter C. Reckless, *The Etiology of Delinquent and Criminal Behavior*, New York, Social Science Research Council Bulletin #50, 1943, p. 42.

on delinquency too.) Indeed, publishers of the newspaper comic strip themselves boast that the example of "Popeye the Sailor" popularized spinach-eating among America's children, and that in the wake of "Bringing Up Father" corned beef and cabbage became a favorite dish. In one community the mothers petitioned the creator of Popeye to stop him from opening cans of spinach with his teeth because their children were imitating him. The idiom of the comics has left its mark on our language, examples being "heebie-jeebies" and "time's a-wastin'" (Barney Google), "goon" and "jeep" (Popeye), "let George do it" (Jiggs), and "Shmoo" (Li'l Abner). The comics have contributed to our song, our drama, and our art. They have invaded the campus (Sadie Hawkins Day) and the classrooms, where thousands of children are learning to read from comic-type workbooks. Many others are studying foreign languages, the social studies, English literature, and the Bible by way of their help. When Milt Caniff, creator of "Terry and the Pirates," staged the death of Raven Sherman in 1942, 1,400 letters of sympathy came to him from comic readers, a number of them accompanied by floral offerings. On the day Raven was buried in the hills north of Chungking, 450 students of one American university facetiously paid tribute to her by gathering on the campus, facing east for a minute of silence.[17]

Evidence of direct effects on delinquent behavior is also claimed. For example, in 1948 newspapers reported that three boys who were six, eight, and nine years of age had tortured a playmate of seven "merely to re-enact a comic book plot." Shortly thereafter the press publicized the poisoning of a woman by an adolescent boy who acquired the idea and the recipe from another comic book. Many look upon such cases as substantiation of the theory that comics suggest delinquent ideas to children and lead them to act out these ideas. With regard to other mass media, many are satisfied by the findings of the Chicago recreation study to which reference was made in the previous chapter. There it was found that delinquents attended movies more frequently than did the nondelinquents. In four neighborhoods with higher delinquency rates all children favored radio crime and

[17] Harvey Zorbaugh, "The Comics—There They Stand!" *The Journal of Educational Sociology,* 18:196–203, 1944.

mystery stories, whereas comedians and variety hours were preferred by boys and girls living in an area with a lower delinquency rate.[18] In Merrill's study,[19] an outstanding and presumably significant difference between delinquents and nondelinquents consisted not in whether they went to the movies, but in the frequency of their attendance. The delinquents attended more than once a week to a greater extent than did the nondelinquent controls.

The Defense

Those who are reluctant to recognize any etiological relationship between the mass media and delinquency use several refutations to support their position. They stress, for example, that since more than nine out of ten American children read comic books, while considerably less than one out of a thousand commits a delinquent act after the comic book description, the argument of the psychiatrists hardly permits a general conclusion. The juvenile can imitate a machine gun, shoot or be shot at with the appropriate histrionics, and play the role of Superman after being to the movies, listening to serials or murder mysteries on the radio, or reading comic books. But there is reason to believe that these are merely play-forms without much meaning or significance in the formation of behavior patterns.

The defendants of the mass media maintain that one must take with a grain of salt what delinquents themselves say about the effects of comics or motion pictures on their behavior. One cannot accept at its face value the plea of a frightened child, hoping to please the judge by his "reasons," that he committed his delinquency because he "saw it in the comics" or "in the movies." Yet such confessions have been quoted as "proof" of the causative influence of mass media.

There are many testimonials by specialists in the behavioral sciences and practitioners in the field of child welfare defending the mass media. Says one: "I am unaware of the existence of any scientifically established causal relationship between the reading

[18] Ethel Shanas and C. E. Dunning, *Recreation and Delinquency: A Study of Five Selected Chicago Communities*, Chicago, Chicago Recreation Commission, 1942.

[19] Maud A. Merrill, *Problems of Child Delinquency*, Boston, Houghton Mifflin, 1947, p. 91.

of comic books and delinquency." And another: "In studying the causes of behavior problems of children for many years, I have never seen one instance of a child whose behavior disturbance originated in the reading of comic books, nor even a case of a delinquent whose behavior was exaggerated by such reading." [20]

The defendants point out that to argue, as has one psychiatrist,[21] that an increase in juvenile delinquency has gone hand in hand with the distribution of comic books is the same kind of fallacy that enables statisticians jokingly to "prove" that the stork delivers babies, simply because storks and the birth rate are more numerous in rural areas.

Conclusion

Evidently it is impossible to come to an unqualified conclusion either in behalf of or against the theory that the mass media "cause" delinquent behavior. It is not simply a matter of subscribing either to one side or to the other. But some theoretical conclusions are possible which are intermediate to the extreme positions involved in the controversy. One such conclusion is that the mass media teach children that violence is a solution to problems in human relations. The point is not that children will tend to resort to violence themselves, so much as that they will come to accept violence, when practiced by others, as "normal." [22]

Another tentative conclusion is that the mass media have a differential effect on the behavior of children, depending on the background and experience of the various children. For example, a child from a high-rate area of delinquency may more likely be influenced by the content of movies than will a child from a low-rate area of delinquency.

A third tentative conclusion is that there is differential response among juveniles to the mass media on the basis of differentials in personality. That is, some people can become sexually excited reading a Sears Roebuck catalogue. Almost anything such people see, hear, or read may suggest a delinquent pattern, providing the necessary personality traits are there. On the other

[20] Frank, *op. cit.*, p. 7.
[21] Frederick Wertham in *Saturday Review of Literature*, May 29, 1948.
[22] Muhlen, *op. cit.*, p. 86.

THE IDLE APPRENTICE TURNED AWAY AND SENT TO SEA: *Plate V in the* INDUSTRY AND IDLENESS *series*

Here the artist shows Tom, the idle apprentice, being rowed down the Thames to a ship and a future of indentured service at sea. The hope of those who are banishing Tom is that a seafaring life will reform him; his removal will of course safeguard society for a time. One of the men taking the boy out to the ship displays a cat-o'nine-tails, as a warning of the punishment that may be expected for breaches of discipline aboard ship. Another man points to the gallows on shore, suggesting what Tom's fate may be if he continues in his present course. No one heeds the boy's weeping mother. In Hogarth's time banishment was a common technique adopted by society both to prevent the repetition of deviant behavior and to protect itself. Society's treatment of crime and delinquency has taken on new forms in recent decades, but banishment is still implicit in many of them. The community may gain temporary protection through banishment, but there is little, if any, evidence of actual reform induced by such treatment.

THE IDLE APPRENTICE EXECUTED AT TYBURN: *Plate XI in the*
INDUSTRY AND IDLENESS *series*

*The ultimate punishment in eighteenth-century England
was the same as that meted out in our society now: execution.
Capital punishment in Hogarth's world took place in public, on
the theory that the dramatic lesson of the gruesome spectacle
would deter any would-be wrongdoers in the witnessing crowd.
But Hogarth's picture of the execution of the idle apprentice at
Tyburn indicates that this theory was false. The spectators are
making a holiday of the occasion. A particularly ludicrous note is
seen in the right foreground, where a child is picking the pocket
of a biscuit-seller. In the midst of the seething, brawling, festive
mob the condemned Tom Idle stands in a cart before his coffin.
Tom's unfortunate mother, covering her face at the right, is almost
the only person grieving in the entire scene, from the disheveled
woman hawking Tom's death speech in the front of the crowd to
the hangman nonchalantly smoking his pipe at the gallows. Execution as a public spectacle has passed from the scene today—indeed, there is considerable evidence that such public punishment
is ineffective in deterring future misbehavior. But society still re-
sorts to capital punishment, occasionally for juveniles.*

hand, if the psychological world in which the child lives is an adjusted one, then nothing external to it, such as the comics, can lead him to delinquency.

Our concern, in the chapter that follows, is the etiological relationship, if any, between American culture and juvenile delinquency. The society as a whole, as it impinges on the juvenile, must be considered in any realistic analysis of juvenile delinquency.

QUESTIONS AND RESEARCH SUGGESTIONS

1. *What is the justification for an analysis and evaluation of the etiological relationship between the mass media and delinquency in terms of the comics?*
2. *What theories are there to explain the appeal of the comics to juveniles?*
3. *Is there any substantial evidence of the direct effects of mass media on American culture other than delinquent behavior?*
4. *Discuss the arguments used by those who are reluctant to recognize any etiological relationship between the mass media and delinquency.*
5. *If it is impossible to be unqualifiedly for or against the theory that the mass media "cause" delinquent behavior, what other position can one take?*
6. *Sample several comic books and make a content analysis of the themes and values they incorporate.*

SELECTED READINGS AND REFERENCES

Blumer, Herbert, and Philip M. Hauser, *Movies, Delinquency and Crime*, New York, Macmillan, 1933.

Frank, Josette, *Comics, Radio, Movies—and Children*, New York, Public Affairs Pamphlet No. 148, 1949.

Muhlen, Norbert, "Comic Books and Other Horrors," *Commentary*, 7:80–7, 1949.

United States Congress, *Juvenile Delinquency*, Washington, D.C., U.S. Government Printing Office, 1950.

Zorbaugh, Harvey W., ed., "The Comics as an Educational Medium," *The Journal of Educational Sociology*, 18:193–256, 1944.

Chapter **XII.** *The Delinquent Culture of American Society*

Two scholars set out to get some descriptive data about unapprehended law-breakers by distributing a questionnaire listing 49 offenses under the penal code of the state of New York. Of these offenses, fourteen were felonies, seven might be felonies under certain conditions; the rest were misdemeanors. All of them were sufficiently serious to draw a maximum sentence of not less than a year. Replies were returned anonymously to insure frankness. The study was not a rigidly scientific one, but was carefully and critically prepared and tabulated. Some effort was made in distributing the questionnaires to secure a balanced racial and religious community cross-section, although this could not be done with precision. Economically the group was probably weighted on the upper income side. Replies were received from 1,698 individuals, 1,020 men and 678 women. Geographically most of the responses came from the metropolitan area of New York, Westchester and Long Island, but there was a scattering from upstate New York, Pennsylvania, Ohio and California. Ninety-nine per cent of those questioned answered affirmatively to one or more of the offenses. The number of offenses per persons ran high.

Personal comments appearing on some of the questionnaires reflected the ethical viewpoint of the individuals. Their rationalizations would not be acceptable in defense of their action if they had been apprehended and brought to court. A housewife over sixty, admitting to false testimony, added this statement: "It made no difference in the outcome, and I did it to spare someone pain." An artist made this comment on the same question: "It was a divorce action and I'm a gentleman." A doctor, admitting to taking a car without permission, pencilled in the word "emergency." A businessman who opened someone else's mail appended this explanation, "Tried to keep my son from making a fool of himself, but he did it anyway." A girl student justified illegal opening of somebody else's mail with the explanation, "She (roommate) opened my mail first." A minister who confessed to making false statements about a commodity that he sold, betrayed traces of his moral struggle in the comment, "I tried truth first but it's not always successful." Annoying letters were sent by a social worker to her husband, by a student to his teacher and by a salesclerk to his boss. A laborer who had broken in and taken property took pains to note that he "put it back later."

Several persons stated that they had had to falsify their religion to get a certain job, others reporting violation of birth control or of gambling laws regarded the laws themselves as stupid and therefore they saw nothing wrong in violating them. Larceny under $100 in value covered such items as towels, a bathmat, a spoon and stamps. One man asserted that his high bill gave him at least a moral right to steal from the hotel where he was staying. Another excused himself for stealing from his employer by observing, "My boss is a jerk." A mechanic who falsified to get someone to sign a document explained that the paper in question was his marriage license. A farmer faced with the issue of whether or not he had been guilty of assault without provocation wrote "no" in the designated space, but added the comment, "Thrashed a lot of men in my time but they all jolly well deserved it." A woman artist decided to call herself guilty of assault but with the qualifying phrase, "Threw ash tray at an unbearable cad." A self-styled criminologist over sixty gave up after reading the questionnaire and returned it with the sweeping comment, "Too much trouble, I've done them all." [1]

An increasingly vociferous school of thought in American social science subscribes to the position that etiology in social problems has failed largely because it has overlooked the proper frame of reference for study and analysis; namely, American society itself. It has probed only segments and only the "outer crust," so to speak. The impelling forces to delinquency inhere deeply in the culture of the American people. This calls for a much broader perspective than is involved in the examination of the family, peer group, or media of communication.

Culture dominates behavior. It dictates what most people will do most of the time. If part of our culture is "criminogenic," then part of the people will engage in delinquency and crime. For example, in a competitive society organized around profit, people will murder for profit. When a competitive society moves toward large-scale production the people will also move toward large-scale murder. Those who support this theory assert that any attempt here to draw an arbitrary line between juveniles and their elders in the population is unrealistic and indefensible, resembling the attempt formerly to see only problems of the individual rather than those of society.

The theory of the "juvenile in delinquent society" is not without its detractors. Some see it as an avenue of escape from more rigorously controlled thinking. This, of course, may be true of any frustrated search for specific answers which leads to wholistic but ambiguous substitutes. Whether or not it is true,

---

[1] James S. Wallerstein and Clement J. Wyle, "Our Law-Abiding Law-Breakers," *Probation*, April 1947, 7 pp.

however, depends on the analyst and the student. Others have
been reluctant to adopt the theory because they maintain that,
under the guise of moral detachment, it actually imputes moral
blame to a reified combination of individuals—all of us. This, too,
is a possibility, especially among those who are adept in the misuse of a theory by moralization and reification. Again, however,
it need not be the case, for the weakness lies potentially in the
analyst and student, not in the theory. Still others detract from
the theory because they believe that it carries the deterministic
premises of social science to a point of absurdity, the point where
human beings are mechanistically conceived to be irresponsible,
passive products of their environment. Here we find a perennial,
futile question: Do we make society or does society make us? The
answer probably is that both propositions in the question are
partly true. One does not exclude the other. *The theory of a delinquent society simply implies that society plays an incredibly
greater role in making the individual juvenile delinquent than the
individual freely determines for himself.*

The structure and functions of American society are obviously
too complex and ramified for an adequate analysis in one chapter.
As a matter of fact, entire volumes devoted to the subject can do
no more than define the outlines and sample the content of such
a vast subject.[2] For the purpose of this book, a detailed analysis
of American society and culture is unnecessary. It should be kept
in mind that we are dealing here with only one aspect—namely,
the alleged delinquent and criminogenic traits of the society and
culture—rather than a comprehensive picture of the American
way of life.

Society, Culture, and Values

The culture of every society comprises learned and socially
shared symbols to which conventionalized understandings are
given. These symbols each stand for objects, concepts, images,
social processes (or norms) and social objectives (or goals) of
varying degrees of concreteness and abstraction.

Social values refer to those cultural symbols which have

[2] See, for example, Harold J. Laski, *The American Democracy*, New
York, Viking, 1948; Robin Williams, Jr., *American Society: a Sociological
Interpretation*, New York, Knopf, 1951.

become meaningful to members of the society in terms of the two criteria of truth and worthwhileness. The social values of a society are so meaningful to members of the society that they accept them largely without the demand for proof and without skepticism. Bernard [3] has suggested that one may test what is and what is not a social value by imagining a person being elected to office on a platform advocating a specific program. If there is no hesitation in imagining that he will be elected, then there is no question that the program contains values held by the society. If there is doubt, the program conflicts with the voter's values. In most American communities it would be impossible to elect a man to office on a program advocating more poverty, disease and ill health, aggressive war, ignorance, and illiteracy. American values can also be inferred from Fourth of July orations, sermons, and the like. A second test of values, therefore, is their triteness. That is, they are taken for granted.

Official and Unofficial Values

Up to this point the reference has been to "official" values. By "official" we mean those values which are verbally acceptable to most adult members of the society and are formally and systematically indoctrinated in children by their parents, the school, the church, and character-building agencies such as the Boy Scouts and the Girl Scouts. In their classic sociological study of Middletown, the Lynds identified the personality traits of hard work, honesty, kindness, friendliness, and considerateness as a few of such values in a typical American community.[4]

Official values are found in the sacred documents of American society. Many of them appear in the laws defining juvenile delinquency. For example, a careful examination of virtually any state law on delinquency would bring out such values as the inviolability of private property, subservience to parents and other authoritative adults, linguistic discretion,[5] and economic and financial "integrity."

[3] Jessie Bernard, *American Community Behavior*, New York, Dryden, 1949, p. 73.

[4] Robert S. and Helen M. Lynd, *Middletown in Transition*, New York, Harcourt, Brace, 1937, pp. 403–19.

[5] That is, usage of Romance or Latin derived words and avoidance of Anglo-Saxon equivalents (four-lettered vulgarity) in describing processes of bodily elimination of waste matter and of reproduction.

But one must also reckon with "unofficial" values. These values are usually informally and unsystematically conveyed to children. Theoretically they are very significant with regard to delinquency. In Middletown the Lynds identified them as the values that cluster around "forcefulness," "enterprise," "shrewdness," and "power," the qualities particularly important in gaining competitive advantage in a business-oriented culture.[6]

Merton,[7] a careful student of such values, claims that the child is exposed to them as he observes the daily behavior and casual conversation of his parents and other adults. The child detects them and incorporates them in his own make-up even though they are frequently implicit in adult communication. The best evidence for this can be found in the language pattern of the child, especially when there are persistent errors in such patterns. An error such as "goodest" instead of "best" indicates that the child has detected the implicit paradigms or models for the expression of plurality, the conjugation of verbs, and the inflection of adjectives. One can infer from this that the child is also probably involved in detecting and incorporating implicit paradigms or models of cultural evaluation even when they conflict with the explicit, official admonitions, advice, and evaluations he receives.

Implicit, "unofficial" values, to a greater extent than explicit "official" values, are related to juvenile delinquency in the sense of being more likely to motivate such behavior. It should be noticed, however, that the following typology of American values, the pursuance of which theoretically involves delinquent behavior, is represented by some "official" as well as "unofficial" values.

1. SUCCESS. In American culture, success is unquestionably one of the most conspicuous objects of desire and emulation, more so perhaps than in any other culture of the Western world. As Williams states it, American culture is organized around the attempt at active mastery rather than passive acceptance. This involves a low tolerance of frustration, the refusal to accept ascetic renunciation, the positive encouragement of desire, the

---

[6] Lynd, *op. cit.*, pp. 423–4.
[7] Robert K. Merton, "Social Structure and Anomie," in *Social Theory and Social Structure*, Glencoe, The Free Press, 1949, pp. 147–8.

stress on power, and the approval of ego-assertion.[8] Success is not exclusively an American trait, but in a land characterized by extraordinary mobility and the absence of rigidly fixed classes, success has a marked appeal to an unusually large number of people.

American culture values upward gradients. We ask how fast a baby is growing, how much a school child is improving, how a man is "going up in the world." We give rewards not so much for achievements as for increasing achievement. We value the distance "from log cabin to White House" because it represents a long upward gradient.

The credo of success in America, it may be said, includes the conviction that, since success begets success, the appearance of success may bring actual success. The result is that individual Americans admit failure only with the greatest reluctance. Like the father in the famous play *Death of a Salesman*, there must be bluster and an appearance of prosperity, no matter how hollow it is. Not only is it difficult for Americans to admit to others that they are merely "getting along," but, with the success doctrine so prevalent, it is increasingly difficult for them to feel that life is worthwhile unless income and position are constantly being bettered.[9]

More than any other people, Americans are taught to believe that hard work and thrift will bring them success. But as American society is presently organized, there is less and less room for upward gradients. And since thousands upon thousands of normal and useful Americans do not have the drive, intelligence, and skill to earn more than a limited amount of recognition and income, feelings of frustration and despondency are easily aroused. When people come to the realization that they cannot attain success by hard work and thrift they are apt to turn to delinquency and crime to achieve the goal, even though few men enjoy the threat of punishment hanging over their head and would rather achieve the symbols of success legitimately.

It is likely that in many societies where the standard of living is considerably lower than in America delinquency and crime

[8] Williams, *op. cit.*, p. 441.
[9] Morris Opler, "Living Patterns in the U.S.A.," *Patterns for Modern Living*, Chicago, The Delphian Society, 1950, p. 567.

rates are far below those in this country because the level of
success that the majority of people elsewhere set up for themselves is not remote from what they are likely to reach. In other
cultures one seldom finds a person whose success aspirations and
expectations reach beyond the achievement level of his parents.
In American society, however, both parents and children expect
successive generations to aspire to and achieve higher levels of
success than the previous generations.[10]

2. STATUS AND POWER ASCENDANCE. Americans, especially
American juveniles, are said to live in a "pressure" culture in
which the question is "How far can I get?" [11] Inasmuch as the
answer is usually thought of not only in terms of success but
also in terms of social status, the struggle for higher status may
be discerned even in the earliest years of childhood. The school
experience, for example, has become meaningful to many children as a struggle for grades, the symbols of position or status in
relation to other schoolchildren. Outside of school, Poster has the
following vivid recollection of his own boyhood:

The battle for status was the chief determinant of our
lives. Status came from skill in fighting and in such key games
as punchball and basketball, but also from a certain indefin-
able quality of personality, the gift of making others accept
and conform to one's style of behavior. Even fighting was
not so simple an affair as it seemed on the surface, and success in fighting was not altogether a matter of sheer physical
skill. The question of who could fight whom was constantly
on our minds, and hardly a day went by without someone
trying to put some newly conceived opinion of himself to the
test. The boys at the very top were more or less unchallenged.
Those at the very bottom were likewise immune so long as
they accepted the humiliations and insults which were their
daily lot. But for a boy lodged precariously in the middle
ranks, life was a tornado of fists and faces, the faces he was

10 Nathaniel Cantor, "Crime—a Political Problem," *Ideas for Action,*
1:51, 1946.
11 James S. Plant, "Social Significance of War Impact on Adolescents,"
The Annals of the American Academy of Political and Social Science, 236:3,
1944.

out to damage on his way up or the fists that were hammering him down to the nightmarish, infra-human realm. . . .[12]

That status-consciousness and the struggle for status in terms of social class are preoccupations of American adolescents as well as adults can clearly be seen in the findings of Hollingshead's study of the teen-agers of a midwestern community.[13] One conclusion concerning the relationship between status-striving and delinquency is that, despite apparent fluctuations in delinquency rates over the years, there are three basic factors underlying American social structure which are constantly conducive to delinquency: (a) inequality in status, (b) competition in school, on the playground, in the community, and for a living; and (c) aggressive individualism.[14]

3. PECUNIARY AND MATERIAL WEALTH.   Money and material wealth are American values so close to success, status, and power that it would seem unnecessary to consider them separately. Success and status have been translated into monetary and materialistic terms. It is often not what a person is that matters, but what he has. The more he has, the greater must be his effort to demonstrate to others how much he has; the less he has, the greater must be his effort to accumulate, by illegal if not by legitimate methods.

In a large measure, however, one may say that money and material goods have been consecrated as values in themselves. It can effectively be held, say many sociologists, that the ideology of pecuniary success best characterizes the basic motivation that spurs Americans to activity and provides them with a sense of significance in their lives. The dollar is dominant if not almighty, so that the desirability of having it and spending it often leads to a minimization of regard for its source, even when other values such as honesty are accordingly sacrificed.

[12] William Poster, " 'Twas a Dark Night in Brownsville," *Commentary*, 9:464, May 1950.
[13] August B. Hollingshead, *Elmtown's Youth: the Impact of Social Classes on Adolescents*, New York, Wiley, 1949.
[14] Louise McGuire, "Social-Work Basis for Prevention and Treatment of Delinquency and Crime; Community Factors," *Proceedings of the National Conference of Social Work*, 1936, pp. 579–89.

The extent to which these values are enmeshed in the lives of delinquents can roughly be measured by the high proportion of known juvenile offenses which are concerned with the illegal accumulation and possession of money and other wealth.

4. RESISTANCE TO AUTHORITY. Whatever one prefers to call it —independence, individuality, nonconformity, freedom—there is in American culture a value that pivots about resistance to authority. Americans tend to resist too many rules and regulations. In contrast to the Hindus, for example, who are intrigued by rules and "red tape," Americans prefer to be free from the control of too many societal norms, and exalt "rugged individualism." The end result in America is a high incidence of nonconformity as expressed in rates of delinquency and crime.[15]

Some historians trace American resistance to authority back to Plymouth Colony, the Boston Tea Party, the Whisky Rebellion, the Abolition movement, the industrial robber barons, straight down to the contemporary phenomena of gangsterism and racketeering. Others, like Frederick Jackson Turner, have seen its origin in the American frontier, a moving, not a fixed, line in American history. Turner was certainly not the first student to note the significance of the frontier in American culture. But it was he who made the frontier central to an interpretation of the American way of life, and who founded a school of frontier interpreters.[16] Today there is little left of the frontier as a physical fact; that is, as a part of continuous land-mass through which the American people can move and which is theirs to develop. But the interpretation is that in a psychological and cultural sense the frontier still operates in such characteristics as the resistance to authority.

Complete subservience to authority in America, in the form of literal observance of *all* laws or other social norms and rules, is subject to ridicule on both juvenile and adult levels. This is nicely portrayed in the popular cartoon whose central character is Caspar Milquetoast. Tufts [17] has suggested that it has become

[15] Bernard, *op. cit.*, pp. 470–3.

[16] See the famous essay of 1893, Frederick Jackson Turner, "The Significance of the Frontier in American History," in Henry Steele Commager, ed., *Living Ideas in America*, New York, Harper, 1951, pp. 73–80.

[17] James Hayden Tufts, *America's Social Morality*, New York, Holt, 1933, pp. 220–1.

a quasi-religious and patriotic duty among Americans to resist restraints placed upon free adventuring. The hostility shared by many Americans against police personnel—the negative connotation of the term "cop" is a supporting point—is largely an expression of resistance to authority, as are many of the attacks on concentration of political power and against centralization of government functions and "controls." We are told that one of the chief goals of adolescents is emancipation, especially from the authority of the family. Achievement of this goal is a long and hard psychic struggle, frequently expressed in deviant behavior such as delinquency.[18]

5. TOUGHNESS. Another American value that appears to be significant for the etiology of delinquency, especially as it appears in the personality make-up of juvenile males, is "toughness." Its importance in the world of boys can hardly be overestimated. "Boys in all the lower-class New York neighborhoods took pride in their toughness," recalls one writer of his boyhood, "but in Brownsville, somehow, we worked at it full time." [19]

Although there is undoubtedly a social class differential in this respect, in most strata of American society an inordinate pressure is placed on boys, from their earliest years, regarding the necessity of "fighting back" and "not being a sissy." Boys are generally taught to use physical violence when the occasion calls for it, as in self-defense. They are frequently ridiculed for any display of sensitivity. Lerner [20] has noted that even when the family does not convey the desirability of toughness to the child, the boy acquires it from all about him. American culture is permeated with the violence of interpersonal relations. Movies carry it as a theme to the point where many children no longer consider a movie a good one unless it has several deaths in it. Crime and gangster programs on the radio and television have it. Pulp magazines have it, and so do the comic strips with their superhuman—and therefore "dehumanized" achievements. The business mentality often has it, setting itself against anything that does not "pay off" in the toughest terms.

[18] Peter Blos, *The Adolescent Personality*, New York, Appleton-Century, 1941, p. 175.
[19] Poster, *op. cit.*, p. 459.
[20] Max Lerner, *PM*, September 17, 1947, p. 12.

6. DUPERY.   In his own struggle for power and success, Phineas T. Barnum, the famous American showman, provided many of his fellow Americans with a supporting slogan in achieving similar goals: "There's a sucker born every minute." The "truth" and "worthwhileness" of these words, and of others such as: "Do others in before they do you in," and: "Everything is a racket," have made an unofficial value of dupery, which, as we shall see below, is known and adopted by a considerable segment of the juvenile population. Its significance in connection with delinquency is theoretically far greater than most adults are willing to concede.[21]

Dupery, as Williams points out,[22] seems to operate in situations where an official or "publicly accepted norm" such as honesty is covertly violated on a large scale, with the tacit acceptance or even approval of the same society or group, at least as long as violation is concealed. Dupery in such case is an alternative norm that is being observed, of different cultural value than the ideal, official value that is being evaded.

One of the most convincing investigations of the extent of adult dupery in recent times was a nationwide study by a man and woman on tour of garages, radio repair shops, and watch repair shops. They utilized a simple experimental method in each case. Before driving in to the garages, they disconnected a coil wire. Of the 347 garages in all 48 states, 129 noted the wire immediately and informed the investigators, either charging them nothing or only a nominal fee. The others, 63 per cent of the total, treated the investigators as "suckers," overcharging them, lying, inserting unnecessary work, or charging them for work not done, for new parts not needed, and for parts not installed.

For the purpose of testing the radio repair shops, the investigators loosened a tube or disconnected a wire in a new radio. Of the 304 shops tested throughout the country, 109 honestly identified the obvious trouble, repaired it and either made no charge or merely a token charge. The remaining shops, constituting a majority of the sample, tried to cheat the investigators by selling

---

[21] One of the earliest and most important episodes that helped establish dupery as an unofficial American value concerned the so-called "Cardiff Giant." For an excellent popular account of this episode, see Alan Hynd, "The Original Cardiff Giant," *True*, 28:41, 71–8, 1951.

[22] Williams, *op. cit.*, p. 354.

them tubes, batteries, and service the radio set did not need, or by charging them for new parts they did not insert. In some cases they even removed good parts in the radio and added them to the supply on their shelves, substituting inferior equipment.

The watchmakers were the most honest of all. The test here was made by loosening the little screw that fastens the winding wheel in the watch. Of the 462 watch repair men investigated throughout the nation, only 49 per cent lied, overcharged, gave false diagnoses, or suggested expensive and unnecessary repairs, whereas 51 per cent were honest, only eight of them charging anything at all.[23]

7. OTHER CHARACTERISTICS OF AMERICAN CULTURE CONDUCIVE TO DELINQUENCY. Although the analysis of selected American values provides a meaningful approach to the relationship among American society, culture, and delinquency, there are other features of the American way of life which should also be mentioned in this context.

a. *American culture is dynamic.* Change, the fact that cultural forms in a new society such as the American are fluid, gives a high degree of mobility to behavior patterns. American children are sensitive to the superficiality in many areas of life regarding "right" versus "wrong" behavior. The same children brought up in other cultures where change is slow and the "right" ways have become firmly fixed in tradition would be less prone to deviant behavior.

b. *American culture offers alternative norms.* A society as complex as is the American finds that alternatives to the "right" way of behavior as defined in delinquency law are not necessarily the "wrong" ways of behavior in the culture of its various subgroups. American society is, in a sense, a mosaic of various ethnic, economic, and regional groups whose conceptions of conformity and deviant behavior by children are occasionally at variance with the legal definitions of such behavior.

c. *Social relationships in American society have become increasingly impersonal.* The shift of American society from predominantly rural to urban community structures has meant,

---

[23] See *Reader's Digest*, July, August, and September, 1941. A summary of the investigation appears in John R. Ellingston, *Protecting Our Children from Criminal Careers*, New York, Prentice-Hall, 1948, pp. 20–2.

among other things, the decline of face-to-face relations as a form
of social control and the rise of what the sociologist calls
"anomie"; that is, impersonal relations. A very widespread hunch
held by sociologists is that this shift from primary to secondary
groupings in American community life has encouraged an increase in delinquency and crime. City life, it is maintained, does
not provide the restraints on personal behavior formerly provided by the rural social structure.

d. *A multi-group society fosters a duality of loyalty and
ethics.* An interesting hypothesis proposed by Taft [24] is that the
various subgroups of American society retain intense feelings of
ethnocentrism which lead them to have one code of ethics in their
relations with the in-group and another code in their relations
with the out-group. Children of one religious group, for example,
have no hesitation about desecrating the church buildings and
cemeteries of the out-group, whereas such behavior never applies
to the buildings and cemeteries of their in-group.

Adult Source of Juvenile Values and Other Cultural Characteristics

Juveniles acquire both official and unofficial values (whether
or not they are related to delinquency) from two general sources:
adults and their peers. But ultimately the source is the adult.
Some of the values children acquire are communitywide. Others
are characteristic of segments such as a particular social class or
ethnic group in the community.

A prominent theory among sociologists is that in every society one or more subgroups take the lead in diffusing their
values throughout the society. In American society, the most effective group in this respect is believed to be the middle classes.
Their preachers, teachers, journalists, and governmental spokesmen advocate the official values commonly prescribed in the
Protestant version of the Judaeo-Christian tradition.

There is also reason to believe that in large part the unofficial
values children acquire have an adult middle-class origin. This
is strongly suggested by the fact that many juvenile offenders say
without hesitation that they do not consider their delinquencies
to differ from the "white collar" crimes of many politicians, busi-

[24] *Op. cit.*, pp. 229–37.

nessmen, and professional groups. Social-psychological experimentation also shows that children frequently do not distinguish between such crimes and their own juvenile offenses.[25]

Aside from the example of law violation, adults may provide juveniles with a delinquency-provoking value pattern in their attitude that laws dealing with intoxication, taxes, gambling, and traffic may be violated, providing the violation is to one's interest and one can "get away" with it. This stems out of the competitive economic system in the world of adults. The system has provided not only the rewards and goals to be achieved by crime, but also patterns for criminal methods and organization. The tendency in business has been toward the organization of larger and larger economic units and the elimination of competition through stifling of competitors. In the same way, adult professional crime tends to be organized on a monopolistic basis, locally as well as nationally.

It is estimated that every 24 hours in the United States adults commit approximately 36 murders, 730 robberies, and 4,200 burglaries. Much of this is organized crime. The Kefauver Investigating Committee reported at mid-century [26] that organized crime was firmly entrenched throughout the country in the operation of gambling as well as such rackets as narcotics, prostitution, labor and business racketeering, black marketing, etc. Although arrests had been made and criminal reputations were documented, the leaders in syndicated crime throughout the country, according to the investigating committee, remain, for the most part, immune from prosecution and punishment. This can be ascribed to what is popularly called the "fix," the direct payment of money to law-enforcement officials on some occasions. On other occasions the "fix" involves the acquisition of political power by contributions to political organizations or by the creation of economic ties with apparently respectable and reputable businessmen and lawyers, and the purchase of public good will through charitable contributions and press relations. The Ke-

[25] Marshall B. Clinard, "Secondary Community Influences and Juvenile Delinquency," *The Annals of the American Academy of Political and Social Science*, 261:51–2, 1949.

[26] *Third Interim Report of the Special Committee to Investigate Organized Crime in Interstate Commerce*, 82nd Congress, Senate Report No. 307, U.S. Government Printing Office, 1951, pp. 1–2.

fauver Committee also found evidence of the infiltration by organized criminals into legitimate business such as the sale and distribution of liquor, real-estate operations, night clubs, hotels, automobile agencies, restaurants, taverns, cigarette-vending companies, juke-box concerns, laundries, the manufacture of clothing, and the transmission of racing and sports news. In some of these areas evidence was found of the use of the same methods of intimidation and violence as are used to secure monopolies in organized crime.[27]

That the structure of adult organized crime is patterned after the organization of business is to be seen in their parallel development over the years. Many years ago the unit of organized crime was a local gang whose activities were obviously predatory, specializing in such specific types of crime as payroll or bank robbery, loft or safe burglary, and pocket picking. During Prohibition new types of criminal organization and activity emerged. The development of transportation and communication in modern times made possible more extensive and more powerful organization. Organized crime took on new characteristics, so that today criminal syndicates cover a much greater territory and engage in a variety of rackets rather than specializing in one type of predatory crime. The modern criminal organization bases its success on monopoly, the guarantee of large profits. The syndicate relies on violence and murder to eliminate competitors, compel co-operation from reluctant victims, silence informers, and enforce its edicts.[28]

It would be a serious error to convey the impression that organized crime is the only adult model for juvenile delinquency. Some surveys intimate, for example, that "amateur" lawbreakers carry off more loot every year than do all of the nation's professionals. Department stores report that their customers and clerks are so dishonest that they have to make price adjustments to allow for the thousands of dollars they lose annually.

One may still doubt that juveniles actually receive and act to any great extent on the values and behavior-models of adults, no matter how reasonable the theoretical conjectures above, and despite the observation that clinical evidence of children's detection of implicit linguistic paradigms suggests that they may

[27] *Ibid.*, p. 5.   [28] *Ibid.*, pp. 144–5.

also be engaged in detecting and acting upon the implicit paradigms of cultural evaluation. Possibly the demand for direct
evidence on this question can be met by the following representative data:

1. Radke and Trager's research on young children sought to
determine the extent to which they are aware of social differences
based on race. Tests employing dolls and interviews were applied
to 242 children (152 white and 90 Negro) in kindergarten, first,
and second grades in six Philadelphia public schools. The subjects
were given different types of clothing and houses and asked to
assign them to dolls representing Negro and white men and
women. Among other findings, the great majority of both Negro
and white children gave the white dolls good housing and the
Negro dolls poor housing. *These responses of the children clearly
indicated that they had acquired the value system of the adult
culture.*[29]

2. In a junior high school publication a cartoon once appeared consisting of these four parts:

a. A traffic policeman is shown stopping a woman driver of
an automobile. She protests in these words: "I had the right of
way when this man ran into me, yet you say I was to blame."

b. Same policeman and same woman. The policeman says:
"You certainly were to blame."

c. Same personnel and car. The woman asks: "Why?"

d. Same scene. The policeman says: "Because his father's
the mayor, his brother's the chief of police, and I'm engaged to
his sister."

*The theme involved here—namely, that personal influence
supersedes justice—is obviously derived from adult sources.*[30]

3. Frederic Thrasher, author of the classic work *The Gang*,
once told a conference of social workers about the amazing
amount of knowledge the gang boys of Chicago had of corrupt
politics. One of his gang informants, for example, had told him of
his ambition to become a criminal lawyer. When the boy was
asked what he would do if he were a criminal lawyer he replied

[29] Marian J. Radke and Helen G. Trager, "Children's Perception of
the Social Roles of Negroes and Whites," *Journal of Psychology*, 29:3–33,
1950.

[30] Henry W. Thurston, *Concerning Juvenile Delinquency*, New York,
Columbia University Press, 1942, pp. 215 ff.

that he would go to the judge's house at night.[31] *The boy apparently had learned well the unofficial adult maxim that "it isn't what you know, but whom you know!"*

4. A well-known juvenile-court judge in a report he made on juvenile courts and probation noted that some of the boys who came to his court asked him, among other things, why children could not play for money as long as politicians stuffed the ballot box, and how much money each alderman was to profit for purchasing a certain site for a public building.[32] *The boys had come to the conclusion, like adults, that "everything is a racket."*

The Conflict of Values

A provocative theory posed by social scientists is that because of the greater degree of cultural homogeneity in primitive and peasant societies, in contrast to the complexity and heterogeneity in American society, there is very little contrast and conflict in values. Accordingly, the so-called simple societies have relatively little problem behavior. The child growing up in such societies does not face the American dilemma of having to choose between official and unofficial values.[33]

It is conceivable, of course, that the culture of a large-scale society could be so well integrated that, as Williams suggests, its basic normative patterns would remain stable for long periods of time and deviations from conformity to the norms would be slight and infrequent. In actual fact, however, no large-scale society is known where such integration exists. Every modern, complex society has a culture containing conflicts and inconsistencies.[34] Thus it is understandable that in Middletown the Lynds

[31] *Proceedings of the New York Conference of Social Work*, Rochester, N.Y., November 1928, p. 231.

[32] Thurston, *op. cit.*, pp. 215 ff.

[33] See, for example, Louis Wirth, "Culture Conflict and Delinquency," *Social Forces*, 9:484–92, 1931; Miriam Van Waters, *Youth in Conflict*, New York, Republic, 1925, pp. 124–5; John Levy, "Conflicts of Cultures and Children's Maladjustment," *Mental Hygiene*, 17:41–50, 1933; Mary J. Shaw, "Social Valuation," in *Man and Society*, edited by Emerson P. Schmidt, New York, Prentice-Hall, 1937, pp. 762–4.

[34] Williams, *op. cit.*, p. 349. Elsewhere Williams points out that "even within a relatively unified and stable culture there is some normative variability because of the *generalized nature of norms* vis-à-vis the specific situations of action, because of the *causal role of non-normative conditions* and because of *individual differences in perception and interpretation*. It is

found that allowances had to be made in the reconciliation of its values clustering around "forcefulness," "enterprise," "shrewdness," and "power," and of those associated with "kindness," "friendliness," and "considerateness." [35] In the United States as a whole, competing definitions of proper conduct in the same situation are such that there is relatively little agreement on the rightness or wrongness of premarital sex relations, industrial strikes, price control, and poll taxes. Even American norms usually thought of as dominant have had to compete with alternative norms, resulting in established or patterned modes of evasion as far as the former are concerned.

For example, prohibition had to compete with the bootlegging and speakeasy industry prior to the repeal of the Eighteenth Amendment. Perennially impersonal, disinterested governmental services clash with political graft, the "fix," and "status justice"; there are, on the one hand, family mores, and on the other, prostitution; in academic life, "cribbing" is in conflict with classroom honesty; in employment one finds promotion by technical competence threatened by nepotism and racial discrimination; in the courts universalistic legal justice faces bias in jury selection; the legal rules regarding divorce are opposed by the illegality of collusion and the "alimony racket"; professional codes confront such practices as fee-splitting among doctors and ambulance-chasing among lawyers; and ethical concepts of truth are contradicted by some advertising and financial transactions.[36]

When we observe specifically the values of American children we find not only that they conflict frequently with those of teachers and legislators, thus leading them to delinquency, but that the child's own multiple group identification (with his family, religious denomination, nationality, social class, etc.) internalizes within him alternative, conflicting values for given situations.[37] If the child is pulled in one direction by one value

---

a fact that in many instances nominally accepted norms are too difficult or stringent for full conformity." *Ibid.*, p. 352.

[35] Lynd, *op. cit.*, pp. 423–4.

[36] Williams, *op. cit.*, p. 357.

[37] See Read Bain, "Our Schizoid Culture," *Sociology and Social Research*, 19:266–76, 1935; Edward Sapir, "Culture—Genuine and Spurious," *American Journal of Sociology*, 29:401–29, 1924; Thorsten Sellin, *Culture Conflict and Crime*, New York, Social Science Research Council Bulletin

and in another direction by a contrasting value, presumably one would have an explanation as to why children who are dishonest in one situation are honest in another. Another possibility is that, contrary to this version of a child torn between the Scylla of one value and the Charybdis of another, the two values involved are compartmentalized in the child's personality. Perhaps the problem of inconsistent values is of little importance to the child because of the intellectual grasp of one value and the emotional hold of the other. Healy and Bronner [38] at one time observed that the delinquent is often fully capable of expressing his conscious *belief* that his delinquency is "wrong," whereas his *feeling* about rightness and wrongness may be quite different.

It is conceivable too that the delinquent's values may be logically inconsistent to the observer but not to the delinquent himself, whose rationalizations dissipate any such apparent inconsistency. The values of a delinquent, seemingly inconsistent, may actually be consistent in that one value applies to one situation and another applies to a different situation. It would be worthwhile to find out how common is the experience of one graduate of England's famous Borstal System who pointed out biographically in later years that "Borstal to some extent revived the school-boy values of fair play and team spirit but their application remained limited to play and teams. Crime . . . remained as attractive as ever. . . ." [39]

Value Differentials between Delinquents and Nondelinquents

It would seem reasonable, on the basis of the discussion above, that empirical research comparing the values of delinquents and control groups would yield significant differentials. There has been this kind of research, utilizing the subject's replies to such questions as: "What makes a good citizen?" and: "If you had one hundred dollars, how would you spend it?" along with his responses to tests of ethical knowledge. But for the most part

No. 41, 1938; Milton L. Barron, "Juvenile Delinquency and American Values," *American Sociological Review*, 16:208–16, 1951.

[38] *New Light on Delinquency and Its Treatment*, New Haven, Yale University Press, 1936, p. 11.

[39] Mark Benney, *Angels in Undress*, New York, Random House, 1937, p. 216.

these have revealed either insignificant or contradictory evidence of value differentials between the compared groups.[40]

This need not be interpreted as conclusive evidence that the values approach to delinquency is fruitless. *For if a distinction is made between values which are social processes or norms on the one hand, and those which are social objectives or goals on the other hand, a clue is available to account for the insignificant and contradictory results in studies of value differentials between delinquents and nondelinquents.* It is quite possible that failure to make the distinction has beclouded the likelihood that the *value-goals of delinquents and nondelinquents are essentially the same, whereas their value-norms or processes differ.*

Goals or objectives and norms or processes are analytically separable. People aspire for goals, while norms are the regulative, socially appropriate means of reaching out for the goals. Norms that society establishes are not necessarily efficient, so that many procedures which from the standpoint of particular individuals would be most efficient in securing desired goals—like the exercise of force or fraud—are ruled out of the area of approved conduct. But at the same time American culture is goal-centered. The emphasis on success, power, status, wealth, and prestige tends to bring on comparatively little concern with the approved or prescribed norms for striving toward these goals. The stress becomes so intense that, at the extreme, behavior tends to escape from normative regulation. *In short, many children in American society center their emotional convictions heavily upon objectives, with far less emotional support for the prescribed processes of reaching out for them. Given such a differential emphasis upon goals on the one hand and norms on the other, the latter become so weakened as to lead to the behavior of children being limited solely by considerations of efficiency. The result is delinquency.*[41]

We turn in the next chapter to the last major aspect of etiol-

[40] See, for example, James M. Reinhardt and Fowler V. Harper, "Social and Ethical Judgments of Two Groups of Boys—Delinquents and Non-Delinquents," *Journal of Criminal Law and Criminology*, 21:364–78, 1930; George E. Hill, "The Ethical Knowledge of Delinquent and Non-Delinquent Boys," *The Journal of Social Psychology*, 6:107–14, 1935; Edward Bartlett and Dale B. Harris, "Personality Factors in Delinquency," *School and Society*, 43:653–6, 1936.

[41] See Merton, *op. cit.*, pp. 126–9; Williams, *op. cit.*, p. 353.

ogy in juvenile delinquency, the impact of spatial and chronological distribution on American children. This will involve a consideration of the relationship between ecology and age status and the problem of delinquency.

QUESTIONS AND RESEARCH SUGGESTIONS

1. *What do the detractors of the theory of the "juvenile in delinquent society" say about it?*
2. *Define the difference between official and unofficial values.*
3. *What is meant by an implicit paradigm? Give an example other than the one presented in this chapter.*
4. *Dupery has been identified as an unofficial value but not explicitly defined in this chapter. How would you define it?*
5. *Give some examples of duality of ethics.*
6. *How can one explain why children are dishonest in one situation and honest in another?*
7. *Does empirical research comparing the values of delinquents and control groups yield significant differentials?*

SELECTED READINGS AND REFERENCES

Barron, Milton L., "Juvenile Delinquency and American Values," *American Sociological Review,* 16:208–16, 1951.

Hollingshead, August B., *Elmtown's Youth: the Impact of Social Classes on Adolescents,* New York, Wiley, 1949.

Levy, John, "Conflicts of Cultures and Children's Maladjustment," *Mental Hygiene,* 17:41–50, 1933.

Lynd, Robert S. and Helen M. Lynd, *Middletown in Transition,* New York, Harcourt, Brace, 1937, pp, 403–19.

Plant, James S., "Social Significance of War Impact on Adolescents," *The Annals of the American Academy of Political and Social Science,* 236:1–7, 1944.

Ploscowe, Morris, "Crime in a Competitive Society," *The Annals of the American Academy of Political and Social Science,* 217:105–11, 1941.

Sellin, Thorsten, *Culture Conflict and Crime,* New York, Social Science Research Council, Bulletin No. 41, 1938.

Shaw, Mary J., "Social Valuation," in *Man and Society,* ed. by Emerson P. Schmidt, New York, Prentice-Hall, 1937.

Taft, Donald R., *Criminology*, New York, Macmillan, rev. ed., 1950, pp. 226–46.

Tufts, James Hayden, *America's Social Morality*, New York, Holt, 1933.

Williams, Robin, Jr., *American Society: a Sociological Interpretation*, New York, Knopf, 1951.

Wirth, Louis, "Culture Conflict and Delinquency," *Social Forces*, 9:484–92, 1931.

Chapter **XIII.** *Ecological and Chronological Factors*

The community in question is adjacent to a center of heavy industry located along one of the branches of the Chicago River—a drab, unattractive and deteriorated community. It is a community of immigrant settlement with the physical characteristics common to the so-called "blighted" or "slum" areas.

For the most part the dwellings are old and dilapidated structures accommodating two or more families. The presence of a large number of old deteriorated buildings provides an appropriate situation for the practice of junking, which is one of the most common initial forms of delinquency in which boys in this neighborhood engage. This practice consists of stealing iron, lead pipes, and lumber from vacant buildings and disposing of them to junk dealers or to residents of the community.

The community is in a process of transition and deterioration, from residential to industrial usage of land. There has been a migration of many families out of the community as they have prospered sufficiently to be able to pay higher rentals in communities of higher economic status. The obvious physical deterioration is suggestive of the low economic status of the population residing in this community. Rates of unemployment, poverty, and economic dependency have been relatively high for many years.

The universally low economic status of the families in this community stands in sharp contrast to the standards of living which are maintained in a large proportion of the communities in the city. In general the families of this community are seriously handicapped in providing for their children the educational opportunity for successful achievement in business and the professions in the highly competitive world outside the community. In this situation, however, they are exposed to the luxury standards of life which are generally idealized in our culture but which are beyond their attainment. They observe older persons in their community who have acquired money and personal prestige in business, in the professions, in politics, or in crime and the rackets. To many of them the fact that they cannot possess the things which they see others enjoy does not nullify their eagerness and determination to secure these things—even by illegitimate means when such means have the support and sanction of the groups to which they belong.

The children living in this community are exposed to a variety of interests, forms of behavior, and stimulations, rather than to a relatively consistent pattern of conventional standards and values. In this community situation, with its confusion of standards, there is more than one type of moral instruction and education available to the child. The diversification and inconsistencies in the patterns of life in this community appear in many forms. There is, in the first place, the disparity of interests, standards, and philosophy of life as between parents and children. For the most part the parents were born in Europe and their attitudes and interests reflect their Old World background. The children, on the other hand, were born in Chicago and their attitudes and interests stand in sharp contrast to those of the older generation. In this situation the parents are often helpless in their efforts to instil into their children the values which to them seem essential to a normal, stable life. Conflicts arise with regard to a wide range of matters pertaining to family life, employment, leisure-time activities, school attendance, and delinquency. To enforce conformity the parents often resort to severe corporal punishment. In the absence of effective community sentiments in support of the wishes of the parents, the severe punishment often has the effect of further alienating the child from the parents.[1]

No analysis of the etiology of delinquency would be complete without considering the influences of ecology and chronology on American juveniles. Few adult laymen disclaim that they themselves are in part a product of their status in the spatial and chronological senses of the term. This could hardly be different in the case of children. Social science makes considerable allowance for the influence of these factors, the testimony of which is the considerable body of data social scientists have systematically gathered about them.

The reason for examining ecology and chronology last in Part Two of this book is that to a certain extent they synthesize and integrate several of the other causal factors taken up in the previous chapters. This becomes evident in the discussion that follows.

The Theory of Ecology

Ecology is the study of the spatial relations existing between organisms, and between organisms and their environment. The assumption in ecology is that there are meaningful patterns in such spatial relationships. Originally developed in the study of plants and animals, ecology was adapted to the study of human life in the nineteenth century. Most of the concepts of ecology—

[1] Clifford R. Shaw, editor, *Brothers in Crime*, Chicago, University of Chicago Press, 1938, pp. 98–103.

such as symbiosis, competition, invasion, succession, and segregation—are familiar tools of the student of sociology and of several of the related social sciences.

One of the fundamental theories of human ecology is that such social problems as juvenile delinquency appear in a pattern of scatter and concentration in space. This pattern is not a product of chance; there are underlying reasons for disproportionate concentrations of delinquents in some areas of a community while only scattered cases are found elsewhere. These underlying reasons are frequently—and erroneously—thought to be spatial and physical characteristics *per se;* that is, the elevation of the land and the type of dwelling determine whether or not the child becomes delinquent.[2] The recurrent call for slum clearance as the solution of the problem demonstrates how popular this erroneous conception is. Adherents of this physically deterministic view fail to understand that professional ecologists do not attribute causation to physical and spatial factors but to related factors that are distributed in spatially similar patterns. It is not the objective space or physical structure of the area that makes a child delinquent. More important are the sociological and psychological traits of the people who dwell there. Objective features are merely symbolic of these more important traits.

The Methods of Ecology

The methods of ecologists who study delinquency are basically the same. Shaw and McKay's studies in Chicago[3] are the best known of all. Court cases of delinquency were plotted on maps of Chicago, usually according to the delinquent's place of residence but occasionally according to the sites of the offenses. Although this alone brought out patterns of scatter and concen-

[2] Essentially this is an expression of geographical determinism, a school of thought which has long been discredited in accounting for motivation in human behavior.

[3] Clifford R. Shaw and Henry D. McKay, "Correlation of Rate of Juvenile Delinquency with Certain Indices of Community Organization and Disorganization," *Publications of the American Sociological Society*, 22:175, 1928; *Delinquency Areas*, Chicago, University of Chicago Press, 1929; "Social Factors in Juvenile Delinquency," *Report on the Causes of Crime*, Washington, D.C., National Commission on Law Observance and Enforcement, 1931, pp. 60–139; *Juvenile Delinquency and Urban Areas*, Chicago, University of Chicago Press, 1942.

tration throughout the city, Shaw and McKay felt that the patterns would be more accurate if delinquency were portrayed with density of population taken into consideration. Therefore the rate of delinquency per square mile for each one hundred children of the same age and sex was computed and plotted on maps of the city. This was done by drawing radials straight from the center of the city along main thoroughfares and noting the variations per square mile; and drawing concentric circles from the center one mile apart and noting the delinquency rate within each circle.

The Delinquency Area

Studies of this kind gave rise to the concept of the delinquency area; namely, the area (not necessarily the only one in the community) that has a high proportion of delinquency per one hundred male children of ages 10 to 16, let us say, in comparison with other areas of the community. Delinquency areas have been found in residential slums around the central business zone and near heavy industry, not only in the Chicago studies but also in other large urban communities, like Philadelphia, Cleveland, Denver, and Seattle. Shaw and McKay found that delinquency rates tend to vary inversely with distance from the center of the city. They also found that as the older immigrant groups move out of the delinquency areas near the central business zone the rates of delinquency among their children decrease.[4] This "gradient tendency" in the spatial distribution of delinquency is one of the major findings of the Chicago school of ecology.[5]

Ecological Correlates of Delinquency

Another major finding of human ecologists is that delinquency in its spatial distribution is highly correlated with such phenomena of social and personal disorganization as population mobility, substandard housing, family dependency, truancy, tuberculosis, mental disorders, infant mortality, and illegitimate births. This comes out of twenty years of ecological research by

[4] "Social Factors in Juvenile Delinquency," *op. cit.*, pp. 60–139; 140–88.

[5] Walter C. Reckless, *The Etiology of Delinquent and Criminal Behavior*, New York, Social Science Research Council Bulletin No. 50, 1943, p. 33.

Table III *New Haven Residential Areas by Predominant Characteristics*

AREA	PER CENT OF POPULATION	LAND USE	NATIVITY	RELIGION	OCCUPATION	INCOME above or below $1,500	SOCIAL REGISTER 1,002	GRADUATES CLUB 849	WHO'S WHO 179	DELINQUENCY RATE	DEPENDENCY RATE
I	8.7	1-family	American	Protestant	Prof. & Bus. Exec.	Above	559	250	182	Low	Very low
II	2.3	2-fam.	Mixed	Mixed	Office-wkrs. & Dlrs & Prop.	Above	105	81	7	Low	Very low
III	4.0	2-fam.	Foreign-born	Catholic	Artisans & Laborers	Below	—	—	—	Average	Average
IV	7.5	2-fam. & bus.	Foreign-born	Catholic	Laborers	Below	—	—	—	Very high	Very high
V	2.9	2-fam. & bus.	Foreign-born	Catholic	Laborers	Below	—	—	—	High	Very high
VI	8.7	2-fam.	Foreign-born	Catholic	Laborers & Artisans	Below	2	—	—	High	High
VII	5.5	2-fam. & 1-fam.	Mixed	Protestant	Laborers & Artisans	Below	2	1	—	Average	Average
VIII	2.1	Vacant & 1-fam.	Mixed	Catholic	Artisans & Laborers	Below	8	1	—	Average	Average
IX	2.1	Vacant & 2-fam.	Mixed	Catholic	Laborers & Laborers	Below	14	8	1	Low	Average
X	2.3	Vacant & 1-fam.	Mixed	Catholic	Artisans & Office-wkrs.	Below	8	—	1	Average	Average
XI	3.0	2-fam.	Mixed	Catholic	Laborers & Artisans	Below	2	—	—	High	High
XII	18.9	2-fam.	Foreign-born	Catholic	Laborers & Artisans	Below	—	—	—	Very high	Very high
XIII	1.1	Business	Foreign-born	Catholic	Office-wkrs. & Dlrs & Prop.	Above	33	6	5	Low	Low
XIV	2.6	2-fam. & 1-fam.	American	Mixed	Laborers & Artisans	Below	8	1	—	High	High
XV	7.5	2-fam.	Mixed	Mixed	Bus. Exec. & Office-wkrs.	Above	95	22	10	Very low	Very low
XVI	9.9	1-fam.	American	Protestant	Dlrs & Prop. & Office-wkrs.	Above	156	29	9	Very low	Very low
XVII	8.5	2-fam.	Mixed	Mixed	Artisans & Office-wkrs.	Half & Half	8	—	—	Low	Low
XVIII	2.1	2-fam. & 1-fam.	2nd generation	Catholic	Pub. Serv., & Dlrs & Prop.	Below	—	—	—	Very low	High
XIX	0.2	Vacant	2nd gen.	Protestant	Artisans	Below	1	—	1	Low	High
XX	0.3	Vacant & 1-fam.	Mixed	Mixed	Artisans & Laborers	Below	—	—	—	Very low	High
XXI	6.6	2-fam.	Mixed	Catholic	Artisans	Below	—	—	—	Average	High
XXII	1.9	2-fam.	Mixed	Catholic	Artisans, Office-wkrs., & Dlrs & Prop.	Half & Half	10	—	3	Low	Low

Key to Location of Areas:

I. Whitney Ave., Prospect St.
II. Orange St.
III. North of State St.
IV. Grand Ave., E. Chapel St.
V. Chestnut St., East St.
VI. East of Mill River
VII. East of Ferry St.
VIII. Fair Haven
IX. North of Forbes Ave.
X. Lighthouse Point
XI. City Point
XII. Howard, Washington, Davenport, Legion Aves.
XIII. Oak St.
XIV. Howe St., Park St.
XV. Dixwell Ave.
XVI. Outer Edgewood and Whalley Ave.
XVII. Westville
XVIII. Fountain to Whalley Ave.
XIX. Pond Lily
XX. Fitch St.
XXI. Upper Dixwell & Shelton Aves.
XXII. Sheffield St.

Shaw and McKay in 21 American cities.[6] To what extent each correlation is causal it is impossible to say. Caution is obviously necessary. It would be foolish to pose the hypothesis, for example, that tuberculosis causes delinquency. But from the point of view of etiology, there is some significance in the fact that two sets of variables have a high correlation, for either set may be considered as a rough index of the other. The accompanying chart of 22 ecological areas of New Haven, prepared by Maurice R. Davie,[7] is very useful in that it presents a concise picture of some of the outstanding correlations of juvenile delinquency. A comparison of the areas of New Haven which have the highest delinquency rates (areas IV, XIII) with those of the lowest rates (areas XVI, XVII, XIX) brings out radically different correlations in land use, nativity, religious affiliation, occupation and income of parents, dependency and membership in the social register, graduates club, and "Who's Who."

Criticism of Ecology

There are students of delinquency like Robison who doubt that the concept of delinquency area has much validity. Their doubt stems from the inconsistency in reporting cases from various areas of the community. Official registration of delinquency lacks the uniformity in procedure necessary for reliability in spotting cases and thereby constructing area rates.[8] In an earlier chapter it was pointed out, for example, that influential parents more frequently are in a position to deal with their delinquent children without recourse to the police and courts than are less influential parents.

A recent report of the Board of Education in New York City [9] noted other reasons why underprivileged areas yield so large a proportion of delinquents compared with privileged areas. The boy who breaks a store window and whose parents refuse, or are

[6] *Juvenile Delinquency and Urban Areas*, Chicago, University of Chicago Press, 1942.

[7] "The Pattern of Urban Growth," *Studies in the Science of Society*, edited by George Peter Murdock, New Haven, Yale University Press, 1937, pp. 133–61.

[8] Sophia M. Robison, *Can Delinquency Be Measured?* New York, Columbia University Press, 1933, pp. 204–10.

[9] *Juvenile Delinquency and the Schools*, a report of the Assistant Superintendents of the Board of Education, New York City, 1952.

unable, to pay for it, easily acquires the label of a delinquent; the one whose parents pay for it is not. The girl involved in sex difficulties in a lower socio-economic home frequently is identified as a delinquent; the one from a home better able to care for her is not. The child who is emotionally disturbed and commits an "antisocial" act is a delinquent if his family is unable to obtain psychiatric care for him, whereas another child with the same problem who received such help is not a delinquent. Finally, the child in a slum area who becomes a nuisance on the street because of the lack of recreational facilities may be labeled a delinquent, while the child with the same drives and similar behavior in a more privileged area where recreational facilities are available, or where the family can afford special facilities, is not.

On the adult level a serious challenge in recent years to the etiological implications of ecology regarding crime is the concept of "white collar crime." Those who have studied white collar crime are unwilling to accept without reservation the great quantity of research findings which link crime with certain neighborhood characteristics, especially the lower socio-economic status of the population. They suggest, instead, that crime is culturally defined rather than culturally determined. That is, not the fact or frequency of criminality but its form varies from one socio-economic group (and area) to another in the community. There are white collar embezzlers to match burglars, black-marketeers to offset holdup men, and mistresses to parallel prostitutes. Is it not also true that the antisocial behavior of the "respectable" white collar population is more likely to be interpreted as constituting less serious offenses and as deserving milder treatment? Does this not cast doubt on research that claims to measure socio-economic and area differentials in crime?

It is quite likely that among juveniles there is considerable "white collar delinquency" analogous to white collar crime among adults. But juvenile manifestations or equivalents of bribery, price-control evasions, and other white collar offenses do not readily come to the attention of the police. Wattenberg and Balistrieri,[10] two students of the problem, decided that an alternative

[10] William W. Wattenberg and James Balistrieri, "Automobile Theft: a 'Favored-Group' Delinquency," *The American Journal of Sociology*, 57: 569–74, 1952.

would be to search for some type of offense which departs from
the usual high correlation with socio-economic and ecological
variables; which is sufficiently common and widespread so that
it is not peculiar to a single neighborhood; and (to avoid argument as to its antisocial quality) which is clearly illegal and
generally condemned. In a study in Detroit, they found such an
offense to be theft of automobiles. The police records of 1,170
boys, all of whom had passed their seventeenth birthday, showed
that during the period when they had been ten to sixteen years
of age automobile thefts were proportionately heavier among
boys of West European derivation than among those of Eastern
European parentage, and proportionately three times as frequent
among whites as among Negroes. Comparison of 230 white boys
charged with automobile thefts and 2,544 others known by the
Detroit police in 1948 demonstrated clearly that the former came
from relatively more favored neighborhoods.

One can agree with the critics of ecology to this extent: as
yet no procedure is available to compute the true volume of delinquency in any area. This will continue to be the situation as
long as the incidence of reported cases is determined in part by
the informal, unofficial factors that were discussed in Chapter III
in connection with the limitations of delinquency statistics. A reasonable conclusion is that "spatial studies which plot incidence
and compute areas therefrom reflect the influence of differential
registration of cases as well as the undermining and selective influence of an area." [11]

Age Status

The implications of the juvenile's position chronologically are
at least as important as his position spatially. A conviction that
emerges from the comparative, cross-cultural study of different
societies is that age-status is a crucial factor in accounting for the
high rate of delinquency in American society, as contrasted to the
minimum incidence of problem behavior in other societies, especially primitive societies.

In primitive societies age grading is usually clean-cut and consistent. Each person belongs to a distinctive age group. His or her
admission into and exit from a given age group are marked by

[11] Reckless, *op. cit.*, p. 34.

definite ceremonial rites. The rights and duties, and the behavior appropriate to membership in the group are explicit. In American society, too, there is age grading as far as the child is concerned, but except for the formality and clarity that characterize age grading in the school system, the child's age group is marked by informality, lack of ceremonial observance, and inconsistency.[12]

Being a child in most primitive societies is a quite different matter from the comparable experience of most American children. In a primitive society the rate of social change is so slow that it is almost unnoticeable from one generation to the next There the individual child's conceptions of himself and others are likely to be virtually the same as those of his predecessors and successors. His conception of himself as a boy dissolves into his conception of himself as a young man, then a mature adult and finally an elder. There is an unfolding, an emergence of his self-image. It is not necessary from time to time for the primitive child to reverse his notions of what a man is and should be, and how he ought to feel. The child can anticipate what he will become as he grows older and can depend on his anticipation. He has a clear picture of what his age status is and what it will be eventually.[13] In American society, on the other hand, the status of the child has clearly been in flux ever since Colonial days. At that time the child's status and his conception of himself were clearly and consistently that of a subordinate. The discipline of the superordinate parents and teachers was rigid, explicitly supported by Colonial law. But since then American society has witnessed a revolutionary change in the status of children. More and more they are considered in terms of equality with older members of the family, largely as a result of the changing arithmetic of reproduction, the influence of American ideology (especially its humanitarian, scientific, and democratic components), and changes in the structure and function of the family.[14]

Delinquency may be viewed as a concomitant of this revolution, for the child as yet has merely a vague conception of his

[12] James H. S. Bossard, *The Sociology of Child Development*, New York, Harper, 1948, p. 316.
[13] J. D. M. Griffin, "Mental Health and National Security," *Social Work in the Current Scene*, National Conference of Social Work, New York, Columbia University Press, 1950, p. 27.
[14] Bossard, *op. cit.*, pp. 661–2.

duties and obligations in the new society. Adults have failed to encourage his participation in sharing the responsibilities that accompany equality. Keeping him half-child and giving him half-adulthood results frequently in deviant behavior such as delinquency.[15]

Witness the problem in America which grows out of the difference between the physical passage from childhood to maturity and the social transfer of the child to the status of an adult. There is reported to be no such problem in primitive societies that ritualize (*rites de passage*) the outstanding landmarks of age transition in the course of the individual's life. In American society such rites are either lacking or practically meaningless.[16] Add to this the prolonged and compulsory school attendance of most American children, and one has a situation in which young people retain the legal status of juveniles after they have become adults biologically and in other respects.[17]

Perhaps this may explain why puberty and adolescence, the extreme end of the spectrum of childhood, are practically synonymous with crisis, uncertainty, and revolt in American society but not in primitive societies. Aside from delinquency, the "zoot-suit" fad among male adolescents, particularly in a few minority groups of low socio-economic status, is a good case in point for some sociologists and psychiatrists. Their interpretations may be summarized as follows:

1. The desire for bizarre clothes is to be expected in adolescence, given its conditions of inadequacy and insecurity. The zoot suit is merely part of the succession of adolescent fads in clothes and appearance which have included gaudy socks, bright-colored shirts, tilted hats, sweatshirts painted with comic-strip characters and zany phrases, and distinctive haircuts.

[15] Marshall B. Clinard, "Secondary Community Influences and Juvenile Delinquency," *The Annals of the American Academy of Political and Social Science*, 261:53, 1949.

[16] The American Jewish *bar-mitzvah* at the age of thirteen for the male child is an excellent illustration of this point. Originally designed to ritualize the transition of the child from childhood to responsible adulthood, it now has other functions. The memorized *bar-mitzvah* speech, with its introductory words, "Today I am a man," is a functionless vestige of older days.

[17] Bossard, *op. cit.*, p. 317.

2. Adolescents crave attention, and the zoot suit meets this need. Few things attract attention so much as an unusual cut of clothes. The adolescent who wears a zoot suit is assuming a basically adult pattern of clothing and giving it an exaggerated twist, for the zoot suit is really an extreme expression of the English drape.

3. In underprivileged areas, and particularly among minority groups, the zoot suit is a badge of defiance by the rejected against the "outside" world and at the same time a symbol of membership in a group. It is simultaneously a symbol of rebellion and a symbol of conformity. It carries prestige.

Regardless of the merit of these interpretations, it is self-evident that older juveniles in America are confused. A large proportion of them have no clear occupational goals or interests. They are without motivation or responsibility with regard to the general welfare of society. They are in many cases too young for employment and too old for school. Much of the problem of juvenile delinquency can be understood within this framework of the ambiguous age-status of the juvenile in America.[18]

This concludes Part Two, which has dealt exclusively with the etiology of delinquency. The effort here has been to avoid, at one extreme, a desiccated, encyclopedic review of the range of thought and research about delinquency causation, and at the other extreme an unwarranted commitment to one "pet" theory. The pattern followed is easily detected. In general, the earlier chapters covered the older, particularistic approaches and theories; the last two chapters represent the more eclectic, sociological perspectives of contemporary criminology.

By now the thoughtful student should have some appreciation of the dynamic and tentative nature of etiological thought about delinquency. He has been exposed to a cross-section of the research and "educated guesses" of the specialists. If he is not satisfied with this etiology, he may be consoled by the observation that most specialists share with him the hope that refinement of conceptual schemes and further systematic research will produce a more adequate etiology in the years to come.

[18] Griffin, *op. cit.*, p. 30.

We now turn to Part Three, which is a survey of societal reactions to delinquency.

QUESTIONS AND RESEARCH SUGGESTIONS

1. *If human ecology is the study of the spatial relationships between human beings and their environment, is it correct to say that ecologists attribute delinquency causation to spatial factors?*
2. *What is the method generally used in studies of ecology?*
3. *Discuss some of the ecological correlates of delinquency.*
4. *What are some of the criticisms of the ecology of delinquency?*
5. *By map, plot the court cases of delinquency in your community and indicate what delinquency areas, if any, emerge.*
6. *Why is it that primitive societies rarely show problem behavior among children which is comparable to delinquency in American society?*
7. *Why do some scholars believe that the "zoot-suit" fad and delinquency are comparable?*

SELECTED READINGS AND REFERENCES

Bossard, James H. S., *The Sociology of Child Development*, New York, Harper, 1948.

Burgess, E. W., "The Growth of the City," in R. E. Park *et al.*, *The City*, Chicago, University of Chicago Press, 1925, pp. 47–62.

Davie, Maurice R., "The Pattern of Urban Growth," *Studies in the Science of Society*, George P. Murdock, ed., New Haven, Yale University Press, 1937, pp. 133–61.

McKenzie, R. D., "The Scope of Human Ecology," in E. W. Burgess, *The Urban Community*, Chicago, University of Chicago Press, 1926, pp. 172–7.

Mead, Margaret, *Coming of Age in Samoa*, New York, Morrow, 1928.

Mead, Margaret, *Growing Up in New Guinea*, New York, Morrow, 1930.

Shaw, Clifford R., and Henry D. McKay, *Delinquency and Urban Areas*, Chicago, University of Chicago Press, 1942.

Zorbaugh, Harvey W., "The Natural Areas of the City," in E. W. Burgess, *The Urban Community*, Chicago, University of Chicago Press, 1926, pp. 219–29.

Part **III.**

Societal Reactions to Delinquency

Jack was in real trouble and he knew it. He didn't think the teacher knew about it yet, but the police had been told. He knew that. Every time the classroom door opened he expected to see a policeman come in. He supposed they'd send him to the reform school, but that didn't worry him as much as all the talking they'd do first, all the things they'd say to him. He couldn't get his mind off that, no matter what he was doing. He was so worried he was going "nuts."

The police were worried, too. Jack had been reported to them for sex play with some younger boys. It was the sort of thing that might never be repeated and police action might do more harm than good. They would have liked to forget the whole episode. But they could not. The situation might prove to be serious. If the incident were repeated and they had taken no action in the first place, they would be open to severe criticism.

Since the major responsibility of the police is to protect the community, in a case like this they may feel compelled to follow a course which they know is not the best as far as the individual alone is concerned. But at that time the police were in a position to make a compromise. They referred Jack to the Community Service for Children and asked for a report and recommendation.

At first it appeared that the case worker from the Community Service who visited Jack's home could not accomplish much. The mother was frightened and defended her child blindly. She felt that the police had had no right to mention the matter to anyone. She said repeatedly that she would not accept this "lying down" and threatened to get a lawyer and go to court herself. Interviews with Jack accomplished a great deal more. He, quite naturally, did not want to talk about what he had done, but he talked freely on other subjects and was willing to see the doctor (the organization's psychiatrist) and explain his side of the business which had been reported to the police.

After a few interviews with the case worker, Jack talked with the psychiatrist, who was able to assure the police that there was nothing to fear from the boy, and that no further action was needed. The Community Service would continue to work with Jack and his family.[1]

An act defined as delinquent by law theoretically should lead the juvenile out of his home to the attention and under the jurisdiction of the juvenile or children's court. But detection, apprehension, and subsequent definition of the juvenile's behavior as delinquent are frequently avoided. This may happen, for instance, if the parents are influential, or if, in some cases, they are able to divert the child away from the attention of the public agencies of police and court. Then, too, the deceptive juvenile who commits delinquency may escape any sort of

[1] *Helping Children in Trouble*, Federal Security Agency, United States Children's Bureau, Publication No. 320, 1947, pp. 2–3.

detection even by his family. How frequently this occurs no one knows, but it is safe to say that among children who actually commit delinquent acts, at least as many are *not* detected and brought to the attention of public law-enforcement and judicial agencies as *are* so handled.

Before an allegedly delinquent juvenile is brought before the court, he is first detected by the police or referred to them or the court by the family, school authorities, neighbors, or a private social agency. The case may be disposed of at this point by referral back to a private social agency or by a lecture or warning to the child and his parents, depending on the nature of the offense and the age of the child. If the child is detained, he is placed either in the custody of his parents, in jail, or in a detention home. During detention there may be a preliminary social investigation and psychological and psychiatric diagnoses of the child's difficulties. A decision is made about whether the court will handle the case officially or non-officially.

Role of the Police

The usual initial step in societal reaction to delinquency is detection and apprehension by the police. Technically, however, many laws give any citizen the right to file a "petition" with the juvenile court [2] "in behalf of" a child [3] who has committed an offense or who is found in a situation that comes within the court's jurisdiction.

Approximately a million children now come into contact with the police as alleged delinquents in a given year. About 750,000 of these are dealt with directly by the police; that is, they are dismissed with a warning or referred to a social agency. The largest number of children are apprehended by the police during the years of puberty.

The police detect and apprehend a larger proportion of the total number of boys than of girls referred to court. Referrals and petitions to court are being made less and less frequently by social agencies, for the latter now feel better equipped than

[2] The term "petition" is indicative of the less vindictive nature of the chancery philosophy in delinquency, as compared with the "indictment" in criminal proceedings.

[3] Psychologically this is rarely the case, for the petition actually functions as a formal complaint *against* the child.

formerly to provide their own services to children "in trouble." They no longer feel compelled to refer such cases to court.

Police work in connection with juvenile delinquency in many communities has come to be looked upon as requiring different organization and tactics from those necessary in the case of crime. Special juvenile bureaus have been established, made up of officers noted for their skill in dealing with children. In these communities any police officer may arrest a child, but only the officers in the juvenile bureau may question him, confer with his parents, or decide to detain him.[4] Conspicuous, too, is a growing tendency in police work to restrict the officer's arresting power in relation to juveniles, especially when the latter are involved in what is considered a minor offense. This is a logical outgrowth of the chancery philosophy of the juvenile court. But it has produced a dilemma in police work, for the officer is now caught between, on the one hand, the principle of the protection of society implied in his power of arrest, and on the other hand the principle of the welfare of the child implied in the chancery philosophy.

Detection and apprehension are not the only functions in modern police work with juveniles. Prevention of delinquency is another function so important that several of the special juvenile bureaus in police departments are called "prevention" bureaus. When the officers in such bureaus are not arresting juveniles for delinquent acts, they are supposed to be engaged in protective, monitory activities which are believed to prevent delinquencies from ever taking place.

The role of the policewoman personifies this modified conception of police work, with its lessened emphasis on apprehension and punishment of delinquents and its heightened concern with protection and prevention of delinquency among "predelinquents." There are now more than one thousand policewomen employed throughout the United States. They were first utilized for protective and preventive purposes on the adult level in connection with the safeguarding of soldiers from prostitutes and the care of young women in unusual social conditions, such

---

[4] But a recent study of 177 cities, each with a population of more than 20,000, revealed that more than one third have not yet made special provisions in their police departments for work with children.

as the Lewis and Clark Exposition in Portland, Oregon, in 1905.
Other early duties required them to be matrons to female prisoners. Caricatures still depict them as tough, manlike personalities.
By the second decade of the twentieth century the stereotype was
disrupted somewhat. The policewoman's role came to be recognized as requiring professional competence. Detection and apprehension of delinquents along with protective and preventive
work with predelinquents were added to the earlier responsibilities. The primary function of policewomen today is to handle
cases in which women and children are involved either as offenders or as victims of offenders.

Women are believed to be better equipped for many aspects
of police work than are men. Juveniles have less fear and show
less antagonism toward them, not only because they are women
but also because policewomen in this country avoid uniforms,
dressing like other professional women, and do not use weapons
except on special kinds of patrol. The present tendency is to require of women a college degree and social work experience
before an appointment to police work is made. In New York City
no woman can join the police force unless she has been graduated
from high school and has had two years of paid training in teaching, nursing, probation, or parole work, or has earned a college
diploma.[5] Course work for policewomen is now offered in several
colleges and schools of social work.[6] At the first training institute
for policewomen in New York State, sponsored by Syracuse University in 1945, the course was planned to meet the needs of
women from different cities where their duties varied somewhat.
Some did patrol work only; others were functioning as detectives,
whereas in other cities the policewomen served as consultants to
agencies dealing with the problems of juveniles and youths. The
early sessions at the institute were devoted to discussions of the
fundamentals of community organization, with emphasis on the
function of a policewoman as an aid to health and welfare serv-

[5] See Mary Sullivan, *My Double Life: the Story of a New York
Policewoman*, New York, Farrar, 1938.
[6] The Delinquency Control Institute of the University of Southern
California offers the only university-operated training program in the country for police officers who are to work with juveniles. It has graduated about
200 persons since it was founded in 1946. A few other schools give some
attention to police work specifically with juveniles.

ices in the community. But the policewomen attending the institute were frequently reminded that they were not social workers. They were an integral part of the social control pattern of their community. It was explained that police duties were clearly defined by law and their primary responsibility was law enforcement. It was further brought out that the police department was not always a proper setting for social work. The policewoman, however, needs to know the social work resources of her community so that she may refer cases to appropriate agencies for the required help. As the course at the institute progressed, opportunities were provided for observation and discussion of various programs actually in operation. Field trips were made to settlement houses, child-caring institutions, clinics, schools, etc. Considerable time was spent at the Syracuse Police Department, where discussions were led by those in charge of the Crime Prevention Bureau, and the Laboratory and Record Department. The chief of police also discussed problems of administration in a police department. Otherwise sessions were conducted at the university on a round-table basis by persons with practical experience in their chosen fields.[7]

Some specific duties of the policewoman are:

1. To make arrests, but at the same time to interview offenders, win their confidence, and study them for the etiology of their cases.

2. To make calls on predelinquents, especially the youngest ones, who are the most promising for preventive work.

3. To patrol her beat on the lookout for children she can deflect from delinquency and protect from adults.[8]

There are many frustrations encountered by all police in their work with juveniles. For example:

[7] *Summary and Evaluation of the Policewoman's Training Institute,* Syracuse University, Syracuse, N.Y., Mimeographed. January 1945.

[8] New York City's policewomen are assigned not only to the juvenile aid bureau, the children's (juvenile) court, and the women's court, but also to the narcotic squad, missing persons' squad, pickpocket squad, shoplifting squad, the District Attorney's Office, and the Mayor's office. When a distinguished European diplomat or ruler visits the city, policewomen are always included as part of the escort. They are also used to guard material witnesses—not prisoners, but people who have witnessed a serious crime and who are guarded so that no one will interfere with them.

1. Salaries are inadequate and advantages are few for police personnel. It is obvious that to attract good applicants for positions in the police department, the salaries, retirement privileges, and pensions need to be adequate. But police personnel are grossly underpaid, and it is frequently the case that when retrenchment programs are initiated the police are among the first to be cut in the municipal budget.

2. Personnel is inadequate in police departments. Virtually all police departments are understaffed. It is obvious that, in direct proportion to the inadequacy of the police force, there is a lack of police coverage of the community.

3. In some communities there are laws restricting the apprehension and detention of juveniles by the police. There are communities where one restriction on police officers is that they must first get the authorization of a judge or some other court officer before an arrest can be made. This is required even though court officials are frequently unavailable to the police, who are on duty twenty-four hours a day.

4. The police do not always have access to juvenile court records. The complaint is that whenever the juvenile court record is kept from the police department, the latter is handicapped in its function of protecting the community.

5. The police are often prohibited from fingerprinting juveniles. Their argument here is that the taking of fingerprints does not involve any stigma, for the stigma comes from the offense committed. The police say that for purposes of identification, the protection of the innocent, and the completion of records, fingerprinting of offenders who are taken into custody should be a regular procedure regardless of their ages.[9]

Detention in Jails

After juveniles have been detected and apprehended by the police, they may be detained pending a juvenile court hearing, although most children referred to the juvenile court by the police continue to live in their own homes while their cases are being considered. About a third of the children awaiting a court hearing

[9] National Conference on Prevention and Control of Juvenile Delinquency, *Report on Role of Police*, Washington, D.C., U.S. Government Printing Office, 1947, pp. 15–17.

are held overnight or longer. Children apprehended by the police and referred to the juvenile court by them are more likely to receive detention than are children referred by other sources. Detention is defined as the "temporary care of children who are removed from their homes pending investigation and decision by the juvenile court." [10] Theoretically, detention of alleged delinquents has two basic functions: to keep the child secure until his case is heard, and to enable the child and his background to be studied in order to determine the kind of treatment needed. Actually children are placed in detention not only to await a first hearing in juvenile court, but in some cases are also sent there as punishment, despite the fact that punishment is not supposed to be the function of detention. In other cases they are there awaiting commitment to a long-term care institution.

Although it has been the philosophy since the first juvenile court was established in 1899 to use separate, nonpunitive detention in so-called detention homes for the alleged delinquent, there has been a carry-over use of the traditional jail for many delinquency cases. Both the National Probation and Parole Association and the United States Children's Bureau estimate that between 50,000 and 100,000 juveniles are detained each year in approximately 3,000 local or county jails and the 10,000 police lockups in towns and cities thoughout the country.[11] In any given day, anywhere from 1,000 and 5,000 juveniles may be found in jail. This means that they share cells (in some jails they are placed in segregated cells) with adult alcoholics, thieves, and prostitutes.

Interestingly enough, there are laws against the jailing of children, modeled after the Standard Juvenile Court Act. Jail detention is forbidden by statute in twenty-eight states and the District of Columbia, but the laws are more honored in the breach than in the observance. Only Connecticut and New Jersey in recent years have claimed not to use jails for juveniles.[12] An outstanding reason for this widespread dependence on jails is

[10] Sherwood and Helen Norman, *Detention for the Juvenile Court,* New York, National Probation Association, 1946.
[11] The total annual juvenile detention population is estimated to be 300,000. This includes those in detention homes as well as in jails.
[12] Austin H. MacCormick and James H. Dooling, "Keeping Children Out of Jails: It Can Be Done," *Federal Probation,* 13:44, 1949.

that there are only about 175 detention homes in the United States. Many police say they have no choice but to detain "dangerous" juveniles in jail. They point to a western state where a juvenile had committed an armed robbery and had shot a police officer. The state law prohibited the detention of any juvenile under seventeen years of age in the police lockup. At the same time sufficient police manpower was not available to transfer this boy to the nearest detention home 165 miles away. Accordingly, he was released after his arrest and placed in the custody of his parents. He then stole an automobile and escaped.

In a southwestern state a sheriff complained that the nearest juvenile detention home was over 500 miles away. The practice in this state is to detain "dangerous" juveniles in jails because of the lack of other facilities. In an eastern state, although district juvenile-detention homes have been set up, the police in some instances must transport a juvenile a distance of thirty-five miles to the nearest detention home. The arrest of a number of juveniles during a given day creates a serious hardship for these police. In short, the police often have no alternative but to detain juveniles in jails.[18]

This may be a traumatic experience for the juvenile, quite apart from the anticipated dread and fear of being jailed. When a juvenile is placed in the cell block of a jail, he may find there a "kangaroo court" organized by the adult inmates, of whom some are confined there awaiting trial, others have already been convicted and are awaiting sentence, and still others are serving short sentences for minor offenses. The "kangaroo court" is composed of the inmates themselves, with a "sheriff," a "judge," and a set of rules and penalties. It imposes on the juvenile newcomer a "fine for breaking into jail." Frequently a fixed amount is stated in the "kangaroo court" rules tacked up on the wall. If the boy has the sum—two, five, or even ten dollars—he hands it over to the "judge," or faces a penalty of being lashed or being forced to do all the dirty work of the cell block at ten cents per day until the fine is paid. There may also be a demand that he participate in homosexual activity.

In 1948 the Osborne Association, in collaboration with the

[18] National Conference on Prevention and Control of Juvenile Delinquency, *op. cit.*, pp. 4–5.

National Jail Association, launched a campaign against the wide-spread practice of detention of juveniles in county jails, 97.3 per cent of which had been rated below 60 on a scale of 100 by federal jail inspectors. To learn some of the practical answers to the problem of the child who must be detained, special attention was given to the states of New Jersey and North Carolina. New Jersey was selected because, with the enactment of its Juvenile Court Act of 1929, detention of its children was prohibited "in any prison, jail, lockup, police station, vehicle, or *other place where the child can come in contact with any adult convicted of crime or under arrest and charged with crime.*" The intent obviously was to forbid all detention of juveniles in jails. But the final phrase (italicized above) was interpreted by some counties to mean that detention was permitted in segregated sections where the child did not come in contact physically with adult prisoners. For the purpose of closing up this loophole, the New Jersey legislature passed an amended law in 1947 which stated explicitly: "No child under the age of sixteen coming within the provisions of this subtitle (Juvenile and Domestic Relations Court) shall be placed in any prison, jail, lockup or police station." The commissioner of the New Jersey State Department of Institutions and Agencies transmitted to state and county administrators his interpretation of the amendment and the basis on which he would enforce it. From the day the amended law was passed the officers of the Division of Inspection stressed the date on which it would become effective and explained not only how but why it would be enforced. Thereafter no counties had the excuse that the meaning of the law was unclear, nor could they argue that only occasionally was it necessary to jail a child under sixteen, or that they agreed with the law but would get around some day in the future to establishing other detention facilities. Apparently it sufficed that there was a state agency to see whether or not children were being held in jails contrary to law, and that the counties knew there were sanctions if it came to a test.

North Carolina was selected because its State Department of Public Welfare for years had struggled vigorously against the detention of children in local jails. The North Carolina approach has been one of a broad educational nature which emphasizes the philosophy that the temporary detention of children is a function of child-serving agencies (juvenile courts and departments of public welfare) and not the responsibility of law-enforcement agencies. This educational approach uses publications, speeches, state conferences, annual institutes, and consultant services. It has resulted in acceptance by practically all of the state's 100 counties of the principle that the temporary care of children apprehended for delinquent behavior is the responsibility of the juvenile court or public welfare personnel. In cases of the detention of children in jails, the county superintendent of public welfare is immediately asked for a full report. The next step is that sheriffs and chiefs of police are sent copies of such correspondence so that they will be informed that the state department is following up on the situation.[14]

In other states the jailing of juveniles continues for a number of reasons other than the shortage of detention homes. In many places it continues because of the myth that to jail is to reform a child. Children are also brought to jail and detained there at some length because state and private institutions are overcrowded, so that children committed to them by the juvenile courts must be held while awaiting a vacancy. A third reason for the continuation of the jailing of juveniles is the fee system whereby payment is made at a daily rate for the care and feeding of each jail inmate. It is to the obvious advantage of the sheriff to keep the jail as nearly full as possible and to have children who are arrested during the evening held for release at least until the next morning.[15]

Detention Homes

Until 1900 or thereabouts the common jail was the only place of detention for children. Today the use of jails for children is increasingly deplored, partly out of sentimentality and partly out of the realization that the jailing of juveniles does not really reform them. Indeed, it seems to make them more determined, more distrustful, more cunning and resourceful in their delinquency. The detention home is gradually replacing the jail. Sometimes it is independent and at other times it is under the direc-

[14] MacCormick and Dooling, *op. cit.*, pp. 40–5.
[15] National Conference on Prevention and Control of Juvenile Delinquency, *Report on Juvenile Detention*, Washington, D.C., U.S. Government Printing Office, 1947, pp. 2–3.

tion of the juvenile court, which it serves in cases of neglected and dependent children as well as in cases of delinquency where the children cannot be released to a parent's or a relative's custody. The detention home began to appear, as one might expect, when children were taken out from under the jurisdiction of criminal law and placed under the jurisdiction of the juvenile court. The "parent" philosophy of the latter, namely, that juvenile delinquents should be cared for as a wise father would care for his children, inevitably led to the decline of jails and the rise of detention homes.

Consistent with this philosophy, detention is ideally a part of the case work process and not a panic reaction to the child's offense. It is supposed to be used only where clinical study of the child (prior to the juvenile-court hearing) is not possible or desirable in the child's own home, or where there is a strong likelihood of further delinquent acts or of running away.[16]

Standards in the use of detention vary widely throughout the United States. Usually they are crescive rather than enacted; they evolve out of the hit-and-miss methods of the police department and the local juvenile court rather than out of careful thinking and planning. In some communities the police place in detention for at least a few hours every child referred to the court for delinquency. In other communities only those children are detained who are charged with offenses more serious than those classified as misdemeanors in adult court. Elsewhere detention is used only in unusual cases, a procedure based on the belief that intensive supervision of the child in his own home is more effective than detention outside the home. But the latter alternative is rare, primarily because probation officers do not have the time to do intensive case work with children during the period prior to the juvenile-court hearing.

As early as 1930, Healy and Bronner observed that the various reasons given for the origin and continued use of detention homes for juvenile delinquents were only partly justified by the results obtained.[17] Most detention homes have been found to

[16] Sherwood Norman, "The Detention Home," *The Annals of the American Academy of Political and Social Science*, 261:159–60, 1949.

[17] William Healy and Augusta F. Bronner, "Juvenile Detention Homes," The *Annals of the American Academy of Political and Social Science*, 151:180–3, 1930.

violate the very same principles that were violated in the child's own home. There is denial of love and emotional security as well as a lack of meaningful activity. This happens because incompetent authorities assume that detention care should provide custody only, that the quality of staff is unimportant, and that programs are unnecessary inasmuch as the children are detained for only a short time. Even in the "better" detention homes surveyed by the National Probation Association, overcrowding has been found to be prevalent and the personnel who handle the children are generally underpaid, untrained, and unqualified for their work. Food is inadequate and days are spent behind barred or meshed windows. Less than half the homes provide for schooling, and most homes lack recreational facilities or programs.

The following description is typical of two types of average or better detention homes. In the first type, there is a substandard building, incomplete segregation of cases, understaffing, lack of trained personnel, and a low budget. In the second type there is a "showplace" building but an untrained staff trying to serve twice as many children as a trained staff could handle well, the result being a rigid system of regimentation.

Here is one where two locked doors substitute for supervision and provide the only segregation day and night for twenty to thirty boys and girls of all ages up to seventeen. Eight or ten girls, including an occasional baby, young dependent children and seriously delinquent older girls roam the second floor quarters locked away from the rest of the building. The dozen or so boys include an eight-year-old neglected youngster, a ten-year-old feeble-minded boy awaiting institutional placement, and the sixteen-year-old member of a burglarizing gang. Except for mealtime and an occasional stretch in the yard they mill around their third-floor quarters far away day and night from the solitary matron on the ground floor. The detention home does what it was planned to do—it keeps youngsters away from adult offenders, keeps boys away from girls, and its barred windows and brick walls have stood firm against most escape attempts. Although boys' and girls' quarters are in terrible disrepair and both gloomy and barren, the place can be made clean enough to meet the eye of the visiting board. The older and most difficult boys and girls often stay in this home for weeks awaiting placement and casting their shadow over dozens of young children who come and go.

Contrast with this idleness and lack of supervision the brisk schedule and close supervision of a large, imposing and well-kept detention home. Here delinquents are carefully segregated from dependents. Thirty to forty delinquent girls from nine to sixteen years of age live together in a perfect fish-bowl under watchful eyes day and night. They do not have private possessions, a private word, or private action. By day a girl may call her own only the clothes on her back, and even these loose garments are especially designed for institutional convenience. She may not own a bobby pin for fear it might pick a lock. At night her clothes are locked from her. By day she does endless scrubbing, polishing, and dusting, and if she runs out of work she may sit, one of thirty or so, in a day-room and go through the cards, checkers, funny book routine again and again. She must line up in silence to be counted and searched several times a day. She must line up to use the bathroom. They wonder why she doesn't run and play when she is taken out into the square walled court-yard for an hour. But there is nothing to play with and if she walks off by herself or with a friend she is ordered back to the group. So she just sits in the sun. What do they expect a girl to do? The average girl spends three weeks here. Anyone who recalls the warm imprint that two weeks in a good camp can leave on the life of a teen-ager can imagine by contrast the cold imprint that three weeks in this detention home will leave. Will it make her want to live a better life? Not a chance. It will tell her a hundred times a day that the adult world distrusts, despises, blames, and hates her. And she will distrust and hate right back. It will tell her that other delinquent girls are kinder and more considerate than most adults and that life is a battle of youth against the world.[18]

[18] National Conference on Prevention and Control of Juvenile Delinquency, *Report on Juvenile Detention*, Washington, D.C., U.S. Government Printing Office, 1947, pp. 4–5.

The detention home obviously is not an undifferentiated unit. Actually there are at least five variations: the boarding-home, the residence-type detention home, the small institution, the large institution, and the combined detention-study home.

1. *The boarding-home* is a quasi-natural home with a married couple who are board-providing parents. It cares for not more than six to eight children at a time on a per diem rate basis. Because of the selective process that is employed, it is believed to insure the minimum of "contagion" from the contacts of the children present.

2. *The residence-type detention home* is one that has the appearance and atmosphere of a natural home, but is really artificially set up and staffed for the purpose of providing substitute care for children. The juvenile court may lease or buy a spacious house for this purpose. Its distinguishing feature as a detention home is that in its physical aspects it is a home but the personnel are placed there to operate it on a professional basis.

3. *The small institution* is a residence-type home which has taken on a few more children, added to its staff, and departed from a family pattern of living.

4. *The large institution* is a detention home in which the relationships between the juveniles and the adults in charge of them are impersonal. There is a considerable amount of regimented routine, and spontaneous activity is discouraged. In some large detention institutions, however, there is a unit plan whereby there is provision for separate living-units to house the various age and problem groups. This serves to reduce the impersonal relations and repressive measures of the larger structure.

5. *The combined detention-study home,* on the one hand, is merely an ordinary detention home with a clinic as an appendage. On the other hand, it does not stop at holding a child in custody and providing an intelligence test and a routine psychiatric interview. It is set up to provide the kind of living in which clinical study will be most revealing. This means spontaneous activity without regimentation in order to reveal the child to the clinic. The clinic guides the detention-home staff in building up a program, in developing techniques of supervision, and in handling behavior problems. It trains supervisors in making significant observations, and it interprets their reports. Social investigation

of the children detained there provides further evidence with which to piece together the etiology of their behavior.[19]

Standards in Detention

A half century of experience in the detention of children has given rise to the following standards of effectiveness, which are believed to apply in general to all types of care:

1. No child should ever be held in a jail or a prison lockup except in rare instances and under special protection.

2. Detention should be controlled by the juvenile court, with the co-operation of the police. A safe guide is a policy according to which police immediately bring children they have apprehended to the juvenile court during the hours that office is open. Inasmuch as this covers only a third of a twenty-four-hour day, the police during the remaining time must have direct access to the detention home, and their judgment regarding the need for detention must be accepted until the court has an opportunity to pass on it.

3. Children who should be placed in detention may be classified in three major groups: (a) Children so beyond control that parents or their guardians may not be able to prevent a repetition of such menacing behavior as armed robbery, assault, and certain sex offenses; (b) children who are in physical or moral danger in their own homes and for whom no other immediate care with relatives or neighbors is possible; and (c) children whose presence in court can only be assured by detention.

4. The length of detention should be as short as possible, less than a week as a rule.

5. Building design and construction should be adapted to the special demands of detention care, emphasis being on cheerfulness, livability, ease of maintenance, flexibility, and ease of supervision.

6. The administering agency should be one that specializes in the field of child care.

7. The program should not only provide good physical and custodial care but should meet the nonphysical needs of children through a varied and stimulating educational and recreational program.

[19] *Ibid.*, pp. 8–16.

8. The staff should be large enough to insure the night and day supervision of small groups, and should be competent to handle the problems of children.

9. Medical examinations should be given to every child admitted.

10. Clinical child-guidance services should be provided, to give first-aid treatment for acute emotional disturbances as well as for more intensive study.

11. Comprehensive and confidential records should be kept to provide information to the court and other agencies, as well as for periodic evaluation of detention practices.

12. The school program should be under the supervision of the local board of education, and curriculum adjustment should be made to meet the individual needs of the children.

13. The public should be continually educated about detention, and its co-operation should be sought, for these are essentials in maintaining an effective detention program.[20]

The next chapter is concerned with the juvenile court, which is in a sense the pivot of societal reaction to delinquency. Although much of the history and philosophy of the juvenile court has already been discussed in Chapter II, there remain to be considered such aspects as its structure, personnel, and procedure.

QUESTIONS AND RESEARCH SUGGESTIONS

1. *Why is it that the police detect and apprehend a larger proportion of the total number of boys than of girls reported to juvenile court?*
2. *Besides detection and apprehension, what other functions are there in modern police work with juveniles?*
3. *Why are policewomen believed to be better equipped for police work with juveniles than are policemen?*
4. *Discuss the handicaps the police face in their work with juveniles.*
5. *Theoretically, what are the two basic functions of the detention of alleged delinquents?*
6. *How do you account for the widespread use of jail detention for juveniles in the face of laws forbidding the practice?*
7. *Differentiate between the five variations in the detention home.*

[20] National Conference on Prevention and Control of Juvenile Delinquency, *Report on Juvenile Detention*, Washington, D.C., U.S. Government Printing Office, 1947, pp. 18–20.

SELECTED READINGS AND REFERENCES

Healy, William, and Augusta F. Bronner, "Juvenile Detention Homes," *The Annals of the American Academy of Political and Social Science*, 151:180–3, 1930.

MacCormick, Austin H., "Children in Our Jails," *The Annals of the American Academy of Political and Social Science*, 261:150–7, 1949.

MacCormick, Austin H., and James H. Dooling, "Keeping Children Out of Jails: It Can Be Done," *Federal Probation*, 13:40–5, 1949.

National Conference on Prevention and Control of Juvenile Delinquency, *Report on Role of Police*, Washington, D.C., U.S. Government Printing Office, 1947.

National Conference on Prevention and Control of Juvenile Delinquency, *Report on Juvenile Detention*, Washington, D.C., U.S. Government Printing Office, 1947.

Norman, Sherwood, and Helen Norman, *Detention for the Juvenile Court*, New York, National Probation Association, 1946.

Norman, Sherwood, and Helen Norman, "The Detention Home," *The Annals of the American Academy of Political and Social Science*, 261:158–65, 1949.

Sullivan, Mary, *My Double Life: the Story of a New York Policewoman*, New York, Farrar, 1938.

Chapter **XV** . *The Juvenile Court*

Into a clean, sun-swept room whose glistening windows front on Oakland's Forbes Street straggled a woebegone little procession, a ten-year-old boy with a smeared face and grubby hands, a tired Italian mother dabbing at her eyes with a handkerchief, and a stout man with a red angry face set in the fixed scowl of one who had a disagreeable duty to perform and who intends to see it through. Bringing up the van, his brass buttons polished to within an inch of brightness, a city patrolman marched, steering his charges toward the long benches at the far end of the room. As they sat down, into the eyes of the boy there crept a look, half scared, half defiant. He edged away from the stout man toward his mother.

"You no good," she said sharply: "Judge, he lock you up.

I tell him you no mind me. Steal and lie and run away! You go to jail, I tell him; I don' care."

Immediately he began to sniffle, rubbing his knuckles into his eyes. The policeman yawned, and the red-faced man stared at the soft, cream colored wall in front of him. In ten minutes—perhaps five—a young man stepped into the room, beckoned to the policeman and the stout man who squared his shoulders resolutely and marched off into the ante-room. A few minutes later the attendant reappeared, and the now thoroughly frightened boy followed him. Again, after an interval, the mother was summoned. Twenty minutes later—maybe longer—the group reappeared.

"Well," the stout man said somewhat grudgingly, "don't let it happen again, Tony. You keep your fingers out of that showcase—"

"No next time! Tony promise no next time," the woman volunteered. "He's a good boy now. No steal no more."

Tony nodded vehemently. The look of defiance had altogether disappeared. So had the fear. Talking together, the three went out of the building.

Behind those doors in a private conference room or in the judge's chambers, a first offender had been set right through three individual interviews in a process very similar to that of a consulting physician. There were questions to be asked, the "why" of Tony to be answered. Just why did Tony steal? Who was the leader of his neighborhood gang? What were Tony's marks in school, and why didn't he like his teacher? There was advice needed to bring about better understanding between child and parent and perhaps a stern warning to be delivered.

A dozen times within the month, scores of times within the year some such scene takes place in the Allegheny County Juvenile Court, aptly called the "children's court." Sometimes the outcome is not so happy. Sometimes the offender is not a ten-year-old, accused of stealing penny candy from the neighborhood grocer, but a fifteen-year-old charged with anything from theft to arson, from assault to grave sex delinquencies. Often enough so simple a method as conferring with the parties involved does not suffice and the offender must be placed on probation, assisted by court officers toward better school and home adjustments, toward a better understanding of his parents. Or if that does not suffice or succeed he must be placed in a foster home or in an institution for routine twenty-four hour supervision and living. But the broad outlines of procedure, varied as they may be in specific cases, some taking months instead of hours to work out, are the same: individual consideration of individual cases with understanding and patience and kindness with at the same time a firm regard for the social objectives of reclamation and rehabilitation—unless permanent segregation is necessary.

Less dramatic but more effective than a trial, this method of quiet talk, seeking through individual conferences the real truth of the story, enables the court to assume its true role as a combination of counselor and parent.[1]

In 1951, of the estimated 350,000 children brought to the attention of the juvenile courts in the United States for delinquent behavior, about 250,000 were referred by the police. The remaining 100,000 were referred by parents, teachers, and social agencies. We have already seen that the juvenile court was established by law for the first time anywhere in the world in 1899 in Illinois.[2] This was the culmination of a centuries-old revolution in the philosophy of the treatment of children. In the opinion of some legal experts the juvenile court was the greatest advance in judicial history since the Magna Charta. Criminologists stress the new general principle it embodies; namely, that individualized justice means individualized treatment—law violators should be judicially treated as individuals, for their own protection as well as that of society, instead of being treated with the punitive and retaliatory methods of the criminal court. Here is the basis of the claim that the juvenile court is the first legal tribunal in which law and the sciences, especially the social sciences, are integrated into a close working relationship. For the idea that individuals have different needs according to circumstance, environment, and personality is a basic assumption of psychology, sociology, and

[1] *The Juvenile Court of Allegheny County,* Pittsburgh, Pa., pp. 1–3.
[2] See Chapter II.

cultural anthropology as well as the philosophy of the juvenile court.

This is quite different from the classical philosophy of criminal law and the criminal court, in which the emphasis is more on the offense than on the person, and on the person's past more than on his future. In criminal courts there is inclined to be an elixir viewpoint of one medicine (punishment) for all suffering from a given disease (offense), the medicine being given in the same quantity to all those who commit the same offense.[3]

The function of the juvenile court is not to prove the child guilty or innocent of a crime. Its functions are to decide whether the child is delinquent or not, to diagnose the "causes," to prescribe treatment, and to supervise the treatment.

Constitutionality of the Juvenile Court

An interesting problem has emerged from the fact that the juvenile court lacks the legal trappings (indictment, attorneys, trial, evidence, etc.) of the criminal court and has taken on many of the traits of a social-work agency. The question is whether or not the juvenile court is a violation of "due process of law" and is therefore unconstitutional. Does juvenile court legislation contravene the provision of the Fifth Amendment that "no person shall be held to answer for a capital, or otherwise infamous crime, unless on a presentment, or indictment by a grand jury"? Instead of the criminal court presumption that a person is innocent until proved guilty, is it not true that the child brought before the juvenile court is presumed to have committed a delinquent act and treated as such with virtually no opportunity to disprove the presumption?[4]

A good case in question is the Federal Juvenile Delinquency Act. In 1938 the federal government stood virtually alone in continuing to try, in the same manner as adult criminals, juveniles accused of violations of federal law. In June of that year Congress passed the Federal Juvenile Delinquency Act. This legislation, like its counterparts in the various states, was enacted in order to

[3] Gustav L. Schramm, "Philosophy of the Juvenile Court," *The Annals of the American Academy of Political and Social Science*, 261:103–4, 1949.

[4] Alexander Holtzoff, "The Constitutionality of the Federal Juvenile Delinquency Act," *Federal Probation*, 3:5, 1939.

be rid of the formal procedure of the criminal court, to reduce to a minimum both detention and the commitment to penal institutions intended for adult offenders, and to eliminate the stigma of criminality as a result of a conviction. It was designed to introduce informal proceedings for children in private chambers in place of a formal trial in open court; to permit the commitment of juveniles to public or private institutions other than penal ones; and to enable the release of the juveniles on parole at any time thereafter. This required that there be no indictment by a grand jury or trial by a petit jury. At the same time, however, it was realized that juveniles as minors had the same constitutional rights as adults, and that without their consent the informal procedure could not be used. Therefore the Act provided that an alleged delinquent could be dealt with as such only with his consent given in writing before a judge. Otherwise there would have to be the usual criminal procedure by indictment and trial before a jury.[5]

The prevailing opinion is that in view of the fact that the procedure under the Federal Juvenile Delinquency Act may not be used except with the consent of the juvenile and that this implies a waiver of prosecution by indictment, there is no invalid infringement of the juvenile's constitutional rights. Just as an adult person accused of a crime may waive prosecution by indictment and consent to prosecution by information, so may a minor waive any constitutional guarantee surrounding his trial. Hence the Federal Juvenile Delinquency Act may be regarded as constitutional.

But what of the various state laws providing for juvenile courts to take care of non-federal violations? These do not have in all cases the federal provisions described above for securing the juvenile's consent to chancery procedure. State supreme courts have maintained that juvenile court treatment in such jurisdictions does not constitute a violation of due process of law either, for the child in these courts is not charged with crime in the first place.

Types of Juvenile Courts

Below the federal level, there is no uniformity in legal provisions and practices of the juvenile courts. Symbolic of this is the

[5] *Ibid.*, p. 4.

fact that the 2,500 juvenile courts in the United States are called by a variety of names: Juvenile Court, Children's Court, Juvenile and Domestic Relations Court, etc. In organization there are four different types of juvenile courts:

1. *The independent juvenile court* administratively is apart from other courts. Technically separate from juvenile delinquency but included in the jurisdiction of the court is the power to deal with cases of neglected and dependent children. The court may be on a city, county, or state basis, but usually it is on a county basis because this is in conformity with our established governmental structure. It is usually located in large urban centers.[6]

2. *The family court* has jurisdiction over specified offenses of children and specified types of family conflict. Like the independent juvenile court, it is found largely in urban centers.

3. *The juvenile and domestic relations court* may be either independent or part of courts with more general jurisdiction. Occasionally it deals with cases of divorce and separation as well as delinquency, family conflict, etc. It, too, is located mostly in urban centers.

4. *The juvenile court as a section* or "session" of a court with more comprehensive jurisdiction is the least specialized of all four types. Its judges, for example, are often merely rotated to it from their roles as judges in probate, circuit, and common pleas court. As one might suspect, this type of court is more common in non-urban centers.

Quarters and Physical Equipment

In most cities the courtroom and its probation officers are located either in the courthouse or in the detention home. There

[6] Half of the states have a state probation commission or a division of the state public welfare or correctional department in which is placed legal responsibility with respect to the juvenile courts in the state, regardless of the subdivisional regional bases. The law in these states usually gives this agency or department specific responsibility to develop and operate the juvenile court's probation services. In some states the agency or department is simply authorized to "co-operate" with the courts, such as in rendering advisory service about standards. In several cases, however, the state agency is not given sufficient funds and personnel to fulfill its responsibilities. See the National Conference on Prevention and Control of Juvenile Delinquency, *Report on Juvenile Court Administration*, Washington, D.C., U.S. Government Printing Office, 1946, p. 9.

are no specific standards for the quarters and physical equipment of juvenile courts. If, however, a court is in keeping with the philosophy of delinquency, the location and arrangement of its courtroom are such as to protect children from publicity and undesirable contacts and to encourage privacy and informality. This is because a juvenile-court hearing is theoretically not a trial to determine guilt or innocence, but rather a consultation to determine what is best for the child, his family, and the community.

A small courtroom is generally considered preferable to a large one because it makes impossible the presence of too many people at the hearings. Many judges go so far as to hear cases in their own offices, where they can meet with the child, parents, probation officer, and possibly a few other personnel informally.

Procedure of the Juvenile Court

The actual procedure at the juvenile-court hearing varies considerably from one court to the next. The following account, therefore, is an abstraction or synthesis of what takes place in several courts.

After the petition has been made to the juvenile court "in behalf of" the child, and he has been subject to a pre-hearing psychological, social, and psychiatric investigation while in detention, the case falls into one of two categories: official or unofficial. A staff member of the court (a referee or a probation officer) determines in a preliminary hearing, on the basis of the pre-hearing investigation, whether an adjudication (in which the child is either adjudged delinquent or not) is to be attempted at a hearing, with treatment to follow (official), or whether adjudication is unnecessary because the case is trivial, the child to be treated immediately and unofficially.

If the case is designated as official because the offense is serious and the child shows deep difficulties, a summons (a formal or legal call to the child and his parents or guardians) to appear at a court hearing is made. The hearing is conducted informally, without opposing attorneys, a trial jury, or a public audience. Present are the judge, probation officer, the child and his parents, and possibly one or two others—a visiting teacher, or a representative of a social agency, or someone who witnessed or otherwise knows about the alleged offense.

The hearing opens as the judge asks the child to tell his story. Following this the judge may want to know about the offense from someone else. Then he may listen to the parents, the visiting teacher, and others. Finally the probation officer presents to the judge a summary of the findings at the pre-hearing investigation and the preliminary hearing.

On the basis of all that he has seen and heard about the case, the judge comes to a decision as to what is the best thing to do for the child. Three questions are decided: (1) Does the child need treatment (that is, should he be adjudicated to the status of a delinquent)? (2) If so, what treatment should he receive? (3) What agency should be responsible for that treatment?

An Illustration of Court Procedure

The following case as reported by the Juvenile Court of Allegheny County [7] illustrates the pattern of court procedure in one jurisdiction, as well as the preliminary steps of apprehension and detention:

FIRST CONTACTS

THURSDAY

Number 12 Police Station received a phone call from a parking lot attendant: "Hurry up! I'm holding a kid that tried to swipe a car!"

The police picked up 15 year old Thomas K——; brought him to the Detention Home by the rear entrance; filled out a form giving the name of the child, his age, the reason for his appearance, and the names of the complainants. The two police exchanged their information sheet with the Detention Home Supervisor, who gave them a receipt for the boy's custody.

Detention Home Supervisor, Mr. Homer, ushered Tom into a glass enclosed interviewing booth. There the boy was asked identifying information so that Juvenile Court files could be checked and his parents notified. New record sheets were made out because Tom had never been previously detained. A bath sheet, a valuables record, and a medical record were made out. Mr. Homer briefly asked Tom about

[7] *Report of the Juvenile Court of Allegheny County, 1945, pp. 2–11.*

the charge initiated by the parking lot attendant. The boy did not deny the theft. His attitude was, "Well! So what?"

Tom accompanied Mr. Homer to the Senior Boys Department where Mr. Brush took charge. Preparatory to taking a shower, Tom's body was checked for vermin, bruises, and other injuries. Mr. Brush recorded on the bath sheet that Tom's left calf had a scratch, which had been received in playing "touch tackle last Saturday." After finishing his shower, Tom was given a medical examination and blood test by Dr. Foster, the court's physician. Mr. Brush followed up the examination by assigning Tom a locker for his clothes and a bed in the Senior Boys dormitory. Tom was issued clean institutional clothing except for shoes.

"Time for school," said Mr. Brush. "School? Here?" "Yes sir. Follow me." Tom followed the supervisor to the classroom where fifteen other boys whose ages ranged from 14 to 17 were already seated. "Mrs. Braun, this is Thomas K——." Mrs. Braun gave Tom a smile and asked his school grade. "Sophomore Academic!" "That is fine. Please be seated." With no time lost Tom was in school again, doing classwork and receiving credit for it.

Tom and the other Senior Boys left the classroom and returned to their dormitory's day room for a few minutes before the dinner hour—just enough time to play a game of ping pong, to wash up, and to find out the names of a few fellows.

Dinner. The boys queued up, cafeteria style; each picked up his tray laden with food and made a right turn into the dining room. Each placed his tray on one of the tables, and stood at his place until all were present. One, who had been there longer than the others, and presumably was more at home, led the rest in a prayer:

> *"God is great,*
> *God is good*
> *Let us thank him*
> *for this food. Amen."*

The last word, although said loudly, was buried in the scraping of chairs and the clatter of dishes, glasses, trays, and cutlery.

The menu: Lamb stew with fresh vegetables, banana gelatin, bread and butter, milk, with all the second helpings the boys wanted—and most of them did.

Tom observed the other boys pick up their trays of used dishes and deposit them on the serving counter where he had obtained the food. The boys stood around until all had finished. Then, like a brigade passing water, the boys began pushing the dining room furniture into the hallway. There were jokes and laughter when some pushed hard, or some missed. In almost no time the room was empty. A colored boy grabbed a broom and began making long sweeps with it. Another boy, a tow head, accused him of taking the easy jobs all the time.

Others appeared with mops and pails. Some boys tried to show off, some did not care, but all did some task to complete the cleaning of the room. The wax was applied quickly and efficiently, the furniture moved back in place.

Mr. Brush beamed, "Good job, good job, let's go!" and the group started towards the Senior Boys day room where they would have free time until the next class.

Miss Stevens was looking forward to seeing the Senior Boys. "Do you want to help me fix Christmas tree ornaments today?" She asked. "It's very simple. Just flatten the tinsel out with your fingers. Start from the strings and work outward. Do the leaves one by one until you've completed the whole ornament." Then she demonstrated. Murmurs of approval. One of the boys helped Miss Stevens distribute the crushed ornaments to the various tables. In a few minutes the entire group seemed absorbed in the stuff of Christmas.

Miss Stevens, who had been repacking the ornaments, glanced at the clock. "Almost finished? Let's put them away and finish up tomorrow." The boys brought up all the ornaments, then waited for dismissal. Miss Stevens, before opening the door asked, "How many want to do some weaving tomorrow?" A chorus of "I do" seemed unnecessary because a pile of colored potholders on the table attested to the craft's popularity. The classroom emptied and the Senior Boys walked into the adjoining classroom for their second session with Mrs. Braun.

"We have a current events class this afternoon," the teacher explained. A small boy sitting on the front seat followed Mrs. Braun's every movement. "Bill, please pass out these papers," and the boy was in action. Another class was on its way.

School dismissed. Tom and the others filed singly out of the room and proceeded to the boy's department day room. Tom was challenged to checkers almost as soon as he entered the room. At last Tom would have some time to exchange information, to brag, or to explain his detention.

Mr. Bowser, an Assistant Intake Secretary, came to the day room. "I want to see Thomas K——." Tom bounded up from his chair. "Here!" and followed Mr. Bowser into a small office.

From the Assistant Intake Secretary's Report: Tom was interviewed in the Detention Home. When asked about his troubles he explained that he can't get along at home. His parents nag him about his bad school marks; never allow him to go out with other boys or to shows. He said that he pays his own way through money he earns working but his father still will not permit him to go. He goes out anyhow because his father works from 3 to 11 and he doesn't listen to his mother.

Statement: Tom, age 15, stated that he was on his way downtown to look for a Christmas holiday job. The weather was wet and cold. As he passed the parking lot he thought he could sit in one of the cars and warm himself. He had no sooner closed the door than the attendant rushed up and accused him of the car theft. Tom admitted he was learning to drive against the wishes of his parents; that he was truant; that he had participated in a joyride previously with a boy whose car ownership was doubtful. Tom seemed to be very much disturbed and upset. He said, "I shouldn't have been in that car . . ." and about that point the tears began flowing. The self-confidence with which the interview had begun melted away.

Tom wanted to go home. Mr. Bowser informed him that the Court Authorities had already reached Tom's family. His parents would be in the next morning to see him.

"See me? Do I have to stay here?" Mr. Bowser then explained that Tom's release depended on many factors: on the report of the police; on his parents' attitude; on the report of the school; but chiefly on Tom himself and on his realization of the seriousness of his behavior.

Mr. Michaels, the Evening Supervisor, announced that it was close to supper time "if anybody wants to wash up."

The boys made a column of twos and waited for Mr. Michaels to start them toward the kitchen. Tom already had a pal, "Boik," who stood next to him—a pimply, long legged, sixteen year old, who listened with his mouth open, but did not have much to say for himself.

The Senior Girls must not have dawdled over their food that night, because the boys, who eat last, were in the dining room ten minutes early. The menu: Creamed cottage cheese with parsley, buttered carrots, Harvard beets, bread and butter, milk. The routine of cleaning followed as in the afternoon.

The Senior Boys went to the gym on the first floor. Within a few minutes basket balls were thumping. Some of the boys were just standing on the side watching. Mr. Michaels blew his whistle. "What is it tonight? Basketball? Dodgeball?" The loudest yell was for dodgeball. Two boys were designated leaders to choose sides. . . .

The game was stopped. Everybody went upstairs to the classroom. Some pretty girls from a club called "The Junior Council" were there with a lot of packages in their arms. The boys quickly quieted down as they took seats. Red, the biggest fellow in the room, gave a wolf call. A few of the boys snickered, but the girls laughed. The announced program: A Bingo game with prizes for the winners.

The hour passed too quickly. The club girls passed out candy, treats to all, even the supervisors. Those who had won candy bars and other favors were showing off, yet none seemed to mind. The boys left the room after they had "policed" it.

Tom and his companions took their showers; flipped some water at each other as well as on themselves. They went to their assigned beds.

Lights out. The talking subsided to whispering; the whispering to the breath of sleep.

FRIDAY

Mr. Giltenboth, the Night Supervisor, opened the door of the dormitory. "Time to get up." The boys were aroused with the usual accompaniment of yawns and stretching. A fresh pair of sox was issued to each boy.

The boys who had been detained longer than one night knew how to make up their cots "Army style." Tom's sheets had square corners and blankets "tight enough to bounce a coin." The routines of the lavatory made the time pass quickly.

Breakfast: Raisins, oatmeal with milk, buttered toast, milk. When everyone was through and the chairs moved out, three boys were picked to scrub the linoleum floor. The others accompanied the Supervisor to the other sections of the Boys' Department. Seven were assigned to the kitchen to help Mrs. Hastings. Others were designated to clean the day room, to wax the dormitory floor, to wipe the windows on the inside of their own department. Tom drew the supply room job. "Snap job," his predecessor told him.

When the chores were completed all the boys with the exception of those assigned to the kitchen went to the classroom. Mrs. Braun returned Tom's algebra paper. The answers on it were all wrong. "Try some arithmetic today; do the problems on the board, Tom." Papers and pencils were distributed, some individual attention given here and there, the class was on its way.

When Mr. Homer peered into Mrs. Braun's classroom, Tom stood up. "I just knew you were looking for me" were the first words he said to him. "Is my Dad here?" Tom preceded Mr. Homer into the office. When he saw his father waiting in the interviewing room he hurried even more. Father and son embraced, oblivious to the door being closed by Mr. Homer.

INTAKE SECRETARY'S REPORT

Tom's father called at the office. He is a youngish man, neat, well dressed, alert in manner. The father stated that he had been contemplating Court action for some time. He said he needed the "power of Law" to impress Tom. Mr. K—— stated that he is not as severe as Tom might indicate, but denied he had been unsuccessful in enforcing rules and regulations at home. "The boy has proven himself untrustworthy at times. He is not careful in the selection of his companions . . . he is a poor student—not because Tom isn't smart, but because he doesn't care."

Mr. K—— stated that the allegations of the police were unfounded "because Tom can't drive." When informed that his son was learning to drive the father seemed surprised. "Guess he'll be wanting to buy a car next."

Mr. K—— then began asking what he could do about the situation. He paused more frequently than he had in the beginning of the interview to phrase his questions. His concern seemed genuine. "Did Tom tell you that he has had trouble in school and with me about his school marks?" When informed that we were aware of the problem, Mr. K—— then volunteered, "I'll bet that's at the bottom of this whole mess!"

The father asked if Tom could be released in his custody. He indicated that he did not object to the Court's interest. The Intake Secretary said that he would check with the police before authorizing release. Mr. K—— could visit Tom if he wished.

Later—Mr. McKnight, the police representative, stated there was no further information on Tom and no objection by the police to his release.

Later—Tom released to the custody of his father. He was informed that there would be a court hearing later.

THE INVESTIGATION

Herewith is the report of the investigation as presented to the Judge the evening before the hearing. (Judge Schramm studies these reports so that he can familiarize himself with each case.)

FIRST APPEARANCE

K——, Thomas (age 15 years)
345 Dormet Street.
Pittsburgh, Pa.

November 30, 1945: Petition filed by Mr. Charles Bowser, Assistant Intake Secretary, Juvenile Court of Allegheny County.

Charge: Said child was brought to the Juvenile Detention Home on November 29, 1945 by officers from Police Station Number Twelve; said child was involved in "attempting larceny of a car." Legal settlement of said child is the City of Pittsburgh, Pa. Your petitioner prays that a hearing be held in Juvenile Court.

Statement of Child: Thomas is a sturdy but unrefined type of boy whose mannerisms and speech suggest recklessness. He is well built, but lean; has regular features from which a skin eruption detracts. Tom squints his eyes. His attitude towards his mother would lead probation officers to believe that he was intolerant of her authority. He was sullen and impolite to her. When the probation officer was alone with Tom the lad was co-operative and responsive.

"It happened on Thursday morning, November 20. I didn't go to school because I wanted to find a job. I'll be 16 pretty soon; so I thought I would get a Christmas holiday job. It's pretty cold these days; so when I passed this parking lot I didn't see anybody around; so I decided to sit in one; warm up and maybe listen to a radio a little. The guy got me before I had a chance to do anything. It was a crazy thing to do, but everybody pushes me around these days, especially Mr. Koller. I don't like school, I don't like him!"

Tom agreed with the probation officer that everybody had to follow regulations, even Mr. Koller. He admitted he wasn't very considerate of the rules of his parents. He volunteered: "—especially about that gang of mine and about learning to drive a car." When asked about his truancy Tom said, "That too!"

Previous Knowledge: He has never appeared before Juvenile Court or any other Court.

School Record: Dr. Koller, principal of the High School, made a general statement. He said Tom was a member of a gang known as the "Hell Raisers" and they were! No day passed that he didn't receive some information on one of them. However he had no direct evidence. He enumerated the following: Breaking a window; interfering with the play activities of small children; jumping street cars; cutting classes. Tom's school marks were:

English	D	Metal Shop	B
World History	E	Physical Education	E
American History	E	Citizenship	E
Mechanical Drawing	C		

Of the total of 67 days, he was absent 23.

Statement of Parents: Mother was emotional during the initial stage of the interview. She spoke of the humiliation which she would suffer as a result of the proceedings and was horrified by the thought of appearing in Juvenile Court. When PO explained Juvenile Court procedure and the general objectives of the Court, mother relaxed and assisted in establishing facts for the investigation.

Mother informed probation officer that both the police and the Detention Home had notified her of the boy's arrest.

She admitted that Tom had caused her some concern, especially his saucy attitude, his street car hopping, and the gang with which he was involved. He ridiculed her attempts at punishment. The father had acted wisely by restricting Tom's use of leisure time and money.

Father came in from shopping just as the interview with mother was drawing to a close. He said he didn't believe that his boy had the right to enter the car, but was sure Tom had no intention of taking it. Tom and he had discussed the matter thoroughly. "Tom had no business leaving school; that's his business now!" Probation officer then informed parents of the doctor's examination. The doctor's diagnosis had been: nine pounds underweight, refractive error, wax in both ears.

Probation Officer suggested that Tom be taken to a clinic for further examination and correction. "It might help his school work." Parents agreed. Father was composed and judicious when discussing problems with Probation Officer.

The father seemed to feel that perhaps he was at fault in that he had not been close to the boy; had taken little part in supervision. He pointed out that he worked long hours, therefore spent little time with his son.

Social History: The family is composed of the parents and two children. Tom is the older. The other son, Paul, is four years younger and doing well in parochial school.

Both the parents were born in Pittsburgh. They have resided here their entire lives. Father has been employed regularly at a mill. Father was an only child. Mother had been working prior to her marriage but has had no employment since that time.

Mother is in poor health, a heart condition. Father stated that mother is very much upset by Tom's difficulty.

Home Investigation: The family rents a small, four-room house, one of a row, in a quiet residential section.

Statement of Police: "His story sounds fishy! There has been a lot of car lifting lately by kids. No, we never saw this kid before."

Social Agencies: No Social Agency has known this family.

Evaluation: Facts revealed in the course of this investigation point up Thomas' inability to meet the limits set up by the community, the school, and his parents. There is some question regarding the adequacy and consistency of parental supervision. Both parents appear to recognize to some degree Tom's inability to meet limitations but are somewhat overprotective. This is evident in their attitude towards Mr. Koller and his criticism of Tom's behavior. They have been unable to accept the constructive help made by the school.

It appears that the authority of the Court may be a constructive factor in assisting Tom to meet some limitations and in bringing the parents to some realization of the possible future if the boy is not corrected.

Recommendation: That Thomas be returned to the custody of his parents on probation.

Reasons: 1. This boy's conduct for several months has shown a definite trend towards habitual delinquency.

2. Remedial measures have already been taken at the probation officer's suggestion for the correction of the eyes.

3. Transfer to a trade school has been arranged by parents.

4. Although parental control has been weak, the parents have been aroused to their responsibilities by Tom's trouble. A better relationship between Tom and his parents seems possible under supervision by a probation officer.

THE FAMILY IN COURT

Court opened for the day at 9:30 a.m. All present were invited to assemble in the Court room. When all had entered the small wood-paneled room, Judge Schramm rose from the long desk that faced the people. He announced quietly, "In opening Court we stand at attention and repeat the pledge of allegiance to the flag." The shuffling of feet stopped; some with emphasis, some in sing-song fashion accompanied the repetition of the pledge; then everyone was asked to return to his seat in the waiting room.

In the buzz of comments in the waiting room were heard: "The judge don't look so bad. . . ." "It's a little room. . . ." "There's no jury or witness stand."

The Court session began without formality. Mr. Downs, the probation officer who had a written report on Tom, walked up to the desk. He named the child, the reason for the Court's attention, and the information which he had gathered concerning the child. He briefly summarized the problem because the Judge had "studied" the case the evening before the hearing. Mr. Downs ushered the parents individually into the Court room. The Judge talked over the boy's problem with them. Tom's school adjustment was discussed, his companions, his behavior on the streets and playground, the remedial measures initiated.

After each of the parents had been in the Court room,

the Judge left his chair. He entered a very small room next to the court room. The plain-walled room was without furniture save for two or three chairs.

Tom was waiting when Judge Schramm entered. He acted surprised when the Judge extended his hand for a handshake. Tom didn't know what to do. He extended his sweating palm slowly. "I've never shook hands with a Judge before." The ice of conversational restraint was broken.

The Judge encouraged Tom to talk about himself—not only about his recent involvement, which he fully admitted, but about the whole story of his difficulties. The more Tom talked, the more he seemed to be gaining in confidence. Tom indicated penitence for his acts; he said that his folks didn't understand him; his father never did talk to him "man to man" like the Judge did. But lately, after he got into trouble, his father was paying more attention. Father and son went to a movie together, the first in a long time. And last week the father "came down the cellar to help fix my brother's sled." Dad saw Mr. Koller so that Tom could go to Trade School.

Judge Schramm spoke solemnly to the boy. He reminded Tom that the circumstances in which he was arrested were extremely suspicious; that "bad company invites trouble." "I've decided that you can go home on probation. An officer of the Court will see you from time to time. Talk over your problems with him." The Judge again shook hands with Tom, then left the room.

Back in the court room: The parents entered the court room together. The Judge told them that Thomas would be on probation. Mr. Downs, the probation officer, would be visiting them.

Juvenile-Court Personnel

The procedure of the juvenile court presupposes skill and training on the part of the personnel. This, however, is not always actually the case.

THE JUDGE. The judge, for instance, is seldom explicitly chosen for his interest in and understanding of the child. He usually has had no training in the behavioral sciences; he has had a legal training which is of little use for juvenile-court work. Generally he is selected by election or appointment, and then primarily to serve other courts. In either method of selection, politics are involved. In some of the larger and better-organized courts the judges are designated by the judges of a court of general jurisdiction from among their own number to give full-time service. Judges in independent juvenile courts may be appointed by the governor or by judges of higher courts, by the legislature or by a city or county government, or by a local juvenile-court committee.

Competent performance as a judge is no guarantee of re-election or reappointment. The juvenile-court judge's status is inferior in the judicial hierarchy and does not lead to promotions as readily as in other courts. The result is that the work is not too attractive to people of outstanding ability. This helps explain why rotation of juvenile-court work is often resorted to in order that no judge shall be deprived of experience in other courts. Obviously the result is often superficial performances in juvenile-court work.

This is not to say that we lack excellent juvenile-court judges. The point is that there are not enough of this caliber. It is widely held that the juvenile-court judge, in addition to legal training, desirable personality traits, and ability to deal with children and their parents, needs a knowledge of social work and community resources and an understanding of child psychology. He needs the ability to convince appropriating authorities and the general public that sufficient funds must be made available. He should give his undivided attention to the juvenile court and not be distracted by responsibilities in other courts. The term of office should be sufficiently long and rewarding to make specialization possible, the recommendation being for a term of not less than six years.

THE REFEREE. Inasmuch as a judge cannot perform all functions in the juvenile court, and is usually untrained in case work, the law in approximately one third of the states provides for the appointment of referees, mostly by the judge. The referee relieves the judge of some important responsibilities. He may preside at the preliminary hearing, and in jurisdictions where the

volume of cases is heavy he may relieve the judge by hearing
cases in certain areas of the jurisdiction or cases of special types,
such as cases involving girls or the less serious cases.

THE PROBATION OFFICER. Probation officers are social workers who assist the judge in carrying out the provisions of the
juvenile-court law. In most cases they are appointed by the judge.
Their duties ordinarily include interviewing persons who come
to the court seeking help or making complaints, conducting social
investigations of the juveniles brought to the attention of the
court, and supervising juveniles if they are placed on probation
by the judge. Many juvenile courts, especially those in rural
areas, lack probation officers. Indeed, as recently as 1951 there
were only 3,716 local probation officers for juveniles, and many
of them served both adults and children. Many also had to serve
150,000 dependent and neglected children coming under the
juvenile-court jurisdiction. The result was that there was an average of one probation officer for every 135 children coming to
court. In several states, full-time and paid probation officers are
found only in the large cities or densely populated counties.
Therefore probation work is the part-time responsibility of sheriffs, bailiffs, welfare workers, clerks of the court, and attendance
officers. Some probation officers are qualified social workers,
whereas others are completely lacking in professional training or
previous experience in social work.

There is an increasing acceptance of training in social work
as preparation for probation work. The professional council of the
National Probation Association recommends as minimum qualifications for appointment to probation work graduation from a
college with courses in the social sciences, and at least one year
of previous full-time experience in a special agency, or one year
of graduate training. Beyond that it recommends graduation from
a school of social work as well as additional experience, especially
for those in supervisory positions.

THE VISITING TEACHER. During the first decade of the twentieth century in New York, Boston, and Hartford, the visiting
teacher came into existence with the function of aiding children
who had problems of school adjustment. The visiting teacher, in
short, is a social worker in the school setting. Children come to

her attention through referral by teachers, principals, social agencies, and the parents. Her work in the juvenile court is largely, although not entirely, concerned with truancy.

JUVENILE JURORS. An innovation in juvenile-court personnel was made in New York City in 1947 by Judge Anna Kross of the "Home Term" Court. This provided for three juvenile jurors to act as advisers to the alleged delinquent, giving him peers to explain his position to the court. Defending the innovation is the argument that it would serve to break down the psychological barriers at a hearing between the alleged delinquent and the adult judge, for the juvenile would no longer feel that he was alone in a hostile, grown-up world. Another argument is that serving as a juvenile juror would provide training in citizenship for children and would give them a sense of real responsibility and participation in handling the problem of delinquency.

Problems of the Juvenile Court

Despite the welcome the juvenile court received at its inception in 1899, it still faces many obstacles and problems. One of the most important is that too much is expected of the juvenile court, as though it were a panacea for delinquency. Another major problem is that in actual practice in many jurisdictions the differentiation between the juvenile and criminal courts is imperfect, for virtually the same methods of procedure are utilized in both cases. This is almost inevitable when the same personnel (judges, probation officers, etc.) who try adult criminal cases are at work in juvenile-court cases. The intrusion of politics, especially in the appointment of court personnel, is largely responsible for the lack of training and interest which these people often show.

Court Procedure in Other Countries

In Chapter II it was pointed out that the invention of the juvenile court in the United States led to legislation in other countries providing for the establishment of special courts or procedures dealing with child offenders. For example, in Japan no separate courts existed for juvenile offenders until 1923, the year when the Juvenile Act of the preceding year became effective. Although the larger cities had already made some provisions for special consideration of juvenile offenders by delegating specially appointed judges and prosecutors to handle juvenile cases, the Juvenile Act provided for the first juvenile courts and stipulated that all persons under eighteen years of age should be regarded as juveniles. The procedure and personnel in Japanese juvenile courts are patterned after the American system. One judge hears the case, assisted by a probation officer who investigates the case. Disposition ranges from a simple admonition at one extreme to institutionalization in a reformatory at the other extreme. Probation is a very common middle alternative.[8]

Under a French law of 1945, courts in France were to be reformed in the following fashion. Judges in children's cases were thereafter to be specialists in child psychology, and the children's jails were to be replaced by centers, homes, camps, and hospitals. Inquiry in cases involving children was to be rapid, and decisions made without delay. First consideration was to be given not to the offense itself but to the child's personality traits, background, and behavior.[9]

Not all countries have adopted the American juvenile-court system. The Scandinavian countries, for example, constitute one important area of the world without juvenile courts.[10] The Soviet Union is another exception. The Soviet theory as far as children are concerned is that offenses and offenders fall into two broad categories: (1) Either the child is very young (under 12), or he is charged with a petty offense, in which cases he or she should not be subject to the experience of arrest and court appearance; or (2) the child is old enough (over 12), or the offense is serious enough to warrant fair but stern consideration. A special juvenile court could not properly handle any of these four situations, Soviet legalists maintain, for in practice the juvenile court makes far too much "fuss" over such things as truancy or petty law infractions, no matter how informally the presiding

[8] *Army Service Forces Manual*, M 354–16, Civil Affairs Handbook, Japan, Section 16: Public Welfare Headquarters, Army Service Forces, July 29, 1944. Prepared for the Military Government Division, Office of the Provost Marshal General, by the Research and Analysis Branch, Office of Strategic Services, pp. 90–2.

[9] Marcelle Kraemer-Bach, "Women in the New France," *Think*, 12:14, 1946.

[10] See Thorsten Sellin, "Sweden's Substitute for the Juvenile Court," *The Annals of the American Academy of Political and Social Science*, 261: 128–36, 1949.

judge conducts the case; and for the younger children (under 12) to appear in any court is too traumatic an experience. On the other hand, older children (12–16) who may commit serious offenses would tend to take their offenses too lightly if asked to appear in a juvenile court.[11]

Future Directions of the Juvenile Court

Despite these basic disagreements between the American juvenile-court system and the systems of other countries, there is little doubt about the secure position of the juvenile courts in this country. They have convinced most interested Americans that they are more appropriate as a judicial agency in offenses involving children than are the regular criminal courts. In the future, however, four questions about juvenile courts will have to be answered:

1. Should the juvenile court continue to have jurisdiction over dependent and neglected children as well as delinquent children?

2. Should it continue to provide and supervise treatment for delinquent children after adjudication?

3. Should the definition of delinquency in law which serves as the court's guide be made more or less specific?

4. What should be the form of organization of the juvenile courts?

The two chapters that follow are a description and analysis of the major dispositions made by the juvenile court in the treatment of delinquency cases. These are institutionalization, parole, probation, and placement in foster homes.

QUESTIONS AND RESEARCH SUGGESTIONS

1. *If the function of the juvenile court is not to prove the child guilty or innocent, then what are its functions?*
2. *Differentiate between the four types of juvenile courts.*
3. *How do "official" juvenile court cases differ from those which are called "unofficial"?*

[11] Dyson Carter, *Sin and Science*, New York, Heck-Cattell, 1946, pp. 183–91.

4. *What is the function of the referee in the juvenile court?*
5. *What is the theory that accounts for the lack of juvenile courts in the Soviet Union?*
6. *Interview a juvenile probation officer regarding his background, training, and duties.*
7. *Examine the juvenile-court system of another society and indicate the key resemblances and differences between that system and American juvenile courts.*

SELECTED READINGS AND REFERENCES

Chute, Charles L., "The Juvenile Court in Retrospect," *Federal Probation*, 13:3–8, 1949.

Eastman, Harry L., "The Juvenile Court Today," *National Probation Association Yearbook*, 1934, pp. 76–89.

Elkin, Winifred A., *English Juvenile Courts*, London, Kegan Paul, Trench, Trubner, 1938.

Killian, Frederick W., "The Juvenile Court as an Institution," *The Annals of the American Academy of Political and Social Science*, 261:89–100, 1949.

Lou, Herbert H., *Juvenile Courts in the United States*, Chapel Hill, University of North Carolina Press, 1927.

National Conference on Prevention and Control of Juvenile Delinquency, *Report on Juvenile Court Administration*, Washington, D.C., U.S. Government Printing Office, 1946.

Schramm, Gustav L., "Philosophy of the Juvenile Court," *The Annals of the American Academy of Political and Social Science*, 261:101–8, 1949.

Sellin, Thorsten, "Sweden's Substitute for the Juvenile Court," *The Annals of the American Academy of Political and Social Science*, 261:137–49, 1949.

Tappan, Paul W., *Delinquent Girls in Court*, New York, Columbia University Press, 1947.

Tappan, Paul W., "Children and Youth in the Criminal Court," *The Annals of the American Academy of Political and Social Science*, 261:128–36, 1949.

Chapter XVI. Disposition and Institutional Treatment

They are not all "the quiet ones" at Wiltwyck. Some of the young boys, unable to hold in their fury at a world they never made, explode in wrath. Take ten-year-old "John Jones." Two weeks ago he stole three knives in twenty-four hours and threatened to kill his teacher and a classmate. Each time a knife was taken away from him he found another. "I'll keep on getting them, too," he boasted. "I am going to kill someone."

Ernst Papanek, the new executive director of the school, headed a staff conference at which the case was discussed. John had been committed by the Children's Court of New York City for truancy, stealing and refusing to obey his parents. Led by Mr. Papanek, the staff decided to gamble on

John. They knew the boy had reason for anger. They knew his father had always punished him severely (John openly declared: "I hate all men"). They knew he had stolen a roll of Scotch tape from the teacher he threatened to kill and that the classmate he threatened was the one who told on him.

Now, two weeks later, the staff was learning that its courageous decision had paid off. Mr. Papanek told how he took John into his office and talked things over with him for a few hours. He said to the boy: "Look. We know that you stole from a teacher. We still love you. We want you here. But you must help us, too. You can't go around throwing knives at people."

Later, when they happened to meet in the hall, Mr. Papanek offered John a candy. The teacher whom the boy threatened got him interested in stacking up books on the shelves of the classroom bookcase. John forgot about knives. No longer did the staff have to watch him night and day to protect the other boys.

A quietly jubilant staff discussed the change. John was taking up boxing. Nervous and energetic, he was using some of his energy in dancing. He was heard singing and laughing with a group of boys. "He now wants to get attention—by pleasing, instead of killing," Mr. Papanek said.

John is an extreme case for Wiltwyck, a non-sectarian and interracial school. The eighty boys at the school, in the wooded foothills of the Catskills across the Hudson River from Hyde Park, have an average stay of one and a half years.[1]

Through the nineteenth century whenever a "guilty" child was believed to have the ability to distinguish between right and wrong, the case was usually disposed of in court by one general type of treatment: punishment. The basis for such treatment was the classical (or free will) theory of human behavior—the theory that crimes are motivated by the calculation of the pleasure involved along with the pain involved, a surplus

---

[1] *New York Times*, February 12, 1950.

of calculated pleasure leading to criminal behavior. By making the act retroactively more painful than pleasurable, punishment was not only societal revenge; it was also believed to be treatment in that it deterred both the offender and onlookers from further criminal behavior.

The establishment of the juvenile court with its chancery, deterministic philosophy led to the decline of punishment as revenge and treatment of children. Punishment came to be looked upon as ineffective, and other forms of treatment consistent with the "patient" approach to delinquents replaced it.

Punishment of adjudged delinquents may be obsolete today in theory, but it is not entirely so in practice. Indeed, when one studies the major types of disposition and treatment, one discovers that they represent degrees of punishment ranging from a minimum in foster home placement to severe punishment in many institutions called reformatories, industrial schools, and training schools. It is also noteworthy that if the judge disposes of a case with no punishment in mind, this is no guarantee that the child feels unpunished. Even if we tell each other that foster home care is not punishment, "it does not remove the aspect of punishment from the youngster's mind. Nor does the vocabulary really remove it from our own." [2]

The treatment and rehabilitation of the adjudged delinquent presupposes knowledge—or at least a theory—of etiology. Delinquent behavior cannot be corrected without having either an explicit or implicit conception of what brought it on. For example, if it is thought that delinquency is a product of situations where there are alternative systems of norms for reaching cultural goals or objectives, then treatment should involve convincing the child to accept the values and norms of the conventional group, either in opposition to the conflicting values or through their elimination.

But, to a surprising extent, treatment does not rest on such etiological foundations. Instead, several "isms" underlie many treatment programs: moralism, the idea that the youngster is inherently bad; scapegoatism, looking for something to blame;

[2] Ruth Gilpin, "Foster Home Care for Delinquent Children," *The Annals of the American Academy of Political and Social Science*, 261:124, 1949.

fatalism, the assumption that nothing can really be done; sectarianism, using one method of treatment to the exclusion of all others; formalism, lack of freshness and ingenuity; dogmatism, a closed mind; and sentimentalism, a "warm" heart without a "cool" head.[3]

An outstanding theoretical contrast between today and the situation years ago in the disposition and treatment of adjudged delinquents is that the disposition is no longer necessarily considered to be terminal. Nor does the disposition place any civil disabilities on the child; nor, legally speaking, does it work against his interest. The theory is also that treatment is related to the individual child's needs. This means that the judge's decision cannot be mechanical in the classical sense of the criminal law and courts' principle of a particular penalty to fit a particular offense. Nevertheless the tendency in practice in many courts is to assign delinquents to a preconceived category; to apply institutionalization, probation, or alternative types of treatment at the judge's disposal with little or no thought or study given to individual differences between the adjudged delinquents. This is often called "classification," and the justification for its use is that it is necessary when large numbers of delinquents must be disposed of in a short time.

Alternative Dispositions of Cases

Although there are several possible alternatives in the disposition and treatment of delinquency cases, four types actually predominate:

1. *The child's case is dismissed, adjusted by restitution, or held open without further action.* Nationwide statistics show that approximately 46 per cent of the boys' cases, contrasted with 36 per cent of the girls' cases, are disposed in this manner. A plausible explanation may be found in the reasons for referral to court. In the boys' cases referrals are more frequently for acts against property, and many of these are adjusted by restitution.

2. *The child is committed to an institution, with the possibility of parole thereafter.* In recent years approximately ten per cent of the adjudged cases of delinquency have been disposed of

[3] Lecture by Paul W. Tappan at a meeting of the Institutes of Probation, February 19, 1949.

in this way, but the proportion has been declining consistently from one year to the next.

3. *The child is left in his own home on probation.* This is the disposition in approximately one third of all cases, and the proportion has generally been increasing from one year to the next.

4. *The child is placed in a foster home.*

The disposition in a given case of delinquency is determined by a number of factors or variables. One, of course, is the presence or absence of a variety of treatment facilities available to the judge. There is often a marked difference between one judge and the next in the number and quality of probation officers he may call on to handle a case load; in the money available to place children in boarding or foster homes; and in the range of types of institutions to which he may commit delinquents.

Another factor is the difference between judges. This was brought out in Frankel's comparative study of the types of dispositions made by four New Jersey judges in three selected years. Quantitative differences were noted, amounting to more than ten per cent, in the use of probation and institutionalization. Two of the judges, especially, showed marked differences in disposition of the same types of cases. Qualitative differences between the judges were noted, such as in the degree of informality of courtroom procedure, agents consulted before disposition, and attitudes toward persons of different nationalities.[4] The variety of ideas held by juvenile-court judges regarding the place of any given type of disposition is reflected in the miscellany of children found subject to it. This is especially true of institutionalization. The one common denominator for children so committed is that they have all been adjudged delinquent, and in most cases there has been inadequate examination into the basis of their difficulty or their need for institutional treatment.

Despite the philosophy that disposition of delinquency cases should be influenced mostly by the personality and needs of the child, and little if at all by his offense, the latter does play a large

[4] Emil Frankel, "The Offender and the Court: A Statistical Analysis of the Sentencing of Delinquents," *Journal of Criminal Law and Criminology*, 31:448–56, 1940.

part in determining the type of disposition. Some offenses lead to more punishing treatment than others, depending on their position in the scale of values held by the judge.

The age of the delinquent is still another factor that affects the type of disposition. The younger child generally is less likely to receive commitment to an institution and more likely to receive probation and dismissal than the older one. Race is another factor, for it has been found that white male delinquents are more often dismissed and less often committed to institutions than are Negro male delinquents, but white girls are lower in dismissals and higher in commitments than Negro girls. The interpretation of the boys' cases is self-evident, but for the girls the explanation is that white judges guard the sexually promiscuous daughters of the dominant race by committing them, whereas the same offense is not considered as serious in the case of Negro girls.[5]

Lastly, the sex of the delinquent and the size of the county where he or she is adjudged affect the disposition of the case. A boy coming to court has been found to have four chances out of ten of being placed on probation, whereas a girl has only two and one-half chances out of ten. Commitment instead of probation is found in a larger percentage of the girls' cases than of boys' cases. Larger counties in general prefer to supervise a case informally rather than remove it from court jurisdiction by commitment to an institution. The opposite tendency is observed in smaller counties.[6]

The Philosophy and History of Institutionalization

Segregating the offender has been a practice throughout the history of mankind. Today segregation of juvenile delinquents takes the form of commitment to training, correctional, and industrial schools, or to institutions called reformatories. The philosophy of institutionalization is not only to "train," "correct," or

[5] Walter C. Reckless and Mapheus Smith, *Juvenile Delinquency*, New York, McGraw-Hill, 1932, pp. 71–6; Edward E. Schwartz, "Statistics of Juvenile Delinquency in the United States," *The Annals of the American Academy of Political and Social Science*, 261:17, 1949.

[6] Benedict S. Alper and George E. Lodgen, "The Delinquent Child in Pennsylvania Courts," *Mental Hygiene*, 20:598–604, 1936; Schwartz, *op. cit.*, p. 7.

"reform" the delinquent but to protect the community in the meantime from further offenses. The assumption in institutionalization is that the delinquent is to be only temporarily confined and that he can anticipate returning to his home. Learning a trade in the institution, conformity, cleanliness, and contact with nature ("green grass, cows, and God's open country") will somehow reform the child and make it possible to reincorporate him into conventional groups upon his release and return home.[7]

Literature conveys to us virtually nothing about the institutionalization of convicted juveniles in ancient times and in the early Middle Ages. The material that historians have been able to cull almost invariably refers to young adults or adults. In the late Middle Ages, however, the first "reformatories" or "bettering houses" were established for convicted and neglected children. Shortly after the Reformation, correctional imprisonment appeared, partly to provide what was thought to be a suitable means of treating convicted juveniles and youths.[8]

In Colonial days in this country, it was commonplace to find children of all ages in local prisons. Even after the states set up their own prison systems, children were confined in them, occasionally in separate quarters but often mixed indiscriminately with adult offenders. Progress in the direction of establishing institutions for wayward children was extremely slow. Until a century ago it was still the prevalent pattern to care for the criminal, insane, dependent, neglected, and diseased in the same institution. Gradually the recognition emerged that the needs of each of these groups were different and that they should be classified and treated on differential bases. But even today, in

---

[7] "Correction" or "reform," however, is often merely a euphemism for what actually occurs in an institution. Commitment is often confined to the most recalcitrant cases and is used frequently only after other alternatives in disposition and treatment have failed. Secondly, it is questionable whether the mode of participation in society can be learned in the regimented atmosphere of an institution. A third point is that the psychology of revenge and punishment is still present, contemporary theory notwithstanding, and such a psychology is considered today by criminologists to be incompatible with correctional treatment. See Arthur E. Fink, *The Field of Social Work*, New York, Holt, 1942, pp. 101–2; Ralph S. Banay, *Youth in Despair*, New York, Coward-McCann, 1948, pp. 205–6.

[8] Thorsten Sellin, "Youth and Crime," *Law and Contemporary Problems*, 9:581, 1942.

many jurisdictions, training schools for delinquents are still virtually dumping-grounds for children who are neglected, mentally defective, pre-psychotic, and physically and glandularly disordered. As many as two thirds of the children in a given training school may really require care in an institution for defectives.

Seventy-five years before the first juvenile court, some separate institutions for juveniles appeared in the United States. These so-called "houses of refuge" were meant to shield children from corrupting contacts with adults. They were introduced under private auspices in New York, but later they were supported by public appropriation. The nomenclature changed from "houses of refuge" to "reform schools," and then to "training" and "industrial" schools. Today every state in the country has at least one separate institution for the treatment of children committed there by the juvenile courts.[9]

In the earliest days the transition from a penal to a rehabilitative philosophy was drastic. As institutions grew in number, the new philosophy weakened somewhat and the old philosophy enjoyed a comeback. In the 1930's the new philosophy had a renaissance. Today, however, institutions are still far from free of punitive characteristics.[10]

At first children in their own separate institutions were looked upon as a homogeneous group to be treated primarily in mass. Increased awareness of individual differences gave rise to programs of individualized treatment in a few institutions.

The trend today is away from institutional commitment toward alternatives like probation and foster home care. In a broad sense one may speak of the nineteenth century as the period of the building of institutions. The twentieth century, on the other hand, especially since the first White House Conference of 1909, has brought on their decline.[11]

[9] National Conference on Prevention and Control of Juvenile Delinquency, *Report on Institutional Treatment of Delinquent Juveniles*, Washington, D.C., U.S. Government Printing Office, 1946, pp. 1, 11.

[10] John B. Costello, "Institutions for Juvenile Delinquents," *The Annals of the American Academy of Political and Social Science*, 261:166, 1949.

[11] Fink, *op. cit.*, p. 92.

Statistics on Institutionalization

At any one time, approximately 35,000 boys and girls can be found in American public and private institutions for juvenile delinquents. About two thirds are in public and one third in private institutions. Many of the early established institutions cared for boys and girls in separate buildings; others congregated both sexes in the same building. Massachusetts and Ohio were among the first states to turn to the cottage plan in the effort to group delinquents in a social setting resembling the family unit at home. Today the average is approximately fifty training schools for boys, fifty for girls, and eleven for both sexes under the same administration. Several states maintain separate institutions for Negro juvenile delinquents. The state institutions vary considerably in size, but most of them accommodate between 200 and 400. The institutional population ranges in age from 7 to 21 years, depending upon the commitment laws and alternative types of disposition available in the state for adjudged delinquents.[12] The maximum age at which juvenile delinquents may be admitted to institutions exclusively for their cases varies from one state to the next. As one might expect, the population of juvenile institutions and the number of admissions to them reflect this variation. Some types of cases, such as sex delinquents and truants, are committed to institutions in some states but are completely avoided in commitments in other states. One may infer that these cases are regarded as very serious in some jurisdictions but not in others. Consequently statistics on institutional population and admissions tend to reflect differences in administrative procedure rather than actual differences in the incidence of certain types of offenses.[13]

Classification of Institutions

There are two general categories of institutions, public and private. Private institutions in turn may be classified into the

[12] National Conference on Prevention and Control of Juvenile Delinquency, *Report on Institutional Treatment of Delinquent Juveniles*, Washington, D.C., U.S. Government Printing Office, 1946, p. 5.

[13] National Conference on Prevention and Control of Juvenile Delinquency, *Report on Statistics*, Washington, D.C., U.S. Government Printing Office, 1947, pp. 18–19.

nonsectarian and the sectarian.[14] The hundred-odd public (usually state) institutions in the United States are, in a sense, the dumping-grounds for communities that do not have private institutional facilities for their adjudged delinquents. They receive, when there is room, cases that have been rejected by private institutions. Such cases are usually Negroes, recidivists, the feebleminded, the psychotic, sex deviates, the physically handicapped, and gang members. While Negroes are accepted, racial segregation is often practiced in the form of a Jim Crow cottage system, even though this is a violation of specific statutes of some states, which prohibit racial discrimination in public agencies.

The average length of stay in public institutions is approximately eight and a half months. The cost of institutionalization varies, as do other expenses, with the fluctuation in prices from one year to the next. It is interesting to note, however, that in recent years it cost some states as much to send and keep a delinquent in an institution as it would cost to send a young person to college.

Private institutions are licensed and inspected periodically by the state departments of social welfare. They are maintained by endowments, tuition, gifts, and a charge to the jurisdiction using them. Commitment by the court to a private institution is made only by consultation with the institution, for the latter reserves the right to screen admissions through an intake worker or a committee. Because of this selective process, private institutions are often criticized for discriminating against Negroes and handicapped, disturbed, and retarded children.[15]

Physical Facilities

Most institutions for delinquents have a mixture of old and new buildings and differ widely in their standards of maintenance and repair. Generally speaking, they present serious fire hazards as a consequence of poor construction, defective wiring, locked and blocked exits, and substandard methods of fire control and prevention. Specialists in institutional housing and facilities

[14] In New York State private institutions are all sectarian because state law requires that dependent and neglected children, as well as delinquents, who are not sent to public institutions be sent to institutions of their own religious affiliation.

[15] Costello, *op. cit.*, p. 167.

maintain that if there are 150 or more institutionalized delinquents, there is need for (1) an administrative center that includes offices for case-work personnel, interviewing, conference
rooms, and the filing of records; (2) a receiving and orientation
unit, to receive children upon admission for a period of observation and orientation, and including physical examination rooms,
shower and dressing rooms, and rooms for psychological tests;
(3) student housing units, each to contain a maximum of 25 children; (4) staff housing units; (5) a medical and hygiene center
containing bed-space on the basis of ten per cent of the total
institutional population; (6) an education center; (7) chapel
buildings; (8) a recreation and entertainment center; (9) dining
room, kitchen, and warehouse; (10) maintenance shops for the
upkeep of plant and equipment; (11) a farm center as part of the
training program; and (12) heating, sewage, and water supply.[16]

Program of Training and Personnel

The program of training in an institution for juvenile delinquents can be divided into four phases:
1. Reception-orientation.
2. Training program.
3. Preparation for release.
4. After-care or parole.

The highest standard for the staff conducting this program
is that they have some training in social work, or at least some
acquaintance with the philosophy and practice of case work.
While cottage "fathers" and "mothers" (where there is a residential cottage plan in which the delinquents are supposed to
live in small, informal groups) are not expected to be graduates
of schools of social work, the expectation is that they have
understanding, sensitivity, and genuine interest in their relations
with children. Instead one finds among the personnel in institutions an unusual number of failures who have left other fields of
work, and people who are insecure and sadistic with regard to
the delinquents.[17] A political turnover in a state administration

[16] National Conference on Prevention and Control of Juvenile Delinquency, *Report on Institutional Treatment of Delinquent Juveniles*, Washington, D.C., U.S. Government Printing Office, 1946, pp. 5–9.
[17] Fink, *op. cit.*, p. 95.

frequently brings in its wake a complete change in the staffs of public welfare institutions, including those for delinquents. Most have no qualifications for their work. They are generally paid less than zoo keepers in charge of animals. Salaries are so low in most institutions that qualified professional workers of all categories—teachers, social workers, recreational and vocational directors—do not bother to apply except in times of economic depression. A salary of fifteen to seventeen hundred dollars per year *per couple* is offered by many states to cottage parents.

Administrative Control

There is wide agreement that state institutions for delinquents should be administered by the state department that has responsibility for other child welfare services, and not by the department concerned with adult correctional institutions. Yet, throughout the various states, there is considerable variation in administrative control. In some states, juvenile institutions are operated by a special division such as a children's bureau; elsewhere, responsibility is in the hands of the same division as that which operates adult correction; in still other states, training schools are controlled by divisions such as the fiscal, personnel, construction, and medical.

Many states have institution boards, usually composed of laymen and a few state officials ex officio controlling the policy of the administration. Although authorities recognize the value of such lay boards in an advisory capacity representing public opinion, they are convinced that the boards should not be the controlling administrative body in this age of specialization and professional techniques.

Organizational structure, it is felt, should enable control to issue down from the governing authority—preferably a state department in charge of other child welfare services—through a specialized division to a professionally trained superintendent. This makes for a direct line and the most effective channeling of legislative and financial needs for the institutions.[18]

[18] National Conference on Prevention and Control of Juvenile Delinquency, *Report on Institutional Treatment of Delinquent Juveniles*, Washington, D.C., U.S. Government Printing Office, 1946, pp. 2–4.

Brutality in Institutions

Despite the nonpunitive philosophy of institutions for delinquents, punishment, even brutality, is not uncommon. In a four-month survey beginning late in 1947 and ending early in 1948, Deutsch [19] found that "adjustment cottages" in some institutions are really disciplinary barracks; "supervisors" are actually guards; "cottage parents" are little more than caretakers and custodians. Whips, paddles, blackjacks, and straps are "tools of control." Isolation cells are called "meditation rooms," and the inmates are referred to as "students."

In many state institutions corporal punishment is officially forbidden, but it is practiced anyway, with or without the superintendent's tacit consent. Even in the "best" training schools children undergo the following:

1. *Duck-walking.* The offending child must grasp his ankles and waddle about like a duck.

2. *The squats.* This is deep knee-bending for a specified period or number of times. Some children are sentenced to 5,000 squats, worked out in intermittent sessions to avoid collapse.

3. *Brick-counting.* The offender stands erect with his nose touching the wall.

4. *Star-gazing.* The offender stands erect with his eyes turned up to the ceiling.

5. *Standing on line.* This involves standing erect in absolute silence, sometimes for hours, often with hands upraised.

6. *Rice-polishing.* Boys crawl on their knees across a floor strewn with rice grains until bleeding starts and suffering is intense enough to satisfy the disciplinarian that "justice" has been done.

7. *The slicks.* This is humiliation by shaving the heads of returned runaways and other offenders.

8. *Burlap party.* Offenders of rules are made to push piles of burlap bags across a floor flooded with water. When the bags are soaked through, they have to wring them and then resume sopping up water with burlap until the floors are dry.

9. *Walking posts.* This is marching between or around posts continuously for a prescribed number of hours.

[19] Albert Deutsch, "Is This Reform?" *Woman's Home Companion,* March 1948, pp. 30–44.

10. *Runaway pills.* Captured runaways are dosed with laxatives to "help them run."

11. *The cold tub.* This is a form of disciplinary "hydrotherapy" in which rule-violators are thrown into tubs filled with ice-cold water.

A "game" played in some institutions surveyed by Deutsch is called "flying home." The idea is to administer a kick or paddlewhack to a boy's backside so sharply and expertly as to shock his nervous system and literally lift him off the floor. Failure or success for the disciplinarian is measured by the height reached by the offending child and the distance he travels.

Excessive regimentation and monotonous food, work, schooling, and recreation may induce severe behavior disturbances in institutions for delinquents. "Rag-sniffing" is one of such disturbances detected by observers. It consists of soaking a rag in gasoline, benzene, floor polish, or virtually anything else that gives off strong fumes. The boy then holds the rag to his nose and breathes deeply until he becomes dizzy and nauseated. Aside from these unpleasant after-effects, the user has a "high" feeling quite different from the monotonous pattern of life in the institution.

Failure of Most Institutions

The majority of delinquents who have been committed to institutions are not reformed or corrected. Institutions generally fail to achieve their goals, for a number of reasons. One is that there are many children in institutions whose problems have too long been neglected and who presently have emotional difficulties so advanced that successful treatment there is virtually impossible, given the prevalent type of program and the quality of staff. Another reason for institutional failure is the admixture of widely different children in a given institution. This limits the opportunities for individual rehabilitation and is conducive to regimentation and monotony. For example, experience with mentally defective delinquents points to the need for separate institutionalization in such cases.[20]

There are still other reasons for institutional failure. The

[20] G. Dybwad, "The Problem of Institutional Placement for High-grade Mentally Defective Delinquents," *American Journal of Mental Deficiency,* 45:391–400, 1941.

dynamic nature of each delinquent's behavior is still too infrequently understood in institutions. The treatment of most children there proceeds with scant life history data and with too limited guidance at each step. Furthermore, little if any coordination is attempted in all that the institutional staff endeavors to do for the children.

In most institutions too much political domination and interference prevails.[21] Much constructive attention is frequently paid to the physical appearance of the institution, but too little of this attitude is directed toward the children who live in it. Consequently, corporal punishment for misbehavior in institutions is still widespread, and reinforces the child's difficulties, whereas the rewarding of good behavior is still relatively scarce even though it has a beneficial effect.

It should be pointed out, finally, that institutions can hardly operate successfully in isolation from the communities to which the delinquents are to return. Failure seems to be inevitable when institutional programs are formulated without any consideration of the social situations to which children must eventually adjust.

An Innovation in Institutional Treatment

Some serious efforts are now being made to overcome the failure of institutional treatment. One conspicuous innovation in recent years is group therapy, also called "guided group interaction."

Group therapy takes what is presently known about human behavior and attempts to apply it, through the medium of group discussion, toward the reorientation of the offender. The purpose of group therapy is to re-educate the delinquent so that he will come to accept the restrictions of society and find satisfaction in conformity to social norms. It involves free discussion by inmate groups of their pre-institutional as well as their institutional experiences. In this manner the problems of the participants are historically traced and analyzed. All topics are proper subject matter for discussion by the group. The effectiveness of the discussion depends on the ability of the leader to encourage un-

[21] See Harrison A. Dobbs, "Are Correctional Schools Evil or Are We?" *Federal Probation*, 14:38, 1950.

inhibited expression and to co-ordinate these expressions into group sessions that have meaning and purpose for the participants.

Group therapy calls for an informal, permissive atmosphere, in which the participants are equals. In New Jersey's correctional institutions, where the innovation has been thoroughly tested, group therapy programs are believed to have had substantial success. This is because both personnel and delinquents become very conscious of each other as distinct personalities; tensions are reduced, even though initially the introduction of the program may increase tension; greater insight is cultivated on the part of some of the delinquents, as measured by psychiatric and psychological examinations; channels of communication are opened between the "world of inmates and the world of administrators," so that the number of complaints about the institution and its personnel decreases; and finally, meaningful social experiences are provided for a greater number of delinquents.[22]

Actually there are four distinct types of group therapy, whether in or out of institutions: (a) *activity group therapy* for children aged seven to thirteen; (b) *analytic group therapy,* for psychoneurotic adolescents; (c) *activity-interview group therapy* for school-age children with very serious problems; and (d) *play-group therapy* for preschool children.[23]

(a) *Activity group therapy* involves a group comprising seven or eight children of the same sex and approximately the same age. Their leader is a specially trained therapist. The children in the group have in common a pattern of rejection by parents, school, or companions. Some are actively hostile and destructive, whereas others have withdrawn into introversion. Their fears and guilt feelings lead to overcompensation by antisocial behavior.

The group meets as a club once a week for a few hours, with the opportunity to release their drives collectively. Provided with arts and crafts materials, they may use these in any way they like, ranging from constructive effort to destruction of materials and furniture and fighting among themselves. The therapist permits

---

[22] F. Lovell Bixby and Lloyd W. McCorkle, "Applying the Principles of Group Therapy in Correctional Institutions," *Federal Probation,* 14:36–40, 1950.

[23] S. R. Slavson, "Group Psychotherapy," *Scientific American,* 183: 42–5, 1950.

the children to act out their aggression and hostility without fear of punishment, criticism, or disapproval. Each child is unconditionally accepted by the therapist with love and support. Eventually definite order and group adjustment evolve. The diffident and fearful members of the group become more outgoing; on the other hand, the aggressive ones take on more subdued behavior. They are now able to assume acceptable social roles because they look upon themselves as adequate. The new feeling of security is applied to other life situations in the course of time.

(b) *Analytic group therapy* places more emphasis on discussion and interviews, and no material artifacts whatsoever are provided. The group's members, under the guidance of the therapist, discuss their common problems with each other, giving each one of them support to uncover his feelings and attitudes. The result is catharsis, the acquisition of insight into one's own behavior, and the sublimation of destructive tendencies.

(c) and (d) *Activity-interview* and *play-group therapy* are both combinations of activity and analytic group therapy. The activity-interview variety is designed for deeply disturbed children who need to talk about their anxieties and internal conflicts as well as to act out their feelings. The therapist needs to apply limitations and controls of some sort. Therefore they are formed into a play group and supplied with dolls, blocks, clay, water, watercolor paints, doll houses, and other toys. Through the play activity the children express their concealed resentments, frustrations, fears, and confusions. For example, the therapist helps a child who tears viciously at a doll to see that he is actually expressing his feelings toward a younger brother or sister who, he feels, has taken his place in the affections of his parents. If the child does not always acquire this insight immediately, repeated incidents and explanations may lead to such understanding. The guilt and fears associated with the prohibited feelings are diminished, and presumably the child becomes freer and happier.

Progressive Types of Institutions

A more basic innovation in institutional treatment is the establishment of modified types of institutions.

HAWTHORNE CEDAR KNOLLS SCHOOL. Illustrative of such modifications is the Hawthorne Cedar Knolls School, sponsored by the

Jewish Board of Guardians in Westchester, New York, and financed by the Federation of Jewish Philanthropies. Its objective is the emotional reconstruction of the child. The term "delinquent" is regarded as archaic and is never used there. Noninstitutional in appearance, its cottages house approximately two hundred juveniles committed there for thieving, violence in home and school, sex offenses, etc. There are no guards, locked doors, fences, or prohibiting signs on the premises. The staff numbers one hundred, and includes cottage parents, schoolteachers, social-work graduates, psychiatric social workers, psychiatrists who visit the institution one or two days a week, medical consultants, and the farm staff. Staff members are assigned to the child guidance clinic, the educational department, or the medical department. A student self-governing council, consisting of representatives from each cottage, functions as a clearing-house for problems and grievances.

A child coming to Hawthorne stays there from a few months to two years (the average is twenty-one months). The pivot point of treatment is the cottage parent. A typical child is admitted deliberately on Friday, to afford relaxation over the weekend with movies, games, and new acquaintances. During this time his file is interpreted by a psychiatric social worker for his cottage parents. This gives them the opportunity to anticipate some of the problems of the child. The first week the child takes several physical, psychological, and vocational tests. A school program is laid out for him and he is set to work also in one of the vocational classes—printing shop, carpentry, sewing, mechanical shop, or farming.

After school the child visits his social worker and discusses matters with him. The child is encouraged to join a school club. Occasionally, as he shows progress, the child goes home for weekend visits. With further progress he may attend the local high school or do salaried work off the premises, returning in the evenings to Hawthorne.

THE GEORGE JUNIOR REPUBLIC. An internationally famous type of institution is the George Junior Republic. The original Republic in Freeville, New York, has been duplicated in other states, in South America, and in Europe. Founded in 1895 by William Reuben George, it was at first no more than a "fresh-air camp" for underprivileged children of New York City. Later it emerged as a coeducational institution, not only for those who had been adjudged delinquent (cases considered amenable to treatment in this type of institution) but also for those in danger of becoming delinquent. The latter cases reach the Republic through the referrals of their own parents, welfare agencies, and sometimes through their own efforts. Technically, no boy or girl is committed to the Republic. Each must agree to "enroll" voluntarily.

The underlying concept of the institution is *citizenship* and the *responsibilities* that accompany it. The institution is a miniature quasi-community for children ranging in age from thirteen to nineteen, with grade and high school classrooms, a residential cottage plan under the care of house parents, a nonsectarian chapel, a gymnasium, trade shops, and dairy buildings. The children are "citizens" and annually elect their own officers: a president, vice president, secretary of state, and treasurer. The president appoints a magistrate, court clerk, attorney general, chief of police, health commissioner, and truant officer. If any citizen does not like the rules he or she may advocate changes by campaigning to amend or abolish them.

The slogan of the Republic is "Nothing without Labor." Every citizen is paid for working and going to school, and in turn the citizen must pay for room and board and for any other necessities. Citizens are permitted to choose the kind of work they want, with the advice of a counselor. The boys usually work on dairy farms and in mechanical trades; girls are required to take a homemaking course developed by Cornell and Syracuse Universities. Some girls work in the bank and in the administrative offices while others become skilled in dressmaking. If a citizen does not work, he or she is brought before the Republic's court and charged with vagrancy. The usual penalty is restriction of social life.[24]

Income taxes must be paid at the Republic, ranging from two per cent on monthly incomes reaching twenty-five dollars, up to ten per cent on incomes of more than eighty dollars a month.

---

[24] There is also a Republic jail where "prisoners" work two hours extra a day without pay, and with the possibility that their citizenship will be revoked.

Everything must be bought with money the citizen earns, the Republic having its own bank and currency. If a boy or girl needs a loan or capital to finance a business project, he or she may apply at the bank where the application is acted upon by citizen-bankers. Any citizen may set up his own business if he or she so wishes, and hire other citizens to work for him.

An evaluation of institutions of this type brings forth both commendation and criticism. In its behalf, for example, one may speak of citizenship, with the active, clearly defined roles it offers juveniles. The lack of this in the lives of American juveniles, as we have seen, appears to be an important etiological factor in delinquency. In criticism one may refer to the transplantation of the value processes and goals of the larger, adult world—competition, status striving, acquisition of goods. A strong suspicion is that there are criminogenic aspects in such a social and cultural environment just as there are in the "outside" world of American society.

THE ENGLISH BORSTAL SYSTEM.   Another type of institution, with a worldwide reputation, is found in the English Borstal System, named after the village of Borstal in Kent, the site of the first such institution. The Borstal System emerged in 1908 from the Prison System of England, its model being the English "public schools." Physically the Borstal schools may vary from converted prisons and hut-camps to "stately homes of England." Until 1946 there was only one Borstal school for girls. Civilian dress is worn, and in some of the institutions there is a house plan involving living in separate cottages under house masters who foster a close relationship with the boys. Each house is supposed to become the focal point of identification for the boys who live there, and the master seeks to indoctrinate them with standards of acceptable behavior. Community participation is encouraged in the institution's activities, to assure the boys that they are not outcasts.[25]

After being sentenced to Borstal training, boys are first transferred to a reception center. The center classifies them and allocates them to one of the Borstal schools. The boys sent usually stay there from two to three years. There are various opportunities for work and they are allowed to spend about a

[25] William Healy and Benedict S. Alper, *Criminal Youth and the Borstal System*, New York, The Commonwealth Fund, 1941.

shilling a week of their earnings. The trades and crafts they may learn vary from bricklaying to baking, carpentering, cobbling, and laundering. During their stay they acquire nothing without paying for it.[26]

If they do not adjust there, they are sent to a detention wing at Wandsworth Prison to do penance. If they are discharged from the Borstal System and get into trouble again they are recalled to the Licence Revocation Centre at Chelmsford Prison for correction and further training.

New Legislation for Institutional Treatment: the Youth Correction Authority Act

Perennial attempts to improve institutional treatment of delinquents are initiated by legislative action. Best known of all in recent years is the legislation enacted in some states, on the basis of a model bill drawn up by the American Law Institute in 1940, and known as the Youth Correction Authority Act.[27] The proposed Act was not radically new. It was conceived merely as a synthesis of selected practices already in effect in a number of different states.

The fundamental premise on which the model Youth Correction Authority Act was based is that delinquency is not a manifestation of the diabolical will of particular juveniles. Rather it is primarily a symptom of our "sick" society. Punishment does not reform the offender nor protect society. The need is for scientific treatment aimed at rehabilitation. The obvious place to begin such treatment is in the community at the early stages of juvenile delinquency. Furthermore, such treatment should be accompanied by preventive action to remove the social and psychological sources of delinquency. This cannot be done effectively without strengthening and improving services to all juveniles and youth.

An advisory committee of the American Law Institute had recommended as early as 1938 that the treatment of an adjudged delinquent or youthful offender should take into account his

[26] Most of the boys are committed for such offenses as theft and burglary.

[27] Official Draft, *Youth Correction Authority Act*, The American Law Institute, 1940.

personality characteristics and other etiological factors leading to his delinquency or offense, rather than depending on the nature of his delinquent act. It had also recommended that treatment should be aimed primarily at the correction of the juvenile or youth's "antisocial tendencies," and that he should be kept under control until such time as it is reasonably certain that he is "cured" of these tendencies. Each person is sufficiently different from others to warrant a study of him before a particular treatment is applied. If it is clear that no particular treatment is necessary and that the delinquent act was merely an isolated incident unlikely to occur again, the juvenile should be released immediately. When the need is for minor treatment, and it is apparently successful, he should be discharged immediately thereafter. But if the "disorder" leading to the delinquency is deep-rooted, prolonged treatment and control of the child should be expected.[28]

Those who prepared the model Act concluded that the state correctional systems were the logical areas in which to begin this shift from punitive to rehabilitative goals. The direct reorientation of the thousands of local jurisdictions seemed an impossible task. Therefore the model Act was concerned only with the procedures for handling offenders after their adjudication and commitment to the state. Even on that limited basis, the American Law Institute doubted that it would be possible to secure legislative action implementing its proposal with regard to the treatment of all age groups. Prospects for the adoption of the Act seemed brightest if the program were limited to the older juvenile and youth groups. Accordingly, the model Act was initially designed to apply to committed offenders between 16 and 21 years of age.[29]

The model Act called for the creation of a "Correctional Authority" in the individual state, made up of at least three members who would serve as administrators of its provisions. Anyone between 16 and 21 years of age convicted in any court, except a juvenile court, would be required to be committed to the Authority. In effect, this commitment to the Authority would be the court's sentence, and it would be the Authority's responsi-

[28] John Forbes Perkins, "Indeterminate Control of Offenders: Arbitrary and Discriminatory," *Law and Contemporary Problems*, 9:624, 1942.

[29] John R. Ellingston, *Protecting Our Children from Criminal Careers*, New York, Prentice-Hall, 1948, pp. 48–9.

bility to determine the length of sentence and the form of treatment.[30]

Four states have enacted legislation based on the model Act —California in 1941, Minnesota and Wisconsin in 1947, and Massachusetts in 1948. The California legislation and its so-called Youth Authority are not only the oldest but enjoy the widest reputation. In most respects California followed the model Act closely, but there were, nevertheless, the following major differences:

1. Under the model Act the judge would not place on probation those persons coming within the age group committed to the Authority. On the other hand, the California Act provided that the courts may grant probation to this age group and may also impose jail sentences up to ninety days.

2. Under the model Act the Authority would be empowered to accept persons from 16 to 21 years of age. In California there is no lower age limit and the state's Authority, in the early years of its establishment, could accept any boy or girl from the juvenile courts if the courts cared to commit and if the Authority cared to accept. Furthermore, in California the upper age limit is now raised to 23 years at the time of apprehension.

3. Unlike the model Act, the California Act provides as a major function of the Authority the establishment or assistance in the establishment of public councils or committees having to do with delinquency prevention.[31]

In subsequent years the California Youth Authority, by amending legislation, was given supervision over all delinquent children and youthful offenders. It was given control of California's three reform schools for boys and girls; and it developed a network of small, camplike schools for delinquents to be committed on a carefully selected basis of age, background, personality, and potentiality. One camp, for example, may have children from the ages eleven to thirteen, and another may have those between fourteen and sixteen. The Youth Authority has also attempted to stimulate communities to establish and operate their

[30] John Barker Waite, "The Youth Correction Authority Act," *Law and Contemporary Problems*, 9:603–5, 1942.

[31] Karl Holton, "Youth Correction Authority in Action: The California Experience," *Law and Contemporary Problems*, 9:655–6, 1942.

own camps for delinquent children, with the state of California paying half the cost of upkeep. At the request of any locality, the Youth Authority sends out its field experts to help develop a co-ordinating council, an organization of community agencies aimed at the control of delinquency by changing some of the conditions that are believed to provoke it.

Conclusion

The past century has witnessed some drastic changes in the modes of segregating and confining juvenile offenders. And it is likely that the chancery philosophy will continue to stimulate innovations in practices of institutionalization. But institutionalization, no matter how extensive its modification, has inherent limitations as a form of treatment. This fact has given rise, ever since the concept of delinquency was established, to a few alternatives in the treatment of delinquents.

The next chapter examines the major alternatives to institutionalization: parole, probation, deferred prosecution, and foster home placement.

QUESTIONS AND RESEARCH SUGGESTIONS

1. *Is the judge's disposition of a delinquency case terminal? Why?*
2. *What are the four major alternative dispositions of delinquency cases?*
3. *How does the age factor affect the type of disposition?*
4. *Why does institutionalization usually fail to achieve its goal?*
5. *What is the purpose of group therapy and what is its procedure?*
6. *Visit an institution for delinquents and analyze its underlying philosophy, organization, and program.*
7. *Study the details of the George Junior Republic and the English Borstal System and show the extent to which each reflects the culture of American and English society respectively.*

SELECTED READINGS AND REFERENCES

Alper, Benedict S., and George E. Lodgen, "The Delinquent Child in Pennsylvania Courts," *Mental Hygiene*, 20:598–604, 1936.
Bixby, F. Lovell, and Lloyd W. McCorkle, "Applying the Principles of

Group Therapy in Correctional Institutions," *Federal Probation,* 14:36–40, 1950.

Costello, John B., "Institutions for Juvenile Delinquents," *The Annals of the American Academy of Political and Social Science,* 261: 166–78, 1949.

Frankel, Emil, "The Offender and the Court: A Statistical Analysis of the Sentencing of Delinquents," *Journal of Criminal Law and Criminology,* 31:448–56, 1940.

Healy, William, and Benedict S. Alper, *Criminal Youth and the Borstal System,* New York, The Commonwealth Fund, 1941.

Mellanby, Molly, and R. L. Bradley, "The English Borstal System After the War," *Federal Probation,* 12:19–22, 1948.

National Conference on Prevention and Control of Juvenile Delinquency, *Report on Institutional Treatment of Delinquent Juveniles,* Washington, D.C., U.S. Government Printing Office, 1946.

Slavson, S. R., "Group Psychotherapy," *Scientific American,* 183:42–5, 1950.

Carl S——, age 18, was the sixth of seven children born to parents described as cultured, well-to-do, and socially prominent. The father, a successful banker, is distinguished in appearance, possesses many admirable traits, but is rigid, cold, domineering, and inflexible. The mother is a gracious person who is well-groomed, quiet-spoken, and self-contained. There are no indications of friction between the father and mother. Their home, located in one of the best residential sections of the community, is large and beautifully furnished.

More youthful appearing than his years, Carl is a tall, thin boy with a ready smile and agreeable manners. He has been marked as the "problem child" of the family for a long time. His early adjustment in school was poor. He was truant frequently, and he was given to lying and taking sums of money from the home. When he was eight years old he was taken to a mental hygiene clinic by his parents for advice and guidance. After repeated failures in school adjustment, a progressive private day school was tried but even the flexible curriculum and focus on individual interests failed to capture his sustained attention.

Carl had one interest—automobiles. He liked to drive them and to work on motors. At 15, he was arrested for operating an automobile without a driver's license, and at 16 persistent truancy and petty thefts brought him to the attention of the juvenile court, but no official record was made because the family arranged a plan for him. In March 1946 he was admitted to a well-known private training school, the father paying $1,400 a year tuition. Carl resented this action, and later contended that the only reason for it was that his father wanted to get rid of him.

His adjustment at the training school was fair for a time. He participated in the student government as a judge, and he did academic work at the eighth-grade level. Nevertheless he ran away numerous times during the next 14 months. Early in May 1947, Carl and another boy made off with the car of the principal of the school. They were apprehended in Virginia, and returned. Both boys escaped from detention at the school and a fortnight later, broke into the home of the principal, and departed in the same car, taking a watch, radio, cash, and clothing. They were apprehended in South Carolina. Neither the school authorities nor the father interceded this time and under the provisions of the Federal Juvenile Delinquency Act Carl was committed to the custody of the Attorney General by the United States District Court for the Eastern District of South Carolina.

At the National Training School in Washington, D.C., tests revealed that Carl had high-average intelligence (I.Q. 112), high-average mechanical aptitude, and high-average manual dexterity. He was assigned to part-time school, in which his work was poor, and to part-time auto class, in which his progress was above average despite less effort than was regarded as desirable. In the National Training

School evaluation this significant comment appears: "Much of this boy's future depends upon his family and their attitude toward him. So far, they have given him little affection and understanding. While he is a capable boy and has at least average abilities, he probably will never live up to the expectations of his parents."

Carl was received at the National Training School in late June 1947. In August, the admission summary was sent to the probation office, and in December the probation office was notified by telephone that Carl was granted parole effective at once and the school hoped he could be released before Christmas. There had been no parole planning. There had been some discussion of the possibility of working out a school program for him, and it was hoped something could be worked out with the parents.

The probation office summary of what happened subsequently is as follows:

"Upon initial contact, the father was obviously displeased that Carl had been granted parole. He felt the boy had been doing fairly well for the first time in his life and the same program should be continued for a longer period in order that settled work habits and attitudes might be firmly established. The boy had been at the National Training School only six months. It seemed very soon for him to come home. Furthermore, the parents had not been consulted. The father accepted the boy's return home as inevitable, but he was not prepared to offer any suggestions as to a parole plan. If we could make any arrangements about a school program, that would be satisfactory. We succeeded in having him participate to the extent of securing the services of a parish priest as the adviser. A tentative school plan was set up after conference with the director of vocational schools and a member of the guidance staff of the department of education. Carl was well known to these people because of their efforts to work out a plan for him a few years ago. If Carl could take an advanced course in automobile mechanics which would fit him for eventual work on a managerial level, he might gain status in the eyes of his family. In any event, Carl would have to participate in any plan decided upon, and he will be interviewed and tested after his return home." [1]

Despite man's ingenuity, there are surprisingly few major alternatives to institutionalization in the disposition and treatment of adjudged delinquents. Furthermore, three of the four alternatives—parole, probation, and deferred prosecution—are meaningful only as tentative substitutes for institutionalization. Implicit in each case is the assumption that if failure in treatment results, the recourse is to confine and segregate the offender.

Parole

Both public and private institutions for delinquents generally assume that there will be follow-up treatment for children released from the institutions. Parole is the usual name given to the follow-up supervision and treatment. Some children are paroled under the supervision of a staff responsible to the committing juvenile courts; in other cases the staff is responsible to the superintendent of the institution that has released them. The institution may turn over the parole supervision of its released children to state or local departments of welfare.

The philosophy of parole is that it is the most effective way to bridge the gap between the institution and the return to the community. Parole is divided into two phases:

1. The determination of when and under what conditions parole is to be granted.

2. The supervision and guidance afforded individuals who are placed on parole.

The parole officer's job is to help find work for the parolee, help him make friends, and guide him into legal recreational activities so that at the end of the parole period the parolee is law-abiding, and reasonably certain of self-respect and self-support. In a model parole program, the parole service begins to operate when the child reaches the institution. While he is there contacts are maintained with the child's family and community through the parole officer. Whatever agency is responsible for

[1] Frank T. Flynn, "Parole Supervision: A Case Analysis," *Federal Probation*, 15:36–7, June 1951.

recommending or granting parole keeps in constant touch with the child's progress. When the agency decides the time has come to grant parole, it may do so since the statutes regarding commitment and parole conditions are intended to permit discretion to the paroling agency.

Where institution and parole services are well integrated, the administrators of institutions rely upon parole experiences to evaluate the strengths and weaknesses in institutional programs, and thereby to modify their programs so as to prepare children more effectively for the return to the community.[2]

Fear that their institutional commitment will be a handicap in school and employment is a major anxiety felt by children on parole or about to be paroled. *The Declaration of the Principles of Parole*, adopted by the Attorney General's National Parole Conference several years ago, expressed the conviction that this can be overcome if the community aids the parolee to adjust vocationally and socially. The parolee's experience may be looked upon by the community as that of a person who has been seriously ill and is now convalescing.[3]

Probation

Laymen often confuse probation, as a form of disposition and treatment, with parole. Although both include supervision and guidance of the adjudged delinquent in the community, parole is a conditional release of an offender from a correctional institution, whereas probation is used instead of commitment to an institution.

Probation is thought to be an outgrowth of the juvenile court. Actually it appeared many years before the court was founded. In 1841 a Boston shoemaker, John Augustus, became what one may now call a "volunteer" probation officer when he served as surety for an alcoholic. In 1878, twenty-one years before the first juvenile court, adult probation was officially established in Boston. Today all states and the federal government provide for juvenile as well as adult probation. It is one possible type of disposition available to all juvenile-court judges.

[2] William J. Ellis, "A Yardstick for Measuring Parole," *Federal Probation*, 7:29–33, 1943.
[3] *Idem.*

A weakening belief in the deterrent effect of punishment, especially in institutionalization, has promoted the growth of probation. Its increased use has made probation perhaps the leading type of disposition and treatment, aside from dismissal and restitution. Legal scholars and social historians regard it as one of the most significant social inventions of modern times. It implements the chancery ideal of individualized treatment, for it considers the offender a unique individual whose needs may differ from those of anyone else.

In addition, a strong argument in behalf of probation is its low cost in comparison with other forms of treatment. It has been estimated that the expenditure by the government for the federal probation system is fifteen cents a day per probationer; on the other hand, the cost of institutionalization may be $2.37 a day per person. This means a saving, if probation is used, of $2.22 a day, or approximately $800 per year. But probation involves an even greater financial asset if the probationer is old enough to work and support himself and his family. For example, in one recent fiscal year, a monthly average of 13,610 probationers in the federal system worked and reported earnings for the year which amounted to $25,976,243.[4]

Probation is a substitute for institutionalization. Its objectives are to give the child a new code of ethics, to provide him with a strong motivation to adhere to this code, and to develop his latent ability. It allows the adjudged delinquent to remain in his community for treatment under the supervision of the court and the controlled conditions which it imposes on a case work basis. General conditions that apply to all probationers are obedience to parents, regular school attendance, keeping of early hours, following of instructions by the probation officer, notification of change of address, and avoidance of disreputable places and people. Special conditions applying to some probationers may include restitution for damages, living with a relative, attendance at a special school, and affiliation with a recommended recreational agency.[5]

[4] Henry P. Chandler, "Probation: What It Can Do and What It Takes," *Federal Probation*, 12:14, 1948.

[5] John Otto Reinemann, "Probation and the Juvenile Delinquent," *The Annals of the American Academy of Political and Social Science*, 261: 116, 1949.

As it is presently conceived, probation has two essential elements:

1. A pre-sentence investigation that gives the court the necessary information for a decision as to whether or not probation will be used.

2. The supervision and guidance of the adjudged delinquent by a probation officer skilled in the art of human relations and in the utilization of community resources.

It differs from institutionalization, then, in that it usually leaves the child in his own home; it is more individualized; it applies the methods of social case work; it uses community resources; and it is less punitive and involves a milder social stigma.

In juvenile cases, unlike adult cases, there are usually no legal limitations on the judge as to who shall be placed on probation. After a favorable decision has been made, it is the pattern to place the individual on probation for an indeterminate period. The understanding is that the probationer will be released if the objectives are met. Otherwise it is understood that probation may be revoked and commitment made to an institution.

Probation Personnel

For some time the trend has been toward the professionalization of probation work by assigning it to trained social workers instead of to unqualified political appointees. One of the most effective organizations in the promotion of professional probation work is the National Probation and Parole Association. Its activities include surveys of probation, the provision of consultation services, conferences, publications, and serving as a clearinghouse of information on all aspects of probation and parole work in the United States.

The usual difficulty in attracting a sufficient number of first-rate people to social work appears in probation work; namely, low remuneration. In New York City in 1952 probation officers were offered the substandard starting salary of $2,960 a year, with selection aimed at college graduates. Some other places that year paid starting salaries as high as $3,600 and $4,000. Yet the cost of living and the attraction of other work much more remunerative than probation work inevitably meant a staff turnover as high as twenty per cent a year. The result has been the use of volunteer probation workers in many localities. The Big Brother and Big Sister Organizations represent such volunteers, supplementing the work of the regular, understaffed probation department of the juvenile court. Some training is provided to volunteers who join either organization before they take on any assignment. In New York City for years a representative of the Big Sisters has been "on call" for every session of Children's Court, ready to help any girl who is in need. Despite all this, at least half of the counties in the United States are without probation services for juvenile delinquents.

Success and Failure in Probation

It is claimed that a juvenile court, adequately financed and staffed, can place as high as 90 per cent of its adjudged delinquents on probation and get up to 75 or 80 per cent success in terms of reaching its objectives.[6]

The difficulties in the path of such a performance are numerous. Probation work is hindered by the fact that the community has been slow to accept the necessity of professional careers in probation. A related difficulty is that, to many laymen, case work practice seems to be irreconcilable with the exercise of authority. The public, despite the philosophy of delinquency, often continues to view the delinquent, even when he is on probation, as a degenerate to be feared and punished. The situation in the probationer's family and neighborhood may be such that there are too many obstacles to overcome; the probation officer cannot remodel all of the child's environment. There is also the difficulty embedded in the court's budget. This affects the size of the probation officer's case load, which in turn affects the quality of service he can provide. A case load may go as high as 250 to 300 probationers, plus many pre-hearing investigations to be made. In the federal probation system the excessive case load is believed to be the most serious handicap confronting the service.[7] The average number of federal probationers under supervision per

[6] Austin H. MacCormick, "The Community and the Correctional Process," *Focus*, May 1948, p. 88.

[7] Harold M. Kennedy, "Report of the Committee on Probation with Special Reference to Juvenile Delinquency," *Federal Probation*, 12:3, 1948.

officer has recently been 115, despite the fact that most correctional authorities suggest a limit of 50 persons per officer for supervision. Under present conditions, probationary supervision becomes superficial and officers must engage in considerable overtime and work under unnecessary strain. A final difficulty is the probationer himself. He may be antagonistic to the probation officer, rejecting all offers of help and refusing to make any adjustments.

Deferred Prosecution

"Deferred prosecution," which resembles probation in philosophy, differs from it by taking place before instead of after court action.

Deferred prosecution is defined as "a procedural method, in worthy cases, involving juvenile offenders, by which the prosecutor holds in abeyance for a definite period, contingent on good behavior, all legal process, where such action is not in conflict with the best interest of the United States, and thereafter the prosecutor either administratively closes the case upon the satisfactory completion of the definite term, or processes the original complaint forthwith where there is a subsequent delinquency." [8]

Deferred prosecution is limited to those under eighteen years of age who have committed federal offenses. Prosecution is deferred for a definite period of time, usually eighteen months, in order to determine whether the prosecutor's faith in the supervised juvenile was justified. Supervision is in the hands of the same personnel that supervise probationers.

This procedure has been approved and recommended to United States attorneys by the Attorney General. One finds it in use in various localities and under a number of different names, but because it has been in operation in the Eastern District of New York at Brooklyn since 1936 it is often known as the "Brooklyn Plan."

Advocates of deferred prosecution maintain that it is one important step in advance of probation, inasmuch as it comes before court procedure rather than after it. That is, satisfactory completion of the probationary status merits release from that

[8] Conrad P. Printzlien, "Deferred Prosecution for Juvenile Offenders," *Federal Probation*, 12:17–19, 1948.

status, but the adjudication of delinquency—a "court record"—
still remains. Successful completion of deferred prosecution leads
to no court procedure; hence no court record. The participant in
deferred prosecution therefore has an additional incentive for
conformity—the avoidance of the delinquency tag that results
from adjudication.

The following case illustrates how deferred prosecution
operates:

A postal inspector apprehends a thirteen-year-old boy stealing mail from a letter box. He brings the juvenile to the office of
the United States attorney along with the parent or guardian.
The assistant United States attorney discovers that the stolen
material consists of chewing gum samples used in an advertising
campaign. The first impression he has is that this may be a case
worthy of deferred prosecution, but he makes no decision. Instead, he informs the juvenile of his constitutional rights, as well
as of the seriousness of the offense, and that further investigation
will be made of him. Then he requests the postal inspector to
take the juvenile to the probation office, and telephones the probation officer, requesting an investigation. He places the juvenile in the custody of his parents or guardians and establishes an
adjourned date (usually a week hence) convenient to all parties.

In the meantime the probation officer takes a case history,
makes a field investigation, and submits in writing to the assistant
United States attorney a report comparable to the pre-sentence
report he prepares for court cases. On the adjourned date all
parties appear in the office of the United States attorney. If the
report is favorable, the assistant United States attorney decides to
grant deferred prosecution, and explains what it entails to the
juvenile and his parent. The United States attorney then makes a
written request to the probation office that the juvenile be placed
under adjustment supervision comparable to the regular probation supervision.

Before the probation office can proceed with its supervision
of the case, it must take into consideration a printed form on
deferred prosecution, consisting of three parts. First is a direction
for supervision, the authority for it, and the terms and conditions
that control it, signed by the United States attorney. Second is a
statement of consent to be read to, and signed by, the juvenile

and parent or guardian. Third and last is the acceptance by the probation office.[9] On the fulfillment of these special conditions, the procedure of deferred prosecution thereafter resembles probation.

Foster Home Placement

The last major type of disposition and treatment of adjudged delinquents is placement in foster homes. The theory, in essence, is that transplanting will reform. Just as it was felt for centuries that a new land where adult criminals could begin a new life not only relieved the mother country of their presence but also gave them a chance to reform themselves, so in a similar way it came to be felt that a new home for delinquent children would have a reforming effect. A foster home is a home established and subsidized by the court or some other agency to care for a small number of adjudged delinquents. The boarding and care of the children is the paid job of the husband and wife.[10]

Like probation, the foster home is more in keeping with the juvenile court than is institutionalization, because it involves a milder social stigma. A truism in the field of child welfare is that the best place for a child is in his own home with his own parents, unless the home is clearly detrimental in its influence. In other words, if probation cannot be done with the child in his own home, then foster-family homes may be used. With the development of more careful observation, supervision, and recording of data, and better techniques of evaluating foster parents, foster home placement of children who have committed delinquent acts is less precarious than was formerly the case.

The most basic consideration in the use of foster-family homes for delinquent children is the extent to which the personality and needs of the child are known. A careful life history provides some of this information. It is important to understand not only the child's own behavior, attitudes, and emotions, but also the attitudes of his family toward him, his attitudes toward them, the kind of setting that provokes the delinquent behavior, and so forth. In general, foster homes are most successful for

[9] *Ibid.*, pp. 19–20.
[10] Ruth Gilpin, "Foster Home Care for Delinquent Children," *The Annals of the American Academy of Political and Social Science*, 261:125–6, 1949.

those delinquents who have a strong need for affection from adults and for individualized attention, and for those delinquents whose habits and attitudes are such as not to make them too conspicuous in a community. Whether or not a foster home is desirable instead of institutional commitment for an adjudged delinquent is also dependent on the community's resources in comparison with those of the institution. For example, the child may need special remedial work in school, which is not available in the community where a suitable foster home is located, but is available in the institution. The same may be true of psychotherapy, in cases where it is needed. Children who do not respond to case work treatment, and those with intense feelings of aggression against adults, are not ready for foster homes.[11]

An interesting case of foster home placement[12] was that of Walter, one of three boys riding in a taxicab who struck the driver with a blackjack and forced him at gunpoint to drive to the country. There they tied him to a post and drove off in the cab. They abandoned the car in another state and slept overnight in a barn. The next morning, after being treated to breakfast by a farmer's wife, they tied her up, ransacked the house, and drove off in her car. After holding up a filling station they were caught, but not before Walter, the youngest of the three boys, had threatened to shoot the arresting officer.

The two older boys were committed to a reformatory for a term of from one to twenty years. The case of Walter, the 15-year-old boy, was heard under the Federal Juvenile Delinquency Act, and he was committed to the custody of the Attorney General for his minority, a period of almost six years. A study of his background made by the Federal probation officer for his pre-sentence report revealed a lifetime history of rejection, abuse, and homelessness.

His mother was married when she was 18 years old. For about five months her husband, a contractor, worked steadily, but he was never to do so again. When there were

11 Herbert D. Williams, "Foster Homes for Juvenile Delinquents," *Federal Probation*, 13:49, 1949.

12 Joseph Vogel, "Reconstructing Youth: Some Case Studies," *Federal Probation*, 6:34–5, July–September, 1942.

three children and another was expected, he deserted his family. Three years later he reappeared, was arrested once for passing bad checks and a second time on a charge of non-support. He deserted his family again, but returned later. In 17 years his wife had nine children and then she died following the still birth of the tenth child. The father deserted the children and was never heard from again.

At that point Walter was five years old; three of the older children had been married; the remainder were placed in a children's home. Shortly afterward some of the children were accepted by relatives, but Walter was placed as a foster child with a family and four years later the family adopted him.

Even before they adopted him, Walter hated his foster parents. They kept him busy before and after school hours with housework. At the age of seven he was put to work in their confectionery store. The foster mother nagged and complained continuously. If the boy took a piece of candy in his mouth, she accused him of bringing about her ruin; when she found him eating a banana, she charged him with stealing. In desperation Walter finally ran away, riding off on another boy's bicycle, but he was caught a few miles out of the city and brought back. Again he ran away, riding a freight. When he returned his foster parents beat him and lengthened his work hours to keep him out of mischief. When he ran away the third time he hitchhiked to Chicago where he remained several weeks. Upon his return his foster parents turned him over to one of his married brothers.

This brother, having already assumed the responsibility for one of the younger children, could not offer much to Walter. Feeling that he was virtually a stranger in this home, Walter fled, wandered aimlessly for a while, and finally returned to his adoptive parents. They no longer cared to be troubled by him and took him to the juvenile court where he was committed, at the age of 12, to a boys' industrial school. During his entire year's stay there he maintained a conduct record of "A" and he was found to have a better than average intelligence, completing the ninth grade without difficulty.

Walter was then paroled to the care of another married brother. He worked about the house awhile and then was sent to the home of his brother's mother-in-law. From there he went to the home of a newly married couple, and then back to his brother. Almost immediately thereafter his brother and sister-in-law became ill and had to be hospitalized. Walter, left alone, drifted about aimlessly and at this time met the two older boys with whom he was seized for aggravated assault against the taxicab driver, kidnapping, armed robbery, and threatening to shoot a law-enforcement officer.

Placed for observation with a juvenile-research bureau, Walter was described as tall for his age, and more mature than the average 15-year-old. He was found to be a capable workman with an intelligence quotient of 111, a feeling of rejection and self-pity. In considering designation for the boy, his excellent record at the industrial school was taken into account. Equally significant was the fact that despite misunderstanding and abuse from his adoptive parents, he had returned "home" again and again.

A foster-home placement was developed for Walter in a small town where his past was unknown. Arrangements were made to pay board through the United States marshal. The foster parents, a middle-aged couple experienced with boys, strived, but not too noticeably, to make him feel completely at home. He continued with his high school education and found odd jobs after school hours, affording him the satisfaction of buying his school supplies and clothes. During the summer vacation he worked in a dairy, saving part of his salary for a college education.

At school Walter's teachers considered him superior to the average student in appearance and in ability to meet people. He participated in extracurricular activities, played on the basketball team, was elected president of the student council and of the senior class.

His foster parents told him that as long as they had a home, he too would have a home.

Other Types of Treatment

Besides the major types of disposition and treatment discussed in the preceding pages, a few others are worthy of brief mention. Some of them, of course, like *psychiatric treatment,* are found enmeshed in institutionalization, parole, probation, and foster homes. Although it is now outmoded to think that all cases of juvenile delinquency require intensive psychiatric study and treatment, psychiatry may benefit the sex offender, the runaway child, truants, and cases of organic brain damage, psychosis, and convulsive disorder.[13]

Psychoanalysis is used to treat some cases of delinquency, but the expense involved precludes wider utilization. It is applied, however, on a short-term outpatient basis, such as in London by the Portman Clinic. The technique includes anywhere from ten to seventy interviews scattered over a period of eighteen months to two years. These psychoanalytic interviews are supplemented by group therapy and play therapy.

Recidivism

To many students of juvenile delinquency, the extent of recidivism is the only accurate measure of the success or failure of any and all types of treatment the juvenile-court judge decides to use. Punishment is especially likely to be followed by recidivism, possibly because punishment does not reform and because it results in social ostracism of the punished. The younger the child is at the time of his or her first adjudication as a delinquent, the greater is the likelihood that there will be recidivism. The type of offense is also thought to be definitely related to recidivism, for a person who commits an offense against property is more likely to relapse than one who commits an offense against the person.[14] Healy, among others, disclosed that a surprisingly large percentage of those who commit delinquency continue to

[13] George E. Gardner, "The Psychiatrist's Role in the Treatment of the Delinquent," *National Probation Association Yearbook,* 1940, pp. 220–3.
[14] Thorsten Sellin, "Youth and Crime," *Law and Contemporary Problems,* 9:584–5, 1942.

demonstrate that behavior after treatment.[15] The Gluecks [16] found that approximately nine tenths of the children whose cases were disposed of by what is alleged to be one of the best juvenile courts in the country continued their delinquent behavior. Their conclusion was that the prevalent practices of treatment were failures.

This conclusion is debated by Merrill: [17] "While few would question the fact that the persistence of antisocial conduct is indicative of unsuccessful adjustment, the use of the fact that the child was brought before the court after committing another offense as a criterion of maladjustment is not so obvious. No clinical psychologist can think of conduct as good or bad, adjusted or maladjusted, in terms of any single item of conduct. The patterns of adjustment are so intricate that no single event can serve as an index. . . ."

In any case, recidivism after treatment has brought personnel dealing with the problem of delinquency to the conclusion that treatment is not enough. Prior to delinquency there is often an early phase of predelinquency, or incipient deviation. It is here, in the area of control and prevention, that societal reaction to the problem of delinquency can be most fruitful. The chapter that follows is an account of contemporary thought and practice in delinquency control and prevention.

QUESTIONS AND RESEARCH SUGGESTIONS

1. *Briefly, what is parole, and what is the philosophy that underlies it?*
2. *Explain the growth of probation and its position as the leading type of disposition and treatment of delinquents.*
3. *What are the hindrances to successful probation work?*
4. *Why can one say that deferred prosecution is similar to probation in theory and practice? Why different?*
5. *Why are foster home placement and probation more consistent with the juvenile court than is institutionalization?*

[15] William Healy, "The Psychiatrist Looks at Delinquency and Crime," *The Annals of the American Academy of Political and Social Science,* 217:67–75, 1941.
[16] Sheldon and Eleanor T. Glueck, *Juvenile Delinquents Grown Up,* New York, The Commonwealth Fund, 1940.
[17] *Problems of Child Delinquency,* Boston, Houghton Mifflin, 1947, p. 271.

6. *Do you agree or disagree that the extent of recidivism is the only accurate measure of the success or failure of any and all types of treatment?*
7. *What form of treatment would you have proposed for Howard L., whose case is described in Chapter I? Why?*

SELECTED READINGS AND REFERENCES

Beard, Belle B., *Juvenile Probation*, New York, American Book Co., 1934.

Chandler, Henry P., "Probation: What It Can Do and What It Takes," *Federal Probation*, 12:11–16, 1948.

Ellis, William J., "A Yardstick for Measuring Parole," *Federal Probation*, 7:29–33, 1943.

Flynn, Frank T., "Probation and Individualized Justice," *Federal Probation*, 14:70–6, 1950.

Gardner, George E., "The Psychiatrist's Role in the Treatment of the Delinquent," *National Probation Association Yearbook*, 1940, pp. 220–3.

McGuire, Louise, "The Essentials of Casework with Delinquents," *National Probation Association Yearbook*, 1935, pp. 39–47.

Printzlien, Conrad P., "Deferred Prosecution for Juvenile Offenders," *Federal Probation*, 12:17–19, 1948.

Reinemann, John Otto, "Probation and the Juvenile Delinquent," *The Annals of the American Academy of Political and Social Science*, 261:109–19, 1949.

Reinemann, John Otto, "Principles and Practices of Probation," *Federal Probation*, 14:26–31, 1950.

Supplee, Rosalie, "Case Work with Offenders," *Federal Probation*, 3:7–12, 1939.

Taber, Robert C., "The Value of Case Work to the Probationer," *National Probation Association Yearbook*, 1940, pp. 167–79.

Timasheff, N. S., *One Hundred Years of Probation*, New York, Fordham University Press, 1943.

Williams, Herbert D., "Foster Homes for Juvenile Delinquents," *Federal Probation*, 13:46–51, 1949.

Young, Pauline V., *Social Treatment in Probation and Delinquency*, 2nd ed., New York, McGraw-Hill, 1952.

Chapter **XVIII.** *Delinquency Control and Prevention*

Laymen, it will be recalled, hold the theory that the most important factor contributing to juvenile delinquency is family life.[1] Yet their suggestions as to the most effective ways of controlling and preventing delinquency are not always consistent with the theory. For example, the same "inquiring reporter" referred to in Chapter VIII asked the following question of five people: "What do you suggest to help curb juvenile delinquency?" They responded as follows:

A sales manager:

"I think the teen-age group suffers from lack of a sufficient number of suitable recreational and entertainment centers where

[1] See Chapter VIII.

they can make friends and spend their leisure time. Also, I suggest that social classes be added to the school curricula for the express purpose of fostering the high ideals of young people."

A company guard:

"I have always thought that if every boy would become a member of the Boy Scouts, who know so well how to engineer his spare-time activities and arrange his participation in worthwhile projects, juvenile delinquency would necessarily diminish greatly. As far as the girls go I think they are too apt to frequent night clubs and adult joints, a matter which could be rectified by the provision of more youth centers."

A housewife:

"I am convinced and have been for a long time that lack of parental supervision is at the core of the juvenile problem. I think that many young people are allowed to run around on week nights more than is good for them and that greater interest by parents in their welfare and activities is necessary to beat juvenile delinquency."

An ex-serviceman:

"Many things contribute to delinquency, including character, hereditary tendencies, and environment. Every child can have a fair chance to become a good and useful adult only when his home and social life are wholesome and constructive. Therefore, I think that the home life atmosphere of delinquents must be improved to successfully combat the situation."

An electrician:

"I believe that young people need a greater number of community centers where they can have a good time with others of their age group. In fact, many of them have remarked to me that they 'wish we had somewhere to go' and I personally feel that this is the crux of the entire situation." [2]

These responses indicate that, along with family control, panaceas such as recreation centers and character-building programs represent lay thought on the control and prevention of juvenile delinquency. Laymen, however, do not stand alone in such superficiality and triteness. Professionals, especially those who seek to promote a pet theory of social control, advance their own "single cures." They advocate such things as playgrounds,

[2] *Syracuse Herald-Journal*, October 23, 1946.

courses in manual training, mental examinations, the erection of better housing, and juvenile clubs as answers to the problem.

Any attempt to reduce the incidence of juvenile delinquency, panacea or otherwise, comes under one or the other of two categories: control or prevention. Delinquency control is not so far-reaching in its objective as is prevention. Its assumption is that the roots of delinquency are so deep and so thoroughly enmeshed in the American way of life that the most practical goal to work for is a partial reduction of the incidence. Prevention seeks to eliminate the problem by obliterating its "causes." Two broad types of action are taken in either case:

1. Modifying the relationship of the juvenile to his environment by removing him from the environment, or, more frequently, modifying the environment without moving the juvenile.

2. Modifying the juvenile's attitudes and emotions in order to alter any behavior patterns that might lead to delinquency.

Before a sample of programs and techniques in delinquency control and prevention is examined, it is well to keep in mind the wisdom of caution in the interpretation of fluctuations of the measured incidence of juvenile delinquency. Such interpretation frequently depends upon the prejudices or purposes of the observer. It has already been indicated, for example, that advocates of a particular control or prevention program are apt to cite a decrease in the incidence of delinquency as proof of the efficacy of the program. When the incidence increases, however, the same advocates point to the rise as evidence that their budgets are too small. Studies of the effects of control and prevention programs indicate that to show any actual effectiveness they must reach children early and continuously for years. Any claim that a sizable proportion of delinquency incidence has been eliminated by a given program or technique in a year or two is incredible. It is much more likely that any measured reduction is the result not of such a program itself but of uncontrolled factors such as the economic trend or seasonal variations.[3]

Another suggestion is that the merit of any program should be weighed in large part by the etiological theory of delinquency implicit in it. It matters little that a program has money, per-

[3] Lowell J. Carr, *Delinquency Control*, New York, Harper, 1940, pp. 49–50.

sonnel, organization, and dynamics if its etiological foundation is weak.

A Panorama of Panaceas

CENSORSHIP OF MASS MEDIA. One of the most popular panaceas seeking to prevent juvenile delinquency is the censorship of the mass media of communication, especially comic books. In New Orleans, for example, a Mayor's Advisory Committee of seventeen civic leaders was organized in 1949 to meet weekly for the purpose of reading comic books, thereby determining their suitability for the juvenile population of the community. The following material was set up as objectionable:

a. *Regarding crime:* Any situations that glamorize or glorify crime; the portrayal of law enforcement officers or agencies as stupid or ineffective; situations in which the crime is overemphasized in relation to emphasis put on morality and justice.

b. *Regarding sex:* Indecent or suggestive attire; any situation or scene having a sexual implication; the glamorous representation of divorce.

c. *General:* Scenes of sadistic torture or extreme cruelty; any situation or scene that presents prejudice against any race, religion, nationality, or established American institution.

Aside from the dubious etiological basis upon which censorship rests, there is involved here a curtailment of freedom of the press, the implications of which advocates of censorship either minimize or do not recognize.

EDUCATION AND PUNISHMENT OF PARENTS. Other panaceas, founded on the theory that parental shortcomings are directly responsible for juvenile delinquency, are the "education" and the punishment of parents.

The program of classes of instruction for parents of delinquents, attendance at which is compulsory, is frequently called the "San Francisco Plan." In 1943 the judges of the juvenile courts of San Francisco established a center for the instruction of "delinquent parents" in order to accomplish what their previous efforts (institutionalization, probation, etc.) had failed to do; namely, deter the adjudged delinquents from further delinquent behavior. The program was subsequently adopted in other communities.

In San Francisco, the series of eight weekly classes is designed to inform the parents about the city's public health, recreational, and other welfare provisions. Lectures are given and group discussions are held on parent-child relationships and personality development of children. When parents are "graduated" from the series, the cases of their children are returned to juvenile court for final review and dismissal. Only those parents who the courts believe will benefit are sent to the center. Some foreign-born parents are sent, instead, to Americanization classes to aid them in establishing "a proper environment for the American home."

The kind of thinking implicit in this program is shared by many people professionally concerned with delinquency. For example, the chairman of the State Probation Commission in an eastern state was asked by an undergraduate student in a course on juvenile delinquency for his opinion on the most effective means of delinquency prevention. The reply the student received was as follows:

> "To begin with, let's propose that the schools, colleges, and the churches get into a huddle and teach the parents of the next generation the responsibilities and duties of being parents and of running a modern home. What we need is to put the HOME in its place in American life; let the HOME run and regulate society, and not the young rascals run the home and the future of our civilization."

Related to the education of the parents of delinquents, because it too scapegoats and overemphasizes the role of parental responsibility, is the punishment of parents by fine or imprisonment. Laws have been introduced in several states increasing the power of juvenile-court judges by permitting them to hear, determine, and impose a penalty on the parents of adjudged delinquents. The efficacy of such punishment has been measured. Judge Paul W. Alexander of Toledo's Domestic Relations and Juvenile Court, after a seven-year study of 1,028 cases, 500 involving the arrest of parents, found no evidence that punishing parents had any effect whatsoever on the control or prevention of juvenile delinquency. There was no evidence that sentencing "offending" parents served to deter other parents from "contributing" to the delinquency of their children. In New York City the levying of a fine upon the parents of truants has been found not to accomplish its purpose. Improvement in school attendance after such court action against parents was discovered to be less marked than in the cases of children whose parents were not fined. A larger proportion of children whose parents had been fined were back in court a second time in the same school year.[4]

CURFEW.   A third panacea is the municipal curfew, which is meant to reduce juvenile delinquency by requiring that children be off the streets after dark. More than three thousand American communities at one time or another have adopted curfew ordinances for this and other protective reasons. One type of curfew law requires that persons under eighteen years of age be home by 10 p.m. Penalties for parents in case of violation include arrest and $100 fine. Some curfew ordinances set different age limits for boys and girls. Others merely forbid loitering rather than total exclusion of juveniles from the streets after a specified hour. Most such ordinances, however, are enforced only periodically, if at all.

The curfew implies that delinquency is an outdoor, after-dark problem, and that darkness facilitates stealth and anonymity. Furthermore, the curfew implies that there is something inherently evil about the night. Actually, of course, there is very little juvenile activity after dark which is precluded during the day, delinquent or otherwise.

VOLUNTEER, PROTECTIVE WORK BY ADULTS.   A fourth panacea to prevent juvenile delinquency is the protective, volunteer organization of adults for the benefit of teen-age boys and girls. In the case of the Big Brother and Big Sister organizations, the work is mainly with the pre-delinquent rather than the delinquent person.[5] The organizations may be either private, as is true of the Big Brothers, Big Sisters, and National Girls' Work Council, or they may be part of the county or state departments of public welfare, or of the state boards of children's guardians. Both types aim to provide adult companionship, and vocational and recreational guidance for pre-delinquents. Occasionally a volunteer Big

[4] Herbert A. Landry, *The Prosecution of School Non-Attendants*, New York, Division of Administrative Research, 1949.

[5] We have seen in the previous chapter that members of both organizations also serve as voluntary probation officers for adjudged delinquents.

Brother serves as part of a child guidance clinic team with a psychiatric case worker, a psychologist, and a pediatrician.[6]

A Big Brother, in a routine situation, meets his "case," who is often from a broken home, about once a week. Acquainted beforehand with the child's problem, the Big Brother arranges a program in which the two share common experiences—attending baseball games or concerts, or visiting museums. This is the point of departure for the development of a relationship in the course of which the child is presumably diverted from his delinquency tendency.

The Big Brother movement is composed of businessmen, merchants, lawyers, and other volunteers. Its etiological basis, one may infer, is that delinquency results from the loss or absence of parents, for the Big Brother is, in a sense, a substitute parent. Unquestionably this is a factor in a number of delinquency cases, but at the same time it does not encompass a very large part of the universe of delinquency cases.

An important experiment in connection with the effectiveness of protective work by adults was the Cambridge-Somerville Study.[7] The study was designed to test the hypothesis that many delinquent boys would be deflected from their problem behavior if they were provided with the continued friendship and counsel of adults who were sincerely interested in them and who could obtain for them access to the community services they required. It dealt with the systematic observation of two groups of boys, 650 in all, whose ages at the beginning of the experiment ranged from six to twelve years. They were divided equally into an observation group "T" and a control group "C," comparable in age, social environment, intelligence, and character. From 1938 to 1945, each boy in group T was subject to the constant attention of a social worker. He was aided in adjustment to school, given medical care and organized leisure, and offered advice along with his parents on a variety of problems.

The control group was not placed under such care. In 1948,

[6] A discussion of the child guidance clinic appears in a subsequent part of this chapter.

[7] Edwin Powers and Helen Witmer, *An Experiment in the Prevention of Delinquency; the Cambridge-Somerville Youth Study,* New York, Columbia University Press, 1951.

three years following the end of the eight-year experiment, a comparison was made between the two groups with regard to the incidence of delinquency. No significant difference was found, which led to the first conclusion that the work of adult counselors was no more effective than the usual forces in the community in preventing boys from committing delinquent acts.[8] Subsequently, however, the following qualifications were made:

1. The execution of the project was seriously handicapped by the war. This brought about so many changes in personnel that the emotional tie between the protected boy and the protecting counselor was affected.

2. The average age of the boy subjects of the experiment, to begin with, was ten and a half years. Thus the experiment had no influence over the important earlier years of childhood.

3. The initiator of the experiment intended to discover whether or not the nonspecialized work of social workers would be sufficient to prevent delinquency. Therefore a deliberate attempt was made to avoid child-guidance and psychotherapeutic methods for group T. This calls for the conclusion that only the ordinary methods of social workers are inadequate for the prevention of delinquency.

4. Some individual case analyses suggest that delinquency may be prevented by the counseling of social workers when the following factors are present: (a) the emotional maladjustment in the family and in the boy is not too extreme; (b) the boy and his parents want help; and (c) the counselor's services are consistently and skillfully related to the source of any difficulty he may have.[9]

RECREATION AND ATHLETICS. A popular solution for the prevention of juvenile delinquency is to provide recreation and athletic activities for children. Its etiological premise is that delinquency is a product of leisure-time inactivity, and it further assumes that supervised clubs and participation in organized sports have a sublimating effect on children.

[8] Edwin Powers, "An Experiment in Prevention of Delinquency," *The Annals of the American Academy of Political and Social Science*, 261: 77–88, 1949.
[9] Lucien Bovet, *Psychiatric Aspects of Juvenile Delinquency*, Geneva, World Health Organization, Monograph Series No. 1, 1951, pp. 46–7.

Early representatives of the recreational-club aspect of this panacea are two welfare agencies superimposed from without on indigenous areas: the boys' club and the settlement house. Developed, controlled, operated, and financed from outside the neighborhood, these agencies have not succeeded in diverting many juveniles from delinquency because (a) they have been too small to influence the area; (b) a small proportion of the children participate in their activities; and (c) they are "foreign" to the area.[10]

A more modern version is "Teen Town." One of its first appearances was in New Orleans where the Council of Jewish Women, aroused by reports of a high incidence of delinquency, decided that the solution was to find a place of recreation for children in the crowded downtown streets bordering the famous French Quarter. Once the house, an old warehouse, was acquired, the children themselves put it in order by cleaning, carpentering, and decorating, under the supervision of adult advisers. "Teen Town" in New Orleans provides recreation for those between thirteen and eighteen years of age. It has a snack bar, lending library, art classes, and a swing band. A Youth Council, made up of officers elected by the children themselves, is the governing body.[11]

Representative of the athletics aspect of the panacea is the American Baseball Academy, which was organized in 1951 to furnish free instruction in baseball by major league players to boys in New York City and eventually in other cities, explicitly for the purpose of "combating juvenile delinquency."

In Chapter X we saw that organized and supervised recreation and athletics on the one hand, and delinquency on the other hand, are not mutually exclusive activities. Even if delinquency occurs during leisure time, this is no evidence that the real etiological basis lies in that period, nor does the fact in itself point to the most effective methods of prevention. Organized recreation and athletic competition do not succeed in solving

[10] Henry D. McKay, "The Neighborhood and Child Conduct," *The Annals of the American Academy of Political and Social Science*, 261:36, 1949.
[11] Mildred W. Wells, *Youth and Your Community*, New York, Public Affairs Pamphlet #108, pp. 7 ff.

the problem of delinquency because delinquents usually avoid supervision or turn athletic competition into a new area for gang tactics.

EXPANDED USE OF THE SCHOOL SYSTEM. It is widely held that public school facilities, if more fully utilized, would control and prevent juvenile delinquency. The opening of school buildings during evenings and Saturdays for recreational purposes has long been a major objective of some state legislators whose theory is that delinquency is a product of leisure-time misuse.[12]

For those who believe that a direct relationship exists between sex delinquency and lack of accurate sexual knowledge, the answer is sex education in the school system. It is claimed, for example, that in communities where proper sex education is given there are fewer arrests for sex delinquency.[13] Another learning experience advocated for schools as a solution to the problem is participation by pupils in self-government. Allegedly it develops a favorable attitude toward law observance.[14]

Still another proposal is that elementary schools prevent delinquency by having the teachers detect early signs of maladjustment. Inasmuch as virtually all children attend elementary school, the classroom is the logical place to screen children for symptoms of behavior deviation. The classroom is also useful because it permits (a) easy detection of mental defects and social maladjustment; and (b) easy observation of infractions of rules. Every school system, it is urged, should have the facilities for a thorough investigation of the child in the first school years, with regard to physical make-up, aptitudes, disabilities, etc.[15]

One of the best-known attempts at pre-delinquency detection in the schools was made by Williams in a survey of ten medium-

[12] Eleanor T. Glueck, "The Family, the School and Crime," *Harvard Teachers Record*, 5:71–81, 1935; *Newark Evening News*, February 15, 1947.
[13] Benjamin Fine, "Instruction in Sex Urged on Schools," *New York Times*, July 24, 1949.
[14] Ralph S. Banay, *Youth in Despair*, New York, Coward-McCann, 1948, p. 56; Rosanna M. Peters, "Children's Attitudes toward Law as Influenced by Pupil Self-Government," *Studies in Higher Education*, No. 31, Purdue University, 1936.
[15] Martin L. Reymert, "Juvenile Delinquency in a Democracy," *Federal Probation*, 7:3–7, 1944; Sheldon and Eleanor Glueck, *Delinquents in the Making*, New York, The Commonwealth Fund, 1952.

sized cities.[16] Of 55,995 children surveyed with the assistance of teachers, 2.4 per cent were identified as "pre-delinquent." These were found most frequently among the thirteen-year-olds. About four times as many boys or girls were listed, the proportion being almost the same as that found in juvenile-court cases throughout the country. Pre-delinquent boys were described as resisting authority more, engaging in more misconduct in school, and annoying other children more than did the girls, whereas the pre-delinquent girls were reported as being more subject to feelings of inferiority, interested in sex, and overdeveloped physically.

The greatest shortcoming of pre-delinquency detection in schools is that very few school systems can answer "yes" to any of the following questions: [17]

a. Is the school organized to evaluate individual differences of its pupils?

b. Are the teachers trained to know the signs of pre-delinquency?

c. Are the teachers concerned not only with the academic progress of their pupils, but also with their attitudes and behavior patterns?

d. Is provision made for visiting teachers, psychologists, school physicians, and other specialists?

e. Does the school system assign its best teachers to classes in areas of high delinquency rates?

As for the other academic panaceas—evening recreation and self-government—they are obviously limited approaches to a very extensive problem.

INTEGRATION OF JUVENILES IN ADULT RESPONSIBILITIES. A final panacea is to integrate juveniles into police work and other community activities such as civilian defense in wartime. The theory is that delinquency is largely aggression against a society dominated by adults; if children can be given a sense of social responsibility they will be less motivated toward aggression. In some communities the program takes the form of an organization of "junior detectives" sponsored by the police department. Boy

[16] Herbert D. Williams, "A Survey of Pre-delinquent Children in Ten Middle Western Cities," *Journal of Juvenile Research,* 17:163–74, 1933.
[17] Donald DuShane, "The School and Juvenile Delinquency," *Journal of the National Education Association,* February, 1947.

members wear badges and carry official identification cards, their tasks being to report to the police any infractions of the law. In New York, Philadelphia, and Chicago, Youthbuilders, Inc., operated by the public school systems, are kept busy trying to find ways to prevent juvenile delinquency. The children open school canteens, campaign to stop window-breakage and vandalism, and so forth.

The selectivity of children who participate in these organizations, and the general superficiality of their programs, do not make for effective control and prevention of delinquency.

There is no clear dividing line between these panaceas and other programs and techniques. The difference between the two is relative; a program or technique tends to avoid the panacea label if it goes beyond the "single-cure" to a multi-dimensional line of attack on the problem. Some non-panaceas, in effect, border close to panaceas when they are promoted to the exclusion of all other possible programs and techniques.

The Child Guidance Clinic

The child guidance clinic came into existence along with the conception that there is often very little to distinguish the delinquent personality from the nondelinquent; that tendencies or symptoms of delinquency can be recognized beforehand in many cases; and that delinquency can be prevented if the total configuration of the child, rather than any particular fragment of his life, is taken into consideration.

Child guidance clinics are organizations where the pre-delinquent problems of children can be diagnosed and treated, and delinquency thereby prevented. Sometimes they function primarily for the diagnosis and treatment of cases of adjudged delinquents referred to them by juvenile courts. They have various names other than that of child guidance clinics: the bureau or institute for juvenile research, service or guidance centers, etc. They are supported by private organizations, community chest funds, and hospitals, or by city, county, and state funds.

The basic approach of the first child guidance clinic established in Chicago prevails today. This consists of (a) a medical examination to ascertain the physical assets and liabilities of the child; (b) psychiatric and psychological study to determine the child's emotional make-up, attitudes, personality characteristics, and intellectual capacity; and (c) the analysis of information concerning his personal history, family life, and social experiences.

Typically, the child guidance staff is composed of psychiatrists, psychologists, and psychiatric social workers in the ratio of 1:1:2 or 3. Whenever possible, a pediatrician is also included.[18] In most clinics the psychiatrist is the executive of the staff.

The process of diagnosis and treatment in a child guidance clinic begins when application is made for service. Generally, the clinic prefers to interview the applying parents alone, at which time they present to the psychiatric social worker their definition of their child's problem. The social worker in turn tells the parents about the organization and function of the clinic. If there is an agreement between the parents and social worker that the clinic may help the child, appointments are made for the child with the psychiatrist, psychologist, and pediatrician, and for the parents to continue their interviews with the psychiatric social worker. Fees are discussed and adjusted to the income of the applicants.

The usual procedure calls for the psychologist to test the child to determine his intelligence and for the pediatrician to give a medical examination. Then arrangements are made for the child to be seen weekly by the psychiatrist, and the parents by the social worker. Conferences between psychiatrist and social worker enable them to check on each other's progress. If the parents had been referred to the clinic by the school or a social agency, these are informed of developments.

Staff conferences furnish an opportunity for the synthesis of the various perspectives of the child by the specialists, and a decision is made about treatment.[19]

Child-guidance clinics have not escaped criticism. It is often said, for example, that the clinics are too slow and cumbersome

[18] National Conference on Prevention and Control of Juvenile Delinquency, *Report on Mental Health and Child Guidance Clinics*, Washington, D.C., U.S. Government Printing Office, 1947, pp. 2–4.
[19] Arthur E. Fink, *The Field of Social Work*, New York, 1942, Holt, pp. 145–7.

to be of much use. Another criticism is that psychiatrists are not easily understood by laymen. Furthermore, the clinic does not always have sufficient skills to be of help in every situation with which it is confronted. On the positive side, however, there is little question about the significance of the child guidance clinic. It is one of the most promising devices yet developed for synthesizing approaches to behavior problems and personality disorder in childhood. It occupies a prominent place in the total array of programs and techniques for delinquency control and prevention.

Neighborhood Area Projects

In Chicago in 1932 a new type of program of delinquency control, thereafter called the *Chicago Area Project*, was organized. It grew out of the conviction of Clifford R. Shaw that most programs had failed because they were uncoordinated intrusions of outside philanthropic agencies into areas of high delinquency in a community, without dealing with all the problems of each area as a unit, and without provisions for the active involvement of the residents of the area themselves. This project came to differ from preceding programs in that it stressed the autonomy of the neighborhood in planning and operating the program; it emphasized the need to train and use neighborhood leaders; it sought to use to the maximum the already established institutions of the area, and it aimed to enlist the active participation of local residents.[20]

There are now several area projects in Chicago, all patterned after the original experimental project, which covered an area of about seventy-five blocks in southeast Chicago. Programs funds are provided initially by a private organization, whereas the department of sociology of the Illinois Institute for Juvenile Research, a state unit, provides personnel and administrative funds. After an area project is established, funds are raised in a citywide community fund drive. The process in each project, briefly, is as follows:

Into each area young men are sent to become acquainted informally, and then to become accepted by the residents. The

[20] Ernest W. Burgess, Joseph D. Lohman, and Clifford R. Shaw, "The Chicago Area Project," *National Probation Association Yearbook,* 1937, pp. 8–28.

young men soon thereafter raise and discuss the problem of delinquency with local leaders to the end of forming a local community council as a sponsoring agency for the area work. As soon as possible all responsibility is shifted to the council, which organizes and operates the program. The council operates clubs and recreation halls, sends children to summer camps, offers adult education, takes over supervision of the area's probationers and parolees, and so forth. The very core of the project is that the people themselves recognize the problem and accept responsibility for solving it. The program is for themselves and their own children. The theory is that delinquency is a product of the area's culture; therefore the logical thing to do is to change the culture of the area through the efforts of the residents themselves.[21]

Another area project, somewhat different from Shaw's, was done on an experimental basis in New York City, under the auspices of the Social Research Laboratory of the College of the City of New York, and directed by Professor Harry M. Shulman. It included a workshop and game-room program, and classes in creative art, woodwork, and metal and leather work. There were three sessions a week lasting three successive school semesters for pupils 10½ to 14½ years of age from four public schools in underprivileged and low-rent areas. The pupils invited to participate in the project were chronic truants, children with personality problems, and children charged with such offenses as arson and theft. Equal numbers of non-problem children were invited to participate. The total constituted an experimental group of 155 children. The trained group leaders were not informed about the identity of delinquents or nondelinquents. Another group of 155 children who were not exposed to the program was set up as the control group, containing both problem children and normal children in the same proportions as the experimental group. In both groups problem cases were obtained from official sources, and normal cases were obtained by serial selection from class roll-books of those children who had never been reported by either teachers or administrators as problems, nor ever dropped below B in conduct throughout their school careers. Each problem child in the experimental group was individually matched for age, sex, race, educational achievement, general intelligence, and

[21] Carr, *op. cit.*, p. 223.

mechanical aptitude with a problem child in the control group. Similar matching was done for the normal children.

The results of the program after three successive school semesters showed that problem children in the experimental group had on the whole a marked decline in symptoms that characterize the delinquent personality, such as sex offenses, stealing, and truancy. On the other hand the symptoms of problem children in the control group worsened.[22]

The Chicago Area Project initiated by Shaw and the "controlled activity" experiment directed by Shulman are not claimed to be panaceas. Each has had limited goals, and in each case cautious claims have been made. Shulman, for example, has said of his own work that, without repetition of the experiment, under like conditions with similar subjects and results, no generalization can be made about the success of the type of program which was provided.

In 1953 a documentary sound film was completed at the College of the City of New York which depicted still another area project to control delinquency, developed by the College's community service division. Entitled "Step by Step," the film followed the various steps the division has been using in handling gang problems along New York's upper West Side. First the aid and interest of community leaders are enlisted. Then the gang is accepted at its own level of interest before it is requested to work with a student group leader. Next the film traces the introduction and acceptance of the student leader whose first job it is to restore tranquillity in the community by arranging a temporary gang truce. This is followed by the student leader's efforts to ease the gang members "back into community life." He remains with the gang while redirecting their behavior.

Community Co-ordination

An outgrowth of area projects is the co-ordination of all effective programs and techniques in the community. The rationale for community co-ordinated programs is that delinquency

[22] Harry M. Shulman, "Delinquency Treatment in the Controlled Activity Group," *American Sociological Review*, 10:405–14, 1945. See also F. Stuart Chapin's account in *Experimental Designs in Sociological Research*, New York, Harper, 1947, pp. 84–90.

is a problem with roots deep in American culture. Therefore the most intelligent approach to the problem is in terms of the entire community. The attack on delinquency cannot be piecemeal nor limited to formal agencies. It takes in the attitudes and behavior of everyone and requires the organized efforts of the whole community. Heretofore programs of delinquency control and prevention in any community have "just grown," without uniform development. Co-ordination tends to make for uniformity of development, reduce unnecessary overlapping of service, and permit specialization between agencies.[23]

Community co-ordination ideally includes the following:

1. *Getting the facts.* This means the collection of census data about the children in the community: the number of children of different ages, sex, race, and nationality background, and their spatial distribution. A sociological analysis of the community is done in such terms as economy, housing conditions, population mobility, ethnic conflict, and recreational facilities. Facts about the way local courts, police, schools, civic organizations, and welfare and leisure-time agencies compare in adequacy and efficiency with accepted standards of service for such agencies and institutions are also collected. Last but not least, facts are collected about the problem of delinquency in the community, such as the number of detected and adjudged delinquents, their traits, and the disposition of their cases.

2. *Promoting community understanding.* This is a public relations task that seeks to give the greatest possible number of people in the community some understanding of the problem of delinquency and the need of a communitywide program to control and prevent it.

3. *Promoting balanced growth and maximum quality of service.* Entirely independent efforts on the part of different agencies are not so effective as joint action, especially after there is agreement as to which are the most important "next steps" to be taken, and mergers, eliminations, and revisions of existing programs are made.

4. *Relating the problem of delinquency to other social prob-*

[23] National Conference on Prevention and Control of Juvenile Delinquency, *Report on Community Coordination,* Washington, D.C., U.S. Government Printing Office, 1947, pp. 1–3.

lems. Any attack on juvenile delinquency as separate or apart from other social problems is unrealistic. Efforts toward delinquency control and prevention are at the same time efforts toward the control and prevention of problems in family relations, education, intergroup relations, etc.

5. *Co-ordination of services.* The crux of community co-ordination is in the co-ordination of services for early discovery of behavior problems, proper referral, and diagnosis and treatment. Some of the specific types of co-ordinated services are: (a) *Social service exchange.* This operates through a central agency in which all participating agencies in the community exchange the information they have about children and their families and integrate their efforts to solve the problems. The central agency has a confidential card index containing information about children and families known to any agency. (b) *Case conferences.* These are regularly called conferences of the workers in the various agencies to discuss and agree upon procedure in dealing with specific problem cases. (c) *Services where problems appear.* School social service departments, juvenile bureaus in police departments, and social service departments in health agencies are illustrations of attempts to get at problems of children in their early stages by providing skilled workers at places where such problems tend to appear most prominently. (d) *Mutual understanding and working agreements.* All agencies in the community which deal with potential or actual behavior problems of children have clearly defined functions. Referral plans and case allocation agreements are jointly developed by the agencies, each of which is thoroughly informed of the community's resources.

6. *Co-ordinated efforts to improve community conditions.* This is the most clearly preventive aspect of community co-ordination. It is concerned with the reduction of those social and cultural factors which are thought to contribute to delinquency. An example of this is the reduction of intergroup tensions along racial, religious, and nationality lines.[24]

Statewide Programs

A number of states now have a program of delinquency control and prevention which is even more comprehensive than

[24] *Ibid.*, pp. 3–19.

community co-ordination. This is the organization of statewide programs. The first states to set up central bodies to plan and supervise comprehensive control and prevention programs are California, Massachusetts, Minnesota, New York, and Wisconsin.[25] In New York state, for example, this was done by the establishment of a State Youth Commission in 1945. State financial aid was authorized for localities to enable them to establish local youth bureaus and to provide recreational and educational facilities for people under twenty-one years of age. The state pays fifty per cent, or up to $15,000 annually, toward the expenses of a local youth bureau, and fifty per cent, or up to $250 annually, for every 1,000 youths who are given recreational and educational supervision. The commission has also organized services that include child guidance clinics, school social work, family case work, group work, youth guidance, and employment counseling. In 1953 more than 830 municipalities, embracing about 90 per cent of the state population, were participating in the program.

The White House Conference

The most comprehensive approach of all, although not necessarily the most effective at the grass roots, is the nationwide approach of the White House Conference on delinquency and other problems of child welfare. The first of these was called by President Theodore Roosevelt in 1909. In 1919, 1930, 1940, and 1950 other conferences were called to consider specific problems, make recommendations, and stimulate action by focusing the nation's attention on the proceedings. The most concrete results that have emerged from these conferences have been the following:

1. *The Children's Charter.* This is a children's bill of rights which the third conference, in 1930, enunciated and which is referred to in the introduction of this book.

2. *The Children's Bureau.* This is a federal agency established in 1912, the first public agency in the world whose function is to consider as a whole the conditions, problems, and welfare of childhood. It has conducted research in the field of child develop-

[25] Lowell J. Carr, "Organization for Delinquency Control," *The Annals of the American Academy of Political and Social Science,* 261:75–6, 1949.

ment, child labor, and community provisions for children in need of all kinds of special care. Its findings and recommendations are published. Congress frequently assigns to the Children's Bureau the task of administering federal laws affecting child welfare. The Bureau also consults with and advises states, localities, and organized groups that deal with the health and welfare of children.

In the summer of 1952 the Bureau began to work with more than 100 national organizations to improve community services for juvenile delinquents. Specific aims of the campaign were: (1) to get better handling by the police; (2) to get children into proper detention facilities; (3) to get more and better probation services for juvenile courts; (4) to get better treatment of boys and girls in training schools; and (5) to work out plans for more effective, better co-ordinated state and local administration of services for delinquent children. As an intensification of the campaign during 1953 the Bureau hoped to be able to develop standards for these services which would be of practical use to such groups as training-school superintendents, juvenile-court judges, and police. The Bureau planned to continue and extend its efforts to enlist widespread support of good programs for both the prevention and treatment of juvenile delinquency.

3. *The Child Welfare League of America.* In answer to the first White House Conference's recommendation that there be established a private national organization for the promotion of child care, the Child Welfare League of America was organized. Its membership has included agencies having direct and indirect responsibility for the foster care of children, and for other children whose homes are otherwise inadequate. Its aim has been to develop standards of service for child protection and care in agencies and in community programs.[26]

4. *National Conference on Prevention and Control of Juvenile Delinquency.* On the nationwide level, too, there is the National Conference on Prevention and Control of Juvenile Delinquency. Organized by the Attorney General and supported by the President, the purpose of this Conference is continually to study and disseminate information about the problem and to foster co-operation among all state and federal agencies attempting to cope

[26] Fink, *op. cit.*, pp. 77–9, 104–5.

with it. The Attorney General has organized a bureau within the Department of Justice which serves to co-ordinate these activities.[27]

All the ingenuity represented in the programs and techniques considered in the preceding pages—all the time, expense, and effort they involve—have not brought forward a drastic decline in juvenile delinquency. There are two theories to account for this situation:

One possible explanation, of course, is that effective use is not being made of the programs and techniques that are available. This possibility does have some support in fact. Carr's study of the functional efficiency of the various agencies and services aimed at delinquency control and prevention in twelve Michigan cities showed that, even on the basis of its own ratings, no community could boast better than sixty per cent of "best practice." Some communities were doing approximately half that well. In all of the communities, the agencies and services for "normal" children rated somewhat better than any of the agencies and services for delinquents.[28]

The other possibility is that the problem of juvenile delinquency is not being approached adequately. Most programs and techniques of delinquency control and prevention penetrate no deeper than the symptoms of the problem. They do not even come close to the underlying etiology. Ideally the prevention of delinquency and related social problems would entail some modification of the social structure and culture of American society itself. It would call, for example, for a reduction in the prevailing exaggerated emphasis on such values as competition and accumulation of wealth. These, we have seen, have led violation of law to become an integrated part of the American way of life. It would presumably require the enhancement of other values that now occupy lower rungs in the scale of American values.

[27] Harold M. Kennedy, "Report of the Committee on Probation with Special Reference to Juvenile Delinquency," *Federal Probation*, 12:3, 1948.

[28] Lowell J. Carr, "Organized Efforts in Crime Prevention," *Federal Probation*, 6:49–50, July–September, 1942.

Rigidity in Social Action

But this is shunned in virtually all of the programs and techniques. The unwritten rule seems to be: Try what you will, but do not tamper with any of the fundamental themes of American society. These are sacred and inviolable. Search out and treat early symptoms of problem behavior, if you will, but make no effort to modify the social and cultural bases that have caused these symptoms to be brought to your attention.

In short, major, drastic changes in the patterns of human relations are, for the most part, taboo in contemporary American society. The American way of life has come to mean, among other things, the correctness of the social status quo. Suggestions for conscious, planned, controlled change are frowned upon as being the "impractical" work of crackpots. Or proposals that "social engineering" be employed to solve our social problems are associated with political subversion or foreign ideologies, and dismissed. The flexibility characteristic of early American society has given way to a fear of, and resistance to, social change.

Sanctioned Action

Only within a very limited sense, then, is further action possible. An example is that proposed in 1940 by the White House Conference for Children in a Democracy. After standards of child health, education, and social welfare had been formulated and recommended by the Conference,[29] question outlines for the review of needs and resources were prepared, with the explicit aim of facilitating action on either the community or the state level. From the very beginning it was apparent that satisfactory question outlines for action in dealing with juvenile delinquency and all other problems of children could not be projected that would be applicable to the situation in each of the fifty-two state and territorial jurisdictions and the thousands of local communities with their varying demographic, social, and economic conditions. Therefore it would be necessary to adapt such items as the following concerning delinquency to the conditions in each locale: [30]

[29] *Standards of Child Health, Education and Social Welfare*, Washington, D.C., Children's Bureau Publication #287, 1942.
[30] See Emma O. Lundberg, *Our Concern—Every Child: State and*

TREATMENT MEASURES.

1. Does your county (or city or district) have a special juvenile court? If not, what court handles children's cases? Does this court use special procedure in dealing with cases of juvenile delinquency?

2. Is the judge who hears children's cases a person who understands children and has a knowledge of social conditions and community services? How frequently does he have hearings for such cases?

3. How many boys and how many girls appeared before the court in official hearings during the last fiscal or calendar year? In unofficial hearings?

4. How many children referred to the court because of delinquency during the year were detained pending court hearing? Were any children under sixteen years of age held in police stations or in jail pending court hearing?

5. Is it the practice to get in touch with the parents before the children are placed in detention? Who is responsible for doing this? Could detention be avoided or shortened if court hearings were held more frequently, or if more adequate social services had been available to determine the need for detention?

6. Who investigates complaints and gives case-work service to children coming to the attention of the court because of delinquency? A court probation staff? A social agency at the request of the court?

7. How many boys and how many girls were committed by the court to state institutions for juvenile delinquents during the past year? How many were assigned to probation officers for supervision?

8. How many children were referred by the court to public or private agencies for supervision or for case work with the families or with the children themselves? Which agencies were used, and for what types of cases?

9. How many boys and how many girls, white and Negro, from your community were in state institutions for delinquent children on a given date? How many were in county or city

---

Community Planning for Wartime and Post-War Security of Children, Washington, D.C. Children's Bureau Publication #303, 1948.

training schools? How many were in private institutions of this kind?

10. While a child is in a training school or correctional institution, is contact kept with his family? Is this responsibility carried by the court, by the public welfare department, or by some other local agency?

PREVENTIVE MEASURES.

1. What public or private agencies in the community are providing case-work services for children whose behavior is likely to lead to delinquency?

2. Are full-time school facilities available to all children in the community, and is there adequate enforcement of attendance laws?

3. Are laws for the protection of children from hazards in child labor enforced?

4. Is the necessary provision made for care of children whose mothers are out of the home because of employment, including facilities for supervised activities during hours when schools are not in session?

5. Are there adequate facilities in the community for leisure-time activities, play, and recreation?

6. Do the schools have visiting teachers, or do they utilize the services of social workers of public or private agencies for helping children who exhibit conduct problems or other difficulties in school?

7. Has any study been made in your community of the possible relationship between juvenile delinquency and the absence of recreational facilities? If so, what were the findings of this study? Are your school buildings and grounds utilized for after-school activities? Is there need for such a program?

8. What is being done by law-enforcement agencies and officials toward elimination and control of conditions in the community which are conducive to delinquency of boys and girls?

9. Does your police department use special procedures in dealing with children? Is this done through a juvenile bureau or by assignment of a special staff to juvenile cases?

10. Do the social agencies, court, and public co-operate with one another in preventing and controlling juvenile delinquency?

Conclusion

Periods of war and prosperity, we have seen, bring rises in the measurement of delinquency incidence and, as one may expect, an intensification of anxiety among responsible adults. Distraction from endemic delinquency, however, develops in the economically deflated and peaceful years. This is so despite the caution that "concern for children cannot be divided into three parts—pre-war, wartime, and post-war." [31]

The children of America comprise roughly one third of its total population. This is an inescapable fact for all those whose concern with such juvenile problems as delinquency relaxes periodically. Another inescapable fact is that the child is an indivisible whole as he grows from infancy to manhood. The child cannot be broken up into parts—one the concern of parents, another the concern of the teacher, a third the concern of public officials, and so on. [32]

It is the duty of the social scientist to add that American society too is an indivisible whole. It must assume an indivisible responsibility for explaining, controlling, and preventing its problem of juvenile delinquency.

QUESTIONS AND RESEARCH SUGGESTIONS

1. *How does one distinguish between delinquency control and delinquency prevention?*
2. *Why are education and punishment of parents considered to be panaceas?*
3. *What was the hypothesis the Cambridge-Somerville Study was designed to test?*
4. *Discuss the merits and weaknesses of pre-delinquency detection in schools.*
5. *Visit a child guidance clinic and trace the procedure used in the case of one child.*
6. *What does community co-ordination ideally include?*
7. *With all the programs and techniques of delinquency control and*

[31] *Ibid.*, p. 1.
[32] *Children in a Democracy—General Report Adopted by the White House Conference on Children in a Democracy*, Washington, D.C., Children's Bureau, 1940, pp. 8–9.

prevention which are available, why has there been no drastic decline in juvenile delinquency?

SELECTED READINGS AND REFERENCES

Burgess, Ernest W., Joseph D. Lohman, and Clifford R. Shaw, "The Chicago Area Project," *National Probation Association Yearbook*, 1937, pp. 8–28.

Carr, Lowell J., *Delinquency Control*, New York, Harper, 1940.

Carr, Lowell J., "Organization for Delinquency Control," *The Annals of the American Academy of Political and Social Science*, 261:64–76, 1949.

Carr, Lowell J., "Organized Efforts in Crime Prevention," *Federal Probation*, 6:49–52, 1942.

Hartwell, Samuel W., "The Guidance Clinic and the Court," *Federal Probation*, 12:3–7, 1948.

National Conference on Prevention and Control of Juvenile Delinquency, *Report on Mental Health and Child Guidance Clinics*, Washington, D.C., U.S. Government Printing Office, 1947.

National Conference on Prevention and Control of Juvenile Delinquency, *Report on Community Coordination*, Washington, D.C., U.S. Government Printing Office, 1947.

Powers, Edwin, "An Experiment in Prevention of Delinquency," *The Annals of the American Academy of Political and Social Science*, 261:77–88, 1949.

Powers, Edwin, and Helen Witmer, *An Experiment in the Prevention of Delinquency; the Cambridge-Somerville Youth Study*, New York, Columbia University Press, 1951.

Redl, Fritz, and David Wineman, *Controls from Within*, Glencoe, The Free Press, 1952.

Shulman, Harry M., "Delinquency Treatment in the Controlled Activity Group," *American Sociological Review*, 10:405–14, 1945.

References

Periodicals Concerned with Juvenile Delinquency

American Journal of Orthopsychiatry. American Orthopsychiatric Association, New York.

Channels. Social Work Publicity Council, New York.

The Child, Monthly News Summary. United States Children's Bureau, Washington, D.C.

Journal of Social Casework. Family Welfare Association, New York.

Federal Probation. Administrative Office of the United States Courts in Cooperation with the Bureau of Prisons of the Department of Justice, Washington, D.C.

Journal of Criminal Law and Criminology. American Institute of Criminal Law and Criminology, Northwestern University, Chicago.

Journal of Social Hygiene. American Social Hygiene Association, New York.

Journal of Criminal Psychopathology. Medical Journal, Monticello, New York.
Mental Hygiene. National Committee for Mental Hygiene, New York.
Prison World. American Prison Association, New York.
Social Service Digest. Joseph Andriola, ed., San Diego, California.
Social Service Review. School of Social Service Administration, University of Chicago.
Survey Graphic and Midmonthly. Survey Associates, New York.
Understanding the Child. National Committee for Mental Hygiene, New York.
Youth Service News. New York State Youth Commission, Albany, New York.

Bibliographies

CABOT, P. S. DEQ, *Juvenile Delinquency: A Critical Annotated Bibliography,* New York, H. W. Wilson, 1946.
CHAMBERS, M. M. and ELAIN EXTON, *Youth: Key to America's Future* (An Annotated Bibliography), Washington, D.C., American Council on Education, 1949.
Clearinghouse for Research in Child Life, *Research Relating to Children,* Washington, D.C., Children's Bureau, Social Security Administration, Federal Security Agency, 1948–49.
Clearinghouse for Research in Child Life, *Research Relating to Children, Supplement No. 1,* Washington, D.C., Children's Bureau, Social Security Administration, Federal Security Agency, 1949–50.
POLLAK, OTTO, "Criminological Research Bulletin, New Series, No. 1," *Journal of Criminal Law and Criminology,* 40:701–28, 1950.
SPECTOR, HERMAN K., *Bibliography on Criminology, Penology and Allied Subjects,* New York, Department of Correction, 1944.
THOMAS, ELIZABETH, *Criminology: A College Library Resources Checklist,* Stillwater, Oklahoma, Bulletin of the Oklahoma A. and M. College, 1948.
United States Department of Labor, *List of References on Juvenile Delinquency,* Washington, D.C., Children's Bureau, March 1939.
United States Department of Labor, *Supplementary List of References on Juvenile Delinquency,* Washington, D.C., Children's Bureau, March 1940.

Index

A NOTE ON THE TYPE

The text of this book has been set in Caledonia, a Linotype face designed by W. A. Dwiggins. Caledonia belongs to the family of printing types called "modern" by printers—a term used to mark the change in style of types that occurred about the year 1800. Caledonia borders on the general design of Scotch Modern, but is more freely drawn than that letter.

The book was composed, printed, and bound by

THE PLIMPTON PRESS, *Norwood, Massachusetts.*

Designed by HARRY FORD.